The

Complete Patriot's Guide to

Oligarchical Collectivism
Its Theory and Practice

By
Ethan Indigo Smith

~Dedicated to Mom, Mother Earth, Lady Liberty, and George Orwell.

Congress shall make no law respecting an establishment of religion, or prohibiting the free exercise thereof; or abridging the freedom of speech, or of the press; or of the right of the people to peaceably assemble, and to petition the government for a redress of grievances.
The First Amendment, U.S.A. Bill of Rights

INTRODUCTION TO INFORMATION

It is all about information. What is oligarchical collectivism? Well, what is Patriotism?

The Theory and Practice to Oligarchical Collectivism is the main source of inspiration for the volume in hand, and its namesake. It is the title of what's known as the book within the book in *1984*, written by George Orwell. George's *1984* is fiction, the volume in your hands is nonfiction.

The book within the book is read by the main character of *1984*, Winston Smith. It is an infamous book about the institutional monopolization of the fictional world, and is contraband. Winston is a typical worker in the regimented and institutionalized world of *1984*, with an unusual job. Winston is employed at the state news office, the Ministry of Truth. His job is to make the bad news good and to embellish good news, and to do so he rewrites history. Winston begins to question the oligarchy he is controlled by, in part because it is his job to rewrite the story.

1984 describes a world where every facet of life is controlled. The book within the book, *The Theory and Practice to Oligarchical Collectivism*, describes the institutional monopolization of entirety and how individuals can empower themselves to counter their exploitation, but Winston is not able to read its entirety before being imprisoned for reading and being in love. This book is the nonfictionalized version of the book within the book, *1984*.

In *1984* there are three super powers at war; Eurasia, Eastasia and Oceania. The sides shift, but the Ministry of Truth insists the enemy never changes. In Oceania there are four classifications of people. The Inner Party is made up of exploitative controllers at the capstone of the pyramid. Below them, in the upper portion of the pyramid, is the Outer Party. They are the ardent supporters of the Inner Party. Below the Outer Party, at the base of the pyramid, reside the Proles. They are the vast majority, generally doing what they're told and stuck, lacking opportunity. Hidden amongst them are the Brotherhood, the righteous rebels of *1984*.

The Theory and Practice to Oligarchical Collectivism, the book within the book, was originally written by Emmanuel Goldstein. Emmanuel (Emmanuel means god is within or with, Goldstein means gold rock) was a scapegoat of the Inner Party, labeled a rebel of the Brotherhood and against the people. Everyone is convinced to hate Emmanuel and his book, as a terrorist and his rant. The book within the book, it is revealed, was adopted and at least partially rewritten by the Inner Party, ultimately it is unclear if the book within the book was Emmanuel's words at all or if it was just an Inner Party fabrication. The book states that there are three kinds of people in the world; the High, the Middle and the Low. The fourth group, that is the likes of the Brotherhood, is apparently omitted.

1984 is an elaborate allegory of a war world where institutions seek control to the point of psychological takeover. The book within the book investigates slanted institutionalized control and was rumored to offer solutions. And yet it was distorted by the Inner Party as a ploy to find dissenters. Perhaps at one time, in the past of fictitious *1984*, the book within the book was real, but by the time Winston read it, it had been twisted by the Inner Party for their agenda. The Complete Patriot's

Guide to Oligarchical Collectivism is what the book within the book would be, in reality, without being flipped and twisted.

I am an individual, lacking institutional representation. I am not in an inner party, outer party or brotherhood associate. Perhaps I am most similar to a Prole, a proletariat, a simple individual in the institutionalized war world. I am not like the fictional Emmanuel Goldstein, but I am more comparable to him than I am to O'Brien, or any other institutional authority.

George Orwell was born in India, as Eric Arthur Blair. George Orwell was Eric Blair's penname. Eric's father worked for the British Government in India, where Eric eventually was a police officer for several years. His father's work and his own employment as a soldier were likely catalysts for his later political interest and insight.

I am Ethan Indigo Smith, an individual author caught up in, and questioning the world. The fictitious authority, the Inner Party in *1984* was unquestionable. Information, mainly lies, was distributed and unquestioningly acted on. In reality, no matter how reputable an individual or institution may be, they should always be questioned. In the twenty-first century, everything may be questioned. When information is available, it can be developed on. When information is unavailable and questions are unasked, stagnancy ensues, lies are probable, and people take ignorant action.

I began writing this with questions. What is patriotism? Why are there widely different interpretations of patriotism? The dictionary definition is clear, but the interpretation sways far and wide. It is a simple and commonly used word; however there is no concrete understanding of its meaning.

I found that there are many answers to every question and many subjects with twisted distorted interpretations. There are many subjects accepted as steady facts, but are actually incomplete and in flux. The term "Orwellian" has come to mean the misdirection or deletion of information, usually with insertion of euphemism for institutional purposes.

I have no formal corporate, religious or government training and no higher education to speak of. I am simply a curious individual. I attended public schools in the U.S.A and learned in the classroom, but I learned to question on the streets, outside of institutions. Schools mostly taught me how to answer their questions; the streets taught me to ask my own. I was never scholastic, but I always had a question, aimed not at necessarily finding an answer, but provoking thought.

The most useful thing I ever learned was not a fact or function, it was to question. Have no fear, look people into their eyes and question. Ignorance is excusable and temporary, if questions are asked. Questions get answers, sometimes many different answers, sometimes other reactions. The Complete Patriot's Guide to Oligarchical Collectivism has no angle, and few biases, other than obvious, curious, pro-individual stance.

Partial and complete answers always present more questions. It is impossible to fully comprehend, and yet always possible to comprehend more. To some questioning oligarchical collectivism sounds like a curios endeavor, to others the idea of a dissident rebel. The distinction is apparent, not through the question asked, but of who is asked the question. A question is just a question until it's posed to someone who has interest in the answer remaining limited in scope. Then curiosity becomes dissent.

What is patriotism? In short, it's support of liberty. The original patriots of the U.S.A. were architects of a system to provide liberty in a nation surrounded by exploitative institutions. The Declaration of Independence, Constitution, and Bill of Rights, or the trinity of liberty, outline and protect individual rights - among institutions.

Many define patriotism in nationalistic, martial and institutionalized terms. Patriotism is pro-individual, concerned with liberty rather than nationality, the actual definition of patriotism is a combination of maternal and paternal sensibilities and could be accurately called matriotism rather than patriotism, for liberty encompasses all humanity not just select nationalities.

When the trinity of liberty was first designed it was infiltrated by flawed tolerations of the time. Greed led to exploitation, slavery, and ultimately more war. Some of the nation's founding powers insisted exploitation should be maintained, that only certain people were individuals with rights, but with tremendous foresight the original patriots also allowed the trinity of liberty to be alterable, and potentially enhanced.

In the past, the spark of liberty was rare and fleeting. The world has still never seen liberty for all, not even liberty for both sexes. Oligarchical collectivism to benefit the few is the standard. Past societies made it so free people were free to exploit those who were not free. The mind was perhaps so conditioned to separate "us and them" that one could not imagine giving "them" liberty. The trinity of liberty is not perfect, but permits progression of liberty.

What is oligarchical collectivism? An oligarchy is defined as the few over the many. An oligarchy can be depicted as a pyramid. Oligarchical collectivism unifies control in pyramidal fashion among many institutions, or pyramid stones. Oligarchical collectivism is the conjoining of slanted institutions to enable their control and exploitation of the many. Patriotism flattens oligarchical collectivism.

Individuals everywhere, unless inhibited by acquired tolerations, prefer liberty. The ideas of the Declaration of Independence, the Constitution, and the Bill of Rights give people hope for liberty and opportunity all over the world. Why is there more opportunity in one place or another? Opportunity is not just a matter of resources; it is a matter of liberty.

The concepts of the trinity of liberty allow for individual prosperity. The ideas also allow for wrongdoers. Many lofty notions have been left dusty on the trail in order to achieve one diabolical objective or another. Sometimes the same institution that promotes hospitality also promotes hostility. The U.S.A. was founded on countering oligarchical collectivism, but is threatened by it.

We are products of our environment. No matter how likeable or noticeable, our perception is subject to information. Our physical composition is acquired by the environment of our ancestors and influenced by present conditions. The debate between nature versus nurture is moot. Such "either or" arguments result in the "us and them" mentality. Two polarized options tend to produce doublethink. The truth is that the environment, nature, nurtures all. The "either or" presentation limits perception.

Everything is political, but first it's biological. The natural elements constantly provide input, resulting in evolution. Information is constantly being processed. Information is inescapable. The physical and mental states are constantly molded by our environment. People are intertwined with the environment, physically and mentally.

Presentation in polarization, as in the debate of nature v nurture, may sound like a logical discussion, but it's limited and limiting. The choice of nature or nurture merely has a nice ring to it. The only sensible answer is that both influence us. One or the other is hyper restrictive.

Everything begins with information. Whether the information is truth, half-truth, fact, distorted fact, belief, opinion, lore, lie, or joke is relevant. Yet the distinction is unknown unless questioned, otherwise it hits one the same. Information is compiled in many forms; cold statistics, hard facts, interpretation, common knowledge, secret code, and on and on. The commonality shared by all types of information is power. The withholding of information creates an imbalance, an oligarchical slant. Information is potentially powerful in many ways, yet it is always powerful based on its availability.

Opinion is derived from information. If one has incomplete information, one has incomplete opinion. People tend to consider and move forward with the attainment of new information, though, not everyone seeks to attain new information. Questioning is essential to liberty and practically instinctual to people. Those who do not seek to question go against their natural psychological inclination.

Everyone is entitled to have an amorphous opinion, changeable relative to new information. Logical change is okay and in all likelihood beneficial. Thankfully people normally question, adjust and proceed with new information, otherwise we would all be skipping around looking for pots of gold at the end of rainbows, and hoping, perchance, to catch sight of the Easter Bunny along the way. Practically everyone is capable of change, but there are many people who prefer to keep their beliefs immovable, ignoring or refuting information that would instigate change.

Humankind is separated from monkeys by questions concerning our environment. Perhaps human ancestors perched up on two feet and asked, "Why is that?" The human hand is powerful tool, but only in combination with thoughtfulness. The truth changes, it was true at one time that you did not read this. The truth sways, as does the perception of it.

Beliefs stem from certain information. People make educated guesses, hypotheses and conclusions based on information of all sorts. New information leads to new conclusions, with everyone, whether the information is true or not, is important, but falsehoods lead to conclusion too. This is why people personally change over a lifetime, and society develops over lifetimes – new information leads to new conclusions. Acceptance of information precedes transcendence of it, further skeptical questioning eliminates falsehoods.

Insects and reptiles behave like programmed computers, regardless of experience. Most mammals behave like computers programmed by experience. People are capable of understanding and surpassing the biological and experiential/political programming through questioning.

People are able to interact with information without bias. To be unbiased one must question those presenting information, one's own mindset, as well as the information. Considering your reaction to the information often leads to better questions of pertaining to the information. Better questions are more likely to prevent incomplete opinion derived from incomplete information.

Today information travels at light speed. Information and interpretation is distributed by individuals and delivered by institutions, media corporations, and other authorities. Important information is mixed with irrelevant and it's available everywhere.

Perhaps, because of its sheer abundance, many choose not to acquire new information. Most don't want to ask and they don't want to know. On top of the overwhelming amount of information, much of it irrelevant, there is also abundant sensitive information. Information concerning actuality that is not pleasing, but is occurring, is constantly ignored. Willful ignorance is utilized to preserve one's comfort zone in the status quo.

Institutional representatives have biased responsibilities, which distort how they proceed with information. They pick which information to contemplate and which to ignore. Institutions are not individuals, yet they have opinions, promote opinions and are awarded some of the same rights as individuals, but have no heart and are not alive. Individuals breathe air and drink water, institutions do not. Institutional interpretation of information is limited to its pertinence to their agenda.

Institutional information is often incomplete and jumbled, and it's predominantly spin, their side of the story. Institutional agenda normally has little to do with the primordial concerns of individuals, such as clean air and water. Institutions recognize institutions. Individuals remain outside of their scope, unconsidered other than as various statistical masses. Institutions have complex goals which are inflexible to basic individual interests. Institutions ignore individuals until enough counter their rigidity, cracking their framework. Institutions either crumble or bend to individual will and always try to ignore people.

Included in The Complete Patriot's Guide is factual information. Not included: all of the facts.

> FACT #1: You do not have all the facts.

No one has all the facts. Even experts fall short of complete knowledge, while time also disintegrates most expertise. Things change. We all have some information commonly agreed upon, and we work from there. All the facts would require too vast a mind and constant update. And yet this is not the primary reason we do not have all the facts, the primary reason we do not have all the facts, is we are not allowed all the facts.

The withholding of information; half-stories, part-truths, mistruths, omissions, misinformation, and outright lies, cast and support opinion. The factual and reasonable are sometimes exalted and sometimes quieted to support opinion and belief. Institutions and individuals use information. In conducting research for the Guide, I learned one can find 'facts' to back up any belief, so I offer no resources. Check the information in the Guide because that's the first step to truth, but don't just question this, question it all. Sometimes essay, and even mathematics may sound correct, but no matter the content or source, information deserves to be questioned. All relevant information should be questioned and all questions should be encouraged. If individuals or institutions do not promote questions, they are likely hiding something.

If the unsourced information provided in the Guide is unbelievable, question it. Check the information, for the numbers may change and may have been previously distorted before I scribed them. I promise that I triple-checked the information, but I also admit that I might have been lied to and being human, I make mistakes. Question this and continue questioning information, including and especially information delivered by institutions.

> "A witty saying proves nothing." ~Voltaire, Philosopher

What sounds right may be, but may be wrong. Remember, just because something is true doesn't make it the entire truth.

> "Information is not knowledge." ~Albert Einstein

To persevere in researching in an openly curious manner, without the weight of prior information, leads to better knowledge. Progression is halted with assumptions of complete information. In researching any subject, there are always many versions of the story. These stories are numerous in variation, but often are presented as being on one of two sides, two extremes. Like two sides of a coin, one side represents the extreme of one set of opinions and the other side represents the extreme opposition. Institutions prefer situations be in polarization, like the two party system in the U.S.A.

> "There are two sides to every question." ~Protagoras

The truth is sometimes an amalgamation of two opposing ideas. The truth often resides as the third side of the coin, the curvature, the ring and edge of the coin, often in coexistence with opposites. Sometimes the truth remains hidden inside the metal itself, but mostly is on that fine line. Truth is usually distinct from the major oppositions, but of both.

Historical fact becomes jaded by people's opinions. Even current events recorded with an arbitrary camera are interpreted and presented differently by one extreme or the other. The names of people and places are lost, changed, stolen and stomped out. There are many sides, perhaps because there are many lies.

Sometimes information is presented in a way, that to those with differing information, it seems distorted, resembling an outright lie. Opposite sides may be part of the same coin, the same truth. The ring or edge of a coin might hold the truth and at times, an alternative coin might be truth. Sometimes people lie or are misled and adopt one side of the coin or another, partial truth taken as the whole truth. Some people base their opinion on a fraction of what they know of entirety.

"Rinse, but don't swallow this. Don't swallow."
~Your Dentist

FACT: Fluoride in topical doses can be effective against tooth decay. Over 60% of people in the U.S.A. live in communities with fluoridated water. Ingestion of fluoride has been scientifically found to risk the health of one's brain, bones, kidneys and thyroid gland. Dental and Skeletal Fluorosis is caused by it and it is a powerful neurotoxin. Fluoride has been found to be beneficial only when small amounts are used topically on teeth, not when ingested. Over 90% of western Europe chose water free of added fluoride. Fluoride is administered to drinking water, not as a mineral from the ground, but as a byproduct of industry.

FACT: Milk is a good source of calcium, for babies. Milk becomes ever increasingly difficult for adult mammals to digest in order to obtain nutrients, including calcium. No being past two years of age is meant to consume milk. Humans are the only species who continue to consume large quantities of milk throughout life. Milk has little to no preventative value against osteoporosis. Pasteurization changes the milk proteins and arguably makes it so bad milk can be sold.

Most milk is more product than nutrient. Milk has little nutritional value to most adult mammals. If scientists observed another animal that sought out the milk of a different creature throughout adult life, they would describe this as strange behavior, maybe a sign of immaturity. Politically speaking milk is for institutions, biologically it is for babies.

Do not take the word of an admitted tea drinking derelict, but moreover, no matter what, no matter the situation or trusted voice never let institutions present unquestioned information. Question this, but remember that most individuals normally have little reason to lie, whereas intertwined institutions and institutionalized individuals on the other hand, have an outrageous assortment of reasons to lie.

If fluoride is administered to the water supply to benefit our dental health, why stop there? More importantly, why start there? Why not add calcium and zinc to the water supply? Calcium derived from kale or some other leafy green vegetable? The reason your dentist tells you to rinse and, most importantly, spit out fluoride, is because it's an accumulative poison which only works topically.

The reason milk from cows has calcium in it is because they graze on greens all day long. The reason people generally lose the ability to digest milk is because milk is for babies. People need calcium every day, but the natural mammalian cycle does not include milk throughout adult life.

There is always more to the truth than one side or another. The milk from cows may be good occasionally, a spot with tea maybe, but there are better sources of calcium. Fluoride may be beneficial when used topically, but there are less toxic ways to protect the pearly whites than adding it to drinking water. In order to observe with an open mind let go of predispositions. Is it not perverse to raise animals for milk which is cooked so it will be safe to ship far and wide? Is it not suspect to include poison in municipal water?

Contrasting information can be divisive. Some will sense that one side or the other must be completely wrong or completely lying, but usually truth, the whole truth is an amalgamation, sometimes of seemingly opposing ideas. If only presented with one side of the facts, the other side and the truth remains unseen. Reputable institutions might speak the truth and still be lying by omission, often telling only part of the story, that part that works for them.

Old oligarchical European institutions conquered the world brutally and killed any who stood in their way. They were headhunters and scalpers and only recognized one another. The oligarchical institutions worked amongst and against each other, and others were simply unrecognized and mostly vanquished. They attempted to monopolize the world, much like the warring states depicted in *1984*.

The violent worldwide conquest and institutional exploitation is known as Colonialism. Eventually the Colonies in the U.S.A. retaliated and after the original patriots defeated the British Empire, George Washington could have been king. Instead he installed elections. Alexander Hamilton arranged for George to be king of a new country, but George declined; he served as president for two terms and then returned to his farm.

The same old empirical mind state that was abandoned by some was adopted by others in the new U.S.A., who did their best to institute exploitation. Freedom was instituted for some, while many others were openly stomped on. The land of the free had qualifications and stipulations for freedom, mostly based on racial distinctions. Freedom is not liberty. Liberty has no such qualifications.

They were stuck in their oligarchical ways and relegated those with high quantities of melanin to a low level of exploitation and slavery. Because American Indian and African people were easily distinguished as a "them" among an "us" they were enslaved, killed and treated as property.

> FACT: In 1850 native indigenous people in the new State of California had no rights, while European and African men were free. Two ranchers in Clear Lake, California kept many local Pomo people as slaves in hostile and abusive conditions. On May 15, the two ranchers were killed in an uprising. Subsequently the U.S.A. Army was dispatched. They surrounded and killed as many as 200 nearby Pomo people, including women and children. No prisoners were taken, few survived.

The story goes that prior to the rebellion, many enslaved Pomo died from starvation and beatings, and a few died simply out of fear. The Pomo people were brutally enslaved, exploited and like the rest of the native people from Cuba to California, and from Canada to Chile, violently obliterated. The Pomo people hardly knew violence until the arrival of institutions. They lived in a land of plenty, where art took precedence over war. The Pomo survived Colonialism, many peoples in the Americas and around the world did not.

Captain Nathaniel Lyon was the leading officer dispatched to find the Pomo slaves who rose up against their oppression. Upon failing to find them, he ordered an attack on a neighboring peaceful village, killing all who they came across. Supposedly, the unit continued their savagery afterwards on random native peoples as they returned from the mission, this is not confirmed. Nathaniel would go on to lead at least one other documented massacre during the Civil War. He later died in combat, fighting for the Union. The U.S.A. Congress passed a resolution of thanks to his "eminent and patriotic services."

The Pomo people were treated inhumanely and retaliated against enslavement, and systematic abuse. Innocent, neighboring men, women and children were then murdered by the U.S.A. Army as retaliation. As unrecognized individuals in a new world of institutions, the Pomo were treated in an inhumane fashion. They were looked upon as less than, and a "them." This is considered to be the first of many massacres of innocent natives by the newly formed U.S.A. Army.

In the early days of California, the government compensated the expenses of hunting forays for Indian slaves with one million dollars from Washington, DC. Anyone could engage in military missions to gather native slaves and was guaranteed reimbursement. This was the exact type of duplicity practiced by all empires before; some had freedom over others. Freedom is a free-for-all, while liberty is indiscriminate for all.

Ultimately, the U.S.A. evolved, but institutions promoted individual participation in a heinous genocide and land theft. People have progressed and developed liberty, but liberty is for all, and when it is not given to all, it does not exist. Individuals expand liberty, institutions initiate the "us and them" mentality based on perception and not truth in order to limit individual liberty. These perceptions are institutionalized and used primarily for gains of strangers.

In *1984* there are four types of people, based largely on social rank. There are the proles, the outer party, the inner party and the brotherhood. In reality there are four types of people understood according to the reaction to information. Idiots do not question substance or relevance. Zealots question in line and in accordance. Elitists question in order to advance power and finance. Patriots question curiously and openly, often enough in prevention of exploitation.

> "Until lions have their historians, tales of the hunt shall always glorify the hunters." ~African Proverb

A BRIEF PEOPLE'S HISTORY

Throughout recorded time, and probably since the beginning of the Neolithic Age, there have been four kinds of people in the world, the idiots, zealots, elitists and patriots. They have been subdivided in many ways, they have borne countless different names and their relative numbers, as well as their attitude toward one another, have varied slightly from age to age, but the essential structure of society has never altered. Even after enormous upheavals and irrevocable changes, the same pattern has always reasserted itself, just as gravity sets equilibrium, however pushed one way or another.

The aims of the four groups are entirely reconcilable. Their behaviors are dissimilar, but their differences fit together. Idiots refuse information, zealots refute information, elitists misuse information and patriots distribute information. Despite dramatic alterations in the world and occasional fluctuations of people from one group to another, the shape of society, the formation of the groups remains the same, just as planetary gravity shapes globes.

Idiots avoid all new pertinent information in order to maintain perspective. Zealots ask certain questions of certain information, ignoring unaligned information in order to maintain perspective. Elitists question information in order to manipulate and reap gains off of those without information. Patriots question information to educate themselves and share it with others in order to progress.

All people, in all of history and today can be fairly understood according to how they interact with information. The way in which people react to new information is the primal and realistically only legitimate guideline to understanding people. Any other labeling of people is at best secondary, and often inaccurate or completely absurd. Historically people have been labeled based on various descriptions and assumptions, and rarely according to how they think.

History contains important information. Despite countless paradigms between a given event and the present, history provides insights. It is tremendously important to dig around established facts, to seek new information, as in archeology, in order to better understand the past and present. It is equally important not to take theory as fact and to question the delivery of said facts. The distant past is always more difficult to decipher and more easily mixed up than recent occurrences.

FACT: Christopher Columbus never set foot on North America. In all his four expeditions he explored only the Caribbean. On his first visit he claimed Cuba for Spain and began hemispherical gentrification, enslavement, and theft. In 1494 he visited Guantanamo Bay, Chris called it Puerto Grande. He died in 1506, fake name and all, believing he found an island near India.

"History is the lie commonly agreed upon." ~Voltaire

Throughout recorded time, people have been divided into groups based on their appearance, their religious beliefs, their heritage, their nationhood, their possessions, their poverty, their schooling, their institutional status, and on and on. Historically these differences have been enhanced or eliminated for institutional agendas of one form or another. Labels based on anything other than interpretation of information are normally inaccurate and used by institutions. The best way to understand individuals is through their reaction to information.

History is the story of many people being manipulated by a few. It is a story of manipulations to maintain situations and revolutions to change situations. History is a story of the oblivious and conscious, the active and passive, the idiots, zealots, elitists and patriots. The pattern has more or less remained the same. The past and present coincide, they are not distinct.

History's mysteries can be cast to the wind, until the known actualities are deciphered and dissected. Questioning the known is required before one can effectively question surrounding unknowns. The conditions of the present is important enough to ponder alone, before or rather than, the mysteries preceding. Mystery is best left aside, until all is deciphered about that which is known, or commonly agreed upon.

It would be a luxury to have all the questions about all the known facts answered. When the luxury of comprehending reality's knowns is attained, then leftover mysteries can be addressed. By questioning actuality instead of mystery many mysteries may be dispelled, mysterious no longer. By concentrating on reality, mystery is surpassed and eliminated.

"A morsel of genuine history is a thing so rare as to be always valuable." ~Thomas Jefferson

The distant past is full of unsolved mystery and wonder. To what extent actuality of the past has been swayed is hard to say, but certainly the presentation of history has been distorted. In our own time interpretation and speculation surround thoroughly investigated, and recorded events. Truth is difficult to obtain about events last year, let alone last century. We can only imagine how history is twisted through the influence of institutions and the biases of historians.

Speculation and interpretation looms about the Kennedy assassinations. Both were witnessed by many, partially recorded and still highly disputed. The extent of purposeful and accidental distortion in history is impossible to calibrate, but looking at recent history allows us to see the likelihood of distortion. The truth sways and is also swayed, manipulated.

"We're not saying there was a conspiracy. All that we're saying is the evidence that was presented as a slam dunk for a single shooter is not a slam dunk."
~Cliff Spiegelman, Texas A&M, 2007
Concerning JFK assassination

FACT: The most important and closest Secret Service guards who were supposed to jog alongside the vehicle were called off minutes before the JFK assassination. The driver of JFK's car turned back twice and braked during the shooting. These events are recorded on video.

Unknowns surround the attacks of 9/11. Unidentified lights adorn the sky and light only curiosity. New planets are discovered and new species are found on Earth. Speculation surrounds the origins of people, our cosmology. The missing link in the evolution of humanity is still debated on. Natural reality provides plenty to question as well as the actuality of society.

Individuals desire the mysterious and institutions tend to inject mystery as to their workings. To have any hope of understanding mystery one must first question actuality. One must first question the elementary before inquiring into the ornate. Reality is the starting point, and an endless subject in and of itself.

A realization of the basics is required before questioning the esoteric; otherwise it would be possible to equate thunder and lightning with the boogeyman. Without knowledge of actuality one can make wild assumptions that might seem reasonable. Without questioning our surroundings, subjects assumed to be realized entirely, may only be known partially, if at all. Without knowledge of actuality one creates mystery where there is none, with knowledge one cancels mystery that once was.

It is easy to find a laymen's answer. As it turns out, every subject has multiple layers, like onions. The more information one acquires the more layers one finds. It is wise to question, and continue questioning. A prerequisite to knowledge, understanding and realization of the basic or complex, is questioning. Great mystery may be a well-kept secret, and is often just a series of unasked and unanswered questions.

People constantly uncover remnants of the ancients that lead to discovery, but lead mostly to more mystery. More answers lead to more questions. People in the past left behind monuments of stone. How people in the past accomplished building some of their architecture is unknown. New information leads to new questions.

World history contains people living primitively in simplistic villages alongside sprawling cities of great expenditure, neighbors in the same time. Hunter-gatherers perhaps practicing subsistent agriculture existed nearby workers with specific talents. Nomadic and fixed tribes subsisted off of their surroundings alongside expansive institutionalized kingdoms.

The elite of oligarchy, monarchy, patriarchy, matriarchy, and all other forms of hierarchy harvested off of individuals, instead of off the land. Despite variations in operation, societies share certain traits no matter the continent or time period. People of the past made stone monuments. The intricacies of their stone testimonials might differentiate them, but performing their construction is shared.

There are leftovers of harvesting and hunting tribes alongside remnants of engineering accomplishments and architectural feats that we are only now capable of contemplating. People of all different wants and ways coexisted at the same time. Whether they were hunter-gatherers or pyramid builders, the mystery of their existence still abounds. What did they know? How did they know? The celestial and architectural knowledge of the Mayan, Aztec, Incan, Egyptian and similar ancient peoples are only recently fathomable. The Gobekli Tepe monument in Turkey, the Piri Reis Map, the Waldseemuller Map, the Baghdad Battery, the Antikythera Mechanism, Mystery Hill in Salem, NH, the Ohio Serpent Mound, the ancient pyramids the world over, are all suggestive of highly advanced peoples.

There are many facts which run counter to established history. Because they go against history, also known as his story, they are little discussed. History is an alterable presentation of one altered version of events. There are anomalies in history, in the history that we've been taught. The known anomalies exemplify the likelihood that there are other unknown anomalies.

History is at best partial truth we have, often only one portion, of one side of the coin. Anomalies suggest that real history may have been swayed. Who can say why, when or how? The dark ages, the inquisitions, the burning of libraries, every war and a whole slew of other occasions have allowed for revision and distortion. What is presented as concrete is often soupy.

The last few centuries provide well documented history, and yet still unknowns are many. Events have been recorded, people quoted, and still in the end, there is plenty of uncertainty. Everything should be questioned, especially when there is a track record of error and anomaly, as in the recording of history. Those who would not question, those who promote unquestioning behavior are questionable. Those who insist that the present story is the entire story, don't know the story well enough, and perhaps act to prevent realization of the entire story.

> "A history in which every particular incident may be true, may on the whole be false." ~Thomas Macaulay, British Politician

The mystery of creation is inconsequential to the current condition of creation. The mysteries of ancient pyramid builders are inconsequential to their legacy, the legacy of a pyramidal system, of the few over the many, of oligarchical collectivism. Mysteries are inconsequential to actualities. Throughout recorded time, there have been pyramid systems regulating class and existence.

Distinction and organization in the past was mostly racial and territorial. The pyramidal oligarchical organization was a mark of grace or a stamp onto the exploited. Some people were branded or tattooed, most had their exploitation stomped into them through generational threat and abuse. Throughout recorded time people have been judged on their appearance, race, sex or some other stipulation.

Some of the oldest known civilizations, Sumer and Babylon, in the area of modern day Iraq and Iran, constructed pyramid systems, with one king, many slaves and everyone else falling somewhere in between as luck or charm would have it. Five thousand years ago, they constructed Ziggurats, stone pyramidal structures with stairs leading to the top.

The pyramids of Egypt are perhaps the most stunning and inspiring. Today speculation surrounds the mystery of their construction. Why? How? The stone construction of the pyramids and the societal construction of the pyramid system still hold secrets, unknowns. There are ancient pyramids all over the world in Babylon, Egypt, and Nubia of course, but also in Greece and elsewhere in Europe, South America, Mexico, Central America, North America, the Canary Islands, Samoa, Tahiti, China and throughout Asia.

Pyramids were generally stone constructions. Today, pyramidal construction continues as institutional format more frequently than it does in stone structure. Oligarchical collectivism is a pyramid system supported by different stones, representing different institutions. Throughout recorded time, institutions have designed systems, whatever distinction or label, whatever dogma or legislation, to keep hold of their power and control the status quo in pyramidal fashion, to insure the continuation of the majority of power being in the hands of a minority. No matter the brand name, be it republic or regime, all institutions are pyramid schemes.

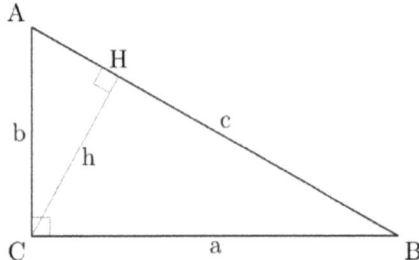

"Reason is immortal, all else mortal."
~Pythagoras

The pyramid system provides more pleasantries and a better view the higher one ascends. Those on the lower levels experience more pressure. In the past people were born into a situation, and there was no leaving that station, the son of peasant would be a peasant, and that was that. Systems of nations were set up to keep the majority held in their place, unquestioning and unmoving.

In the past, no matter one's place in the pyramid, ignorance prevailed and served well. Most had no desire to question or were kept so ignorant it was difficult to perceive questions. Serfs were just lucky to be alive and often grew accustomed to the local oligarchical enforcement. Pyramidal autocracies violently ruled most of the world. Those at the base worked the hardest and were forced to pay upwards.

If born into nobility at the top, one would receive the best education of the day and most likely would still be ignorant. Oligarchies set up education as a privilege and program too. The best education of the past taught that those in the base were a "them" among an "us" to the point some of the base believed it.

Education was more institutionalization, propelling the notion that certain people were more valuable than others. This led to war, genocide and slavery. Institutions taught individuals to understand others according to their race, or anything other than their reaction to information, how they think.

The people in the lower portion of the pyramid were deprived and repressed so that they did not know how to question or what to ask, or dared not to. Those in the base of the pyramid were happy to have a bowl of gruel without a beating. It was difficult to see other ways of interaction in order to properly question. Anyone who was so bold and brave enough to question the system would get their tongue cut off, or worse. Lacking questions perpetuated the system.

Those at the apex of the pyramid system were comfortable, so rocking the boat with questions would be foolish. The only questions among the elite pertained to maintenance of the status quo. The royalty, nobility and clergy were often free to perpetuate exploitation and not responsible for their wrongdoing. Typical individuals were so beaten down or held so lofty, that just asking a question was out of the question.

> "The few who could understand the system will either be so interested in its profits, or so dependent on its favors, that there will be no opposition from that class, while on the other hand, the great body of people mentally incapable of comprehending the tremendous advantage that capital derives from the system, will bear its burdens without complaint and perhaps without even suspecting that the system is inimical to their interests."
> ~John Sherman, U.S.A. Senator and politician 1848–1898.

Throughout recorded time, individuals have been left unconsidered next to the functions of institutions. It took centuries of individually instigated progression to enable individual rights among the mechanics of elite institutions. The U.S.A. wasn't the first nation to sanction the right of individuals to question and to steer their country. The original patriots were not original in their attempts at liberty, only original at attaining it.

> FACT: Thomas Hobbes was a political philosopher born in England, 1588. Thomas penned "Leviathan" among other works. The book was about the basic rights of people relative to formations of people, institutions and authority, which he named leviathans. His political theories angered royalists of the time, though many people supported his revolutionary ideas of basic rights.

The Magna Carta is a collection of documents written in 1215–1225. Parts were copied from the Charter of Liberties, written in 1100, England. These documents provided people with Habeas Corpus, protection from being jailed for nothing, but it mainly addressed royalty, nobility and clergy privilege. It was written as a legislation to prevent the King of England from taking advantage of church officials and other nobility. Those at the base of the pyramid were mostly unconsidered.

The Charter limited the power of kings over the bishops and barons. These documents were mostly concerned with the privileges of the haves, relative to the despotism of the king, the have-all. The Magna Carta inspired the original patriots, but the documents were limited in scope and mostly recognized the institutionalized rather than all individuals.

The 1689 English Bill of Rights set forth certain rights for certain individuals as well; many concepts were shared by the Colonies. Yet the rights were prescribed only for certain individuals. The Colonists believed they were included in the English Bill of Rights, but soon it became apparent they were not.

The original patriots used ideas from England, but they also had other influences. The Haudenosaunee as they called themselves for generations, now known by the name they became associated with by outsiders, The Iroquois, directly influenced the original patriots. The exact etymology of the word Iroquois is unknown, but in all likelihood, the word was once derogatory. The Iroquois Nation of Haudenosaunee is a generations old democracy that was long established. The Iroquois Nation influenced and assisted the European newcomers to North America, formerly known as Turtle Island.

The newcomers, as illustrated by Thomas Jefferson, essentially advocated the genocide of indigenous peoples, while at the same time looked to many of them as exemplary of tribes forming one common league. The Colonists not only adopted native knowledge, but also, at the same time legalized the theft of their land and institutionalized their expulsion and murder. This must have required a certain amount of doublethink.

The trinity of liberty was influenced by native ideas as well as European concepts. These ideas formed the foundation of the U.S.A., and were themselves a paradigm. Meant to insure the liberty of colonies among empires, they have since changed the world. Individuals have set on a course for increased liberty ever since, for the documents allow progression. The Declaration of Independence was meant to inspire the Colonies to shun the blood right of kings, and has gone on to inspire generations to seek liberty. And the Haudenosaunee influence cannot be overlooked.

Through the trinity of liberty individuals countered the framework of generational, global, oligarchical collectivism. The original patriots questioned and rejected the status quo. Throughout recorded time, nearly everywhere, were fiefdoms, kingdoms and oligarchical empires. Any place and people that weren't designed in such a way, or were weaker, were rolled on and capitalized on. Empires set sail on the Seven Seas to institutionalize the world over, and were then challenged.

The Declaration of Independence was an open letter to the royal and noble oligarchical collectivism of King George III. It stated that the people had enough and would no longer support their oligarchical collectivism. They demanded liberty. They could taste liberty, being far from the dominant European institutions and they could see liberty exemplified by the autonomous indigenous, and they announced their discontinuance of institutionalization.

The Declaration of Independence was a direct insult to George III and the well cultivated oligarchic and monopolistic institutions. It is a declaration of discontinuance. The Colonists, people without an actual nation to call home, began flattening the slant of the empirical exploiters with an open declaration. The Declaration of Independence boldly questioned the King's actions and announced that the royal exploitations were detested and that they desisted.

The Bill of Rights protects the basic rights of individuals in a complex institutionalized world. They are elementary rights preventing exploitation of one, under another. No institution or individual can supersede the Bill of Rights. It exists to protect individuals from religious, corporate and government institutions. People around the world aspire for the universal rights the trinity of liberty assures. The Bill of Rights was arguably written with the hindsight of The Revolutionary War, with the knowledge of what rights needed to be secure and counters institutional exploitation by providing individual rights.

The Constitution provides framework to a government of the people, for the people and by the people, an institution with checks and balances to guarantee that all actions are questioned and all powers limited. The Constitution did not set up the most effective government, but attempted to set up the most impartial and fair government. The Constitution is adjustable, it develops along with people; its laws are changeable so the government acts without interfering with the individuals and on their behalf.

The checks and balances restrict institutional monopolization, or oligarchical collectivism. Liberty allows for progression; development is possible via democratic principles within republic structure. Processes are questioned at every turn and no one individual or entity is given complete control. The Constitution keeps power among many offices that ideally function together in partnership. It put into place the complexities of cooperative government in liberty.

December 16, 1773 Boston Tea Party.
1775–1783 American Revolutionary War.
July 4, 1776 Declaration of Independence signed.
June 21, 1788 The U.S.A. Constitution went into effect.
December 15, 1791 Bill of Rights adopted.

The Boston Tea Party was one of the original protests and patriotic acts that led to U.S.A independence from English oligarchical collectivism. The Boston Tea Party engaged questioning the situation, the monopolistic taxation of the tea, trees and other commodities. After communication, the original patriots openly ceased support and proclaimed their reasoning in the Declaration of Independence. Then the original patriots set up a system that was stable and yet, changeable to allow development.

The trinity of liberty provided equality and limited institutions among individuals. Royalty and familial power were more or less banished. Ideally people were valued on their merit instead of their heritage. The documents provided a government that could be questioned and improved upon, but conditions were not ideal. Today the phrase "all men are created equal" is acceptable in ways that it originally was not.

FACT: In 1834, the Tennessee Constitution was changed. What once read "the freemen of this state have a right to bear arms for their common defense" was changed to "the free white men of this state have a right to bear arms for their common defense."

"The soldiers never explained to the government when an Indian was wronged, but reported the misdeeds of the Indians." ~Geronimo

---

There were setbacks and underhanded exploits, but the documents intended to provide everyone the ability to rise above their circumstances. Today, whoever can reflect, question and speak whatever they want. Anyone can choose any path and take it, so long as it does not harm others. Therein lays the responsibility of true liberty, overcoming the wrongdoers.

Freedom is not liberty. Freedom means one is free to ignore exploitation, free to let it happen, free to profit from it and/or free to prevent it. With liberty comes responsibility because liberty is for all individuals.

The trinity of liberty was a response, and instills responsibility. The documents intended to empower individuals and to cast off the royal and elite grip. The Bill of Rights prevents institutional exploitation by providing explicit rights to individuals to prevent specific exploits, but still these rights were not applied universally, they were exclusive, relegating some to caste existence.

The trinity of liberty was a response to exploitation, directly experienced and known historically. The exploitations of elite monopolistic institutions were disbanded. And yet, certain individuals and institutions infiltrated what was designed for individuals and institutionalized situations in to favor oligarchical collectivism. Liberty is pliable, but also permeable.

The original patriots questioned and renounced the wrongdoing of institutions despite global establishment. They questioned what was wrong swore them off with the Declaration of Independence. Despite the wrong being the global status quo, despite the majority tolerating it, despite it being beneficial to some, they stopped sought to stop the exploitation.

Who knew how King George III would react to their gallant words? They stood up for what is right, without consideration of the drawbacks to standing up against the exploits of empire. They made themselves independent of wrong by ceasing it, simply because it was the right thing to do. The original patriots chose to stand up to British exploits because it was the right thing to do, not because it was a battle they wanted or one they counted on winning.

The trinity of liberty made the state independent of any royal family, church, corporation or other institution. The trinity of liberty also makes institutions accountable, including government institutions. Until then, oligarchies were predominantly familial institutions and always had supportive churches as well as lucrative corporate charters. Church and state had been joined at the hip and corporations were their whips, and they were unquestionable. The trinity of liberty allowed for open inconsequential individual worship. But it prevents churches from intertwining with government because when institutions collectivize oligarchy is cemented. The trinity of liberty provides freedom for religious interpretation and more importantly freedom from religious institutions.

To question oligarchies was disallowed. Protesting was practically unheard of. The Bill of Rights guaranties the right for individual interpretation of God in whatever manner one sees fit. It provides the right to gather and communicate and the right to make public any information. It guarantees the right to question and petition the government and any institution under its governance. The First Amendment provides for the freedom of speech and the freedom to question all, but it is more than that. It is the First Amendment because it enables and supports all the other following Amendments and covers the most important material relative to individual empowerment.

The Second Amendment gives people the right to bear arms, the right to possess the same might as institutional authorities. This is meant to level the slant. The original patriots were reacting to the violent age-old battle between institutions and individuals and attempted to level the field. The Second Amendment is for self-defense certainly, but also to influence institutions to listen to people who might be armed when they question and protest. Also, if the First Amendment rights do not work, the Second Amendment and following Amendments back it up. The Bill of Rights is in a specific order for specific reasons.

Because British soldiers were invading homes with accusations and forcibly procuring provisions and housing from colonists, the Bill of Rights disallowed unannounced entry. The Bill of Rights prevented institutional search and seizure of property without justification. These were reactions to protect individuals over institutions without concern for institutional agenda. The Third and Fourth Amendments protect these liberties.

Because oligarchical institutions had always confiscated property as punishment the Fifth Amendment gives individuals the right to eminent domain. Because of the difficulties in receiving a fair trial for individuals, the Bill of Rights addressed trials in the Fifth, Sixth and Seventh Amendments. One need not speak if one doesn't want to and one has the right to a trial by a public jury.

The Eighth Amendment prevents institutions from holding individuals without possible payment of bail. It also prevents excessive institutional fines and cruel punishment.

The Ninth Amendment ensures that these are not to be the people's only rights. The original patriots knew very well how institutions flip words and intentions. The Ninth Amendment ensures the intention behind the Bill of Rights is clear. No one down the line can ever say that people do not have the right to clean water because it is not written in the Bill of Rights.

The Tenth Amendment puts power in the hands of people and state representation. The Bill of Rights provides liberty, and direction to protect and progress liberty.

The disdain of royal oligarchical infallibility led to the formation of a democratic republic, the likes of which the European world had not known since the ancient Greeks. The Greeks had an exclusive freedom, democracy for Grecians and slavery for everybody else, a quality the early U.S.A. shared with ancient Greece.

FACT: The original draft of the Declaration of Independence, drafted by Thomas Jefferson on hemp paper, included a denunciation of the global slave trade; this was removed from the final document approved by Congress. Thomas, a slave owner, wrote: "He has waged cruel war against human nature itself, violating its most sacred rights of life & liberty in the persons of a distant people who never offended him, captivating & carrying them into slavery in another hemisphere, or to incur miserable death in their transportation thither."

FACT: Edward Rutledge was a Continental Congressman and the youngest signer of the Declaration of Independence from South Carolina. He was a lawyer educated at the Temple, at Oxford University. He led the Southern States in their refusal to vote on the document until the grievance concerning slavery was removed.

The design of the U.S.A. was such that it was left open to all types of forces, including from institutionalized individuals. No longer would one man or one family be able to claim the divine right of kings, but only certain individuals had rights. Every freeman had an equal say, but freedom was exclusive. Originally only white men were considered to be born free because of institutionalized corporate agendas, because of psychological flaws, that transposed freedom for some, as liberty for all. Exclusive liberty is an oxymoronic impossibility.

Ideals that gave no man absolute power over another were radical concepts to most then. Throughout recorded time institutions were violent and slanted oligarchies. Rarely was power vested among people and not a primary royal family ordained with power through God. The same people who eventually fought off the most powerful army and navy of the world in the name of liberty, owned people as slaves; that's how radical the idea was.

Benjamin Franklin and Thomas Jefferson were the primary architects of the trinity of liberty and both were slave owners. Ben was also a Grand Master Freemason. Ben had international connections through the club, such as in France, who helped the founding of the U.S.A. Slavery is a steeply slanted pyramid system, Freemasonry is pyramidal as well. Ben and Thomas wrote opposite ideas to the old world, they also wrote opposite ideas to much of their own behavior.

On many occasions Ben and Thomas met with the Iroquois federation. The generous indigenous people offered resources and information on how to live in the new continent and also ideas on how to live together. Their cooperative autonomy was an inspiration. The ideas of localized government and consent of the people within a greater federation were Iroquois ideas. The notion that a federation of small states provided power and protection for one another was exemplified by the Iroquois.

The ideas of Greek democracy and Roman Republics inspired the foundation of the U.S.A. But the Iroquois were a well-established, peaceful, yet powerful democracy that faced opposition not only because there were corrupt influences that sought to take their resources, but also because of institutionalized biases based on appearance.

Throughout recorded time, people have been divided based on their appearance, birthplace and apparent alignment. People have been harmed, exploited, enslaved and murdered because of numerous conceived, nuanced differences. The differences in appearances have been magnified to mean all sorts of absurdities. People have been subjected to judgment and harm, all because of how they looked or where they lived. The only way to fairly understand people is according to their individual mentality.

It is not how people look that defines them, but how people think. There are four distinct types of people in the world. Idiots only question irrelevance, zealots only question in accordance with their preconceptions, elitists only question to advance their own situation, and patriots openly question all information. To understand people based on anything other than their mentality is at best marketing or polling and normally just a Neanderthal or cavemen notion of division.

FACT: William of Ockham was an English Friar born around 1288. He was a logician and philosopher noted for numerous intellectual contributions. He is associated with, but did not originate the theory of Occam's Razor. The Razor theory supposes that entities must not be multiplied beyond necessity. Occam's Razor is symbolic for cutting away extra and superfluous descriptions. "Plurality should not be posited without necessity."

"Make everything as simple as possible, but not simpler." ~Albert Einstein

The original patriots installed the idea that information and reasonable and logical thought had precedence over the power of the right of kings. But people still had biases and tolerations that allowed for exploitation based on appearance. The Revolutionary War was as much a war over the freedom to think as it was a war for the freedom from certain oligarchical exploitations. If the British Empire won, they possibly would have been free to exploit and monopolize entirely. The U.S.A.

allowed progression and protection from exploitation and from being defined by appearance or heritage or other arbitrary standards.

Many of the original patriots, those at the Boston Tea Party and the signers and architects of the trinity of liberty were Freemasons. Freemasonry is pyramidal; however in those times it was counter to the pyramidal system of the royal oligarchies. Freemasonry, despite its design, countered the pyramid system then conducting exploitation and monopolization.

The original patriots promoted reasoning in intelligent discussion where one was free to speak. They shared information about engineering and God and everything in between. The Freemasons had to exchange this information in secret, so much of it counter to the oligarchical dogma.

The Boston Tea Party was the catalyst for further protest and ultimately revolution against royal monopoly. The planning for the Boston Tea Party took place, at least in part, at the Green Dragon Tavern, a meeting place of Freemasons in Boston. Ideas of the autonomous natives, concepts of questioning, belief in rational thought and historical examples of liberty inspired the original patriots to create a country free from royal despotism.

> "Tolerance implies no lack of commitment to one's own beliefs. Rather it condemns the oppression or persecution of others." ~John F. Kennedy

Tolerance might be ambivalence or acceptance, negative or positive behavior. When one is ambivalent to evil one has acquired negative tolerations. When one is open and accepting of individual differences one has positive tolerance. The tolerant indigenous people welcomed the European newcomers. The European newcomers acquired negative tolerations concerning the murder of native peoples.

Well before 1776, there was a confederation of states with localized power and unified representation in the new world. Truly the U.S.A. is the land of the free and always has been. Despite indigenous Americans subsequently experiencing the worst and most institutionalized genocide and gentrification in world history, they were originally an integral part in inspiring the trinity of liberty, and physically enabling the survival of many European newcomers.

The ideas of the trinity of liberty were, and perhaps, still are ahead of its time; more accurately ahead of most people in its time. The wording, "All Men" now equates to everyone, not just white guys with land and loot. Basic freedoms and privileges are now adorned to all.

It took generations for the word "men" to mean human beings, but finally it does. The U.S.A. has evolved into a country that would not have anything to do with the country of the original patriots. In some ways, we have surpassed them. The U.S.A. has evolved to the point where people might consider the thirteen Colonies as repressive and exploitative as the monarchies existent around them. Liberty allows for progression.

The romantic story of the immigrant to the U.S.A. typifies this notion. It is the idea that anyone can come to the U.S.A. and walk streets paved with gold, open opportunity. The U.S.A. offered liberty and open equality that was unavailable elsewhere. In the U.S.A. a pauper could essentially become a king. Starting with nothing in the old world meant one was sure to end up with nothing, in the new world one could end up with it all.

The liberty people experience today is a magical exception in history. In the old world, one was overtly forced to worship one way, live one way and stay in one place. Oppression was normal. The glorious and rebellious nation of the U.S.A. was founded against empire, but greed and corruption infiltrated. Land was taken away from people who already lived there. The liberty enjoyed in the U.S.A. has a bony underside.

Basic liberty was already legislated in parts of the Americas. The new arrivals removed them and then pronounced their own legislation which relegated many as "them" and others as "us". Progression was allowed and yet the early U.S.A. was no less empirical than most other nations of the time. A partial version of liberty was provided to the privileged and revoked from others. Many people in the past tried to hide from institutions and avoid being implicated as a "them". Others were violently confronted and forced to defend themselves like Chief Sitting Bull and William Wallace.

FACT: Chief Sitting Bull was considered a visionary among the Sioux. He envisioned and foretold of U.S.A. troops attacking his village, but his people defeated and killed them. Soon after the vision George Custer raided the village, his troops were annihilated at the Battle of Little Bighorn. Sitting Bull went on to perform briefly with Buffalo Bill.

"Each man is good in his sight. It is not necessary for eagles to be crows. We are poor…but we are free. No white man controls our footsteps. If we must die…we die defending our rights." ~Chief Sitting Bull

The trinity of liberty provides for power to rest in people's hands. Power rests with local people who communicate with locals. Power is not automatically in some ultimate, distant, royal, infallible family and their nobility, it is nearby. Any and every person has the right to take hold of the reins of regional and national institutions and influence their course.

The flexibility for laws to evolve allows people to progress as well. Overt and covert racist slavery is wrong, but it took action and legislation to outlaw and eliminate institutionalized slavery. Nearly every culture from Asia to the Americas practiced slavery in one form or another for centuries. Open legislation outlawed racist intent and institutions. Progression was allowed to happen.

Women should have always been allowed to vote, but at least the trinity of liberty allowed for the progression. They had to demand it first though, through women's suffrage, whereas women held positions of power in the Iroquois Nation.

Temperance is essential in order to develop and progress. Encouraging legislation of change has progressed equality. The most noble of people get power because they earn it, not because they seek it. The most noble develop change and give up power when alternatives are available.

Any and all people now have access to all positions in the U.S.A. This was, and is, an extraordinary concept that provides great benefits with occasionally not so great consequences. Potentially evil and malevolent people have access to all, as well as the compassionate and benevolent.

Any ideal, great and godly, or vile and defiled, can gain popularity and focus if it has the predominant number of people's acceptance or the acceptance of persons of prominence. Anyone can rise up in the U.S.A., even the despicable. All people, despite local tolerations, lean toward what is right and therefore evil must distort truth, tolerations and situations, to conduct and coordinate their evil. The evil are free to do so and people are free to ignore it, or follow it, or respond to it.

"I cannot accept your canon that we are to judge Pope and King unlike other men with a favorable presumption that they did no wrong. If there is any presumption, it is the other way, against the holders of power, increasing as the power increases. Power tends to corrupt, and absolute power corrupts absolutely. Great men are almost always bad men, even when they exercise influence and not authority: still more when you superadd the tendency or certainty of corruption by authority. There is no worse heresy than that the office sanctifies the holder of it." ~Lord Acton's Dictum, John Acton, English Historian

Absolute power corrupts absolutely. That is why the original patriots separated church, state and corporate. It was a reaction. The original patriots knew from experience once these institutions linked, absolute power was possible and the exploitation of individuals was all but sealed. The U.S.A. was founded on Lord Acton's Rule.

Absolute power corrupts absolutely and some power corrupts some. It is not that all people of power are corrupt, or that they always become absolutely corrupt. It is that the corrupt tend to seek power in the first place. Not all people, once in a position of power, become absolutely corrupt. It just seems so because the corrupt gravitate to power and the corrupt in power seek to empower others who are similarly corrupted. The corrupted in power absolutely empower more corrupt. They need more corrupt people around to maintain their corruption.

Corruption happens all the time. Every day there are multitudes of random stories of one prominent institution or institutionalized individual acting on corrupt greed. They embezzle, extort, bribe, con and operate any number of scams to contrast law and distort information to con people. The most successful corrupt gather other corrupted around them in order to keep their corruption clandestine.

There are many sorts of corruption, but most corruption transpires unnoticed. Corruption benefits the few off of the many and always revolves around lies and the distortion of information. Corruption results in the less corrupt and more honest being restricted to the outskirts of power play.

"In war truth is the first casualty." ~Aeschylus, Playwright

In 1296, Scotland was controlled by the English monarchy. Scottish people were routinely imprisoned, punitively taxed and expected to serve King Edward I. All the land was corrupted and slanted to benefit the few over the many. William Wallace was a simple Scot who fought against the royal monopoly.

The unverified story goes that William crossed paths with English soldiers one day after fishing. The soldiers demanded all the fish he had. King Edward had monopolized everything in Scotland; there was not a fish that swam or a bird that flew which was not owned by the King and all the King's men. Wallace offered a portion of his fish, but refused to give the soldiers his whole catch. There was a confrontation and William ended up beating them and possibly killing one or more. In 1297, William Wallace killed an English Sheriff and officially became an outlaw.

William and his peers began battling the English oppression and exploitation with swords. "Oppressed by the burden of servitude under the intolerable rule of English domination," (from Declaration of Arbroath) the Scottish people gathered together and rose up against exploitation by English royalty.

> SYMBOL – FISH
> The fish is symbolic for fertility, freedom and happiness. It is symbolic of fearlessness, the ability to travel in dangerous waters unafraid. Early Christians adopted the fish as a symbol. Around the time of the birth of Jesus, the age of Pisces began.

On September 11, 1297 at Sterling Bridge, William and the Scottish surprised the English forces and ultimately celebrated victory. William and the outnumbered Scots used Sterling Bridge to reduce the advantage of the English forces. Thousands of English soldiers perished. After the battle, William was knighted and made into a respected leader. He is known as Scotland's greatest patriot.

> "This is the truth I tell you: of all things freedom's most fine. Never submit to live, my son, in the bonds of slavery entwined." ~William Wallace Family

In the medieval world everyone was obsessed with the pyramidal hierarchy of personal classification. The kings believed they were ultra-men, descendants of God. They believed that those outside their family were beneath them. Whatever situation one was born into was likely to be the same when one passed. People stayed in their place or the hierarchy would find a place for them, six feet under.

The extraordinary military achievements and the assumed personal magnetism of William, gave him power in steering Scottish policy, even over some Scottish nobility. This was an exception to the rule. William attempted to improve his situation as more or less a commoner. He came from a respected family, but was not nobility. He was educated though and a brave leader who stood up to exploitation conducted by royalty.

After years of battles and diplomacy, in 1304, Scottish leaders recognized King Edward as overlord. Only William refused to submit. He was captured in 1305, turned in by fellow Scots and brought to London for trial. William was charged with being an outlaw and traitor and sentenced to immediate execution.

> "I could not be a traitor to Edward for I was never his subject."
> ~William Wallace, at his trial

William was dragged by horses for miles, hung, removed before he passed out, and then disemboweled. They chopped him into pieces and threw parts of his body into a fire, then cut his head off and put it on a pike atop London Bridge. There's a message there – rise up and we'll kill you. As a matter of fact, we'll bloody kill you three times and continue to torture your shell after. The royal authority instituted such punishment to instill fear in any who would question or act against their authority. William was a patriot and is a hero to this day because he selflessly fought for people against oppression and corruption.

> FACT: First known declaration of independence is the Scottish Declaration of Arbroath, 1320.

War for Scottish independence continued for most of the thirteenth century and eventually a treaty was signed that held, sealed with the marriage of Scottish and English nobility. The only way they would let people in is if they were related. One was either in the family or serf to the family. Either one was zapped with the blood right of kings directly from God or unequal.

The only way they could recognize the Scottish nobility as peers was to marry them in, then they could be imparted with the divine right of kings. This was the most acceptable means for royalty to quell a lengthy, country wide insurgency. Throughout the world, marriage of royalty maintained control within selected groups. There was no way the oligarchical monarchical authorities would capitulate to common people, but they would acknowledge other royalty.

SYMBOL – FASCES is Roman for bundle. It is a bundle of rods tied up, central among them, an axe. Originally it was displayed before Roman magistrates as a badge of authority. It is symbolic for individuals joining together with the axe controlling individuality and actions amongst the rods. It became the root word for fascism when the symbol was adopted by Italy and the axis (axes) powers. It also, at one time, appeared on U.S.A. dimes, with Liberty on the other side. Today the fasces is replaced by the torch and, Liberty, who appeared opposite, by Dwight D. Eisenhower. A fasces or mace is still in the House of Representatives. There is one at the Lincoln memorial, on the seal of the Knights of Columbus and on the crest of 71st infantry regiment from New York.

"If all that Americans want is security, they can go to prison. They'll have enough to eat, a bed and a roof over their heads. But if an American wants to preserve his dignity and his equality as a human being, he must not bow his neck to any dictatorial government." ~Dwight D. Eisenhower

Today, William would most likely get blasted to bits like anyone else on the present technological battlefields. Today, the axe and sword are no longer the preferred tools of exercising free will. Because mechanisms of warfare have improved, anyone can be efficient on the battlefield; great strength and charisma are not required. It is practically impossible for individuals to raise arms and battle oppressive institutionalized overt might with overt might alone. Anyone with fingers and eyes might use a gun well.

To go to war is considered a last option for individuals as it may mean their end. People normally need to be convinced to go to war through pushing and prodding with fear and desperation. To fight for reasons other than self-defense and preservation requires tolerations to evils and institutionalization.

People go to war when they are convinced there will be victory and glory, that they will live as heroes, or that dying is better than living. People mandate war when they are convinced their institutions will benefit or that without war they would be threatened. Two choices polarize, but there are always more options other than fighting or fleeing.

William was extremely courageous and gave up everything in the face of the royal English oligarchy, which took control of everything. He attempted to free his people from forceful exploitation by force. He resisted the English soldiers and steel with the might of his sword and his courage, inspiring people like no nobility or royalty of the time could. He fought to cast away the oppressive oligarchical monopoly.

Today raising arms against the powers that be, no matter how exploitative and aggressive their oppression, is probably not the best option. Institutions have built up vast forces and armies to squash violence and engaging in violence enables them to engage in violence with near limitless and technologically superior resources.

There are many ways to resist. William went to war with a broadsword many would not be able to swing. He had immeasurable courage and displayed it eloquently and physically. In his time, the only way to overcome exploitation and oppression was to revolt at arms. Attacking the attackers is often like giving your big brother an excuse to hit you.

Mahatmas Gandhi probably could not have wielded William's sword. Gandhi practiced nonviolent resistance and would have yielded the entirety of his catch back into the waters from where the fish came rather than oblige or attack. Gandhi did not battle, but matched William's stature of heart and ability to fight exploitative powers. William yielded nothing to institutions, Gandhi yielded nothing as well.

A vegetarian, Gandhi never attacked anyone. He freed millions from institutionalized oppression via nonviolent activity and discontinuance of institutional support. He fought against the same empire as William, only through peaceful resistance and non-cooperation. Gandhi battled the remnants of the same type of empirical institutions as William did with sword and the original patriots did with musket, only Gandhi never raised his arms to harm. Gandhi used compassion and his senses to speak out against, and dismantle institutional oligarchical collectivism.

A man of small stature and great principal, Gandhi freed South Asia from British empirical rule. Through peaceful nonviolent protest he rattled the might of the Empire on which the Sun never set. Gandhi peacefully dismantled the deeply entrenched continental oligarchical collectivism.

> "Generations to come will scarce believe that such a one as (Gandhi) ever in flesh and blood walked upon this Earth." ~Albert Einstein

In the 1850s Britain took control of what is now India. India was already conquered, and essentially under British rule prior, but the corporate soldiers of the British East India Company previously owned and directly governed the region. India was a corporate plantation. The Company at one time owned India, Pakistan, Sri Lanka (Ceylon), Malaysia, Hong Kong, and Singapore. Britain took over South Asia and it officially became an English Colony.

The Company organized monopolization wherever they went, whether in India or the East Indies. They stole and enslaved, then sold whatever they could all around the world, all under the auspices of the British royalty. At one point The Company was allowed to coin their own money, declare war, wage war, make peace and other privileges normally attributed only to states.

From timber and textiles, cotton and silk, to tea and opium, The Company and the British Empire owned all. The sea salt in India, as plentiful as the sand, was monopolized by the Company and Britain. Opium though, was among The Company's most profitable cargo.

The Company was largely responsible for the illegal opium trade and held a monopoly on the junk. The trade ultimately led to the Opium Wars and the seizure of Hong Kong, which further opened up the opium market. The Company also made fortunes from the slave trade. The Company was ultimately disbanded. The Company ruled South Asia until it was no longer fit to do so and was completely dissolved of rule by 1857.

FACT: Elihu Yale was one Briton who made his fortune with The Company. Elihu was Governor of Madras for The Company. He donated a carton of goods to a man in Connecticut, representing a small learning institution in 1718. The contents of which were sold for 560 pounds sterling. In gratitude the institution named the new building this money funded, Yale. Eventually the entire institution was named Yale University, despite being more largely assisted by the contributions of Jeremiah Dummer.

COMPANY FLAG
The Company flag flew for over 200 years. The corporate flag has red and white stripes along with St. George's cross. The Company was granted royal English charter on December 31, 1600 and was completely dissolved January 1, 1874. On the eve of their disbanding, The Company elite formed the East India Club that exists today at 16 St. James Square, London.

The Company flag makes the flag of the U.S.A. look a lot less original. The design depicted is from the beginning of the 1700s. Why is there a correspondence in the flag design? Who did Betsy Ross work for?

Francis Hopkinson was a signer of the Declaration of Independence who is given partial credit for the design of the U.S.A. flag. Francis also participated in the design of the Great Seal of the U.S.A. He was successful author who penned many poems, essays and books. His book *The Prophecy* colorfully described and criticized the royal monopolization of the Colonies. Francis' writings were widely influential in inspiring people to cut ties with the royal monopoly.

The people of India were directly involved in The Company's final exit from India through the Indian Sepoy Mutiny of 1857 and further rebellion. The people of India were fed up with being enslaved workers in a royal monopoly. The Company was out, but India was not yet free.

Richard Blair, George Orwell's father, worked for the India Civil Service in the Opium Department for a few years in the early 1900s, before returning to England. Eric Blair, or George Orwell, served as a Policeman in Burma briefly in the early 1920s. George later fought in the Spanish Civil War in 1937 where he was shot in the throat by a sniper, but survived. He wrote about his experiences in the Spanish Civil War in "Homage to Catalonia." The Spanish Civil War is often noted as build up towards WWII.

During the Spanish Civil War, Germany and Italy supported the Nationalists while the Soviet Union supported the Republicans. Many foreigners participated in the war, on both sides, George fought for the Republicans. Approximately five hundred thousand people died in the war. In 1939, the Nationalists installed a dictatorship and went on to execute thousands more.

When The Company left India, the British rule instituted was not necessarily better for the Indian people than Company domination, in fact, it was more organized and sometimes more harsh. Though British rule was not without its benefits, it was still repressive. Gandhi had the opportunity to go to university in London and became a lawyer for instance. Names changed, but not much more, new offices were now in the name of the Crown, not the Company.

Later, while living in South Africa, Gandhi experienced racism and came to the conclusion that there was global discriminatory exploitation. He would recall being asked to move for a white man to sit down on a bus in apartheid in South Africa. There he developed his ideas of peaceful resistance. Gandhi organized and led an Indian stretcher-bearer unit during British conflict with the Zulus in 1906. The Zulus protested and rebelled against unfair taxes and the British stomped out their rebellion. Gandhi later called the military action a manhunt. In September 1906, Gandhi first theorized Satyagraha. It is the practice of peaceful resistance and non-cooperation, literally translated as the pursuit of truth.

Gandhi influenced generations and was himself influenced by many, including the Russian writer Leo Tolstoy, author of *War and Peace*. Leo served in the Crimean War in an artillery unit and later became a pacifist. He also wrote *The Kingdom of God is Within You* about nonviolent resistance to war and oppression which Gandhi held dear. In 1908, he wrote *A Letter to a Hindu* openly suggesting that the only way India would be free of British rule was through peaceful resistance.

> "Everyone thinks of changing the world, but no one thinks of changing himself." ~Leo Tolstoy

Gandhi returned to India in 1915 and criticized British repression, but also the violent Indian retaliations. He began implementing peaceful non-cooperation to protest exploitation. Gandhi announced a Declaration of Independence in January 1930. He called for a boycott of all foreign goods, especially British goods, but criticized violent action.

In March 1930, Gandhi began the Salt Satyagraha. He marched over two-hundred-twenty miles to the coastline to harvest tax-free sea salt. British authorities reacted to the inspired illegal trade of salt by arresting 60,000 people. Gandhi variously spent over 6 years of his life in prison. Many compared the salt of India to the tea of Boston. It was reported that Gandhi himself reflected on the Boston Tea Party as he was harvesting the salt. Observers at the time also compared the two events.

Gandhi called for boycott of the British educational system and courts. He recommended that people resign from government and forsake British titles. Once he was attacked, and refused to press charges on his attackers in the British courts. He called for the abandonment of the caste system and quickly gained admiration worldwide.

> FACT: Now mostly outlawed, the caste system in India still exists, but is declining. It is a multidivisional pyramidal system of classifying people by their heritage. There were numerous classifications ranging from the Brahmin, the high society, to the Dalit, the class so low they had no official class. They are ostracized in every way as the untouchables.

The oligarchical structure of the Indian caste system was well suited for the pyramidal control The Company and the British instituted. The pyramidal arrangement worked perfectly with what the new controllers instituted. It is theorized that the caste system was first implemented by other invaders of India centuries prior, who placed themselves atop of course.

When the Company left, the British authorities debated on keeping the overt control or adopting covert control. They opted to stay as the face of authority and the overt control did not work. Because of the peaceful and popular protest inspired by Gandhi, the British ultimately left South Asia unto itself. In 1947 India became independent and the exploitative rulers sailed back to their island. India was no longer a transnational corporation in service to a monarchical empire. Gandhi inspired individuals to stop participating in exploitation which led to their emancipation.

There was great chaos after the British controllers left. Other institutions and individuals were after power and violently attempted to get it. There were "us and them" separation based on racist and religious concepts. After hundreds of thousands of deaths from tribal and religious battles, Britain divided independent India into two main parts, Muslim Pakistan on August 14, 1947 and Hindu India the next day. The violence and potential violence spawned the division. On January 30, 1948 Gandhi was assassinated. To this day, the nuclear nations routinely shoot at each other on the tense Kashmir border.

> "What difference does it make to the dead, the orphans, and the homeless, whether the mad destruction is wrought under the name of totalitarianism or the holy name of liberty and democracy?" ~Gandhi

> "There are many causes that I am prepared to die for, but no cause that I am prepared to kill for." ~Gandhi

In the U.S.A., thanks to the trinity of liberty, one can do whatever one wants so long as it's responsible. Liberty is the idea that one can step wherever, as long as someone else isn't being stepped on. Hindu, Muslim, Jewish and Christian can live side by side and are obliged to forget their historical or contrived differences and abandon the "us and them" mentality.

The most magical stories of the U.S.A. are about people who were exploited and then allowed opportunity to become exceptional. Hard work and maybe a little luck has produced prosperity for countless. Anyone could win; anyone could go from zero to hero. These stories are magical because of the symbolism of the caste system being cast to the wind.

There is fair opportunity in the U.S.A. Sadly and unfairly, equal rights are a rare and innovative idea in the history of the world. Such corrupted influences and tolerations reached into the trinity of liberty as well. Only recently is liberty for all beginning to come to fruition. And still to this day institutions act on interests for ends other than individual independence.

There is opportunity to rise up in the U.S.A. People have the right to question, communicate and proceed in whatever legitimate venture desired. No matter one's heritage or predicament there is always the ability to excel. And yet questioning is required to maintain and progress this. Questioning institutional presentation is a free individual's ace in the hole among established institutions. Questioning excels individuals and progresses society.

In most places and most times, only the few could get ahead. Among institutions there was no equality only oligarchy. The many were relegated to be stepped on as the elite passed by. Now anyone can shout, "Don't tread on me!" The streets are not paved with gold, but there is potential. It is vastly difficult to navigate the road to success which sometimes leads into dark alleys of failed attempts, but there is hope and possibility. There has never been unlimited opportunity, and there has been institutional exploitation in the U.S.A., largely based on race, but there is in theory opportunity for all in the U.S.A. There is opportunity because the original patriots decreased institutional slant, and made oligarchical angles less acute.

Today most in the world have no access to clean drinking water. The most clean, and the most dramatically filtered water still contains industrial soot, a patchwork of pharmaceuticals and a collage of various mined petrol and atomic toxins that do who-knows-what, to you-know-who. Pollution is seen as the cost of doing business.

If the original patriots, who threw the Boston Tea Party and drafted the trinity of liberty, were prevented from having clean water for their tea, what would they do? If the water for their family, crops, livestock and tea were tainted by institutional processes, what would the original patriots do? Definitely something.

The original patriots actively rebelled against exploitation after questioning the situation. They expressed their independence of the exploitative British monarchy, parliamentary and company, altogether discontinuing their dealings with them. They protested and peacefully disengaged without accord. King George III only made the exploitative grip tighter, resulting in escalation of tension and war. The original patriots ultimately tried to create a government with universal accountability, as a counter to the infallible monarchy. But first the original patriots questioned the situation and tossed the means of their exploitation into the sea.

William and Gandhi were equally courageous patriots. Both conducted patriotic acts to confront exploitation as best they could. William was patriotic in his time and represents the confrontational side of the patriotic spectrum. Gandhi was patriotic in his time and represents the peaceful side of the patriotic spectrum. The Boston Tea Party epitomizes a patriotic act, peacefully confronting abuse. The specifics of the Boston Tea Party may contain some unknowns, mysteries, but what is known is enough. The Boston Tea Party is an archetypal story of patriotism.

THE DESTRUCTION OF TEA AT BOSTON HARBOR.

THE BIG STEEP

In the late 1700s individuals in servitude to oligarchies began to question exploitative conditions and revolt against harsh treatment. Around the world there were revolutions, spurred by the exchange of ideas. There were revolutions in Scotland, The Caribbean, The Americas, Russia and France. People grew tired empirical control and wanted fewer restrictions, but the few at the peak of the pyramid tightened their grip and increased their hold.

Monarchical exploits initiated global shipping institutions. Monopolization and institutionalization expanded all around the world. The Sun never set on the British Empire and other European monarchies violently tried to keep up.

To question the authority of oligarchical institutions was a veritable death sentence in most places. To suggest that their power was not absolute and not absolutely derived via God, could get one absolved of life. Yet people the world over began to question. At first in whispers over tea and eventually people boldly and loudly questioned the institutions among them. People broke free from the shackles of fear holding their tongues. Questioning and communication instigated revolution.

FACT: Caffeine is a psychoactive stimulant. In small doses it can have a positive effect on one's physical performance and stimulate mental focus. It also produces faster reaction time and heightened short term memory.

It is hypothesized that caffeine and the café were essential in the advent of free thinking and open communication of enlightened ideas, ideas of liberty. The café provided just the right stimulant, in just the right environment to enable communication. The café may have been the first place where people openly proclaimed their resentment of monopolization and special privileges of the royalty, nobility and clergy.

CAFFEINE HISTORY
3000 BC: Chinese began steeping and drinking tea. Yerba maté and cocoa consumed by South Americans for unknown thousands of years.
~1500 AD: The Sufis began to drink coffee to stay awake and meditate.
December 1600: Queen Elizabeth I commissioned The British East India Company for expeditions to Asia. They were to seek out the best tea, opium and other spices to bring back to the British Isle. For years tea is so expensive only royalty partakes.
1601: The Company embarked as the world's first multinational corporation. It extorts, enslaves, and murders for profit until 1858.
1610: The Company marketed tea as a medicinal beverage. As the years passed there was so much tea in England and Europe that it became affordable and popular.
1650s: The first coffee houses are opened in London.
1670: Charles II granted The Company the privilege to act on its own, soon it ruled South Asia. Charles II also created the Hudson Bay Company, which colonized much of Canada.
1675: King Charles II attempted to ban coffee houses, but the proclamation was revoked immediately.

By the late 1700s there was a major tea market established in the Colonies. At the time, most in England were quite fond of coffee, while most in New England preferred tea. Some Colonists felt increasingly exploited and began to express their dissatisfaction. Individuals resented the laws of the distant monarchy and their local authorities. Tea was not the only commodity that was being unfairly taxed. The Tea Act was just one of many exploits enacted by the King. The Pine Tree Laws, the Stamp Act, the Townsend Act, and the Sugar Act all subjugated and exploited the Colonists.

Throughout the 1700s many Colonists considered themselves to be essentially Englishmen. And as Englishmen, they believed they were entitled to the rights provided by the English Bill of Rights, but the perception of the English institutions was that the Colonists were not English and therefore did not have the same rights. Freedoms were afforded to a few according to pyramidal classifications, outright liberty did not exist.

No Taxation without representation was a theme even in the early days of English Constitutional documents, when less than five percent of the population was allowed to vote. This idea was originally exclusive and not meant for the likes of Colonists in the far off new world.

"Taxation without representation is tyranny." ~James Otis

The Pine Tree Laws were made to produce gains for the empire, but moreover maintain and expand control. No matter who supposedly owned the land in New Hampshire, if there was a white pine tree that was yay tall and twelve inches wide, it was the King's tree. Obviously American Indians were unhappy about this, but newcomers too chose not to obey the law because they felt exploited. King George III intended to monopolize the land and sea, and all commerce therein. The straight pine trees were used for the masts of ships for the King's Navy and Company John vessels.

During this time a Deputy Surveyor of the King's woods found that the owner of a mill had chopped down some of the King's trees in Weare, New Hampshire. He informed the Sheriff, and on April 13, 1772, the Sheriff and his Deputy rode into Weare to collect the fine from the logger, a prominent member of the community, under threat of imprisonment. It was late when the Sheriff and logger met, both agreed to meet again in the morning to settle the fine then. The Sheriff and Deputy rested the night while the logger made other arrangements.

The logger and his peers might have been up all night, hyped up on high-grade cameillia sinensis, tea, for they disguised themselves with coal blackened faces and armed themselves with pine switches and went to the inn where the sheriff slept. Just before daybreak they woke him up with a beating. When the deputy tried to help the sheriff, they beat him too. They strung the two up, cut the hair off of their horses and sent them out of town on their devalued steeds. Known as the Pine Tree Riot, a white pine tree stands in the area commemorating the event. Eight men of Weare were identified through their thin disguises and were eventually caught, tried and to the disdain of the sheriff, ordered to pay a small fine.

Months later, in May 1773, the Tea Act was passed. This gave The Company a monopoly on tea in the Colonies. The Tea Act made tea more affordable to the Colonists, but it also gave The Company monopolization of the product.

The Company monopolized tea to increase their power and maintain their grip. At the time, The Company was facing financial troubles and needed an income boost. The recent costs of the French and Indian War, (also known as the Seven Years' Wars and The War of Conquest, among other names, fought in 1756) along with rampant starvation in the Asian

Colonies financially devastated The Company. The French and Indian War was fought all around the world, but was concentrated in the Americas, over its resources.

FACT: George Washington and those under his command fired the first shots of the French and Indian War. George was known as a bold and impulsive young officer. The British and Natives fought the French and other Natives for seven years. George hoped to become a British officer for many years. When the promotion did not come, he became a farmer, until the Revolutionary War.

The British Empire owned South Asia and had virtually removed the French, the major alternate empire, from the Americas. Monopolization was instituted and expanded. Some people grew dissatisfied and expressed their dissatisfaction in terms the powers would understand. At times patriots defy law to directly and symbolically express, "no more, shove off." Exploitation instigated people to throw boat loads of perfectly good tea into the sea to express exactly that.

Rebellion, civil disobedience and nonviolent dissent arrived to Boston Harbor. In addition to the ubiquitous exploitation of the King and The Company other events precluded the big steep with the same tone as the Pine Tree Riot. The Boston Massacre occurred only three years prior. Five colonists were shot and killed by British soldiers; six others were injured.

The Boston Massacre started over an unpaid wig bill. Words were exchanged, snowballs were tossed and the situation escalated. The event was marked by capitalizing on the situation to stir up more resentment of the soldiers, who were already seen as bullies by many. The Boston Massacre was used to influence how people perceived events. Paul Revere was involved in the antiestablishment propaganda producing a famous engraving of The Boston Massacre.

Overt oppression was increasingly perpetuated on the Colonists, who believed they had the rights of English people. Boston was especially rebellious and problematic for the authorities. The Boston Massacre was a small massacre compared to the massacres of indigenous people at the time. These massacres were conducted on an exponential scale and labeled expansion, battles, treaty violations, and many names other than massacre and murder. Language is key to the presentation.

Paul was possibly present at the tea toss and an Adams family member, Samuel Adams, may have assisted in planning the event. The Boston Tea Party wasn't only about tea; there was an array of transgressions precluding and surrounding. There were mounting questions concerning Colonial exploitation and repression. Tea became the catalyzing symbol.

The original patriots planned their civil disobedience, perhaps while drinking tea at the Green Dragon Tavern. It would be against the law, but no violence and no thievery was part of the plan. It was a protest and not meant to advance anything except statement. There would be destruction, but no violence, no theft. There would be insult, but no harm nor theft.

In order to be a patriot, first one must question the tea. Why is there a monopoly? Why is it sanctioned by the King? Why must we pay for war? Why should we serve to benefit the distant monarchy? Who benefits? To obtain knowledge of the possibility that tea is being used to exploit requires questioning.

After questioning, the original patriots communicated their information. They let the community know that the tea they enjoy, leads to their exploitation, and the profit of uncaring Company strangers. No matter how pleasing the tea is, if it is enabling exploitation, patriots question, reject exploitation and literally or figuratively toss it into the sea.

Most everyone enjoyed tea though also identified with the sentiment of the boycott, but the boycott could only expand so far. Over eighty percent of the Colonists were loyalists, people who supported the King and willingly consumed the tea. The vast majority just wanted a little tea before milking the cows or making swords. Most people were unconcerned who supplied it or who was exploited in its distribution. An alternative supply of tea from the Dutch and Colonists was available, but The Company tea was less expensive.

Mobilized and committed colonists continued to boycott and voice their dissatisfaction, but it was insufficient; many simply wanted an inexpensive warm beverage. The Company monopolized their drink, authorized by the Parliament's laws and King's orders, certified by church officials. Eventually though the ambivalent drank hibiscus or coffee.

On Dec. 16, 1773, citizens of Boston and members of the Sons of Liberty, a group of freedom fighters and Freemasons, walked boldly and nobly past excited onlookers, some were dressed as American Indians. They boarded the Dartmouth, Eleanor and Beaver, which held The Company tea. There had been an ongoing dispute and the colonists had refused to let the tea into Boston, and the British refused to let the ships leave, so in oceanic limbo the ships anchored. They boarded the ships, broke the locks on the cargo holds, hacked open the tea-chests with tomahawks and tossed them into the harbor.

They were not disguising themselves as Indians. They were identifying themselves with the autonomous American indigenous individuals. Many of the participants were well-known members of the community. They were not trying to hide; they would have donned hoods if they were intending to commit clandestine crime. Instead they identified themselves as indigenous because they identified with them, to make a statement, not because they were trying to conceal their identity.

Prior to taxation without representation and resentment of exploitation, most Colonists were proud to be loyal to the empire. Most believed that they were among the "us" and not the "them." As they were treated unfairly, like a resource, like consumers and producers, more began to reject the ways of the oligarchical model. People craved independence, reflected and symbolized by dressing like the independent indigenous individuals.

The natives provided inspiration. The Iroquois and other tribes were and always had been independent, free of institutions. In dressing like indigenous, the Sons of Liberty symbolically expressed they were no longer English, they were symbolically acting out in support of liberty. They knew very well, after all, that even coal blackened faces would not disguise their identity, let alone a little face paint and feathers in their hair. The donning of native attire was possibly as much of a statement as the tossing of the tea itself.

The welcoming natives were admired for their cooperative independence and through them the Colonists saw there were alternatives to the kingdom. Part of the separation of church and state in the U.S.A. comes from the welcoming Native indigenous who accepted such diversity. The churches the newcomers were accustomed to supported various monarchies that were exploiting the Colonists while the natives welcomed and accepted those with other beliefs, yet kept their own traditions.

The Colonists realized religious institutions were propagating oligarchical collectivism, their exploitation led them to look for alternatives. Churches gave official holy validation to kings and the colonists rejected that. Kings and royalty were not holy whatsoever in the U.S.A. In fact, the King's Company, endorsed by the church, was their exploiter. The welcoming native ideas were adopted by the Colonists who had only known rigid conformity to monotheistic institutions of church, state and company and their institutionalized representatives; the clergy, royalty and nobility.

FACT: The Iroquois Confederacy began as early as 1142 AD. On June 11, 1776 Iroquois Chiefs met with Continental Congress, and on the same day the Congress decided to pen a declaration. During this meeting, the Haudenosaunee, People of the Long House or Iroquis gave John Hancock an Indian name – "the Great Tree." They also wished the Iroquois and the new democracy on the land would "act as one people and have but one heart." On June 28, the first draft of the Declaration of Independence was presented to Continental Congress. During the Revolutionary War the centuries old Iroquois Confederacy split, some Iroquois sided with the British and others with the Colonists.

The Sons of Liberty made their way past protesters and onlookers who very well recognized the locals, despite their garb and who very well understood its symbolism. They made sure that the people of Boston saw them turn the harbor into a tea pot. Forty five tons of tea went into the drink that evening.

This ignited similar acts of resistance at numerous ports, because people saw them, knew who they were, and supported the protest. It was a destructive and aggressive act, but no one was injured, spare some who attempted to pocket tea and were beaten away. It was a nonviolent act of defiance, not a robbery, and not anarchy. Many identified with their message partly because nothing was stolen, and no one was killed.

The initial boycott expanded into protest, then civil disobedience, which cocooned into the Revolutionary War when the institutions would not yield to the individuals. The institutional agendas were more important than individual's voices. War erupted when oppression continued when the institutions insisted and individuals resisted oligarchical exploits.

If King and The Company would have treated the Colonists with fairness, The Company would have sold their tea and the King might have kept his Colonies. If the authorities had capitulated then and there, the following war could have been prevented. Instead, overt control was instituted. The Intolerable or Punitive Acts were installed and the institutions tightened their grip. There were more exploits and Boston was especially punished.

The monarchical authority made infallible by the church and supported by its rising corporation were all empowered and emboldened by the rich resources of the Americas, and they would not yield. More civil disobedience resulted, then more royal restrictions, and ultimately the Revolutionary War.

PINE TREE FLAG
The newly formed Sons of Liberty who dunked the tea dressed as indigenous people, erected a post called the Tree of Liberty. The head of the Iroquois government was called the Pine Tree Chief. One of the early concepts for the U.S.A. Flag was the Pine Tree Flag. Many versions of it were used throughout early New England.

The Boston Tea Party was a disruptive, destructive, and bold act. The tea was sunken into Boston Harbor. Dried tea has no feelings; the act was destructive, not violent. People and living things are capable of feeling violence, not boxes of previously plucked and dried plants. It was a statement, a destructive and nonviolent message. The King ignored the message. If only his majesty and nobility were closer to Boston, they might have been able to read the tea leaves in the Harbor.

There just was too much money, too much gold, too many trees and too many resources in the Colonies, for the King to loosen his grasp. There was too much wealth equating to power residing in the new world for the empire to capitulate to the people's desires. There was no way the powers of the old world would submit. If the Colonists wanted fairness and equality then they were going to have to fight for it.

The Boston Tea Party was an act of civil disobedience which brought only punishment, more restrictions and more taxation. The King was in charge and was inflexible, only capable of flexing overt oppression and military might.

> "A riot is, at the bottom, the language of the unheard." ~Martin Luther King Jr.

The Company was desperate for income; it had overextended itself in attempts at global monopolization. The business of exploitation and plunder was costly. Slavery and opium smuggling would soon solve all their income woes. In 1773, The Company needed money and the Colonists were a threat to their income; a threat to their monopoly on trees and tea. In Boston Harbor the Colonists rocked the boat.

After the Big Steep, Benjamin Franklin offered to pay for the destroyed tea out of his own pocket. At the time he thought that destroying private property was violent. Later, he withdrew the offer.

> "The Colonies are now in open rebellion. The die is now cast.
> The Colonies must either submit or triumph." ~King George III

This was no casual remark. No formidable world power could stand up to the Royal Army and Navy, let alone a ragtag group of farmers and peasants, let alone a small portion of them. Historically, no one could stand up to British might. It's well known King George III suffered from mental illness, but he was considered less out of his mind than the Colonists who challenged his military.

King George the III passed new laws in efforts to clamp down on the rebellious patriots and colonists. They did not work, more people felt burdened by the restrictive laws. The money flow would continue to grow and provide power or the Colonists would die trying to prevent it. The Punitive Acts were meant to quell the growing unrest in the Colonies, but served only to promote sympathy for revolution.

> FACT: Before the arrival of Europeans half of the U.S.A. was old growth forest. One of the oldest aspen trees is at least 80,000 years old and covers 105 acres in Utah as one root system. The Pando root system has survived 80,000 years of Earth changes and is possibly the oldest being on the planet. In the high mountains of California, at 10,000 feet are the Bristlecone Pines, the oldest among these trees is over 4,700 years old.

The Acts took away governing authority from the Colonies, especially Massachusetts. They permitted His Majesty's soldiers to be tried for crimes back in England. George III increased the number of soldiers in Boston and tightened his grip on the Colonies. The Colonists felt increasingly violated. The Quartering Act gave the right to His Majesty's soldiers to be provided lodging in Colonists' barns, empty houses and gave them access to other supplies. This infuriated many and sparked new resistance. This type of oligarchical exploitation was taken into account when the Bill of Rights was manifest.

> "A man does what he must – in spite of personal consequences, in spite of obstacles and dangers and pressures – and that is the basis of all human morality." ~John F. Kennedy

The Boston Tea Party is a celebrated act of civil disobedience, exemplifying and reflecting the practice of peaceful and proactive patriotism. The monopolization of The Company and King George III, backed by church is a clear example of oligarchical collectivism. The institutionalized monopolization in pyramidal fashion was represented by the tea, and the Colonists collected the commodity and tossed it overboard.

Patriots questioned the monopoly on tea to realize it was a tool for exploitation. They stopped drinking tea and encouraged others to do the same by informing them, followed by public protest. The authority has the choice to reconcile the exploitation or reconvene it. If they suppress the protests or continue their exploits, they expose their true intentions to monopolize. If they are wrongdoers and exploiters, patriots figuratively and literally throw their tea into the drink, to be tea no more and deal with the consequences.

> "Those who make peaceful revolution impossible, make violent revolution inevitable." ~John F. Kennedy

On April 19, 1775 Colonial Militia and British soldiers began battling at Lexington, and then Concord. The British sent troops to confiscate arms. The revolutionaries took cover and shot at the British soldiers, others charged their ranks. The revolutionaries were labeled terrorists for their tactics, the day of the mysterious first shot and subsequently afterwards. The Colonists surprised the British and themselves, they won the first battle. The British were defeated at Lexington.

After subsequent battles the Declaration of Independence was ratified on July 4, 1776. On September 11, 1776, British and Colonial officials met, a Lord Howe demanded the Declaration of Independence be retracted and cancelled, Benjamin Franklin and Edward Rutledge refused. War ensued, officially ending September 3, 1783. The thirteen Colonies became a union and the taboo number has been celebrated since.

> SYMBOL- **13** On the Great Seal of the U.S.A. and other U.S.A. symbols the number thirteen is celebrated. The original thirteen Colonies are noted as the reason to celebrate the number. In some circles the number is considered so cursed that hotels and other buildings skip the thirteenth floor. It is considered to harbor luck, both good and bad. 12 or a dozen is seen as a perfect, well rounded number, while 13 can be seen as a transgression, one step too far or more than perfect, good or bad. Jesus and his twelve disciples equal 13. There were 13 tribes of Israel. There were originally 13 signs in the zodiac. 13 was considered a powerful ritualistic number by the Celts before they were conquered by the Romans, the Romans denounced 13 as unlucky.

Friday the 13 is considered bad luck since Friday October 13, 1307, when the King of France ordered the capture and execution of all Knights Templar. These Warrior monks fought in the crusades and were the first international bankers. In their inquisition and execution, all their possessions and riches were confiscated as standard practice. The Templars had stately wealth that was sought after by many, including French royalty.

When pilgrims went on their journey, they would deposit their money with the Templars in Europe and then would later withdrawal it from the Templars in Jerusalem for a fee. The Templars gained so much power that King Philip IV might have considered them a threat and conspired for their downfall. Philip clandestinely planned their persecution, and manipulated the Papacy to allow it. Philip went after the Templars simply to eliminate his debt to them, (Philip similarly exiled all Jewish and Lombard peoples from France and took ownership of their property in 1306) but the Templar gold and their fleet of ships disappeared. It is speculated that fleeing Templars would have gone to Scotland.

Centuries after William Wallace and the Scots fought for rights under English Crown abuse those who had fled persecution of the old world were inspired by the autonomy of the natives and opportunities of the new land, and eventually revolted. The Company and the King would not let go and eventually the splitting of ideas clashed in war. The people wanted liberty and intended to move forward; the oligarchical institutions wanted to keep things angled to their benefit.

> "They that can give up essential liberty for a little temporary safety, deserve neither liberty nor safety." ~Benjamin Franklin

The authorities answered the disobedience with repression, which caused more individuals to agree with the sentiment of the Big Steep. The original patriots represented themselves as a group of individuals who sought liberty among global institutions. The original patriots represented no nation at the time, for they did not yet have a nation. Patriotism is not nationalism, it is not jingoism. The original patriots were a loose group that held high a notion, not a nation.

They were acting out of liberty and countering engrained exploitative measures. In order to proceed with liberty, the Colonists had to first cease support of exploitative institutions. This was symbolically expressed at the Big Steep when individuals threw the fuel of their exploiters overboard. There was no further plan and none needed; all that the original patriots were trying to accomplish was to express their dissatisfaction of the exploitation.

The authorities could not let go of their overt and direct control over the new world and war for independence ensued. There was no one to marry in, no American nobility to speak of, to include in the royal family and the royalty would not let their overt control be questioned.

By questioning, communicating, speaking out, ceasing cooperation and taking action, the original patriots put into practice the unchanging essence of patriotism. Patriotism's fundamental engagement is to question, or depending on one's point of view, practice dissent. If something is so unfair or so ignored that questioning becomes dissent, then there is likely some form of exploitation taking place. When the clock is broken, merely asking the time can be interpreted as dissent.

If the overt powers appeased the civil disobedience, there may have been no revolution and no resulting Bill of Rights either. The First Amendment protects questioning authority and the Second Amendment ensures protecting oneself from overt aggression of authority. The entirety of the Bill of Rights was a response to the despotism of the oligarchical pyramid system. The Bill of Rights is a preventative against future such stomping of individuals by oligarchical institutions. The Bill of Rights is intended to protect individuals from institutions, including supposed royalty who believe they have the right to tread wherever, and on whomever.

DON'T TREAD ON ME An early version of the U.S.A. flag is called the Gadsden flag. The rattlesnake was adopted because of its power, its warning and its nativity to North America. Benjamin Franklin made the country's first political cartoon with a rattlesnake in thirteen pieces expressing unity, along with the slogan "Join or Die." Ben did not want the eagle to represent the U.S.A. as it was a "bird of bad moral character."

"...– always there will be the intoxication of power, constantly increasing and constantly growing subtler. Always, at every moment, there will be the thrill of victory, the sensation of trampling on an enemy who is helpless. If you want a vision of the future, imagine a boot stamping on a human face – forever." ~George Orwell, 1984

GAS IT!

If there is any commodity today comparable to tea in 1773 it's dino juice, bubbling crude, burning water, black gold, Texas tea, petrol. Texas tea is comparable to black tea as both are liquid. They are more comparable and similar in that tea was, and oil is, a means of exploitation. Tea was a tool for exploitation centuries prior, while Texas tea is today, only in an exponential fashion. The potential of tea to exploit was minute next to petrol to do the same.

There was merely a casual physical dependence on tea. There is an overwhelming, ever infiltrating, global, industrial, institutional and individual dependence on petroleum products. It is not a natural dependence, it is an institutionalized dependence. Today tea, coffee and all things caffeine make up the most widely consumed beverages. Coffee is second only to petrol in global trade. Yet, tea, coffee and caffeine, are but a sideline venture in terms of global use and exploitation, compared to petrol and octane. Caffeine may be part of a nice drink, but petrol is literally and figuratively in everything.

Today petrol is needed in order to obtain and distribute everything, even petrol itself. The movement of people is dependent on petrol. The tea business and every other business are all dependent on petrol. Nearly all individual and institutional energy needs are met by burning petroleum products.

FACT: Over 30% of world's electricity comes from burning coal.

Humanity revolves around petrol. The status quo of today is interconnected with fossil fuel; it is everywhere, in everything. All institutions and individuals are dependent on it and use it. Petrol is everywhere, burned up and spilled into in the environment. Take a breath, have a sip – it's in there. It is one of our greatest detractors and greatest liberators. With it we have fueled war and the means to explore. There is no getting away from it, whether one lives next to a processing facility or in wild seclusion.

Petrol is our liberator. Through its octane, people are enabled. People can drive thousands of miles in a few days or simply race cars in circles. People can fly around the world in hours. People can transport every whim and wish wherever. Petrol has enabled and inspired architectural feats equivalent to the seven wonders of the ancient world.

Petrol is decayed carbon matter buried under extreme pressures. The decaying mass is pressurized and over time, creates carbon fuels. Coal is essentially oil that has not aged as long and liquefied. A less acceptable theory is that instead of being pressurized and decayed biomass, fossil-fuel is from much older, Earth forming, geological processes. Either way, petroleum is a nonrenewable resource and practically all of the world's industry, farming and transportation are dependent on it.

FACT: Many new chemicals and previously unknown substances came into existence as a result of petrol experimentation. Many petroleum products such as plastics could be replaced or manifested through other renewable, less toxic resources. A short list of petroleum products includes: asphalt, antihistamines, aspirin, cosmetics, disposable diapers, linoleum, insecticides, fertilizers, pesticides, trash bags, bubble gum, shaving cream, crayons, plastics, synthetics, deodorant, dyes, shampoo, toothbrushes, toothpaste, paintbrushes, paint, stain, sun glasses, rubber cement, carpeting, preservatives, lotion, lip balm, balloons, toys, and on and on.

Petrol is our detractor, because it fuels destruction. Without petrol the ability to go to war would be diminished, the capacity to wage large scale war would be eliminated and often any reason to go to war in the first place would fail to materialize. Is it worth it? What time is it?

Petrol is a detractor because of the resulting pollution. The consequences of abundant and constant use of petrol are leading us to who knows where, but it doesn't appear to be a clean and accommodating place. Future generations will perhaps wonder at the intense consumption of this time period. People may wonder how we could have used such a dirty fuel at all, or perhaps how we could have used so much.

Many wars since WWI have been waged over petrol and all have been fueled with petrol. The Persian Gulf War in 1991 was absolutely about oil. Iraq invaded Kuwait to reclaim oil. Kuwait, once part of Iraq, was partitioned by the colonizing and monopolizing British Empire. Iraq claimed that Kuwait was siphoning oil from fields on their land. During that war a few hundred U.S.A. soldiers perished while tens of thousands of Iraqis, both combatants and innocents were killed. It was a war for oil; oil is precious for it powers machinery of profit and control.

Oil enables the exploitation of people. It disrupts ecosystems and beings through its toxicities, as well as enabling war. The result of the global use of petrol is directly a polluted environment. Indirectly, the global use of petrol results in war and reinforces oligarchical collectivism.

Tea was not nearly as integral to living in 1773, as oil is today. In 1773, the commodity of tea and the surrounding institutional exploitations came to symbolize institutions treading on individuals. Today the symbolism is the same, only exponentially magnified in petrol. The oligarchical collectivism, the institutional integration of petrol are much more significant than tea was.

Tea was seen as a means for slanted exploitation and the people reacted to the wrong of the increased slant. All of the other related and unrelated unfair taxes and exploits did not go unnoticed; they were despised as well, but the tea became the symbol and catalyst for action.

Why then is oil not seen in the same manner? It is all pervasive, it is everywhere. Tea provides caffeine, while oil provides octane. Both are powerful resources of revenue, but the power of octane dwarfs caffeine. Petrol and its accompaniments perhaps make things so easy that people ignore or choose to remain unaware of its exploitative capability and environmental side effects. If caffeine was addictive as opium or cocaine, if tea powered as much as petrol, the big steep might have never happened. Great addictions result in great tolerations and the Colonists would have been waiting at the docks with their life savings for a fix. Petrol is this addicting. Petrol equates to everything, so people forego everything for it.

The similarity between tea and oil is somewhat constricted as the scope and power of octane is near limitless compared to that of the healthful beverage. Tea provides nutrients and prevents illness, while petrol supplies power and denies clean water. Tea was exploitative to North Americans and Asians, but it was avoidable, petrol is not. Tea was exploitative directly, while petrol is exploitative directly and indirectly. If one was disgusted and sickened by tannic acid in tea, one could avoid it, but there is no avoiding petrol and its sickening accompaniments, it's everywhere.

Despite all the wrongdoing perpetuated by the Crown, the item that represented the perpetuation of exploitation was tea. Tea was enjoyable and healthful, a hot drink in a cold world. A hot drink, to which there were alternatives in the expanse of the Americas. It wasn't until the abandonment of tea that new distinct and equally enjoyable alternative beverages were enjoyed by the Colonists. Herbal teas were harvested from the vast expanse of wild plants in the new world, introduced to them by the local indigenous people.

That was the new world, continents and oceans, an entire hemisphere open and new, undiscovered, never previously institutionalized. Wealth of wondrous proportions captivated and catapulted the pyramidal European Monarchies. European institutions recognized only other European institutions and stomped and swept over the Americas. Genocide was instituted, but also wild and random. European institutions and individuals plundered, murdered and then claimed discovery. Thanks to the trinity of liberty, empires were slowed somewhat in the New World.

Today there is a different new world, though no new previously unknown isle has been discovered. Today, it is literally a new world, an altered environment. Every hemisphere is changed in this new world, rather an altered world, manifested by global pollution and environmental destruction at the hands of mankind. The new world is the petrolithic era.

All sorts of great successes and horrible setbacks have been accomplished with petrol as a fuel and resource resulting in all sorts of consequences and calamitous conditions. The petrolithic era is represented by a distinct layer of polluted sediment on the Earth and all the elements. The pollution preceding the petrolithic era has also laden the waters and air and all life on the planet. The petrolithic era is a distinct, physically detectable time period leaving a permanent mark on the Earth.

> "Sufficient evidence has emerged of stratigraphically significant change (both elapsed and imminent) for recognition of the Anthropocene – currently as a vivid yet informal metaphor of global environmental change – as a new geological epoch to be considered for formalization by international discussion." ~Geological Society of London

Cities and nations are built to accommodate petrol powered machines. People have steered the Seven Seas in gale storms and at great depths with petrol. People have been catapulted into outer space with petrol. People have risen parts of the world to magnificence with petrol. Pollution and smog ride the tide and wind. The legacy of the petrolithic era may not be the cities, highways, but the pollution and depleted resources.

FACT: Many structures in ancient Babylon were built using asphalt. The tower of Babel itself is said to have been built with asphalt.

Asphalt is a petroleum product. People in Persia, Asia and Japan used petrol millennia ago for fuel and building material, but the petrolithic era began much later in history, when petrol became a worldwide phenomenon, a permeation encompassing and surrounding everything, reaching into all the elements through and through. The petrolithic era began with the unheralded globalization of, by and for petrol.

Petrol pollution has been growing since the early 1900s, the ongoing effects of which are still being calculated and accumulating. Petrol and its accompaniments are all pervasive, measurable in every climate on the planet, detectable in every stratum. Millennia from now, the consequences and conditions of the petrolithic era will be a stain in this geological layer, physically defining the time.

Rudolf Diesel was born in France in 1858, the same year The Company handed control of South Asia to governmental authorities. Rudolf invented different types of engines and received his first patent in 1893. He was a dreamer, a thinker, and a doer and was nearly killed when one of his early engine designs exploded. He had to spend months in the hospital and suffered throughout life due to the accident.

After years of work, he perfected the Diesel engine. Rudolf moved to the U.S.A. to make and sell them in the biggest market. Originally, his design used and was intended to use, a mixture of bio-fuels. Rudolf promoted and advocated bio-fuels to power his engines, along with petrol if it was locally accessible. At the time, petrol was the alternative energy source, as bio-fuel is today. Bio-fuels, renewable resources were the accepted, sensible norm.

Rudolf believed that his engine would enable individuals. He envisioned his engine would be powered by locally available fuels to enable local industry. Rudolf never wanted to use petrol. Of course if petrol was accessible locally, he wouldn't argue its use. Still to name a petrol fuel after Rudolf is insulting and misleading. He became a powerful business figure when the Diesel engine exploded on the world market instead of on him. His ideas for bio-fuels were not environmental or extraordinary departure, just sensible.

Rudolf and his invention eventually were caught up in the arms race leading up to WWI. Before his death, he was paranoid and suffered several nervous breakdowns. He was of Germanic heritage, but did not support the German build-up to war.

While crossing the English Channel on the S.S. Dresden, Rudolf disappeared, lost at sea. He was on his way to sell his new technology to the British for their submarines amid the arms race leading up to WWI. It is unknown whether Rudolph committed suicide or was murdered; either way, Rudolf disappeared at sea. Ten days later, possessions were removed from his presumed corpse and the badly decomposed body was set off to sea. There are better ways to kill oneself than submit to the sea, but there are not many better ways to murder. After Rudolf died, people would forget about the bio-fuels. The petrolithic era began September 30, 1913, when Rudolf mysteriously disappeared.

"The fact that fat oils from vegetable sources can be used may seem insignificant today, but such oils may become in course of time of the same importance as some natural mineral oils and the tar products now." ~Rudolf Diesel

Rudolf intended his engine to be powered by bio-fuel and/or petrol, enabling individuals worldwide. He did not intend his engine to be used specifically with petrol to enable global institutions. Today, petrol is presented as the standard while it is just one option. Petrol is the best option for institutions, bio-fuels are the best option for individuals and independence.

At the beginning of the 20th century, John D. Rockefeller, of Standard Oil, was the world's wealthiest individual and the U.S.A. was the world's major supplier of petrol. John D definitely made petrol standard. At the 1900 World's Fair, one of Rudolf's engines was featured running on peanut oil. After Rudolf's death, the petrol would flow, the submarines would go and the bombs would blow. The petroleum business began to globalize, as did weapons manufacturing and sales. The War to End All Wars began after the June, 1914 assassination of the Archduke Ferdinand by a member of a Serbian secret society. Yet in reality, the war was bound to happen and sprouting before Rudolf ate his last meal. Since the death of Rudolf and WWI, war and oil have been as intertwined as math and science.

Rudolf opposed the use of his invention in German submarines, but after his death, Germany gained access to Diesel technology. Petrol became the fuel of choice for the German submarines. One such German U-boat sunk the RMS Lusitania on May 7, 1915, killing over 1,000 people, including some 128 U.S.A. citizens.

President Wilson merely protested. The U.S.A. practiced isolationism until April 6, 1917 when Congress declared war on Germany and entered The War to End All Wars. Perhaps it took that long to convince people to go to war. Ultimately conscientious objectors in the U.S.A. and Britain were imprisoned. The Espionage Act and the Sedition Act made stating facts, or anything deemed disloyal towards the U.S.A., a criminal act.

In different parts of the world there were different reasons to raise arms. War had been expected, and prepared for and fought for many ends. India fought for the United Kingdom, expecting to receive self-governance in return. They did not get it. While India remained loyal to fight, Russians left the front and revolted at home against their royal oligarchy in 1917. Millions died in fighting there and subsequent starvation separately from WWI.

FACT: During WWI, German agents and Kaiser Wilhelm II tried to ignite Jihad in the Middle East against Britain. Turkey obliged and declared Jihad against England, France and Russia. The Ottoman Empire and the German Empire eventually fell side by side, but not before the Ottoman Empire vanquished roughly 1 million Armenian people.

For four years, man killed man at nearly every corner of the globe in every manner imaginable. Those souls that fought in the war were hence known as the lost generation. Many survivors suffered mental trauma and were permanently tweaked; many more lost limbs and were otherwise disfigured. WWI was fought on old battlefields with old fighting theories in the new petrolithic era. Thousands perished charging impenetrable machine gun fire, mortar and artillery under the threat of being shot by a superior if they refused.

Many zealously believed they were on the killing fields for God, or against those who believed in a false God. Many zealously fought for a king, whom they believed was exalted by God or against those that believed in such royal order. Old warring techniques used with new weaponry of the petrolithic era resulted in charge and slaughter. Many of the slaughtered and slaughterers on both sides believed that they were pursuing the greater good.

During and following WWI, bio-fuels and any alternative to petrol became a load of hot air. Many battles of WWI were waged over oil. Warring institutions knew very well its power and potential. Rudolf's engine, powered by local biofuels, to empower local individuals, was shot down like so many people in the trenches of WWI.

When the War to End All Wars ended, petrol became the institutional choice. The petrolithic era enables and benefits institutions. Petrol is limited and is mined, refined and distributed by elite institutions. Bio-fuels are grown, renewable and near limitless, open to all. Petrol enables institutional control, oligarchical collectivism. The petrolithic era has been an affront of pollution and war since its inception. Petrolithic pollutants fuel war, and war fuels further use of petrol and reasoning for violent conquest.

The global burning of petrol creates C02, but also pollutes and poisons every part of the Earth in a mostly subtle fashion depending on one's powers of observation or one's location. C02 is one factor of pollution, the likely major contributor to global warming, but there's more. The burning of fossil fuels is completely toxic as are its additives and accompaniments. Bio-diesel has a more complete combustion than petroleum diesel and less toxic accompaniments. The exhaust, in turn, is cleaner than petroleum diesel. Today, petrol and its accompaniments are in every drink and every breath. Our water contains the toxic leftovers of energy oligarchies, those of petrol fashioned after WWI, and those of nuclear age after WWII.

Some places experience direct and destructive pollution, while others receive an accumulation of dispersed and diluted poisons that casually and slowly add up. Petrol is spilled, burned, morphed, sprayed and shipped on every continent and across every ocean. Petrolithic toxins are everywhere, in quantities both casual and overwhelming, whether noticed or not.

Petrol and its byproducts will accompany every living thing physically, until its global distribution is ceased and cleaned. It has been distributed across the environment and has been deposited in every stratum of the Earth. It is gathered and consumed by people, but it affects every living thing on the planet. Petrol and its spooky accompaniments can be found in water of deep and remote wells and in ice of the most remote glacier, atop the highest mountain, in the most distant lands.

Our mutual ancestors were affected by their environment. Factors such as the amount of sunlight, the mean temperature, and the local flora and fauna affected development. Past environmental factors made us who we are today. We continue to be affected by our environment, by the sludge in our food, the toxins in our water, and the particulate in our air. The recorded changes transcribing the future are not merely of light and heat. The main factors for environmental change arrive through the global use and ingestion of poisons. The consequences are sometimes seen, but mostly unseen and steadily accumulating.

When and if, archeologists of the future, thousands of years from now, dig down to the layer of sediment we exist in today, they will find a global, poisonous layer of soot and muck splattered in the strata of this time period, the petrolithic era, which led to the nuclear age. The intense global use of oligarchical energy has accumulated to form a distinct layer forever imprinted on Earth. For whatever reason what we know may be lost in time, but the pollution of the petrolithic era will persist as a physical layer indefinitely. Perhaps generations in the future they will know that civilization created such conditions or maybe they will hypothesize that an asteroid hit the Earth and spit up all the chemical/nuclear debris.

FACT: In 2004 the U.S.A. burned 140 billion gallons of gasoline. Automobile exhaust contains many poisons including benzene, formaldehyde and sulfur dioxide.

The petrolithic era has resulted in endless pollution, and fuel for endless war. Petrol also fuels industry's overdevelopment. This too, is sometimes blatant and other times difficult to see and understand through the presentation or misrepresentation of conditions. Clear cut forests cannot be seen from the road. Overdevelopment is the result of petrol's power used in a poorly planned manner. Dependence is instigated and independence eliminated.

Civilization's growth is currently dependent on resources that have negative consequences to development of life. Despite creating necessity for more resources, despite creating actual and imagined dependencies on resources, distribution is jaded. Clean water alone is difficult to obtain for most of the world and growing more difficult.

The physical residuals of petrol and its accompaniments are ubiquitous. The poisonous deluge and the thorough destruction of Earth's fragile ecology is the most impending consequence of the petrolithic era. Sickening pollution is the most blatant consequence and global warming possibly the most dooming.

Global war fueled by petrol is the most abrasive and obvious example of having the fuel to do what is possible and not proceeding with what is practical. With unlimited fuel, vast poisons and constant war arrive. Petrol enables overdevelopment. Petrol also allows for reckless war.

Quicker construction, faster transportation, accelerated exchange of goods and services, overall accelerated development, exchange of information, and increased destruction of physicality all result from the fast pace of the petrolithic era. Vehicles are capable of tremendous velocity, while information zaps practically instantly.

With the advent of the World Wide Web, the speed at which information is distributed is limited mainly by the rate at which one can consume it. Everything glides forward at an ever-increasing pace, physically and mentally. Change is constant, slow like an old mule drawn to green fields and also, in increasing frequency, swift and sudden like a stampede of stallions.

Without oil, institutions and individuals would not have instigated many undertakings, both benevolent and malevolent. The two world wars would have been local and minor without petrol. Certainly they would have been less destructive and maybe they would not have happened at all.

The Japanese attacked Pearl Harbor because the U.S.A. stopped oil shipments to Japan. Petrol fueled and reasoned WWI and WWII. The petrolithic era is a toxic, instigated by earthly chemical poisons. It is mechanized, institutionalized and chaotic structure that provides for war. WWII ended in Europe only when the Nazi war machines ran out of fuel. Their synthetic fuel facility was destroyed and they failed at attempts to conquer and pillage more oil, finally their tanks stalled. The allies bombed Germany's fuel depots and prevented the Nazis from acquiring more fuel.

People cast our ancestors as barbarians and yet, it was only in the 21st century that bombing cities became possible, then acceptable. After WWII, most European cities were ruins. After WWII, two super powers emerged and another war began, the Cold War. Troublesome Germany was split in two. The USSR represented the east side of Germany and the U.S.A. represented the west.

Within this time is another epoch, the information age. The information age is completely manmade. Often information is not actual, existent solely in people's minds as reflections of reality. Today, information may exist only in electrical format, but move as fast as light and be relevant and concrete as a hefty book on the most immediate matter.

SYMBOL – SWASTIKA
The swastika symbol is used by cultures all around the world, from Hindu to Hopi. It is a form of the cross. It symbolizes peaceful tidings and happy travels across the Earth. The Nazis flipped its meaning, their swastika went the other way. Instead of peaceful, carefree travels, their swastika meant violent travels with intent to monopolize the world.

Today, secrets, science, news, events, paradigms and bullshit are all circulated via multimedia machines. Today it is possible that anyone, not just those in elite institutions, can be among the most informed people in world history. In the past, information was strictly distributed to only a few, if shared at all. Today, there is a vast amount of information available, however some pertinent information is restricted, and a lot of less pertinent information is distributed. Many people who want to know relevant information might not be permitted access to it. Many more people don't want more information pertinent to their conditions or may believe they know all they need to know.

The premise of the Cold War was one of information, a war in which direct conflict between the nuclear nations would be apocalyptic. There were proxy wars, stealthy battles, communistic versus democratic wars the world over, yet directly, between the two nuclear nations, it was a battle of information. Both super powers fought armies that had support from the other in some way, but never fought each other directly. The Cold War was a war fought with information and disinformation.

The Cold War was fought with secret files, secret weapons, covert manipulation, lies and spies. Information is power and in the Cold War, it was the main weapon. It was a space race, an arms race and a race to capture hearts and minds. Secrets could make or break battles of information. The information age began at the advent of the Cold War when the power of information and at times just information, was the main device of war.

> FACT: After WWII many Hitler henchmen found employment with the U.S.A. and other western nations. Reinhard Gehlen was Chief of Intelligence Gathering on the Eastern front for Hitler and subsequently recruited by the U.S.A. as a spy for the CIA. Walter Kopp – operative, Hans von Ohain – USAF, Arthur Rudolph – NASA and Wernher Von Braun – ASA. These and many others began work with the U.S.A. and many more began working for the USSR.

The information age expanded with radio, telephones, television, computers, pagers, cellular phones and the internet, but it began with the secrecy of the Cold War. The information age began with the global war of information. Now despite secrets, it is easy to obtain new information, society is frequently exposed to potential paradigms. There is an overload of information, yet still some is unavailable.

> FACT: Johannes Gutenberg is credited with inventing the movable type printing press. His invention made news and books available in Europe and is considered to have instigated the Renaissance and later scientific revolution.

> FACT: The first computer was the International Business Machine, by IBM. These punch card machines were used to keep track of prisoners in the Nazi regime and organize slave labor. The numbers categorized people. Slave laborers received tattoos on their arms, these were their international business machine ID codes.

Information is everywhere, just as petrol is everywhere. Though some ancients used oil and all ancients used information, the petrolithic era began with the death of Rudolf and the initiation of global petrol use and global war. The nuclear age began with the first atomic detonation. And the information age began with the birth of a worldwide battle of information and secrets.

The information age began with the legislation of the National Security Act, July 26, 1947. The Act created the CIA and morphed and expanded the military industrial complex. Since then information, disinformation, lies, half-truths and secrets have been used in worldwide power play and metadata is increasingly collected.

> FACT: One of the first missions of the CIA was research into mind control. The Agency experimented with LSD, this included dosing unknowing U.S.A. citizens and observing their delirium after poisoning.

The Cold War was a war of secrets. Both sides presented the sleek and shiny portion of the status quo for show and hid or built over the crumbling and rotting underbelly. Fittingly, as the information age arrived, the consequences of the petrolithic era were beginning to bear fruit. Environmental catastrophes however were considered inconsequential to victory and national prosperity. Extinction of other species was a small price to pay.

WWII heralded the ultimate manmade environmental catastrophe: atomic bombs. Information on this horror was well distributed. Obliterating cities to smithereens, vaporizing people and perma-frying surroundings was presented as a necessary evil toward the greater good. Tolerations for total and violent environmental destruction were instituted –for the greater good.

Whole cities were obliterated instantly. This fear of violent obliteration and environmental destruction was and is delivered persistently. There were still many unknowns about nuclear bombs, but the knowns were frightening enough. Nuclear invention sped the information age, powering it with atomic fear. Nuclear knowledge presented reasoning that not knowing, was better than knowing. Being killed was possibly a better option than surviving nuclear war.

Nuclear information is well-known and would strike subtle fear into generations. The potential to be instantaneously killed or morbidly radiated is more frightening than many a gloomy fate. A war to end all was now possible; perhaps nothing is more frightening. The bombing of the cities of Hiroshima and Nagasaki, Japan ended WWII. The information on the devastation of nuclear bombs would circulate creating fear, but also manifesting the logic that avoiding information was logical.

The understanding of the term blast radius and the effects of radiation became as well-known to school children as the story of George Washington crossing the Delaware. When the actual facts are as dire as such death and destruction, avoiding information might be practical. Yet, if it is actual, if it is real, it is important to know about. If the subject is disagreeable, it cannot be changed by ignoring it. If there is a frightening situation, the only way to surpass it and the fear is to question it and face it. Many of the ideas and phrases used by the nuclear experimentation industry are Orwellian misleading euphemisms. Spent fuel is one, there is nothing spent about it, it needs to be actively cooled and cared for a long, long time. Depleted uranium for ammunition is another example of a misleading idea, there is nothing depleted about it.

If there are dangerous miscreants tricking people in a certain way, it is important to know about their tricks. If there are bombs out there that can destroy all life, it might seem sensible to hide at first. One may not want to know, but one should. One may want to hide, but there is always the possibility of evil, and hiding in a cave, solves nothing.

FACT: After WWII, the U.S.A. and USSR began experimenting with different radio waves and their effects on people. The U.S.A. Embassy in Moscow was repeatedly attacked by varying radio frequencies, sickening and maddening many.

The information age eventually would have occurred, independent of the petrolithic era, but as it happened, the information age began in the petrolithic era and grew with the nuclear age. The nuclear attacks magnified the escalation of the information age. Fear is always induced by information, normally false evidence appearing real. The nuclear attacks spread fear of very real events and information circulated faster with the heightened fear.

The nuclear age is invisibly global. There have been thousands of atomic and nuclear detonations into our atmosphere, waters and earth. There has also been the most severe meltdowns/meltthroughs/meltouts imaginable of multiple reactors in Japan. The nuclear age is capable of making us no more. We are still escalating into the information age and like it or not, we are sliding deeper into the petrolithic era and nuclear age. Their consequences are globally apparent and accumulating.

These oligarchical energy systems burden us all with cancerous toxins and looming, radiating poisoning. There is likely no petroleum or nuclear product that cannot be replaced by some renewable and cleaner alternative, including energy. Yet if the use of petrol and oligarchical energy were to cease tomorrow or be vastly curtailed, the consequences and conditions of piling toxins would persist.

Petrol is power. Information is power. Today acquiring information is easier than ever, information is available to all, but not all information to everyone. Unfortunately there are still too many secrets. Too much information is kept from too many. Information is more powerful when it is kept from some. Information has the potential to sway opinion. This is why there are secrets, because if people knew differently, they could conclude differently. Controlling petrol is powerful, controlling information is total power.

It is difficult to obtain some information. Secrets may remain secrets for centuries even though the information existed. At the same time there is an overabundance of information; a potential for information overload. There is also occasional overload of petroleum pollutants. Institutional presentation of information is ground shaking paradigm mixed with bogus inconsequence. The petrolithic era makes drastic change and the information age delivers news of the changes among other inconsequential information.

Many people don't want to know the information available, information that concerns them, let alone the secrets that may, or may not be pertinent at all. Paradigm or otherwise, people may ignore information, but no one can ignore pollution. Physicality does not and cannot ignore information in the environment.

The petrolithic era is a constant, mostly subtle bombardment of pollutants and poisons. The petrolithic era is physically detectable measurable, and globally layered, it is impossible to ignore and will likely be impossible to hide.

There is also a constant bombardment of information with its own subtleties as well. Its change into the information age is undeniable, but it is not globally layered and calculable in the earth, sea, air and ice, as is petrol defining the petrolithic era.

PATRIOTS AMONG IDIOTS

"The message is that there are known knowns. There are things we know that we know. There are known unknowns. That is to say there are things that we now know we don't know. But there are also unknown unknowns, there are things we do not know we don't know. So when we do the best we can and we pull all this information together and…and we then say well that's basically what we see as the situation. That is really only the known knowns and the known unknowns. And each year we discover a few more of those unknown unknowns. And I, I, it, it sounds like a, a riddle." ~Donald Rumsfeld

Despite the hysterical choice of words and blatant omission, Donald spoke the truth in near poetic manner, albeit the incomplete truth. Donald and other institutionalized figures typically present partial truth as complete. Overlooked and unsaid information is normal for institutionalized individuals like Donald. Donald failed to emphasize that the various knowns and unknowns are not static. Situations may shift obviously or discreetly from unknown to known and also, more importantly, from known to unknown. There are subjects that people believe to know in total, which can totally change.

Another clear omission by Donald is that there are also unknown knowns. There are four forms of information in this respect, not just three. An unknown known is information that one has and another does not know about. These are knowns which are dismissed and where actions are taken as if the knowns are unknowns. Politicians like Donald do not want to address the fourth aspect of this cross reference, for politicians tend to use the unknown knowns, or secrets, for their pursuits.

And each year we discover a few more of these unknown knowns. Donald had become an expert at fashioning certainty from iffy information and acting on limited evaluation and presentation that was not supposed to be known, more commonly referred to as lying. Donald never wanted to remind people that supposed facts may turn out to be fiction and that there were some things he knew and pretended not to know.

FACT: Donald Rumsfeld acted as Chief of Staff for President Ford and was replaced by Dick Cheney. He immediately became Secretary of Defense for President Ford. He later performed roles under President Nixon, served 4 terms in the House of Representatives, was a special envoy to the Middle East for President Reagan, and was U.S.A. Ambassador to NATO, before becoming Secretary of Defense for George II. In his younger days, he was a pilot in the U.S.A. Navy, and attended Princeton University where he was roommates with Frank Carlucci, Secretary of Defense for Ronald Reagan. Frank was replaced by Dick Cheney.

An important aspect of information that prompts questioning is the fact that known knowns may alter into different known unknowns or become unknown unknowns, revealing previously unrecognized other unknown unknowns in the process. That is to say, what is taken for granted as fact is often a gross miscalculation or falsehood and sometimes questioning may not get the answer desired or expected, but leads to other questions and information. The truth may change, and reveal other things.

Known knowns must be questioned to be sure, for sometimes facts are just belief, and what was a fact does not always remain fact. Things change gently, shit happens too. People may have untrue information and they may lie, requiring questioning. It is essential, but difficult to decipher and separate what is fact, from what was fact and also separate fact from belief. Individual surveillance of situations is needed as well as questioning the interpretations of others, for things change.

"There is nothing permanent except change." ~Heraclitus

The known unknowns are what we know that we don't know, subjects we have a limited knowledge of and realize that our knowledge is limited. Many people gravitate toward the unknown unknowns, creating assumptions and false evidence appearing real. The known knowns and the known unknowns are the most worthy subjects to question.

Some people seek information about known and/or unknown circumstances, but many more choose to avoid all types of information altogether, all the time. It is crucial to first categorize information as known and unknown. Then question the knowns, for finding answers to knowns often answers questions of the unknown.

Many people choose to avoid relevant information and remain ignorant for a variety of personal reasons. Sometimes they think they are too good for new information, many more think they are not good enough for new information, and others are simply afraid of the consequences of information. It is their right, but it is also their flaw. Curiosity killed the cat, but curiosity made man. To remain ignorant about important subjects is a sign of manipulation in the information age. Lack of curiosity killed the man.

If the information is there, it could help, but it is often ignored. One should inquire about that which directly and indirectly effects one's life, liberty and pursuit of happiness. If one does not question information one likely has been manipulated, for it goes against the grain of every instinct, in every living person not to question. It is contrary to primal self-preservation to avoid information. People are naturally curious about everything unless brainwashed to some extent. Only the seriously coerced, and institutionalized do not question.

There are manipulated idiots, those who don't know they are idiots. There are also manipulative idiots, idiots who try to get others to be idiots along with them. Instead of remaining ignorant because one has been manipulated, one chooses to remain ignorant in order to perpetuate manipulation. They know that they should know, but realize if they pretend to not know, they can continue to advance. People remain idiots because they have been tricked to believe it is to their benefit.

There are open secrets, information that is known, but people know that they are not supposed to know and proceed accordingly. This willful blindness secures individuals and institutions from direct responsibility and enables them to enable themselves. If one has a billion dollar corporation, selling a product that is carcinogenic to individuals, then willful ignorance maintains profits. One is idiotic to smoke cigarettes and ignore information about their cancerous properties. It is no longer idiocy when one has the information and behaves as if ignorant. It is elitist if one knows the negative health consequences of smoking, but behaves as if one is ignorant in order to profit. Idiots really are ignorant, while elitists pretend to be ignorant.

You are likely not an idiot. Reading itself decreases the odds of being an idiot, yet reading alone does not necessarily abandon all cast of idiocy. Idiots are not simply people who are ignorant, people who do not know, just as patriots are not defined as avid readers. Idiots remain ignorant and promote ignorance, refusing to question and learn. Idiots seek to avoid information on all situations and conditions that directly concern them. Idiocy is the refusal to question relevant conditions and circumstances.

Idiots refuse new knowledge. Idiots want to keep their worldview, ever comfortable in certain confines within the status quo. Idiots ignobly lack questions. By continuously seeking and accepting new information an idiot is an idiot no more.

Idiots refuse to question and refuse to consider new relevant information. They are a diverse group. One idiot might resent the lifestyle of another. The commonality is that all idiots refuse relevant information. They have too much to think about already or know that there would be more to contemplate if they questioned. Where the idiot exists serves the idiot just fine, whether they admit it or not. Idiots have widely varied beliefs. Their cohesion is not in what they believe, but that they refuse all new relevant information. They are in their comfort zone and know that new information could lead them to formulate new opinion.

> "If we choose, we can live in a world of comforting illusion." ~Noam Chomsky

One may be ignorant about infinite subjects and yet, not be a complete idiot. Only adamant refusal of pertinent information qualifies one as a complete idiot. A mechanic may not want to discuss iambic pentameter, and a poet may not want to learn about internal combustion. The mechanic and the poet are not necessarily idiots. One or the other may find the alternative subject uninteresting and perhaps would rather acquire information that is more relevant to their life.

Disinterest or ignorance does not equate to idiocy. It is not what is thought, but how one thinks that qualifies mentality. Ignoring pertinent information makes one an idiot.

> FACT: Leukemia rates among children and cancer/rare disease rates among individuals in and around the town of Fallon, Nevada are distinctly higher than elsewhere in the U.S.A. Cancer rates among officers at Fallon Air Force Base are noticeably higher as well.

Individuals in Fallon, Nevada, do not necessarily want to know about the high rate of cancer in and around their town, but they should. People in Fallon may like to kick back with some freshly brewed iced tea and watch the movie Top Gun while taking a bath, but they better know better. They don't want to know about the potential jet fuel spills, waste sites and unknown unknowns on the base that may be contaminating the surrounding groundwater, but they should. They don't want to know about that, but they have to, because it concerns their wellbeing. They have to question, and their questions in this case, happen to fall onto an unaccountable, unquestionable institution of the petrolithic era, the U.S.A. Military.

FACT: U.S.A. military activity and training has extensively polluted San Diego, CA, Colonie, NY, Oklahoma City, OK, Concord and Cape Cod, MA, San Antonio, TX, Memphis, TN, Isla De Vieques, Puerto Rico and Rocky Fats, CO, St. Louis, MO just to name a few inside the U.S.A. The U.S.A. government began a program of Base Realignment in 1989. Since then over 350 military bases have been closed.

"The world is a dangerous place, not because of those who do evil, but because of those who look on and do nothing."
~Albert Einstein

Only complete idiots would choose to ignore the high rate of cancer in Fallon, Nevada, or another similarly contaminated community. Only idiots would not want to learn about the cancer-prone area, because cancer is an uncomfortable subject. Only idiots would drink tea from tap water while taking a bath in Fallon.

Polluting water is simply wrong; there is no reasonable contrary argument. If the water is polluted in attempts to protect, if the defense works what then? If there is no clean water, what then? There are some things that people know, no matter how idiotic they are, no matter how burdened by tolerations. People know pollution is wrong and killing is wrong. Perhaps this innate knowledge is buried under a lifetime of tolerations, but people know.

People, despite regional distinctions, know the difference between right and wrong. It is an intangible instinct. Tolerations of wrong are built through conditions, prejudices are learned, and acceptance and participation in wrongdoing must be institutionalized. Interpretation of right and wrong changes, tolerance to evil sways, but the distinction of good and evil is ever. Tolerations to wrongdoing are learned and local.

The distinction between right and wrong is the only static in the universe. What is right always has been and always will be. What is wrong is and always will be. Truth changes, tolerations of right and wrong morph, situations sway, but right and wrong stay the same. People innately know the difference between help and hinder. Before and sometimes despite encouraged tolerations, people seek to help over hinder. People need to be convinced to hinder; tolerations must be acquired to perform malevolence.

FACT: Yale researchers, among others, concluded that babies 6 to 18 months young tended to want helpful toys as opposed to those that hindered. Practically every baby wanted the helpful toy as opposed to the negative toy. The babies were also able to distinguish the hindering toy from neutral toys. 100% of the 6 month young babies chose the helper and 87% of the 10 month young babies chose the helper. Preliminary research showed correlating results with babies 3 months young.

The essences of the world's religions all contain certain parallels. All religions, before subdivision and influence of tolerations, contain a mutual measure of morality. All religions share concepts at their pure core, they all relay the same sense of goodness in their least interrupted essence.

Ignorance of the law is no excuse, because the law is supposed to be based out of a standard, universal self-evident morality. Right is right and wrong is wrong, no matter the law. Laws are supposed to be from this essence, though at times right and wrong do not correlate with legal and illegal.

When people go hungry, any theory is obliterated. Without food, all is hard to grasp, and right and wrong are soon forgotten or unseen. When the environment is extreme, extreme tolerations result. When protein is plenty theory is applicable, but when food is in limited supply, tolerations ensue and morality is abandoned. Theory and morality are moot. People need fresh water and food. Every person knows what is right and what is wrong. If they don't, they usually end up in a mental hospital, or more likely prison.

A healthy individual is born with ten fingers and ten toes, as well as a complete, innate knowledge of the distinction between right and wrong. A person can be born physically deformed, missing a finger or mentally deficient, without the ability to make moral distinction. Normally though, one loses fingers living and acquires tolerations of wrong in life too.

Ignorance and tolerations are no excuse, only mental illness is an excuse; the inability to distinguish right from wrong.

> FACT: Estimated that 1 in 6 in U.S.A. prisons has mental illness. The U.S.A. leads the world in mentally ill per capita.

Some in jail and outside of it were born missing a moral finger or two. The inability to know right from wrong is rarely congenital though, mostly it is acquired through life's accumulated tolerations. Most people in jail do know right from wrong and also know legal from illegal, two distinct subjects. People can be born with mental illness, but more likely it develops during a lifetime of accumulated tolerations.

There is no way to legitimately justify any evil for the purpose of any good, but depending on people's tolerations it is possible to believe as much. Wrongdoing is enabled by tolerance and is often conducted on behalf of one institution or another. Institutional representatives proclaim that they committed wrong despite knowledge it was wrong because they believed that it was right for some abstract institutional objective. The notion of "wrong for right" exists, but it is a continuously failing notion, like marching to war in order to prevent war.

> "Preventive war was an invention of Hitler. Frankly, I would not listen to anyone seriously that came and talked about such a thing." ~Dwight D. Eisenhower

> "I have never advocated war except as a means of peace." ~Ulysses S. Grant

Individuals know the difference between right and wrong automatically. Unknowing the difference takes time. People view right and wrong differently. The distinction between right and wrong is not different, only the perception of it. Tolerations are a measure of one's flexibility to wrongdoing. How much wrong one might ignore, endure and engage in measures tolerance. Tolerations allow for atrocity whether it's because a child is threatened or one needs new shoes.

People normally only commit wrong when under severe pressure; harm to themselves, their relations, possessions or commonalities. If people know the facts, if the actualities are presented without bias, people will not bother to see their children off to war or leave them behind for war, unless they have acquired certain tolerations and there is a threat.

People innately and instinctively know what is right and what is wrong, but only accurately when all the information is available. Otherwise tolerations may be built upon and played on to propagate wrong. Information lends to a better perspective despite acquired tolerations.

What is right is forever, while truth remains forever sought. The distinction between right and wrong stays, while truth sways. No matter what information is presented wrong will continue to be wrong, only the tolerations for its activity change.

It is the defining gift of man to be able to question and answer. Every question has answers and every answer has more questions. Everything is worthy of questioning and everything is worth questioning again, as things change, except right and wrong. Right and wrong are known and obvious, if all information is available. Possessing all information is a rare and fleeting occurrence, making it possible to steer opinionated action.

Idiots refuse new information, they don't want to know who is doing wrong or that there is wrong being done. Idiots do not want to know because then they will have to do something with that knowledge. The change may be as little as adjusting their critical thinking to include another parameter or drastic as moving out of Fallon. Idiots aspire to keep their ignorance so that they can exist in a more simple bliss. Idiots are the cogs in the machine that have no idea what the machine does.

> "I don't think it is the function of Congress to function well. It should drag its heels on the way to decision." ~Barber B. Conable, Jr. U.S.A Congress, President of World Bank

Congress should drag its heels on the way to decision because it should promote time to debate to find the best course of action. Congress might make better decisions by figuratively dragging their heels on the way to decision, using time to question instead of reacting without investigation. The reason innate curiosity exists is to find answers and better situations. Questioning seeks truth and when one finds information that is not the whole truth and nothing but the truth, more questions are required. When one finds real confirmable information and answers, more questions might be conjured of subjects directly and indirectly relative.

Congressional Representatives constantly regret they did not have more time to understand, or more time to read the legislation, that things might be different if there was more time. Why were they in such a hurry? Where is the imperative to continue in such a rush, that legislation is not read and questioned? When time is restricted and questions are quelled situations are not automatically slanted, but certainly suspect.

People may be wrong in their actions because they are presented with certain information under certain circumstances. In the case of the Iraq invasion, after 9/11 and the anthrax attacks, after being presented with official proof, representatives took action. The majority were so sure of themselves and the resourced information from reliable institutions, that they refused to question and vilified those who did. They made a snap decision that everyone was convinced was the only pertinent course, the lesser wrong among so many more potentially greater wrongs and dangers.

> "Our government has kept us in a perpetual state of fear – kept us in a continuous stampede of patriotic fervor – with the cry of grave national emergency. Always there has been some terrible evil at home or some monstrous foreign power that was going to gobble us up if we did not blindly rally behind it by furnishing the exorbitant funds demanded. Yet, in retrospect these disasters seem never to have happened, seem never to have been quite real." ~General Douglas Macarthur

Idiots are fools; the nuances are rarely debated. The meaning of patriot, despite dictionary clarity, leaves its exact definition open to opinion. Words used to define patriot are themselves words that hold and relate images and opinions. The actions which define patriot are entirely a matter of opinion formulated. The Iraq invasion was presented as a patriotic option. War is often presented as patriotic, yet war is not involved in the definition of patriot.

Practically no one of authority and only a small minority questioned the official documents presented to justify the Iraq invasion after 9/11. The information was considered to be as good as gold and officially stamped, but it was false, a wrong answer, and wasn't further questioned. No one questioned and as in all wars, more and more people are thusly dead.

Many actions, despite obvious or stated good intentions may be labeled patriotic to one group or another. Some actions are always patriotic, such as questioning. Some actions are nearly never patriotic, as is refusing questions and refuting alternate answers. Patriots support the U.S.A by questioning the interests and actions of their representatives, peers, elected officials, and everyone else.

Patriots know the interests of the country are what the people say they are, not what institutions dictate. This is the original, special aspect of the U.S.A.; there is no patriarch or sacred institution commanding patriots. All people are equal and need only support and defend the trinity of liberty in order to be a patriot.

Patriots love and support country; in the U.S.A. the original and most powerful way to practice that love and support is by questioning and further questioning the answers. Questioning is the right that countless authoritarian oligarchies have tried to suppress for if institutions can prohibit information they can influence tolerations and control.

Institutions extol their virtue. They profess their finesse at accomplishing benevolence within the status quo, presenting solutions within their own invented framework that would benefit them. Institutions develop and foster trust and/or dependency among individuals.

Idiots are certain that marijuana is detrimental because it is illegal. They know their edible Genetically Modified Organisms, mass produced milk and meat is safe because it has been inspected by institutions. They know that pesticides are safe because they were approved by institutions. They know that our military is a purveyor of democracy because they give kids chocolate. They know that the energy corporations intend to supply renewable solar power because they say so. Lacking questions lead idiots to trust institutions before individuals.

The most heroic, patriotic solutions have been prospected and proposed by individuals. Individuals have surmounted walls and problems great and small, by simply questioning. People in a loose group and lone individuals with nothing, have changed everything. People came up with the basic idea of liberty and people upheld it. No institution expelled exploitation of individuals by royalty, ministry or nobility. Change for the benefit of people is, always has been and always will be instigated by individuals.

Liberty's gains result predominantly in spite of institutions and not due to them. Individuals progress, while institutions maintain. The original patriots were masters of questioning and/or dissent. They were rebels, they had long hair and grew hemp. They wrote poems and political articles, they communicated over tea. They probably got drunk on homemade beer and had loud discussions about current events. They questioned motives with reasoning and observations if facts were unavailable. The Company, the King, the churches, the monarchies, everyone and everything was questionable and debatable. Free debate along with open questions and criticism, allows for the progression.

Patriots question and debate new conclusions. The same question may be a simple inquiry one day and dissent the next. Questions may be curiosity to some and treasonous to others. "Why do people support exploitative oligarchies?"

Idiots never ask relevant questions and choose to remain ignorant. Their curiosity is dead, depleted or overloaded, they are like sheep. When lambs need help they do not cry out, their instinct to remain quiet overrides their need to cry out. When idiots need information they do not inquire. They know that every new bit of information is another potential paradigm and want no part of it.

There are the haves and the have-nots, and the famous and the common, and idiots are among them all. The prerequisite to being a complete idiot is avoiding questioning pertinent information. They learn only what is prescribed by their employer or other institution and no more. The prerequisite to being a patriot is questioning, the act of questioning and acquiring information negates idiocy. Patriots begin by simply questioning the conditions of their environment. The more people question events and conditions the better situations turn out. Questioning can find better options, but before better options there are often darker truths. Questions potentially uncover the underbelly of the status quo. Yet the truth must be sought even if it means learning that sleek, shiny jets are fueled by a cancerous mixture that leaves lumpy, tumors.

FACT: Toms River, New Jersey experienced a spike in brain cancer. A study concluded that pollution was the cause and three corporations reached financial settlement with numerous families. Camp Lejuene, a military base in North Carolina experienced a spike in leukemia and lymphoma. The problematic tap water at the base was drank and used by hundreds of thousands of personnel and their families between 1957 and 1987. Woburn Massachusetts, Wilmington Massachusetts, Fulton County New York and Libby Montana are all examples of places where massive amounts of pollutants led to severe sickness.

Idiots continue doing what they are told and what they are accustomed to because it is a more comfortable option to questioning and change. When everything is lovely, there are no questions for idiots to ask. When there's trouble idiots hide and do not inquire.

Patriots simply question, as a right and responsibility. The freedom to question via the First Amendment and the other rights provided in the trinity of liberty grant people the ability to progress. Questioning may reveal horrors, but only questions lead to solutions. Lack of questions instigates nothing, save lack of progression.

The original patriots defied the exploitation of institutions on behalf of those who were locals to their area. The original patriots had no country to fight for. Patriots are not jingoes.

There was no nation of the U.S.A. when the Boston Tea Party occurred. It was individuals against institutions. The ideas of the U.S.A. impel and nearly ordain questioning, the primal act of patriotism. Patriots support those throughout the world who need it, they do not support those that exploit throughout the world. Patriots question and defy the status quo, the powers that be, the King and all the King's men, The Company, the Pope, the President and anyone else for that matter, foreign or domestic.

Just because one served a national or military institution does not automatically qualify one as a patriot. Making war for a national institution does not define patriot. Working for the government in any fashion is not a deciding factor. Singing the national anthem is no qualification either. A flag in the front yard does not exemplify patriotism.

Nowhere is it said that one must shed blood to be a patriot. The greatest grunts in the Army and most heroic pilots in the Navy do not automatically qualify as patriots. Enlistment, wounds, capture, torture and even death battling foreigners on foreign soil do not automatically qualify patriotism. War heroes and patriots are two totally different labels. No one in the military is automatically a patriot, though many certainly are and could be patriots.

FACT: John Sydney McCain III was born in U.S.A. owned, Panama. John III comes from a long line of U.S.A. Navy and military men. One of his ancestors, John Young, served George Washington. Later, another ancestor ran a plantation of slaves in Mississippi and enlisted in the Confederacy. John II served the U.S.A. Navy and Pentagon for over forty years. John II was commander in chief of the U.S.A. Pacific Command during the war in Vietnam, while his son was captive. John III experienced the effects of napalm first hand at the USS Forrestal Incident, where 132 sailors died. Months later he would begin a whole other unique experience, spending over five years broken and beaten as a POW in North Vietnam.

"It is lamentable, that to be a good patriot one must become the enemy of the rest of mankind." ~Voltaire

There are four types of people in the world. There are idiots who lack questions. There are zealots who question how to get the answers they desire. There are elitists who question how to use others to get their desires. And there are patriots who question out of a desire to be informed and inform others. Patriots have participated in war as have all types of people, but warriors are not necessarily patriots and patriots do not necessarily war against others.

DEFINITIONS AND ARCHETYPES

"If a thousand men were not to pay their tax bills this year, that would not be a violent and bloody measure, as it would be to pay them, and enable the state to commit violence and shed innocent blood. This is, in fact,

The dictionary is the only book that both poet and lawyer might share a frequency in researching. The dictionary is useful in making precise evaluation and presentation of language. Yet often, like any group of words, there is room for interpretation of the definitions. Despite the sureness of print, the interpretation of "patriot" varies. Opinion, derived from prior information, reflects even the interpretation of definitions in the dictionary. The surest book in print, excluding mathematical text, still leaves wide room for individual subjectivity.

The dictionary definition of "patriot" has changed over time, the presentation of the word simplifies as the world becomes more complex. This simplification may result in increasing disparity in the meaning of "patriot" as opposed to more clarity. Perhaps all language is being simplified. Words with dwindling and deprived definitions that leave room for contrived opinions might be on the increase. Patriot is a word that perhaps will always have wide disparity of interpretation. Differing ideas about the same word exist.

The definitions are more divergent than one extreme supporting the actions of William Wallace and another supporting Gandhi's way. One exemplifies the peaceful warrior and the other side the battling warrior, but both aimed at canceling exploitation. The divergent definitions are often not even in the same spectrum, the differing definitions mix up attributes of the idiot, zealot and elitist with patriot.

The meaning of words arrives from more than just the dictionary definition. Actions and images can define words sometimes better than other words. Sometimes events and stories define subjects and situations better than words. Definitions can only transmit meaning so far, stories and experiences define words before definitions.

Recent forces of language have reevaluated words and terms in order to become politically correct. These forces revise language and terminology to pacify distasteful subjects. Supposedly, this change in language is to eliminate the negative influence of terminology. Language is corrected, but it is also euphemized and simplified, a dangerous and negative influence itself.

Language also expands, there are new inventions and new conceptualizations requiring new terminology. The 1972 Watergate scandal instigated the resignation of President Nixon under sure impeachment in 1974. The Watergate is a hotel. Now any political scandal is a gate, which is a just circumstance. However a gate is an opening into a new area, a doorway, so it is symbolic as well. Language expands and contracts on developed or disregarded ideas.

There is another force in language that shortens and simplifies definitions and explanations. Because people like to read the simplified version, they get it. The meanings of many words have shrunk, have undergone political correct reform and have been euphemized.

Definitions, terminology and language morphs, but it does not morph on its own. Depending on how certain institutions would like one to perceive certain information, they present it in different terminology. In war, the supreme negative, all subjects are given glorious euphemisms. Annihilation is pacification. Accidental murder is collateral damage and friendly fire. Battles are called engagements and murders are called casualties. They make massacres sound like pleasant pool parties. The forces of language label anew, seemingly to allow idiocy and zealotry a comfortable perimeter, safe from information.

In all likelihood, if undesirable information makes it to idiots and zealots, it will be through gentle euphemisms. In WWI it was shell shock, in WWII battle fatigue, in the Korean War operational fatigue and in Vietnam it became post-traumatic stress disorder and now it's just PTSD. All refer to a combatant effectively losing their marbles from exposure to explosions and death. People without any physical wounds may be as badly hurt as people who lost limbs from war. To bomb cities and the people within them is to pacify a region. Disgusting savagery is turned into gentle, unremarkable words. To whom are casualties casual?

There are wordsmiths who enjoy wealth and prosperity in exchange for their clever use of euphemistic language. Wordsmiths are salaried to manifest terminology that dresses the dire and diabolical in roses and smiles. They manifest their prose and unique way of looking at things for corporate marketing and sales, political campaigns and other institutional agendas.

"When you speak of the 2005 legislative agenda, do not be afraid to wax poetic about this link between American icons of freedom and opportunity and the very legislation that you are discussing. It will not seem trite. It will not appear sordid. Indeed, it will resonate with a power that cannot match that of your words and phrases. Language is your base. Symbols knock it out of the park."
~Frank Luntz

Manipulation of emotion replaces explanation. Logical information becomes secondary to the manipulation of emotion. If information is unquestioned, everything is what they say it is. If feelings are unquestioned, then everything is based on emotion. Emotion is predominantly a reaction, and reactions are predominantly fear based.

The same word, image, or event may have different meaning to different people because of different information possessed and accepted, like patriot. The dictionary is important as a definition, but what one feels is the major guideline to interpretation.

DICTIONARY DEFINITIONS OF PATRIOT
Webster's Dictionary 1956: One who loves his country and zealously supports its authority and interests.
Reader's Digest Great Encyclopedic Dictionary 1967: One who loves his country and zealously guards its interests; especially, a defender of popular liberty.
American Heritage Dictionary of the English language 1969: A person who loves, supports and defends his country.
Webster's Dictionary Designed for Home School and Office 1984: One who loves his country and upholds its interests.
Webster's Dictionary 1986: A person who loves and loyally or zealously supports his own country.
Random House Dictionary of the English Language 1987: A person who loves, supports and defends his or her country with devotion.
Webster's Definition 1992: One who loves his country and upholds its interests.
American Heritage Dictionary of the English Language 2004: One who loves, supports and defends one's country.
Webster's Definition 2006: One who loves his or her country and supports its authority and interests.

What one feels about a word is partially based on what one feels about the words used in its definition. The inference is clear, but interpretation is based on individual experience. If two people have the same experience and one finds it thrilling and the other finds it frightening, then not only do they have a different perspective, but they influence and steer a different perspective among others as well. Despite the concrete definition of actuality, interpretation may differ. One person may refer to the art of warfare, while another may refer to the horrors of war.

"For to win one hundred victories in one hundred battles is not the acme of skill.
To subdue the enemy without fighting is the acme of skill." ~Sun Tzu

There is no art to war on the battlefield. The art of war is in strategy, not in murder. Art is creativity, making something from nothing, while war is supreme violence, making nothing from something. To make a foe into friend, to subdue the enemy without bloodshed is artful, all else is just shedding blood.

"Well, that depends on what your definition of 'is' is." ~Bill Clinton

The etymology of the word patriot developed from patriarchy, and the idea of the fatherland. If one was a countryman, then one was of the patriarchy and served as a patriot under the patriarch. Practically all nations were oligarchies and most often patriarchies. To be a patriot was to serve the king or whoever was at the apex of the pyramid. The patriots were the people in and for the patriarchy. States, nations, fatherlands, were controlled normally by one king, one father to all. That was the design of most all nations; patriots were people of the king and kingdom, people of the patriarchy.

The design of the U.S.A. rejects kings and kingdoms. Patriots in the U.S.A. serve no king, no patriarch, no president, no institution and no individual. Patriots in the U.S.A. serve the trinity of liberty, no individual or institution comes before the principles in the trinity of liberty. These principles serve patriots and patriots serve them.

As time spins ever forward, the definition of patriot changes and develops. During this development, the concept in support of authority is included in the definition. Authority described here is not the ultimate authority we all must answer to, but the authority of national institutions. The authority of the U.S.A. is not an institution, not a king; it is the trinity of liberty. The authority in the U.S.A. is the Declaration of Independence, Constitution and Bill of Rights.

Patriots, if necessary, defy Earthly authorities through the real divine right of people. In the U.S.A., patriots cast off kings and those who pose as kinglike. People have the right to cast off any institution through prescribed means in order to protect life, liberty and the pursuit of happiness. People have the right to an equal playing field regardless of the institution in their way, even the bloody king or a centuries old church. All institutions in the U.S.A., including the government are trite, relative to the trinity of liberty.

I,_____ do solemnly swear that I will support and defend the Constitution of the United States against all enemies, foreign and domestic: that I will bear true faith and allegiance to the same; that I take this obligation freely, without any mental reservation or purpose of evasion; and that I will well and faithfully discharge the duties of the office on which I am about to enter. So help me God. (So help me God is optional.)
U.S.A. Federal Military Oath of Office.

The first promise in the oath of office is to support and defend the Constitution from enemies, no matter who they are, no matter where they are. It is a promise to be a patriot of the Constitution. The Constitution manifests itself for the sovereign people of the U.S.A. Patriots do not serve any institution; they support and defend the ideas of liberty and equality. Patriots do not support and defend government, churches, or corporations, but a set of ideals that exist to hold individual liberty secure.

Those who take this oath may not be patriots at all. Just because one takes this oath does not make one a patriot, just as a rectangle has four sides, but is not a square. Civilians, people outside of military institutions may lack that oath, but may have made a similar promise. Patriots need not to take oaths. Oaths, like so much certified information, may be institutional promises and empty words.

The U.S.A. Military Oath is a promise to be a patriot of the ideas, laws and words of the Constitution. The original patriots knew if everyone had freedom, wrongdoers would have freedom, potentially threatening the design of that freedom. This is why they made so many checks and balances in the design of the government, so that no one branch, no one entity could supersede or envelope the others. Domestic enemies are distinct because they are possible and likely.

It is not possible to crown oneself king of America. Checks and balances provide for the ability and opportunity to question, if not making the act outright obligatory. The trinity of liberty allows itself to be amended and evolve; people are allowed to seek answers and truth to progress. The law of the land accommodates questions and answers. The liberty of the land enables infiltration of domestic manipulation as well, necessitating questions. Liberty is not freedom, freedom is generally a free for all, liberty attempts to limit the free for all, while providing open equality.

"Patriotism is supporting your country all the time and your government when it deserves it."
~Mark Twain, Penname of Samuel Langhorne Clemens

Many events and many words leave room for interpretation. Patriots are often mixed up with the other characterizations, for interpretation is all up to individual experience. Many people believe that the government represents the trinity of liberty and has all the answers, while others believe that the people represent the trinity of liberty and can find all the answers. Patriot is a powerful word, no matter one's specific interpretation. The characterization is an archetype, as are the other powerful words involved in its definition. These words stand as much as images, as print. The words involved in the definition of patriot stand out on their own and carry significant and colorful emotional weight too. Certain words evoke imagery and archetypal symbolism on their own. A picture paints a thousand words and some words paint a thousand pictures.

Symbols are archetypes. Symbols may be seen every day, but there may be something more, something that the eyes might typically miss. There are times when the mind doesn't cognitively see what is right there. Like when one loses their key and then later finds it in plain view. Certain images and certain words have power among everyone. Certain people are affected differently than others and some more substantially. Some people notice and some don't, but are all affected by imagery and symbolism.

There is a really funny joke about two brothers, where one dies on a bridge. It is hilarious. Actually there is no such joke, but if one has a brother that statement would be interpreted one way, differently than if one had a brother that was dying. If one had a brother that died recently and was in mourning the suggestion of the joke would be interpreted differently. If one doesn't have a brother one might be disappointed by the fact that there is no joke. Different people are affected differently, but they are affected nonetheless. There are many types of archetypes ranging from the simple to the complex. Shapes are archetypes. These symbols affect people whether they notice it or not. Simple lines and shapes might have a profound symbolic impact, noticed or not.

The circle is symbolic for life, the Earth and the perfection of creation, reality. It is symbolic of God or universal energy in natural and balanced seasonal cycles. It is symbolic for creation and fertility and of the connections between all people, plants, animals, places and things. Every celestial body in the solar system is circular and set in oval orbit.

Cipher is another word for zero or ring, which is represented by a circle. Cipher is also a word for a secret coded message. Ciphers arrive predominantly in text and sometimes via images with concealed meaning or symbolism. A cipher is also a ring or circular group of people. A circle is perhaps the most complex symbolic form. It is simple, common, yet nearly impossible to calculate or perfectly replicate. Universal energy is constantly circular. The circle is symbolic for nature and nature's perfect imperfections. The circle represents a cipher or secret because the circle is a cipher in itself.

Universal energy and balance is circular, balance is nothing, zero. Nothing is not only the lack of possession, but is also a lack of debt. There are just as many billions of negatives as there are billions of positives and yet only one zero. Cipher is zero; the secret or cipher is that zero equates to circular balance.

Pi is as infinite perhaps as the reflections and symbolic interpretations of the simple circle. The yin and yang symbol is interpreted to represent the balance that opposing positive and negative forces not only balance, but also transform into one another. Within the circle all things are connected.

SYMBOL – SQUARE
The square is symbolic of order, man's ability to form and construct perfect right angles. It is symbolic of the four directions. A square can represent Earth as well, only normally an Earth manipulated. The square is a manipulated and constructed form. A block or square is essential in order to form a pyramid base.

SYMBOL – TREE
Different trees are celebrated by different cultures, with subtly varying meanings. The pine, palm, oak, fig, ash, cottonwood, acacia, ceiba, and more are used in creation myths and religious stories throughout the world. Trees are important in creation and religious theories one and all, throughout the world. The Tree of Life, The Tree of the Knowledge of Good and Evil and the World Tree are examples of the archetypal tree. Trees are seen as unification. The roots are underground in the underworld. The stem is on the ground in the Earthly plane and the branches reach to the Sun and into the heavens.

Trees are one of the oldest symbols or archetypes of one thing representing another more complicated concept. Trees bring together spirit and dirt, the physical and the ethereal. Different stories and myths bestow different characteristics to different trees throughout the world, but they perpetually bestow creation and knowledge. Today we know that trees are givers of life in more than spiritual symbolism and more than in supplying raw materials for people. Not only do trees supply wood, food and medicine, trees produce oxygen and help supply our very breath. Trees and plants absorb carbon dioxide, releasing oxygen and water into the atmosphere.

FACT: Ocean plankton produce more oxygen than all the plant life on terra firma.

SYMBOL – CROSS
The cross is a symbol of man and man's ability to manifest. It symbolizes the four cardinal directions and has come to symbolize the crucifixion of Jesus. Before the crucifixion the cross represented the form of a tree. A circle is the symbol for the universe, creation. A cross inside a circle is symbolic of man's creation and travels in all four directions within God's creation, cooperatively. It is symbolic for balance like yin and yang. A cross beginning in and extending outside a circle is symbolic for man exceeding said creation, a domination over Earth, nature, creation.

Archetypes are as simple as two intersecting lines and as complex as the formula to a perfect circle. Archetypes are as remedial as the square and as intricate as an individual's persona. Archetypes are those ancient manifestations and reactions that seem as fate and are actually determined by the unconscious. Archetypal information is something that just is or seems as much.

Archetypal variations and interpretations morph and shift, in near limitless fashion, but share power and unconscious origins. Archetypal information and archetypal reactions to information are from the unconscious and forever influential. The power of symbols is present like a shadow in the light, but only noticed in certain conditions, when conditions are just right and one is facing the right direction.

Sometimes completely different shapes share certain references, for instance both the circle and the square are symbolic for completion. The circle is symbolic for natural cycles while the square is symbolic for regimentation. People base their actions and opinions on information. If people only understand one shape, if people only know one way of operating and living, that is how they will proceed.

"The healthy man does not torture others – generally it is the tortured who turn into torturers." ~Carl Jung

---

"A more or less superficial layer of the unconscious is undoubtedly personal. I call it the "personal unconscious". But this personal layer rests upon a deeper layer, which does not derive from personal experience and is not a personal acquisition, but is inborn. This deeper layer I call the "collective unconscious." I have chosen the term "collective" because this part of the unconscious is not individual but universal; in contrast to the personal psyche, it has contents and modes of behavior that are more or less the same everywhere and in all individuals." ~Carl Jung

---

Archetypes arrive via the collective consciousness, ever present in individuals. They are ideas in flux, and yet also in line with ancient operational characterizations. Interpretations vary, but their influence is steady. Archetypes are those symbols of all sorts that span centuries with little change in their depth despite shift in interpretation and reaction. The power of archetypes and symbols exists whether they are noticed or unnoticed. Archetypes are those recognizable and unrecognizable symbols that initiate emotional and intellectual response in people. They are those concepts that stand as unshaken through time as the Pyramids of Giza. The meaning of archetypes may sway and morph, age in the wind, but their power remains. Symbols are felt like the sounds of cymbals. Alone they are powerful and crashing, but sometimes with accompanying music their sounds might go unnoticed, but are still crashing.

Archetypes are so influential that people seek, adopt and become archetypes themselves. Examples of archetypal characters: divine child, mother, father, damsel in distress, dunce, sidekick, clown, guide, healer, hero, victim, warrior, soldier, mentor, mystic, poet, jester, rebel, royal, slave, king, villain and nemesis, among many, many others. Patriot, idiot, zealot and elitist are archetypal characterizations as well, defined by their reaction to information and not their title or persona.

Patriots openly question. Patriots are portrayed as farmers, as armed citizens and countrymen. Farmers survey and manage the Earth and farm, while patriots survey and question nation and society. Patriots openly obtain and distribute information to others.

Idiots are happy-go-lucky fools, careless, distracted and drunk by whatever is trendy and comfortable. Idiots are the fashionable, yet timeless ignoramuses. Idiots are passive, aside from actively avoiding and refusing all new and relevant information.

Zealots are stern and march in line. They die or kill before they admit defeat of idea. Zealots are loyal, even to their demise and actively aggressively obtain information that confirms their beliefs and refute any countering information.

Elitists conceal certain information and reveal distractions. They are a silhouette just visible in the shadows or behind a curtain. They are the smiling and lying. Elitists clandestinely obtain information and manipulate others with it.

There are thousands of character archetypes that arrive from stories, fables, myths, events and imagination. However there are only these four characters concerning the reaction to new information. Throughout recorded time, they have been assigned different labels, but there are four different types of mentality.

Information acquired and recognized, interpreted and forgotten is hit upon with symbols contemplated by the conscious and subconscious as well. Archetypes sometimes rest quietly, and yet are stunning and stirring in their power over people's thoughts and emotions.

Symbols and all information affects people even if unnoticed. Archetypes abound and shape how people think. Emotional reaction and interpretation to archetypes often precedes thoughtful interpretation. Archetypes influence thought, but that thought is preceded by emotion. That emotion influences the thought. People have been taught to think and feel in certain formats, unknowingly adjusting their archetypal unconsciousness. People's thoughts and emotions are shaped by archetypes and symbols, known and unknown.

The awareness of the potential power of archetypes enables one to question the thoughts and emotions that arise from them. If the powers of archetypes are known, then one is able to question and perceive emotions and thoughts, not be constricted to simply reacting to them.

A master philosopher (Nasrudin) is sitting among his disciples, when one of them asks him the relationship between things of this world and things of a different dimension.
Nasrudin says "You must understand allegory."
The disciple says, "Show me something practical – for instance an apple from paradise."
Nasrudin picks up an apple and hands it to the disciple.
"But this apple is bad on one side – surely a heavenly apple would be perfect."
"A celestial apple would be perfect, but as far as you are able to judge it, situated as we are in this abode of corruption, and with your present faculties, this is as near to a heavenly apple as you will ever get." ~Nasrudin Tale

Archetypes and symbols affect and shape mentality and may not even be noticed. The power is the same, noticed or not, just as minute particles of petrol affect and bond to people. The results of manmade environmental destruction affect people who may not even notice, as well as symbolism.

Just as one may get cancer and not know why, one may choose to behave in a certain way and not know why. One may believe a wrong is right and not know why. One may believe in an institution and not know why. Archetypes are as complicated and infinite as pi and the human mind. Symbols and shapes represent archetypal information, as well as complex personalities. Reasoning is normally derived from some elusive archetypal notion, story or experience.

"A belief proves to me only the phenomenon of belief, not the content of the belief." ~Carl Jung

The act of questioning is powerful and can dissect surrounding and personal archetypes. This means not only paradigms of thought, but paradigms of emotion. Logic is unfixed and possible to progress, it is changeable through questioning. New thoughts mandate new opinions, and more new thoughts. To question is to seek the truth, and so far the search for truth is endless; with new answers always leading to new questions. To question is of the essence and also seeks it.

To accurately define patriot, it is important to explore the other words involved in its definition. These are diverse, divisive and powerful words on their own. Support, defend, authority, interests, liberty, zealous, and country are all archetypal words themselves involved in the definition of patriot. Patriot and the words in its definition are archetypes which inspire imagery.

SUPPORT AND DEFEND

The foremost action of a patriot is to support and defend. There are many forms of support. There is verbal, fiscal, physical, material, martial and informational support. One can defend many ways as well. All too often, to support and defend is insistently defined as bloodshed on behalf of nation or other institution. It is assumed that to support and defend is to raise arms and equipment for war. There are many ways to support and defend.

To stand up for, and when necessary, fight for the trinity of liberty of the U.S.A. often demands no money or weaponry. To support and defend the U.S.A. does not require bloodshed. It sometimes is a whole lot more and a whole lot less than financial, material or martial activity.

It is a substantial part of the oath those who work for the government take. It is also a promise required of those who would seek citizenship in the U.S.A. Actions that support and defend liberty might be as simple as living peacefully and continuing to allow others to live peacefully.

> I hereby declare, on oath, that I absolutely and entirely renounce and abjure all allegiance and fidelity to any foreign prince, potentate, state or sovereignty of whom or which I have heretofore been a subject or citizen; that I will support and defend the Constitution and laws of the United States of America against all enemies, foreign and domestic; that I will bear true faith and allegiance to the same; that I will bear arms on behalf of the United States when required by law; that I will perform noncombatant service in the armed forces of the United States when required by law; that I will perform work of national importance under civilian direction when required by law; land that I take this obligation freely without any mental reservation or purpose of evasion; so help me God.
> ~Oath of Citizenship of the U.S.A

Of course, whoever takes this oath doesn't automatically qualify as a patriot, but nonetheless the first promise after renouncing foreign powers is to support and defend the Constitution. To become a patriot one must ask questions, inquire. Questioning supports and defends. Support and defense is often interpreted as doing battle, however it is not the same and distinct in this oath. To support and defend is an entirely different promise than the act of bearing arms on behalf of the U.S.A. or serving the military in any capacity. In the oath of U.S.A. citizenship, where it is important to be clear, these are distinct and separate subjects.

Many people have died for the U.S.A. in war, but not necessarily in support and defense of the Constitution. How many soldiers have died fighting a potential threat to the Constitution? How many wars have been conducted defending the Constitution, Bill of Rights and Declaration of Independence?

The original copies of the trinity of liberty are housed in the Library of Congress, Washington, DC, in atomic blast proof casing. Is war a way to support and defend the trinity of liberty? The Constitution may be defended in some wars, but in war it is never supported. Sometimes after war liberty arrives, but in war liberty is gone. Some wars are fought for ends other than support and defense of the Constitution, although the same means are employed no matter the cause or pretense.

> U.S.A. SOLDIER COSTS FROM MILITARY CONFLICTS
> War in Iraq, almost 4,200 Killed In Action, some 30,000 Wounded In Action as of late 2008.
> War in Afghanistan, almost 630 KIA and over 1,600 WIA
> Vietnam War, over 58,000 KIA, some 150,000 WIA and almost 2,000 MIA.
> Korean War, over 50,000 KIA, some 103,000 WIA and over 8,000 MIA.
> World War II, over 400,000 KIA, some 600,000 WIA.
> The War to End All Wars, over 116,000 KIA, some 204,000 WIA.
> Civil War, over 200,000 KIA, some 400,000 WIA, many others died from disease.
> Spanish–American War over 3,200 dead, most from disease.
> War for Mexico, over 13,000 KIA, some 4000 WIA.
> War of 1812, over 2,200 KIA, some 4,500 WIA, and 17,000 died from disease.

It is important to memorialize the people who fought and died. It is equally important to remember that millions of civilians died along with them, innocents with nothing to gain and everything to lose. Almost four million Vietnamese died in the war in Vietnam. Innocent bystanders and noncombatants experience the brunt of war, as well as, and perhaps more than soldiers on the front line. Poisons leftover from war in Vietnam and the atomic bombings the world over linger and harm people born into a peaceful world. The harmful aftereffects of war linger for generations.

Perhaps twenty million civilians were killed in WWI, along with eight million other soldiers from various armies. WWI was a monarchical and empirical battle, as all previous wars in Europe had been. Only WWI was different. It was the first war fought in the petrolithic era. This allowed the war to grow to a gross and global scale through new machinery made with and powered by petrol. WWI was fought with pre petrolithic era tactics and post petrolithic era weaponry. Armies were vanquished as a result.

> "Have the horrors of world war done nothing to open our eyes, so that we still cannot see that the

The War to End All Wars was a wishful sentiment and as it turned out, an inaccurate title. The official armistice came into effect on 11/11, 1918 at 11:00 am. The war was so horrible and ruining that people thought or hoped it would never happen again. Treaties and arrangements were made towards a unified world government.

WWII eliminated the original name of WWI when war erupted again out of Europe. Seventy million people died in WWII. Many were servicemen who similarly pledged an oath to raise arms, but most were innocents caught up in empirical megalomania. Germany processed their coal reserves into gas, in a process called hydrogenation to fuel their WWII war machines. Without petrol, they would have never been able to prepare for war, let alone instigate it. When the hydrogenation bases were bombed and in ruin, Hitler's war machine grinded to a halt.

In war, soldiers and civilians are stirred into events and circumstances beyond normal comprehension and reason. Soldiers support and defend their fellow soldiers and not necessarily the Constitution while on the battlefield. The artillery and gunfire cause mortal peril, soldiers are concerned for their hides and not ideas, such as those of the trinity of liberty.

The military actions in Iraq, Vietnam, Korea and the War for Mexico were not in support or defense of the Constitution. WWII was arguably fought over preservation of people's rights and against institutionalized, murderous monopolization. Arguably some wars were waged to defend ideas in the Constitution and trinity of liberty, but no war supports it. The ideas of freedom and liberty are suspended during war. The essence the Constitution prescribes is disbanded, not supported in war.

New England did not participate in the War of 1812, refusing to send militia or financial assistance. This war was not a threat to the Constitution in the eyes of New Englanders; they saw it as a threat to certain trade and expansion, not worth warring for. State militia made up the predominant military force then, and New England refused to send soldiers.

In 1846, the War for Mexico was waged to take land and expand, imperialistic in makeup. This war was guided by the idea that the nation was entitled to take land that might be used more efficiently. Manifest Destiny was the idea that the U.S.A. should expand from sea to shining sea. The idea of Manifest Destiny was depicted by Columbia, a personification of the U.S.A. Columbia was a practical doppelganger of Lady Liberty or Freedom. Of course they all only look alike, real liberty would never motivate war, while Columbia guided people westward in a violent takeover.

The wars in Korea and Vietnam were proxy wars and useful only in degrading the reputation of the U.S.A. and creating division and borders. The U.S.A. military fought against armies indirectly representing the USSR and communism. These wars were waged over ideals; communism versus democracy was fought among individuals with institutional support and advancement.

The War on Terror was also a battle of ideas. Terror is an act, not a side; terror is employed by all sorts of armies and miscreants alike. The War on Terror as labeled by George II, and war in general, is presented as a way to support and defend the Constitution, however there are better ways to support and defend than to kill and maim. The global War on Terror was a war against an idea; only war perpetuates the idea and act of terror. War is terrible and terrorizes. With or without state coordination, a war on terror can endlessly perpetuate itself. War causes terror and terrorists use tools of war to terrorize.

President Barack Obama renamed the War on Terror to the Overseas Contingency Operation. Instead of a confusing confrontational label, the war or operation was given a more euphemistic name, but still remained equally confusing. Being contingent suggests the likelihood or possibility of an operation not an ongoing actuality.

Before the War for Mexico the U.S.A. Military numbered around 6,000; it soon increased to 115,000. At the time, the State Militias contained the majority of enlisted soldiers. The people who already occupied the land were conquered and killed. Constant and rigorous gentrification of indigenous Americans continued westward. Manifest Destiny inspired many people to agree with, tolerate and even participate in the conquest. People believed manifest destiny ordained Columbia, who looked a lot like the Angel of Liberty, yet was anything but, to expand the country from sea to shining sea.

| "Disobedience is the true foundation of liberty. The obedient must be slaves." ~Henry David Thoreau | FACT: Henry David Thoreau was jailed in 1846, in protest of the War for Mexico, he refused to pay taxes. He spent a night in jail and was released when a relative paid what he owed. He later authored Civil Disobedience. Henry was an inspiration to Gandhi. |

Mexico and Mexicans were vilified then and arguably have been ever since. Their immigration is suppressed, and yet, they are some of the only indigenous immigrants, and arguably deserve special privilege as such. Perhaps if they stopped, then they would be invited with benefits or at least protections.

Cesar Chavez was born in Arizona, 1927. Cesar wanted to cease all immigration as a way to get rights for those working in the fields, believing that boycotts were the only way farmers and individuals could voice their opinion among powerful institutions. Both Henry and Cesar believed in discontinuing support of institutions in order to change.

> "The first principle of nonviolent action is that of non-cooperation with everything." ~Cesar Chavez

FACT: Ulysses S. Grant served in the War for Mexico. He later believed the war was unjust, empirical and merely an attempt to create more slave states in the U.S.A. He fought in the Civil War and ultimately became General of the Army of the United States. Later, as President, Ulysses was blamed for his role, mainly out of ignorance, in the financial panic in 1869, known as Black Friday. As a private citizen, Grant was later swindled by Ferdinand Ward.

Many people were against the idea of a war with Mexico, not only because it was imperialistic, but because it would serve to expand slavery as well. The war did expand slave territory, and in doing so, helped lay the groundwork in the build up to the Civil War.

One does not have to be enlisted or commissioned in the military or be employed by government to support and defend the Constitution. Being in the military and pressing buttons for them does not mean one supports and defends the Constitution. Many people have sacrificed themselves in war, sometimes zealously and sometimes patriotically and often for a stranger's agenda. The agenda differs from war to war and battle to battle, but rarely if ever, does pressing buttons or killing people support and defend the Constitution, or liberty.

The Iraq War, or war obviously benefits weapons manufacturers and oil corporations and elusively, perhaps, something else, something more. Perhaps war is done to control, as it always was. All wars are composed of the greatest ideals of the day and compromise even the minutest of beliefs.

By questioning, one exercises the rights provided by the Constitution. The right restricted by countless controlling institutions throughout all time. By enacting the rights in the Constitution, one supports the Constitution. By writing off and ceasing support of institutions that suggest one not employ those rights, one defends it. To question and speak when no one else will is patriotic. To question and further disrespect wrongdoing performed by authorities that undermine the Constitution would make the original patriots proud.

Anyone who suggests that it is un-American to question any institution is, in fact, being un-American. To question is to engage liberty. To question is to perform that which was denied to so many for so long. To question is to employ the right so many have supposedly died to protect and keep. The act of questioning supports and defends the trinity of liberty.

It is always people who fight and die in war. People lose and sacrifice life and time to war. Yet war rarely ousts or harms institutions. War profits existent institutions on both sides of war. Peace treaties perpetuate nations after war. Germany continued on as an institution despite having been conquered in war and despite committing perhaps the most heinous atrocities in European history. It was split in two, but now is the institution of Germany again.

Wars are discussed among institutions, and fought among men. Revolutions are manifested by peoples' rejection of institutions. War is the oldest function of institutions, but revolution is a function of individuals. War is always violent and costly, while revolution does not have to be violent and costly.

Revolutions are about the removal or transformation of institutions. Technological revolutions relegate what once seemed crucial into useless. People used to trade animal skins for a living. Societal and institutional revolutions, like the fall of the Berlin wall, deem once essential institution into arbitrary space for rent.

Revolution begins as a popular desire to stop the wrongdoing of institutions or abandon their out-of-date functions. There is not always a replacement offered, just the sentiment that the current system must be ceased. Institutions will not proceed without a plan. They do not make any movement without a set operation set within the status quo. People will abandon and shun wrongdoing without further plan, just as the original patriots did at the big steep and with the Declaration of Independence.

Humanity is adaptable, but institutions are not. Institutions tell people that it would be difficult, next to impossible, to function without them. People become convinced that they could not function without institutions and that they are dependent on institutions. In actuality it is institutions that are dependent on people.

War maintains the status quo, throughout history institutions have gone to war. Various reasons are presented, but always war is made to maintain the status quo. One war has led to another and another and ultimately directly into the current war. Every war has set up the next war and propagated the same institutions or the same type of institutions. War continues, while revolution starts anew.

"To kill a man is not to defend a doctrine, but to kill a man." ~Michael Servetus, Theologian

A republic, a free nation does not drop liberty with its artillery. Guns cannot shoot democracy, they only can shoot at democratic people. Positivity never arrived by the trigger and there are often better ways to support and defend the trinity of liberty than picking up a gun and pushing buttons in the status quo.

When the military speaks of maintaining stability, they really mean maintaining the status quo. The maintenance of stability is in part, the continuation of money flow into the same hands. War furthers the interaction of death and destruction between many, and advances an elite few. War is never won. Victory in war is only postponement and arrangement of future war. Every war today has its roots in state conflicts, religious conflicts, colonialism and corporatism stretching back centuries. War is fought by people who believe in state, church or company, and every war occurs as a result of manipulation in order to achieve institutional objectives. To support and defend is many things, but war is war.

General Smedley Darlington Butler died in 1940 as the most decorated enlisted individual in the U.S.A. His father, Thomas Butler, was a Representative from Pennsylvania for 31 years until his death in 1928. Smedley enlisted in the Marines when he was just sixteen. After basic training, he wound up at Guantanamo Bay, during the Spanish–American War, where he was nearly shot in the head by a Spanish sniper. Later, he was shot twice during service in the Boxer Rebellion when Chinese people violently reacted to multiple occupying, colonial institutions. The U.S.A. supported European colonial institutionalized counterparts there. Smedley served in many conflicts and ultimately became an outspoken critic against war. He wrote the powerful book entitled, "War is A Racket."

"I spent thirty three years and four months in active military service and during that period I spent most of my time as a high class muscle man for big business, for Wall Street and the bankers. In short I was a racketeer, a gangster for capitalism. I helped make Mexico and especially Tampico, safe for American oil interests in 1914. I helped make Haiti and Cuba a decent place for the National City Bank boys to collect revenues in. I helped in the raping of half a dozen Central American Republics for the benefit of Wall Street. I helped purify Nicaragua for the International Banking House of Brown Brothers in 1902–1912. I brought light to the Dominican Republic for the American Sugar interests in 1916. I helped make Honduras fight for the American fruit companies in 1903. In China in 1927, I helped see to it that Standard Oil went on its way unmolested." ~Smedley Butler

"There are only two things we should fight for. One is the defense of our homes and the other is the Bill of Rights. War for any other reason is simply a racket." ~Smedley Butler

Smedley, also known as the Fighting Quaker, and Old Gimlet Eye, supported his country and troops. He spoke at, and was a supporter of the Bonus Army Protests. The Bonus Army was a group of WWI soldiers who petitioned and protested in Washington, D.C. in 1932 for early access to their promised war bonuses. It was a protest of veterans that was eventually, forcefully busted up by future veterans.

Smedley battled around the world, and ultimately came to the conclusion that there were only a few things worth fighting over. He battled everywhere, but perhaps his most famous battle and the most debated, took place on U.S.A. soil. It was no communist, fascist or Nazi threat either – or maybe it was. Smedley uncovered and exposed an attempted corporate takeover of the U.S.A., by corporations based not abroad, but within. Smedley is controversially credited with exposing an attempted coup in the U.S.A. by corporations.

In 1933, a corporate conglomerate apparently approached Smedley. According to Smedley covert representatives from corporate institutions approached him to lead a veteran army of 500,000. Smedley exposed JP Morgan, DuPont, Chase Manhattan Bank, US Steel, General Motors, Goodyear and of course, Standard Oil in a plot against the U.S.A. government.

In 1934, a Congressional Investigation verified Smedley's evidence of the plot to overthrow President Roosevelt and turn North America into a corporate conglomerate, much like South Asia of the past. Congress found that Smedley's accusations concerning the attempts were true and accordingly, no further action was taken.

Times have changed; people used to be incarcerated for plotting crime as diabolical as overthrowing the U.S.A. government. Today people are monitored and incarcerated for much less than that. Perhaps since this incident, the FBI has been monitoring dangerous plotters, poets and musicians alike for decades as standard operating procedure.

Jose Padilla was involved in a plot to detonate a dirty bomb in attempts to overthrow or destabilize the U.S.A. government. Jose was involved in plots against the U.S.A., but has been in contemplation with himself alone, in solitary confinement, since May 2002. He was arrested when he returned from an international trip to meet likeminded terrorists in Afghanistan, Egypt, Saudi Arabia, Afghanistan, Pakistan and Iraq.

> FACT: The Liberty City Seven, incarcerated June 2006, were involved in a conspiracy to blow up and take down the Sears Tower in Chicago. The Seven, in attempts to acquire weapons, explosives, boots, contacts, anything from anyone, met up with an FBI agent posing as an Islamic radical. They had nothing, but the apparent intention to do terrible crime. Eventually one was acquitted, but was held by immigration to await deportation hearing. There were two mistrials.

They busted the Liberty City crew for crimes they were thinking about committing. Times definitely have changed. In 1993 the FBI supplied explosives to terrorists to attack the World Trade Center. The FBI (founded in 1908 in part to regulate interstate commerce) reasoned that they had to commit a crime before they could be convicted of committing a crime so they supplied explosives and then announced they knew who used them.

Times have changed. Perhaps the reason the Liberty City crew were guilty of thought-crimes was a matter of convenience. They were individuals and it was convenient for them to go down. It was also convenient to supply ordinance for the 1993 attack on the WTC. Perhaps the institutions Smedley indicted, walked away because indicting and trying them would have been inconvenient.

To support and defend is many things. Often the interpretation of support is limited to delivery of material and information, while the interpretation of defense is limited to military action. To support and defend the trinity of liberty often means to no longer support and defend institutional wrongdoing. To support and defend sometimes requires dropping tolerations to institutional actions. To support and defend sometimes means ceasing maintenance and repair of certain institutionalizations.

INTERESTS

> "The Constitution is not an instrument for the government to restrain the people, it is an instrument for the people to restrain the government – lest it come to dominate our lives and interests." ~Patrick Henry

In the expanse and diversity of the U.S.A. and the entire world, there are a multitude of different and at times conflicting interests at play. People around the world perceive things differently and believe different things altogether. One person might possess a countering idea to another's idea or have a total alternative notion.

People's interests are forged in an array of brilliant and occasionally dull tones the world over. A mechanic may not have the same interests as a poet, but despite preferring different means they seek the same ends. Everyone, that is everyone in their right mind, seeks life, liberty and the pursuit of happiness. Everyone wants what is right and good; everyone wants and expects liberty and basic rights. Everyone needs clean air and fresh water, if that is granted, all else follows.

Everyone in their right mind would have institutions among them only in order to ensure their safety, happiness and benefit. If people knew otherwise, the institutions would have to present counter information or expect to be countered. The interests of all people are to live without the sufferings some have endured, with the liberties some have enjoyed, and the ability to pursue happiness that some have been honored. The broad interests of people can be outlined in such commonalities and are insured by ideas in the trinity of liberty. If provided information people will naturally, in an overwhelming majority lean toward what is right, unless heavily burdened by tolerations and manipulations.

If presented with overwhelming economical information, people will act on that instead of other information. If one is always presented with information in terms of economic impact and correspondence, then one will tend to think about things always in economic terms.

There are three general types of institutions created by people. They are government, corporate and religious institutions. Institutions are ostensibly set up to promote and make safe the individuals' life, liberty and pursuit of happiness. Institutions all present themselves as of, for and by the people. But once an institution is established, people tend to become just a subject of, or participant in greater institutional interests.

The more pyramidal the institution, the more restrictive and exclusive their provisions are. The steeper their slant, the more regimented their agenda and the less they can be relied on by people. The trinity of liberty is the design, the base architecture that counters and levels the slant of pyramidal institutions.

The interests of the trinity of liberty are the basis of the U.S.A. Prevention of individual exploitation by institutional oligarchical collectivism is a key concept in the trinity of liberty. Originally the design of the trinity of liberty left business out of government and as much as possible, government out of business. Originally it was also deemed that government be apart from church and church stay separate from politics and business. One intention of the trinity of liberty is to separate the institutions, to keep them from intertwining in order to prevent exploitation.

This is a deliberative reaction to the exploitation the colonists experienced. Many institutional transgressions over individuals were observed, and the trinity of liberty was a preventative measure to institutional exploits over individuals. The trinity of liberty was a reaction based on stopping wrong and implementing the right. The original patriots knew there was a better chance for people to attain and maintain liberty if the institutions were separated. They observed the intertwined, monopolization of the European monarchies, all of their pyramidal exploits and takeovers. They intended to prevent institutional monopolization and manifested the trinity of liberty to restrict, cancel and counter exploitation and monopolization. Some institutional exploits were eliminated, however others took their place.

Institutions always sway towards intertwined monopolization, motivation and action. Individuals tend to seek independence. Government is intertwined with business and businesses are wholly dependent on government policy. Church relies on business and government relies on church. Pyramidal institutional connections, oligarchical collectivism, must constantly be surveyed, targeted and cleared like some weed in the garden.

FACT: As of August 2008, $85 billion dollars has been spent on outsourced military contracts in Iraq.

"I am for freedom of religion, and against all maneuvers to bring about a legal ascendancy of one sect over another." ~Thomas Jefferson

Institutions which were originally arranged for people, because of agendas, come to recognize only other institutions. Institutions assist individuals through institutions first and many times individual assistance gets lost. Institutions work through other institutions and often individuals trust institution over other individuals. This divergence is not orderly, but instigative of chaos. Uplifting institutions rarely uplifts individuals, but always uplifts the institutions. Complete trust in institutions puts machines in charge of the living's wellbeing. Institutions have entirely different interests from individuals; seeking different means through uncaring and mechanical ends.

Institutions are intertwined and embedded into and among one another like so many stacked blocks and pyramids formed into one expansive pyramid. Institutions are formations of individuals, however institutions are capable of outlasting individuals and through this and many other factors, are able to impress a sense among individuals that the institution is greater than the individual. This sense of greatness contributes to the institutionalization of individuals within the institution. Individuals within institutions increasingly behave as machines, individuals burdened by tolerations.

Institutions exist to benefit people and are at the will of the people in the U.S.A. Institutions also exist for selfish agendas they do not let on about. When their agendas outweigh their benefit, people disregard them. If institutions are found to exist for merely themselves or the promotion of other institutions, then they shouldn't and probably won't exist. And they know this.

Institutions do not experience life, liberty, or happiness, and therefore, only pretend to pursue it. Institutions do not experience anything, for they are not alive. Institutions should not have the same rights as individuals; moreover they should not have the right to pretend that they are alive and in pursuit of happiness. People are alive and experience life, Institutions not at all.

People within institutions are in control; they steer machines. A CEO or other institutional official will look past what people would want, and accomplish what institutions would want. People work within institutions, but not as people, they act as the institution itself. Such institutionalized officials place more value on the architecture than the people within it. This is part of the status quo.

It is the old concept of might is right, but one might not notice it today. It is the few above the many. The status quo is the architecture that is stacked up against many and for few. The status quo is the continuation, without conclusion or destination, of unending monopolization. The pyramid system is the status quo, accompanied by the archetypal nemesis.

The status quo is the pyramid system which has sufficiently, albeit cruelly, functioned for millennia. Within the conditions, conflicts, confines and consequences of the petrolithic era; environmentally the status quo can continue no longer. Institutions seek to maintain operations, yet petrol cannot be maintained. Petrol is limited and excessively polluting.

The status quo is the development which was once prized as prosperity and now is protested as excessive. It is the same pyramidal course that has steered people for millennia, instituted in a time that requires something other than the same course, mainly because of past pyramidal operations. The status quo is the promotion of institutional interests rather than the individual interests.

The interests of institutions and the institutionalized operate in conjunction within the status quo. Their interests whether they like or not, or know it or not, are in accordance with the pyramidal status quo. The status quo exists, transmits and has set up the pyramid system society is in, since before Mesopotamian Ziggurats and North African Pyramids were drawn up. The interests of institutions are to maintain the pyramid system; to ensure that they can monopolize and hold their monopolization.

The status quo results from conduct and actions taken in keeping with the pyramid system. Whatever the differences and nuances, whatever progression has taken place, the status quo is that same pyramid system of control benefiting the few over the many. The status quo is the interaction between policy of institutions and pursuits of individuals. It is the pyramid system upheld by institutions and only vaguely adjusted for thousands of years. The petrolithic era is a result of the constant institutionalization of the pyramid system.

> "Status quo, you know, that is Latin for the mess we're in." ~Ronald Reagan

The status quo is maintained by institutions to benefit institutions, while touting future benefit to individuals. No matter how things change, they remain the same. This has been true for generations because the status quo is that unchanging system that enacted throughout recorded time. Some things changed and some things did not, now everything has changed, except the status quo, the mess we're in, which has grown deeper. It is indeed a new world; in the petrolithic era no matter how things change they will never be the same. Petrol and its accompaniments have perhaps permanently, and definitely negatively, altered the environment.

The exact interests of institutions are infinite and yet, all intend to profit and prevail in a pyramidal fashion within the status quo. They shun change that would shift or dismantle their monopolization paradigm after paradigm. No matter how situations call for discontinuance or change, the pyramidal status quo grinds on. Institutions uphold the status quo, which is to keep doing what we've been doing, maintaining a pyramid system. There are new words, new labels, but the pyramid system is that old villain, the archetypal nemesis accompanying all hubris. There are consequences to living out of balance.

The status quo, the pyramid system has delivered assistance and reaped horror throughout history. In the petrolithic era the environment can no longer accommodate institutional continuation, yet they insist. The status quo is institutional agendas presented as collective individual interests. The pyramid system is the continuation and expansion of institutional prosperity and not people's prosperity.

The status quo is the confines, the construction and constriction of the pyramid system placed on people in their life, liberty and pursuit of happiness. The status quo results in institutional interests being placed over individual interests. The status quo batters, displaces and dismantles that which just is for profit and monopolizing agendas. The status quo is that which is right for some and wrong for many presented as right for all. It changes presentation and discourse in order to maintain course, but the status quo is pyramidal. And it is in nearly every institution's interests to maintain it.

Institutions are neatly fitting blocks within the pyramidal system that is the status quo. The pyramid system is perpetuated by the oligarchic interests of institutions. Individuals tend to be circular and amorphous, never fitting neatly into the pyramidal status quo and institutional design. When individuals lack indoctrination via institutions, they tend to want what is right not only for themselves, but for others as well. Institutions want what is. Institutions are designed for inconsequential, monopolistic growth. People seek gains, but institutions seek to gain all. Highly institutionalized people become like institutions in and of themselves, profiting not only for happiness, but, for control.

People want what is right and are interested in what is right. Institutions and the institutionalized rightly want everything. They perform masquerades and adopt personas to hold the perception they are essential and benevolent. They have aliases and speak with different tones among different people. They need the support of people and always promote their benevolence and belittle their extractions and exploitations. The more unscrupulous the institution, the more effort and money they invest to maintain strong public relations and/or conceal portions of reality.

The status quo is the pyramid system within an otherwise circular and amorphous world. The status quo, like the ancient pyramids, stands through centuries of human development and change, looming in the background, yet evoking sway of great magnitude.

The status quo permits institutions and institutionalized to halt the progression of happiness that individuals seek in their own pursuits. This happens seemingly both knowingly and unknowingly. People want life, liberty and the pursuit of happiness and attempt to better themselves and their children through change. Institutions want to control life, take liberties and sell happiness through continuation.

Institutions seek to maintain the status quo. The status quo in the petrolithic era has led us to great discoveries and corresponding greatly irrational acts of unsustainability, both benevolence and malevolence. The status quo is the unchanging design of institutional procedure through multiple paradigms which call for change. In the petrolithic era, all the people's voices demanding change are perhaps eclipsed by Mother Earth's own voice revealing, slowly or suddenly that the status quo does not suit her.

For thousands of years people have diluted their waste with the help of Mother Earth. No more. We have reached the point where any attempt at dilution, is now saturation. Water is polluted with knowns and unknowns. The essential substance of life is growing more impure. If any individual had an interest in the right to clean, fresh water, they lost. Clean water is more rare than gold in some parts of the world.

> FACT: A wide assortment of pharmaceuticals including, but not limited to antibiotics, hormones, painkillers and psychiatric drugs; have been found to be in the drinking water of at least 41 million people in the U.S.A. Over 60 different pharmaceuticals and byproducts were found in water in Philadelphia.

For thousands of years institutions and individuals have warred, conquered, exploited and enslaved people they labeled "them". Institutions and the institutionalized often behave and monopolize like Amazon ants, only able to perform tasks such as war and taking slaves. They are unable to feed themselves, and grow their own food, but excellent at harvesting off of others. The more institutionalized one becomes, the more tolerations one develops and the more likely one identifies with machines more than human beings.

It was more feasible to drop bombs, including atomic bombs on cities in WWII, than to directly battle. Today, it is more feasible to war rather than to communicate and to annihilate rather than confront. The status quo continues through the institutionalized ability to enact wrong in a said attempt to do right. Interests change, but many interests are rooted in the same old conceptualization of the status quo, the pyramid system.

The status quo continues through institutions using individual's interests and tolerations to evil to convince them that a lesser evil is less evil. Change is always present; both negative as well as positive change. The lesser evil is perpetuated through institutions presenting a much more dire option if the lesser wrong is not enacted. Institutions play off of fear of potential future to initiate actual exploits. What are your individual interests? Besides clean air, fresh water and liberty that is.

> "A man will fight harder for his interests than for his rights." ~Napoleon Bonaparte

LIBERTY

> "Democracy is two wolves and a lamb voting on what to have for lunch.
> Liberty is a well-armed lamb contesting the vote." ~Benjamin Franklin

In the petrolithic era, the only way to survive the status quo, let alone attempt to change it, is to be a well-armed lamb. To be well-armed is to be well-informed. A well-armed lamb holds relevant information. Information is conducive to cunning and swift-thinking lambs, lambs that cannot be trapped, or eaten for lunch. The well-armed lamb diffuses any reason or inkling to be hunted by being well-informed. Knowledge is power. Individual ignorance is strength to institutions.

People are not lambs or wolves though, some only seem like one or the other at times. People are capable of being peaceful and making decisions based on information other than emotion, instinct and hunger. Humans are capable of many different behaviors even when hungry or being chased. Wolves always gorge on food and lambs never cry for help. People are capable of much more than wolves and lambs.

"Our thinking and our behavior are always in anticipation of a response. It is therefore fear based." ~Deepak Chopra

People are able to prepare and forecast the actions of themselves and others, whether through correct intuition or absurd paranoia. No animal would seek liberty, fairness, freethinking and equal access to resources. No wolf would allow it and no lamb would stand up for it. Only people could design liberty. Only people can protect the lambs and sheepish from the wolves and ravenous, whether by vote or by protesting situations such as the outcome of a vote. People are capable of logic and compassion. With liberty comes safety for the lamb and restraint of the wolf in all people.

"Liberty has never come from government. Liberty has always come from the subjects of it. The history of liberty is a history of resistance. The history of liberty is a history of limitations of governmental power, not the increase of it." ~Woodrow Wilson

"If liberty means anything at all, it means the right to tell people what they do not want to hear." ~George Orwell

Liberty is interaction between people without impeding on one another, responsibly doing whatever. It is the freedom to choose and the freedom to enact that choice; it is also the freedom not to choose and not to act. Questions, communication and speaking out not only enable and benefit liberty, but are never harmful to real happiness. One's opinions and actions can be contrary to another's, contrary to the majority and even contrary to the powers that be and one can express them to anyone, anywhere. One can express one's logic or love whenever and however one sees fit no matter who it offends. But that is the only line one can cross; revealing something to someone that doesn't want to hear or see, is the only intrusion one can make on another.

In liberty one can do whatever one wants as long as it does not hinder or impede others. This is the main aspect of liberty, and to promote liberty one can never be silent or silence others. No one has to listen, but everyone can speak. In liberty one is free to proceed so long as one does not harm others.

People may vocalize their thoughts and no one has to care. One can speak publicly and no one has to listen. One can write and no one has to read. Anyone can speak and communicate; one only has to stand up to do so. When liberty arrives, it arrives onto all, all are permitted to speak and yell. And everyone is given the same rights without restrictions; one only has to stand up to keep them.

Those convicted of crime, no matter how felonious or horrendous never lose the right to speak. One might lose a lot of things if one gets convicted of taking liberties over another. One may be imprisoned and lose literally practically every possession, but in principle, one never loses the right to speak. They can take away the podium one speaks from and limit those who would hear, but one never loses the right to speak. They can take away the right to vote and bear arms, but not the right to speak.

One can't invade someone's personal space or private life, but that's okay because they must accord others with the same mutual respect. Unless one has been convicted of certain crimes, one keeps one's rights. One must respect everyone, as they must be respectful too, but otherwise party and pursue. Liberty is the activation of the Golden Rule. The Golden Rule is a fundamental principle of all the world's religions, a constant amid variation. If the instinct to do the right thing was imprinted on people, it is similarly worded.

GOLDEN RULE
Blessed is he that prefereth his brother before himself. ~Bah'ai
Treat no others in ways that you yourself would find hurtful. ~Buddhism
Therefore all things whatsoever ye would that men should do to you, do ye even so to them, for this is the law and the prophets. ~Christianity
One concept sums up the basis of all good conduct...loving kindness. Do not do unto others what you do not done unto yourself. ~Confucianism
This is the sum of duty: do not do unto others what would cause pain if done to you. ~Hinduism
What is hateful to you, do not to your fellow man. This is the law: all the rest is commentary. ~Judaism
None of you truly believes until he wishes for his brother what he wishes for himself. ~Islam
Respect for all life is the foundation. ~The Great Law of Peace, American Indian.
The heart of the person before you is a mirror. See there your own form. ~Shinto
The basis of Sufism is the consideration of the hearts and feelings of others. If you haven't the will to gladden someone's heart, then at least beware lest you hurt someone's heart, for on our path, no sin exists but this. ~Sufi Master
Whatever is disagreeable to yourself do not do unto others. ~Zoroastrianism

All the world's religions contain similar lessons and words. This is the innate, self-evident, universal morality. The Golden Rule is also the basis of liberty, meant to preserve fairness among distortions and tolerations. Liberty is not freedom, though in liberty there are certain freedoms, liberty is peaceful and righteous. To be maintained, liberty must be expanded and conditions must be questioned and communicated.

"If all mankind, minus one, were of one opinion, and only one person was of the contrary opinion, mankind would be no more justified in silencing that one person, than he, if he had the power, would be justified in silencing mankind."
~John Stuart Mill, British Author, Member of Parliament

John wrote the book "On Liberty" first published in 1859. In it he proposes that the individual is sovereign over self. John eloquently related the Harm Principle, the notion that one can act so long as it does not interfere with the happiness of, or bring harm to others. He also theorized that factors and authorities in society might steer people to enact wrong by influencing perceptions of morality. John proposed that in liberty there is only one condition that requires forceful power to be exercised; in prevention direct harm to self or others.

Today individuals are granted liberties, and institutions are treated with many of the same rights, privileges. Institutions are not individuals, nor are they anything remotely similar, yet many of the same rights and privileges of individuals are also allotted to certain institutions.

One cannot force people to question subjects that might be paradigm or irrelevance no matter how strongly one feels others should know. One has the right to question and investigate situations of relevance, but one is also allowed privacy in personal comings and goings that are irrelevant to others.

One cannot inquire into people's private comings and goings. Likewise, individuals and institutions are not permitted to invade another's personal space, property or private life, except some individuals in some institutions are sometimes allowed to track others. Equally strange is that when hypocritical actions are taken that subvert liberty they are proclaimed to be taken in attempts to preserve liberty.

Most institutions have overwhelming resources compared to most individuals. Many institutions use their power over people to further their institution and not for people as a whole. Institutions perform feats of withholding information and also become experts at gathering information on others. Information strengthens individuals and institutions.

Institutions are afforded practically the same rights and the same liberties as individuals. Yet institutions are ultimately lifeless property, conglomerations and formulations. Institutions only seem alive because they have been extolled liberty. Liberty is that force from the essence that gives people hope and potential. It is also the magic that gives life to logos and corporate characterizations. If institutions were not entitled the magic of liberty, they couldn't pretend to be alive. They would be considered property, machinery and not friendly or necessary masqueraders.

Among the many rights liberty provides, that to some with extreme tolerations would seem privilege, is the right to gather together. Liberty provides the right to gather and protest peaceably, which may or may not affect another's otherwise daily routine. Nowhere is one's daily routine guaranteed, but the right to gather is specifically assured. The trinity of liberty specifically allows peaceful gatherings and associations with a purpose or without. One has the right to gather and communicate freely, no matter how it impedes some corporate institution's business plan.

In order to support and defend, sometimes it is best to stop. The point of peaceful protest is to eliminate apathy and instigate people to think. When people are delayed, frustrated and angry, they think and perhaps question the conditions and not only the kooks causing their delay. The defense of the daily routine, the assurance of the regular commute and the transaction and commerce is not guaranteed in the trinity of liberty. The right to peacefully assemble together is, and it's first and foremost in the trinity of liberty, in the First Amendment.

NON-LETHAL CROWD CONTROL DEVICES

M1029 40 millimeter non-shrapnel producing projectile. Used to enforce buffer zone and street clearing.

M5 modular crowd munition is designed to be fired in the center of adult threats, producing flash bang and strong, non-penetrating blows with multiple sub-munitions (600 rubber balls). Used to enforce buffer zone and demonstrate a show of force.

M1012 and m1013 cartridges for 12 gauge shotgun, designed to inflict less than lethal trauma. Used in security and crowd control.

Diverse assortment of acoustic and wave weaponry. Different designs and tones may be heard or felt, they cause spatial disorientation, pain, annoyance and possibly death.

Rubber bullets, bean bags, flash-bang grenades, smoke bombs, tear gas, pepper spray, water hoses, shields and good old fashioned batons for beatings, are all used as non-lethal weapons that all can be lethal when misused and used aggressively.

Liberty allows one to do anything except take liberty of and over another. Liberty allows people to stand up together. Liberty allows one to take up arms if one's safety and liberties are threatened and taken. But who decides who is being taken and who is taking? Only individuals were originally given rights, because otherwise institutions might manipulate the idea of liberty for their own interests, integrations and intents.

Liberty is generous equality provided to all and not restrictive fairness. Original attempts at liberty were legislated for some over others, but that is not liberty, only a trite attempt, and an untrue reflection of. Despite individuals steering toward the greater good, institutions attempt to adjust and morph, overtly or covertly, purposefully and accidentally to maintain the status quo.

Until an individual or institution proves that they cannot handle liberty by impeding on the liberties of others they are afforded rights and protection of the trinity of liberty. If they are criminal, they lose many of those rights, but someone has to stand up to the crime first.

Since the initial inception of legislated liberty for individuals among institutions, institutions have pressed to acquire the same rights. Institutions do so by adopting the personification of an archetype or a specific individual to represent them and gather empathy. Liberty is for individuals, not institutions.

SYMBOL – LIBERTY

Lady Liberty is the Roman Goddess of Freedom, Libertas. She is perhaps derived from even more ancient characters. Lady Liberty is a welcoming mother archetype, the guardian and embodiment of liberty. There is a statue of her or her sister Freedom atop the U.S.A. Capital Dome. There are many statues of liberty throughout the world including an 85 meter statue of her in Volgograd, Russia. Both the Swiss (Helvetia) and the Swedish (Mother Svea) have national figures akin to Libertas if not different personifications of her. The most well-known depiction of liberty is the Statue of Liberty at the mouth of the Hudson River, on Liberty Island.

In Tiananmen Square 1989, there were individual protests, riots, institutional beatings and shootings of individuals. During the protests, art students erected a statue of Liberty. She is the archetypal mother of patriots, country being the archetypal father. In Russia, Liberty is the mother of the land. WWII, their war with Germany, is referred to as the Great Patriotic War. Prior to WWII the invasion of Napoleon and French forces was named the Patriotic War, in the U.S.A. it is the War of 1812. Now in Russia, it is called the Patriotic War of 1812.

"When liberty comes with her hands drenched in blood it is hard to shake hands with her." ~Oscar Wilde

---

Institutions rally popular support, especially nations for war, by evoking patriotism. Patriotism is less often defined than it is used. Institutions stomp out gatherings of individuals and claim those that assemble to be anything from hippies to traitors.

In June 1905, thousands of striking workers and their families marched into the Imperial Square in St. Petersburg to deliver a petition to the Russian Royal Family, the ultimate authority of the nation. They were greeted by soldiers who began shooting and killing hundreds, possibly thousands. It became known as Bloody Sunday and bloody it was, but it was patriotic as well. People gathered to protest and petition a disagreeable situation brought about by the controlling institution. The steeply slanted authority reacted extremely and violently.

After some time of complex revolution, rebellion and war, in July 1918, the Royal Family was assassinated while under house arrest. Rasputin, their mysterious medicine man, was assassinated a year and a half prior. Rasputin apparently left a note predicting the family's demise. The Asian continental pyramidal system of serfdom ended and another form of oligarchy was instituted.

Rigid authority would have no protests or gatherings. People get bashed, jailed and shot, simply for gathering together. Throughout recorded time, institutions have marched over and murdered individuals who gathered to question or protest conditions. In St. Petersburg, in Tiananmen Square, at the Boston Massacre and elsewhere, people named and unnamed, known and unknown, have been beaten and blasted for questioning and gathering.

The trinity of liberty provides and guaranties people the right to gather peacefully and further to defend themselves if that right is threatened. Authority historically dislikes and disbands gatherings and still openly stomps them out, in part because of the presentation and communication of information. Authority is manifest in the U.S.A. to promote and protect liberty. And yet branches of authorities often do otherwise.

In the U.S.A. authority exists not to maintain the stability of institutions, but to maintain the respect institutions have towards people and their liberty. U.S.A. authority is designed to prevent one from taking liberty over another.

Liberty allows individuals to peacefully gather and proclaim and exclaim what they think around like-minded individuals, and enables people to inform those who do not share the same opinion, those that may not have the same information. People get told off and people get turned on to new information when people peaceably gather.

The trinity of liberty also provides that individuals don't have to tell anyone anything as private as their opinions. The convicted and incarcerated, those in the military or on parole may lose certain liberties. For instance, the convicted and enlisted lose freedom of movement. Everyone else has total liberty including the right to gather and the freedom of movement, the right to traverse unmolested. Everyone may come and go as they please or stop when they want for reasons imperative or arbitrary.

FACT: The DOD set up the Information Awareness Office after 9/11. The intention of the office was to "imagine, develop, apply, integrate and transition information technologies, components and prototypes, closed-loop, information systems that will counter asymmetric threats by achieving total information awareness." The IAO morphed into the Total Information Awareness Program and changed the logo that gathered so much publicity. In 2002, it was reported that TIA had been given $200 million towards developing computer dossiers on 300 million Americans.

"Any society that would give up a little liberty to gain a little security will deserve neither and lose both." ~Benjamin Franklin

---

FACT: Sprint and Microsoft joined to create business mobility framework. Their employees, via their personal devices, can be located in real time. There is also the Sprint family locator.
Disney Mobile's family locator tracks and maps an individual's personal device.
The FBI has begun remotely activating mobile phone's microphones to eavesdrop on nearby conversations. Also they are capable of turning on built in microphones in automobiles, like OnStar, to listen in on occupants' conversations.
The ability to activate microphones, cameras and personal computers exists as well.
The DOD has agencies that observe every American's every exchange.

Say "hello". Achieving total information awareness sounds very Zen, and like it would feel good. Until it is realized what information is from their institutionalized perspective. It is not Zen-like information of reality and the universe, but rather information arranged by interconnected, big brother institutions concerning the travels and traverses of individuals. Information is power.

Clandestine surveillance of people everywhere, all of the time is increasingly technologically possible, but is it needed? Does such tracking and surveillance infringe on what it is meant to protect? Just because something is possible, does not mean it should be done. The technology is available and some corporate institutions of private industry are likely inspiring it in order to simply prosper, while others may push it for other reasons. They convince legislators that certain individuals are treacherous and that all must be surveyed. They convince people that others are malevolent and all must be watched over.

The trinity of liberty guards against infringement of people's privacy through unreasonable search and seizure. Unless there is an ongoing crime being committed one should be impervious to both specific investigation and mass surveillance. This is your right and your liberty as an individual. The Bill of Rights is a building block to the foundation of the U.S.A. attempting to level millennia old pyramidal slant of institutions. When these principles are abated, the slant grows steeper, liberty slides.

Today it is technologically possible for the everyday shmuck to be a spy. Tools enable people to spy on others without their knowledge. While certain government institutions with the assistance of corporate institutions can also legally spy on people and research their every move with near limitless resources. Not only is random, all-encompassing surveillance legal just in case, but it is being actively instituted as a constant measure.

> FACT: The FBI has implemented the development of a global biometric recognition program. The $1 billion program will be able to track and recognize people through their physical characteristics, such as one's face, eyes, body type and the unique way one walks and talks. There have been many cases alleging repeated of the Patriot Act. The Patriot Act gives the FBI the ability to demand and obtain telephone, bank, credit card and library records without a warrant or probable cause. AT&T, MCI, and Sprint and numerous corporations provide information to the NSA.

Supposedly there exists a secret cooperative between the U.S.A, the UK, New Zealand and Canada, called the Echelon. It is supposed to be a secret global monitoring and surveillance network. Satellite antennas worldwide are utilized, covered by radomes (shells) to protect them from the elements and eyes.

Described as a big brother program, the UK Independent reported in 2008 that the UK government planned to keep track of every email, phone call and website visit by everyone in Britain to combat terrorism. The information is kept using the latest, most sophisticated technology. The option was disputed and presented as one of many, this plan representing the most draconian. In 2006, there were already over four million security cameras in Britain. Some of the monitoring cameras are paired with microphones allow security to make requests and give warnings.

Liberty is for all individuals, for all people. Liberty allows what is right, instead of what the mighty will allow, liberty is legislation of the Golden Rule. No sheep and no lamb can know liberty, because they are unable to speak up and stand up together. Only people can do that. No wolf can know liberty because they are unable to make accommodations and know sheep can know liberty because they are afraid to operate outside the herd, only can people can know liberty.

No institution can ever experience liberty either because they are not alive to experience anything in the first place. When institutions are given the liberties of individuals and rights of living beings they attempt to enact pack mentality, rigid conformity, servitude or worse. Freedom for institutions is eventual slavery for individuals.

> "From the most foul well of indifferentism flows that absurd and erroneous opinion, or rather delirium of liberty of conscience." ~Pope Gregory XVI

ChoicePoint is a corporation that provides intelligence informational support to institutions. They were involved in the 2000 Florida Presidential election. They maintain records on billions of individuals and institutions which they distribute variously. ChoicePoint provides an institutional service, providing information on individuals. They obtain and distribute information to the few who purchase the information on the majority toward refined manipulation. Individual progress is enabled with liberty and often disabled when liberty is shared with institutions.

AUTHORITY

The authority is the law of the land; the legitimacy and the means to enforce laws in whatever form they arrive. Authorities are the professional institutions that physically keep order and they are also the professorial institutions that present official information. Most authority consists of institutions that enforce that which is authorized and trusted in. There are many forms of authority in life, one's parents, teachers, counselors, employers, police, courts, politicians, military, but in the U.S.A. all authorities derive their power from, and are marginalized next to the trinity of liberty.

Throughout recorded time authorities and powers that be have almost always been the same type of institution, with only a few rare exceptions. Regardless of intense or minute differences in presentation, regardless of geographic location, label or identification, the structure of institutional authority remains the same. The design of the world's governments, foundations, churches, corporations and so on, are all pyramidal. Authorities are normally institutions or pro institution; yet the source of legitimacy for all authorities and institutions in the U.S.A., the trinity of liberty, is pro individual.

Whether republican or communist, totalitarian or otherwise, institutionalized authority is always pyramidal. The power of rule has always been in the hands of few, sometimes it is exchanged and sometimes it is kept within a cabal. People at times progress, including the powers that be, but individuals and institutions as well derail progression, including the powers that be. The powers that be are rarely pro individual, but rather powerful institutions that enhance their power by expanding or taking authority.

Authorities variously act as if they were above law and that their ends justify the means. However in the U.S.A. there is no institution or individual above the trinity of liberty. Police, priests, the President, nobody is above the authority of the trinity of liberty. Certain officials sometimes conduct and present themselves as if they were the ultimate authority or above authority, but they are not, not in the U.S.A., not with liberty. Individuals within institutional authorities are just as capable and perhaps more likely with power to authorize and commit harm in one way or another.

It has always been patriots who have questioned and when necessary, stopped the trespasses of authorities. When institutions act as if they are the ultimate authority and commit flagrant or subtle exploitations, it is patriots who question, distribute answers and stand up to them. There are patriots who are part of certain authorities and members of various institutions, but being part of an authority or institution does not automatically make one a patriot.

It is always individuals who initiate and instrument progress, who defy institutional and individual powers when they abuse conditions and situations. The trinity of liberty not only provides for anyone to stand up and speak out against harm, but also ensures the protection of those who stand up and stop wrongdoing. Authority tends to hold course, for to sway the boat jeopardizes their hold on said authority. All authorities are housed in various institutions, but in the U.S.A. they all must answer to the authority housed in the National Archives. If any authority bypasses the trinity of liberty they lose their legitimacy in the U.S.A. and become just another power to be held to scrutiny.

To have authority means one authorizes events and authors information. Authorities order action and also deliver information. Institutions authorize and confirm information. No fact or history is considered a known known until verified by certain authorities. In the U.S.A. ideas are made into law and sometimes later revoked when they are challenged and found to be counter to ideas in the trinity of liberty. Laws sway according to conditions, while liberty is constant.

> "Unthinking respect for authority is the greatest enemy of the truth." ~Albert Einstein

Unthinking respect for institutional authority is the enemy of truth because machines lie and distort information for their own purposes. The trinity of liberty was written to counter and eliminate oligarchical collectivism; institutional interconnection to empower the few over the many. The state is directly supportive of corporations, financial institutions, religious institutions, foundations of various sorts and other states, each supporting the structure of the other. Individuals participate with and support institutions, institutions do not always reciprocate. What is best for individuals is often exchanged for what works best for institutions.

Now, it is law that corporations and other institutions are entitled to the rights of individuals. Institutions have more power, are garnered more respect, and often face fewer consequences for greater infractions. Corporations are granted exceptions, by society at large, merely because they are larger generators in the economy than Joe Schmo. Because of economical or material dependence, institutions frequently achieve forgiveness and exception for their trespasses. Institutions are afforded privilege and are also near everlasting; after all, they are tools without heart and some institutions are thousands of years old.

> "And they came to Jerusalem: and Jesus went into the temple and began to cast them that sold and bought in the temple and overthrew the tables of the moneychangers, and the seats of them that sold doves. And would not suffer that any man should carry any vessel through the temple. And he taught, saying unto them, Is it not written, My house shall be called of all nations the house of prayer? But ye have made it a den of thieves. And the scribes and chief priests heard it, and sought how they might destroy him, because all the people were astonished at his doctrine." ~Mark 11:15–18

Jesus, often referred to as a carpenter, cursed a leafy, fruitless fig tree on the way to town and when Jesus arrived to the Jerusalem temple, he tore it up. Jesus was patriot. Like those at the big steep, like Gandhi, Jesus shook up what he saw as tools of exploitation. Jesus voiced his dissatisfaction of institutional connections by overturning the tables of the dove vendors and moneychangers. This act has been described as a violent one, except tables and money do not experience violence. Doves likely lost feathers; the money exchangers may have lost count or even lost money in the mix up, people were furious, but no one was hurt, feathers were ruffled, but no one was hurt, not a toe was stubbed.

Institutions intertwining and collaborating over individuals is nothing new. It's a pyramidal partnership of blocks which precisely interface to make the status quo, oligarchical collectivism. The situation is like a fire that has been burning for thousands of years, no one today started it, they only fuel it. Why would they sell doves at the temple? Why would moneychangers set up shop at the temple? It was Passover when Jesus went to town and the holiday was lucrative for people selling sacrificial and ceremonial needs, but especially lucrative to the Temple that taxed transactions and ultimately Roman authorities as well. Jesus, as the story goes, was a threat to the interconnected institutions.

Power and authority are wholly distinct. Throughout recorded time, power has been derived particularly by possession of information and resources. In the U.S.A, authority is derived from the trinity of liberty. Its power arrives from people's mental and physical ability and their trust in the founding documents, backed by a few marines of course.

From inside the pyramid, it is easy to confuse power for authority; both are on upper levels and at times coexist. It is easy to mistake power and authority as the same, but they are not. Power is conjured from many sources, but in the U.S.A. legitimate authority arrives via the trinity of liberty, which is meant to protect and elevate all those with beating hearts.

> "Liberty is not collective, it is personal. All liberty is individual liberty." ~Calvin Coolidge

Police and other authorities do not always serve the trinity of liberty; they do always protect the day-to-day functions of powerful institutions within the status quo. Police, the physical enforcers of local law and authority, not only enforce law, but they enforce the status quo. Every time people gather and are forcefully evacuated with swipes of batons and non-lethal attack, police are acting as an authority serving the status quo and not protecting individuals or the trinity of liberty.

The freedom to stop and peaceably assemble was so valued by the original patriots that it is part of the First Amendment in the Bill of Rights. People have the right to peaceably assemble and petition the government or any other institution or individual. This is part of the most basic and most valuable principle of the trinity of liberty, yet police stomp out such gatherings regularly. And authorities that go against the ideas in the trinity of liberty become simply powers for scrutiny.

> FACT: May 1, 2007 police in Los Angeles march on and clash with peaceful protesters and reporters. May Day is International Workers Day. When the Occupy Wall Street movement began to nationally catalyze their protest, there was national and local rally by institutional powers to belittle and squash the movement.

There is a difference between individuals and institutions. Individuals have beating hearts and feelings. Institutions are machines. There is a difference between power and authority. Power requires no authority, just might. Power is sometimes as real as a wielded stick and other times results from long-held fears that allegorically yield to twigs.

Institutions and individuals are treated differently. If an individual steals a hundred dollars from someone on the street, face-to-face, they go to jail. If institutions steal a hundred dollars from one hundred thousand people in a clandestine manner, that theft might be practically excused on reimbursement, perhaps a fine too and all is well. If institutionalized crime is not legitimized, it is certainly treated differently. Why aren't institutions effectively jailed when they are used to initiate and commit crimes? Why aren't individuals given the option of paying a fine instead of doing time?

Authorities are institutions with the legal ability to enforce the law and distribute official information. People with such responsibility become institutionalized and do not act as themselves, but as the institution and they're as fallible as anyone. Authority is derived ultimately from law; however, authority can be derived from money or other power. People gain so much wealth, information and operate in mechanical fashion so frequently that they effectively become institutions onto themselves.

Police officers are the most frequently observed officials of authority. Police agencies assist people, but also serve institutional interests, often before individuals. The police often preserve worker and consumer traffic and protect the flow of money. They serve and protect the regular daily commute, the status quo. Police primarily act in trained mechanized order, not necessarily in coordination with the trinity of liberty.

FACT: Critical Mass Rallies began in San Francisco, in 1992. People in Seattle, New York and hundreds of other cities participate. The rallies were designed to bring attention to the need for more people to commute on bicycles instead of in cars. They are suppressed and violently disrupted by police as recently as July 2008.

Instead of bringing attention to how beneficial biking can be in the inner city, Critical Mass Rallies brought attention to how brutal police can be. The police serve the status quo and the function of institutions within it. The Critical Mass Rallies disrupted of normal business hours, disturbed the status quo. The arms of authority act to maintain that which is authorized and authored by existing institutions and stopping traffic cannot be allowed.

Police officers are lifesavers in an emergency. When there is not an emergency, many individuals in various law enforcement institutions use intimidation, physical force and coordinated violence for a variety of reasons. Cops are great, generally speaking, but cops beat people and get people beat for no other reason than being in the wrong place at the wrong time, perhaps with the wrong quantity of melanin, generally speaking. At Critical Mass Rallies bikers felt powers of authorities and depending on one's location and appearance one might face the same bluntness.

The fire department is called when there is a fire, and firefighters are great heroes because they arrive and do the job only trained and coordinated individuals can do. Police officers are great heroes when they arrive to the call as well. The question is who called them to Critical Mass Rallies? Who called them on May Day, 2007 in Los Angeles? Who ordered them to prevent the May Day gathering and the Critical Mass Rallies? Who ordered the use of non-lethal violence against the OWS movement? Who organized their national dispersal?

The U.S.A. military has been likened to the police of the world, the world's democratic enforcer. One can only wonder about the specifics of military action and work abroad, but if it is akin to inner city police work, it is no wonder there are people who are angry at the foreign policy of the U.S.A. The U.S.A. military would not treat foreign protesters in a foreign country as police in the U.S.A., in inner cities, treat protesters here, exemplified by numerous occasions during the occupation of Iraq and Afghanistan juxtaposed with the treatment of OWS protesters.

Powers gain real authority through the perception of people who believe in that power as authority. Authority in the U.S.A. is gained through decree, the rule of law. It seems the police serve institutional interests at home, and they can confuse power and authority. It seems the military serves corporate and state institutional interests abroad to protect the status quo.

Police and military authorities act to enforce policy and not necessarily to uphold the law. They often act to serve and protect powers of the status quo. Statement of intent is a load next to the results. Benevolent intentions are nothing compared to malevolent actualizations. Certain institutions mean what they say, but because so many do not the entirety of all institutional presentations are questionable.

"Military men are dumb, stupid animals to be used as pawns for foreign policy." ~Henry Kissinger

Stated intent is a pile next to the results and normally just an advertisement of sorts. Petrol is the oil of the economy, without it much within the status quo would come to a grinding halt. It is easy to convince people to continue when otherwise, all known would be lost in great friction. Without oil, all would be lost according to their presentation. The institutions at large would have us believe and correctly so, that it would be the end. It would be the end of their institutional prevalence, the end of a presented dependence on oil and an end to formations of oligarchical collectivism. Petrolithic and nuclear fuels fashion pyramidal authority and oligarchical dependency.

Without petrol, the current design of trade, shipping, manufacturing and industry would come to a grinding halt. There would be an exodus of Vegas. Do we need to be as dependent on petrol as we are? Why are people importing food from thousands of miles away if it could be grown locally? Why aren't farms using electric tractors? Why aren't other vehicles using solar charged electric batteries? Why aren't the lights of Las Vegas powered with solar electricity? Maybe, it is because people would not be as dependent on institutions.

If there were suddenly no more oil, or considerably less, prices would skyrocket and availability would diminish on everything from milk to silk. Some products might not be available at all. There could be fields of grain ready to harvest and without oil, there would be no way to harvest it all, let alone get it anywhere. People are wholly dependent on oil for everything, including practically every meal.

Authorities regulate the distribution of information and resources. Authorities are institutions that enforce the status quo. Authority is the police and the military, but it is more than that. Someone has to call the police, and someone else has to order them to arrive and do whatever it is they do. Authority also exists behind the police, sometimes they too are just powers, though in control of people with sticks. In the U.S.A. it is people who give true authority their powers. In the U.S.A. the people decide. And yet there are other powers that be.

Elitist institutions masquerade as benevolent and refuse to admit that they might have negative consequences. Some do not care one way or another, what people think; they build and grow their institutions without regard. Many elitists, normally of unknown identity, use emotional information to conjure degradation of others for some institutional advancement and maintenance.

> "Behind the ostensible government sits enthroned an invisible government owing no allegiance and acknowledging no responsibility to the people."
> ~Theodore Roosevelt

> "The public be damned."
> ~William Henry Vanderbilt

> "If a man have a stubborn and rebellious son, which will not obey the voice of his father or the voice of his mother, and that, when they chastened him, will not hearken them: then his father and his mother lay hold on him, and bring him out unto the elders of his city, and unto the gate of his place; and they shall say unto the elders of his city, this our son is stubborn and rebellious, he will not obey our voice; he is a glutton and a drunkard. And all the men of his city shall stone him with stones, that he die: so shalt thou put evil away from among you; and all Israel shall hear, and fear." ~Deuteronomy 21:18–21

The ultimate authority in U.S.A. is the trinity of liberty, no individuals or institutions supersede the ideals and rights in the trinity of liberty. All other legislation is directly and ideologically subject to the trinity of liberty. All authorities in the U.S.A. exist under the trinity of liberty, and ultimately the people.

The ultimate authority in the U.S.A. is intended to safeguard us from exploitation by empowering individuals. The trinity of liberty is intended to place power in everyone's hands and not just some people's hands. But with liberty one must be resolute to keep it; responsibility and accountability are essential to just preserve and maintain liberty. The trinity of liberty empowers individuals, but the trinity of liberty cannot stand up for itself.

When institutional authorities mask operations behind closed doors conditions are questionable. When the enforcers of institutional authorities wear masks, conditions are questionable. When the presentation of authorized information masks information, conditions are questionable. Questioning the institutional arrangement is required to maintain accountability. Accountability justifies authority whereas masked meetings, masked enforcers and masquerading facts eliminate accountability.

ZEALOUS ZEALOTS

> "The foolish reject what they see and not what they think;

the wise reject what they think and not what they see." ~Huang Po, Zen Philosopher

The wise accept information on actuality, seen, heard or otherwise sensed and learned. They do not accept rumor, irrelevant perception, opinion or speculation, even their own. The wise concentrate on observations of reality while voiding rigid beliefs, imagined absolutes and assumptions in totality. Some people believe so passionately in a concept that they cannot accept conditions that are not in line with their beliefs. Zealots may hold belief so firmly, that even when shown actuality that disproves their beliefs, they refute it.

At times, some people support the authority of institutions so passionately and unquestioningly that they not only accept concepts without question, they lay down their very lives for them. Their support is so intense they see no reason to question. They have already come to a conclusion despite being presented with new information or being confronted by it. Unquestioning support is uniform solidarity, deaf zealotry. Solidarity can be heroic and can also be more accurately blind allegiance. To show solidarity with what is right under any condition is heroic, to act uniformly without question is zealous.

Zealots support ideas that run counter to their very existence because the institutions they believe in support these ideas. Zealots choose not to question certain information that runs counter to their beliefs, thus developing unquestioning support for institutions. All war is detrimental to all participants, yet individuals proceed.

Institutions enact and engage in all sorts of deviousness in the name of one thing or another, that really no one in their right mind would think was…right. Yet, since institutions present themselves as right and countering institutions as wrong, the potential wrong they perpetuate goes unquestioned. Institutions conduct benevolence and brag, and they also hide malevolence.

Zealots act with solidarity to drive a cause that they believe is bigger than those who they run over for it and bigger than themselves. Mighty goals influence tolerations to willingly trample people to fulfill institutional agendas. Zealots refute information that goes against their beliefs, they refute what is right and what is true to hold their perspective.

Soldiers return for multiple tours to stand with their fellow soldiers, the individuals they know, not the necessarily the institutions they know. Their solidarity is heroic, despite the fact that they are tolerant to wrong, despite the fact they believe good will come out wrong. They don't question, they institutionalized to just follow direction. And when they perhaps come to know that they were put in situations by institutions, for institutions, but nonetheless continue, it's often for their fellow soldiers. This display is heroic, but only within the status quo. Soldiers prefer to believe what they are doing is right, because otherwise it is unthinkable; the institutions they fight and die for, somehow spun evil into good.

Zealots go straight ahead as do heroes occasionally. Zealots do not hesitate to act on behalf of institutions that they identify with. Zealots proceed unquestioningly, ignoring conditions, even life threatening situations, to the point that it might seem fearless or heroic, but they are simply proceeding zealously. Heroes are definitively unafraid and might march in the same direction, but heroes distinguish themselves by going in their own direction, or ahead of everyone else, or stopping.

"He who joyfully marches to music in rank and file has already earned my contempt. He has been given a large brain by mistake, since for him the spinal cord would fully suffice. This disgrace to civilization should be done away with at once. Heroism at command, senseless brutality, deplorable love-of-country stance, how violently I hate all this, how despicable and ignorable war is. I would rather be torn to shreds than to be a part of so base an action. It is my conviction that killing under the cloak of war is nothing more than murder." ~Albert Einstein

"We know where they are. They're in the area around Tikrit and Baghdad, east, west, south and north somewhat." ~Donald Rumsfeld, on the subject of WMD

War, killing, terror, bombs, why? And to what end? What is the goal, if not financial profit and physical demise? Perhaps it is for a prophet. Perhaps war is simply to control, maintain and monopolize? What are the results? Who benefits from the conditions and consequences? Cui bono?

Hitler grew out of the rubble, dust and brutality of WWI. Osama Bin Laden gained prominence out of the chaos and destruction of war in Afghanistan. It is unfathomably difficult to conceive the hatred and warmongering rising out of the death and destruction in Iraq. The people there have been through decades of tortuous rule by Saddam Hussein, war with Iran, a decade of embargos, and a decade of war and occupation. What tolerations have people been burdened with in the area around Tikrit and Baghdad, east, west, south and north somewhat?

People cannot prevent exploitation with terror, just as people cannot prevent terror with war. The result of terror is war, and the result of war is terror. The commitment to override what is right, what one knows deep down is right, for institutional agenda is zealous. Right never results from wrong, only by stopping wrongdoing is right found. Wrongdoing with good intentions is still wrong.

Most zealots are soldiers, not necessarily enlisted, but soldiers on a mission they see as profound. They fight for a cause they believe in and may or may not benefit from. Normally their ideas, by design or accident, do not benefit them, but someone or something else.

Zealots seek new knowledge, but only information that correlates with their worldview. They refute information that does not sanction their beliefs and support their actions. Information that brings to light wrongdoing by them or any institutions they support is ignored. New information that is counter or alternative to zealots disturbs them and the status quo. No matter the information received by the zealous, if it does not fit their preconceptions, it is dismissed. Wrong is ever presented as right by institutions and is often right for institutional benefit, but wrong is never morally right.

> "As long as people believe absurdities they will continue to commit atrocities." ~Voltaire

Zealots do not question aspects of the status quo that are disagreeable to their world view, they simply continue, as if on a perpetual march. Zealots refute information that may be beneficial to them if it goes against their preconceptions. It does not matter whether their beliefs are well founded or absurd, if they refute new information based on prior assumptions, they are zealots. Zealots are sternly incapable of dealing with certain new information as new information could potentially change their course and beliefs.

> "What is morally wrong can never be advantageous, even when it enables you to make some gain that you believe to be to your advantage." ~Marcus Tullius Cicero

Zealots are confused with patriots and some who act zealously may be patriots, as the two qualities at times intertwine. Patriots may be zealous at times, but zealots can never be patriots. Patriots may behave zealously, but only in zealously questioning and disseminating information. Zealots act based on biases, while patriots seek unbiased truth. Zealots refute certain information with tremendous passion and act fervently with incomplete information. Zealots claim patriotism, but it's more rigid institutionalization.

Without questioning all information, they cannot be patriots. Zealots end up going the wrong direction without incomplete information. Without questioning their own procedure, their acts can be used to exploitative ends. Zealots will not take the first step toward patriotism, to openly question. Zealots are fanatical about certain subjects, and intensely hold their mindset and direction.

> "Force, violence, pressure or compulsion with a view to conformity are both uncivilized and undemocratic." ~Gandhi

Zealots are aggressive and act usually in line with what powerful authorities dictate. To be fanatical one has to be convinced of a certain set of beliefs that are logically challenged. No matter what counter is presented, zealots continue with their set of ideas, whatever they may be. Without asking questions, zealots continue down the road of fanaticism, whatever the cause, usually benefiting various institutions.

Zealots march continuously in line with the status quo. Patriots realize that conditions, consequences and conflicts must be pondered, which requires pause. Thinking, stopping and simply asking questions have inspired powerful acts in the world.

Some would ask, "Why?" Why step out of the institutionalized procession? A valid point, an equally valid point is, "Why not?" Why not stop the procession? Patriots stop and ask questions. Zealots only ask questions that lead to answers suitable to their zealotry. Zealots march forward and refute contrary information. Patriots react when they know something is not right or untrue. A question may be as simple as an inquiry of the time, and as complex as the location of WMD in Iraq.

Patriots respond when they get the wrong answers relative to actuality and zealots react when they get wrong answers relative to their perspective. Zealots react, possibly erratically, when they know something is not right with their perspective, when they have information that is impossible to refute. Zealots ignore or effectively stomp out counter information. Patriots continue searching for information and later decide what they believe and zealots decide what they believe first and hold that belief regardless.

The golden rule of liberty is foundational in the U.S.A. No institution or individual can prevent people from questioning. No authority can take away our unalienable rights to life, liberty and the pursuit of happiness. No institution can remove the right to question, but the right must be exercised to be kept, liberty must be expanded or it will be contracted. The original patriots wanted people to question all things great and small without consequence. Patriots want open progression, responsible and compassionate freedom, liberty. Institutions prefer individuals do not question anything of consequence because they want to control everything of consequence.

> "The fool wonders, the wise man asks." ~Benjamin Disraeli

> "One who asks a question is a fool for five minutes; one who does not ask a question remains a fool forever." Chinese proverb

Information is power for many reasons. Its main power though is engaged when one has information another does not. Information is powerful because people want to do what is right. If institutions can restrict and provide certain information, they can reduce the initiative to ask questions, and increase the likelihood of certain responses. They can convince people their actions are righteous through presentation of enough partial truth or false information. People know what is right and gravitate towards it the more they know. But, often they are convinced that what is right is in the wrong direction.

> FACT: The EPA in a June, 2008 email, instructed employees not to speak with congressional investigators or answer questions from reporters.

If people have adequate information, they are able to form an accurate picture and proceed in a better planned direction. If people know the environmental facts, they might formulate a different opinion about actions concerning the environment. If people know there is exploitation among their tea leaves, they stop drinking it. If people know that others are being exploited in order for them to drink what they enjoy, they might not enjoy it and toss it in defiance of the exploitation. Perhaps people would boycott many drinks and products if they knew more of their origins. People might throw their chocolate milk into the ocean, like the Boston Tea Party, if they knew more about the about cocoa and cattle.

How much can we trust institutional information? How much institutional, official information is manipulated and/or restricted? One EPA report states that agriculture runoff is the primary cause for polluted waterways.

> CHOCOLATE
> Nearly half of the chocolate that North Americans consume is from the Ivory coast. The majority of these cocoa farms use child/slave labor. Nestle and Hershey's buy the large percentage of what they produce. The corporations profess they are doing their best to promote family farms.

It is concerning they refer to the chocolate farms as family farms and others refer to them as slave plantations. Both these statements could be true at the same time. One's chocolate was possibly harvested, for all intents and purposes, by a family farm, with families of slaves working on it.

Enjoy your hot cocoa and buy fair trade/organic. Patriots are concerned for the wellbeing of all. Just as a driven and galloping horse will naturally do its best to avoid trampling a person, a person, as well, naturally wants to avoid treading on others. Unless blinded by tolerations and driven by institutions, horses and humans alike share the tendency to avoid treading on others. To ensure the wellbeing of others ensures one's own wellbeing.

In *1984* the young Winston Smith craves chocolate. In the post atomic war environment, perhaps chocolate is even more enjoyable as the taste might offer a moment away from the insanity and poverty he faced. Winston Smith, like a clichéd adolescent, steals the chocolate. Only he steals it from his sick sister and mother. On returning home he finds that his sister and mother are gone and rats are in their stead. This incident of course, traumatizes young Winston and he, like we all do, to one extent or another, through one incident or another, develops fear and guilt. Fear and guilt trap us, burden us and when boiled down, are the emotions institutions use to their benefit the most, because when afraid and guilty we need help.

> "This trafficking in human beings has intensified, persons put into slavery because they depend on certain criminals who take possession of these human beings…"
> ~Cardinal Renato Martino

> FACT: According to National Geographic, there are more slaves in the 21st century than were seized from Africa in four centuries of the trans-Atlantic slave trade.

> FACT: The amount of food shipped internationally tripled 1961 through 2007. The average ingredient on the early 21st century, North American dinner table was shipped nearly 1,500 miles.

Prejudice is ignorance perpetuated by tolerations and acceptance of incomplete information. Prejudice is learned, but it is not factual. Racial segregation is institutionalized racism. Slavery has always been propped by racists who find it easier to extort and exploit one who is perceived as, or is noticeably different than themselves. Prejudices are efficient tools for the status quo to maintain the pyramidal system. Prejudices promote ignorance, compartmentalization and refusal of information. In order to be a racist, one has to be zealous, choosing information that corresponds to preconceptions even when faced with countering reality. Not all zealots are racists, but all racists are zealots.

In the U.S.A. one can choose to remain ignorant. To be prejudiced requires disposal and refusal of information on actuality contrary to racist beliefs. Preliminary decision, based solely on the cover of the book, is as sensible as a preliminary strike, based on a perceived threat. Racism is decision and action out of ignorance; it is the most obvious and prevalent example of zealotry. When encountered with new information differing to their perspective, racists and zealots do whatever it takes to disprove and clear that information.

Ignorance is legal. People don't have to listen or learn and anyone can speak. Even evil is entitled to voice in the U.S.A. Liberty covers all or none. Liberty is not partial and has no exceptions. One can choose to be ignorant. One can choose to march inline to an unquestioned destination. One can choose to stay shut, not ask questions and ignore conditions.

The trinity of liberty provides that no individual or institution can suppress and exploit anyone or any group, as long as that group won't tolerate it. Rosa Parks and many nameless but equally brave people stepped out of line. Rosa decided not to participate in her own exploitation and degradation any longer. She stopped. The law was wrong, but zealots enforced and supported it because it was beneficial to some and by breaking the law she called attention to it.

> "During times of universal deceit, telling the truth becomes a revolutionary act." ~George Orwell

Rosa was a patriot; she questioned the wrongdoing of the bus company and the tolerations of everyone. She observed the situation on her commute and questioned it, perhaps pondering from her seat. Then she acted. She acted by sitting, but Rosa took a stand. Instead of reacting in anger or violence, Rosa stopped participating and catalyzed change. She had a lonely, peaceful sit in. Her action was inaction, nonparticipation.

Most people knew the policy was wrong, but tolerated it, excluding racists and those who benefited somehow from the racist status quo, they promoted it. Many rallied behind Rosa and by simply stopping, people forced the institutions to change. The bus company and eventually every authority all over Alabama capitulated to Rosa and others who sat and folded their arms in defiance.

Rosa was arrested that day and then again for organizing a boycott. She catalyzed immediate change and subsequent change. People loosely organized ways to help provide alternative transportation so the strike would be successful. Some cab drivers charged the same price of a bus ride, under threat of being fired. When the flow of money was threatened, the law of segregation was dismantled.

Without violence, threat or standing, Rosa made her stand. Rosa and others nearly drove the transportation corporation out of business, resulting in change in policy and law. One person questioned and stopped, creating a catalyst. Rosa was not without friends however.

Months before she protested, Rosa attended Highlander Folk School where she learned about Gandhi and the power of peaceful protest. The Highlander School was founded in 1932 and trained labor rights activists and organizers and then transformed into doing the same for civil rights. Martin Luther King Jr. attended the school. Most involved with the school were labeled communists. Today, the school is primarily concerned with economic and environmental issues and the overall negative effects of globalization oligarchical energy, in Appalachia.

> FACT: More than one third of the coal produced in U.S.A. is from Appalachia. The Appalachian Region is one of the poorest parts of the U.S.A. Large amounts of resources are mined and extracted from area mountains, but the most locals do not benefit. Recently mechanization has meant a loss in jobs despite continued mining. The mountains, blown apart and bereft of vegetation now allow runoff causing poisonous flooding. Drinking water in many parts of Appalachia is comprised and air quality is poor.

Zealots and patriots are often mixed up. One holds a transfixed love of a national or regional institution, while the other holds an open love of country. One questions with an amorphous opinion, while the other is transfixed in opinion despite information counter. Zealots believe they always have the correct answer, while patriots always try to find the answer. A patriot in West Virginia would boldly question coal extraction while a zealot would blindly support it.

Zealots, whether consciously or not, think that patriotism is supporting their government, or other institutions that claim to represent country, unquestioningly. Their interests are whatever the government or institution dictates, and they portray institutional interests proudly. They are essentially more like patriots of a patriarchy, than they are patriots of a nation of, for, and by the people.

Zealots are profoundly trusting of institutions they empathize with, while aloof and extreme towards individuals. Zealous and unquestioning behavior is basically jingoism and a cousin of blind allegiance. Zealotry has led to the exploitation and degradation of principles and peoples. The opinions of zealots are a biased jumble steering them away from questioning certain information.

> "In our country are evangelists and zealots of many different political, economic and religious persuasions whose fanatical conviction is that all thought is divinely classified into two kinds – that which is their own and that which is false and dangerous." ~Robert H. Jackson, Supreme Court Justice

Patriots question all information, all sources of information, and all institutions and individuals. Patriots in the U.S.A. question to ensure institutions and individuals operate within the bounds and intentions of the trinity of liberty. The right to ask difficult questions is enabled and promoted by the trinity of liberty, asking difficult questions is patriotic.

Undefined and unrestricted support is what authorities seek. The power of authorities is given to them through the support of people. Often they gather their power through mislabeled patriotism, zealotry. Unquestioning support for a perspective resulting in mental limitations or physical destruction is zealous. Zealots perform wrongdoing because they are convinced it is somehow right or will result in advantages. Zealots leave behind all that is good for a chance to glimpse what they believe in. Zealots actively and gladly engage in evil for a chance to enhance ideas they hold dear.

> "Our country! In her intercourse with foreign nations may she always be in the right; but our country, right or wrong." ~Stephen Decatur

This quote has been simplified and morphed into "our country, right or wrong" and "my country right or wrong." This simplification actually flips the original meaning. Through presenting a partial quote and not the entirety, the meaning may be distorted. This quote reflects the possibility that our country could be wrong, but it is our country nonetheless. It does not demand that people act on behalf of country whether right or wrong.

The morphed notion is zealous and serves institutionalized interests to do wrong. Zealots are more active than idiots and ask certain questions. They are more easily convinced to be more aggressive, and are quick to take action. Zealots are fanatically transfixed and only accept information to further their belief. Patriots have in the past took aggressive and zealous action, but only after all else was exhausted, only after thorough questioning.

> "If on any pretense or no pretense he shall refuse or omit it – then I shall be fully convinced of what I more than suspect

already – that he is deeply conscious of being in the wrong; that he feels the blood of this war, like the blood of Abel, is crying to heaven against him; that originally having some strong motive – what, I will stop now to give my opinion concerning – to involve the two countries in a war, and trusting to escape scrutiny by fixing the public gaze upon the exceeding brightness of military glory – that attractive rainbow, that arises in showers of blood – that serpents eye that charms to destroy, – he plunged into it, and has swept on and on till, disappointed in his calculation of the ease with which Mexico might be subdued, he now finds himself he knows not where." ~Abraham Lincoln, Mexican War Speech

Institutions claim authority and dictate to zealots, who unquestioningly act on behalf of authorities and institutions, at times to their own demise. When presented with information that is alternative to their views, zealots cast it aside to maintain their official and institutionalized stance. They disregard any information that is counter to their belief or not provided by an institution that has their prior support. Zealots continue the authorized institutionalized program so long as institutions dictate. They ask a limited group of selfish questions, accepting only some answers that correlate with their preconceived and established opinion.

Zealots make war easy and tremendous. They will forgo even their own selves, their own flesh and soul without first questioning. Zealots plunder, murder and lay down their lives in strange lands in unknown circumstances without questioning the situation, all for strangers' strange institutions. Zealots make war possible.

Zealots started global drug trafficking, initially in opium, and eventually in all sorts of narcotics. Zealots pushed their poison, smuggled and sold dope, simply as a matter of capitalism, simply to make loot. Zealots sold it, and most likely it was idiots that smoked it. Zealots aren't concerned about the effects of opium on someone outside their circle.

People are dehumanized in the interests of amassing wealth. Hundreds of years ago, the Chinese were vilified in Europe, lending tolerations to conduct brutality. Supplying the Chinese with opium was profitable; someone was going to smoke it, better in Shanghai than Salisbury.

Zealots ignore the fact that smuggling dope is wrong and has negative consequences. China might as well have been Mars, full of cannibal Martians. People were not considered people, or equals to whatever inner circle was doing the considering, be it English, German, Spanish, Christian, Hebrew or Muslim. This is the greatest, most deliberate way to set tolerations on people. If there is an "us" and a "them" it is easy to influence and control both the "us" and "them." Zealots find ways to justify selling hard drugs that hurt people in order to elevate themselves in the pyramid system.

Zealots locate justification in order to initiate and continue tolerations, but find it hard to locate or contemplate information counter to their perspective and tolerations. Zealots will find a way to convince themselves and others that wrong is right and right is wrong.

The Astor family smuggled an estimated 10 tons of opium in 1816 alone. The Forbes family, Cabots, Russels, Cushings, and many others were big-timers in the dope game. This drug money has grown in value over the generations. The ultra-rich get richer, and some of their holdings were founded and compounded on dope money.

Many private families made loot from opium, but the real profiteers from the opium trade were monarchs and royalty. The Elite of Britain and Amsterdam became ultra wealthy via dope money. Shippers and smugglers made so much money they were like a new royalty, but the established states made fortunes that dwarfed their newfound wealth. Corporations and nations gained wealth and power from drugs and druggies.

OPIUM IN BRITAIN
In 1821 De Quincey published "The Confessions of an English Opium Eater."
In 1878 the Opium Act was passed in an attempt to reduce consumption on the island, while at the same time continuing to be the world's biggest pusher.

FACT: Cocaine is legally used as a local anesthetic, medicinal cocaine. Originally it was touted as a cure all, much like opium. Medically, it is used infrequently as there are now alternatives, but it is still acquired and used. The world consumes about 600 metric tons of cocaine annually; the U.S.A. consumes about half of that. U.S.A. annual illicit cocaine profits: $35 billion.

FACT: There were two opium wars with China. The first from 1839–1842, was fought and won by the British to legalize importation of opium and to keep their status as the world's number one pusher. China just wanted the pushers, government controlled monopolies, out of the country. The second Opium War was waged from 1856–1860 in unison by several western countries to prevent China from threatening their dope money. The U.S.A. enabled and profited from the Second Opium War.

The Columbian cocaine cartels are impressive, but they have nothing on the British Empire when it comes to drug smuggling. To the cartels' credit, they have been forced to go largely underground. Arguably, they are winning the War on Drugs, as they are profiting as a whole, while their opposition only spends money. The outcome of the War on Drugs is taxpayer money spent and criminal money earned. Cocaine may have some covert state help, but overtly it is illegal and warred upon and yet, it is everywhere.

All across South Asia, opium was a state regulated and cultivated crop. The Company obtained tea plants from China and began to grow it on their Asian plantation, now India and Pakistan. All of South Asia was Company farmland. Along with Chinese tea, the Company also grew enough poppies to dope up all of China. The Company developed complete dope monopoly, not one ounce of opium left the South Asian plantation without The Company getting its cut.

Recently in similar tactics and incidents, perhaps learned through a history of The Company, a new company, The Agency, the CIA, began smuggling operations. Their front company, called Air America, supposedly smuggled heroin in and out of South Asia to obtain money for, and to manipulate proxy wars, particularly those in Afghanistan and Vietnam. While they were transporting supplies, dropping off food and transporting diplomats, they were also smuggling dope. Opium production increased massively with the arrival of the CIA in Burma after 1958 and Afghanistan in 1970 and again in Afghanistan, subsequent to 9/11.

> FACT: Many people who served in various institutions during the Vietnam War have stated that Richard Armitage was involved in the Phoenix Program, a covert operation in Vietnam. Richard denies any involvement. Richard served in Vietnam as an advisor to the DOD. He also served in Iran until November of 1976. He then moved to Bangkok and ran his own import/export business. He served Reagan as Foreign Policy advisor, worked for the Pentagon and the DOD. He was a signer of The Project for a New American Century. He received Knighthood of the British Crown in 2005. He served as Foreign Policy Advisor to George II. He ultimately resigned the post and later admitted that he was the source of Valerie Plame CIA leak. Shortly after he resigned, Richard was elected to the board of directors for Conoco-Phillips and lobbied for L-3 Communications Corporation, specializing in surveillance and intelligence.

> "Further, the process of transformation, even if it brings revolutionary change, is likely to be a long one absent some catastrophic and catalyzing event – like a new Pearl Harbor."
> ~The Project for a New American Century, part V: Creating Tomorrow's Dominant Force

Opium has had all sorts of institutional assistance over the years; cocaine as well. In the 1980s The Agency was instrumental in importing cocaine into the U.S.A.; the profits went to arm Nicaraguan rebels. The cocaine cartels had some government assistance, mainly that of covert operations. Gary Webb broke a story in The San Jose Mercury News that found The Agency supported Nicaraguan rebels with coke money from drugs imported into Los Angeles. After the story, Gary killed himself by shooting himself in the head, twice.

Zealots refute information concerning the malevolence of an institution they support, like The Agency smuggling drugs. Zealots don't question anything a reputable institution tells them, including Gary shooting himself in the head, twice, with a .38. They peel apart any information that does not suit their handed down ideas. They proceed in a straight institutionalized direction. Highly questionable subjects are ignored if they possibly interfere with zealous perceptions. Zealots find reasoning to ignore and belittle information, convincing themselves and others they are ignoring information logically. Zealots imply that coincidence dominates for one; they also believe that the past is separate from the present.

> "Where liberty is, there is my country." ~Benjamin Franklin

Patriots exclaim "Right, with institution or without" instead of, "My country right or wrong." This solidarity of/by/for the people and has led to heroic, catalyzing principles, ideals and actions. Following institutions, whether wrong or right, leads to mechanization and institutionalization if unquestioned.

Questions inspire people to step out of line and proceed with what is right, instead of proceeding where they are told. It has inspired people to stop and change. It has inspired peaceful acts of resistance and allowed for liberty's expansion. Questioning allows for imagination.

> "Imagination is more important than knowledge." ~Albert Einstein

Most know what is right and naturally want what is right, but sometimes the tendency is buried under so many tolerations that it is seemingly gone. If one constantly blindly continues, it is hard to understand wrong and question alternative directions other than the direction presented. Some are too distracted or scared of the facts to see what is right; others have so many tolerations they can only focus on what is straight ahead. People are inclined to what is right, but because of accumulated tolerations the inclination is swayed or altogether dispersed.

> I pledge allegiance to the flag of the United States of America and to the republic for which it stands, one Nation under God, indivisible, with liberty and justice for all.
> ~Pledge of allegiance – "The flag" was changed from "my flag" and "under God" was added in 1954.

> "It is dangerous to be right when the government is wrong." ~Voltaire

Patriots are concerned for their own wellbeing as well as for their peers. Patriots are not transfixed on any one belief or goal and not out to prosper by underhanded methods. They are so bold as to question the king and the king's companies, the supposed ultimate authorities. Patriots do not fear questioning in whispers or screams among the status quo. Patriots might ask uncomfortable questions of actuality, tolerations, inclinations and direction.

> "A patriot supports his country always and his government when they deserve it." ~Mark Twain

Patriots act unselfishly to preserve what is valued above all else – life, liberty and the pursuit of happiness. Patriots at times zealously cast aside simple, primal wants and requirements like food and that basic instinct of self-preservation to uphold liberty. Herein lays the confusion between patriots and zealots. Patriots proceed with as much passion as zealots at times, in their questions and acts to preserve liberty. Zealots act to preserve their perception and determined course without questions.

In certain circumstances, like the Revolutionary War, zealotry and patriotism end up going the same direction. Although at times they march the same in the same direction, patriots passionately question, while zealots passionately refute questions and answers which are counter to the continuance of their perspective. Patriots will let go, stop and question, while zealots hold their perspective and continue in ordained direction without question.

Zealots are intently focused and transfixed on ideas to the point that they lose track of everything else. Nothing else matters, everything fades into the background, including simply questioning where they are going. Zealots lose sight of everything basic in attempts to obtain complex ends and keep their perspective.

COUNTRY LOVE

The U.S.A., like other nations, is a formulation of people, structures, land, and principles. Nations are built on ideas and on Earth by people. The country is comprised of great natural wonders that provide. In the U.S.A. there are forests, plains, mountains, blue hills, mineral springs, fertile valleys, great rivers, pristine lakes, desert oases, grand canyons, wide open air and big skies. The U.S.A. is blessed with an assortment of rich environments. A nation, the country is literally the country, the Earth and all its elements. The nation of the U.S.A. is blessed with abundant resources and liberty.

> FACT: 18% of the world's fresh water is in the Great Lakes.

Reality and the elements are part of the country, people are another component. The U.S.A. is a hybrid mix of people from all over the world, a blend of countless ethnicities. Hybrid animals and plants tend to take on the best genes of both parents, called hybrid vigor, and the U.S.A. has the potential to be such an ascended descendent. People, in all varieties, are as vital a part to a country as the Earthly elements upon which it is built.

People have worked the land to reap its rewards, sometimes in cooperation and sometimes in conflict, with the Earth. The nation is the country, the tilled, vast fields that stretch to the Sun and also the constructed cities where super-skyscrapers loom and block out the Sun. Not only is the nation a combination of natural resources and people, but also what has been manifested on it. People have accomplished great technological achievements, enormous architectural feats and great works of engineering public and private infrastructure.

The greatest feat and the most important component of the U.S.A. as a country, is its base, the trinity of liberty. The manifestation of liberty, and within it the permission of its evolution, is the special ingredient in the melting pot of the U.S.A. The principles, the trinity of liberty, combined with Earthly elements and people make the country.

At the core of the U.S.A. is trust in the trinity of liberty. Without trust, they are just old documents. The principles permit progression and prevent exploitation within the U.S.A. The trinity of liberty is the basis of the U.S.A. It attempts to ensure that institutions cannot step over, step on or ride individuals.

The trinity of liberty is comfortable to trust. Drafted in the late 1700s, the concepts were hard to completely accept for many. Ultimately the papers were distorted by temporal tolerations perhaps instigated for institutional gains, specifically that of conquest and slavery. However, despite occasional hypocrisy and manipulation, the trinity of liberty became the primary example of liberty and freedom to the world. The trinity of liberty allows itself to change and progress, temporal tolerations could be temporary. Intended to free the Colonies from repression, the ideas inspired liberty around the world.

The Colonies were repressed and exploited; as was the norm across the globe. In Russia and throughout Asia, Europe, and practically everywhere there was an established institution, there was exploitation. The native indigenous people provided a glimpse of life where institutions had not monopolized their slant.

A nation is made up of many things, all of which can be categorized into three components. The country is the geographical area, all the resources and the structures. The second part of a country is the national family, the inhabitants. The principles and laws are the third component. In the U.S.A. the Earth, people and the trinity of liberty compose the country. All nations are made up by these components in an assortment of people, terrain and laws. All are people, and all is Earth, no matter how different in appearance or resource, but not all national designs allow for liberty, not all national designs are accepting and accommodating.

Political figures, religious representatives, corporate executives, commissioned officers and an assortment of institutionalized individuals claim a love for God, family and country. At the same time a lack of love and disdain for God, family and country is accused of all sorts of groups and individuals as well.

Family is one's relations, but as far as this sentiment is concerned, the national family is our neighbors and peers. The national family is comprised of people recognized and unrecognized, sharing a mutual place. Family is every other person breathing the same air, at the same time, as you.

> FACT: China is the world's biggest air polluter as of 2007. The air on the west coast of the United States and Canada, and as far east as Utah and Colorado, occasionally experience dust storms from China.

The country is the actual land and water around and abound, the physicality, that patch of dirt that people prize and plight. Country is our environment that nurtures, natural and unnatural. Country includes the construction on the land. The country is the air, water and soil, the reality here long before people or principle, and the reality that will still be, perhaps when principle and people are not.

God, in this expression, is God's liberty, the trinity of liberty. Love is intolerance to wrongdoing. Love is the ability to navigate through multileveled complexities and retain intolerance to evil. Having love for God, family and country means that one has intolerance to wrongdoing committed against peer or stranger, against land or river. The trinity of liberty legislated the loving Golden Rule.

The three components of the U.S.A. are not your God, but the mutual concepts of the Golden Rule. It is not your country, this land is our land. It is not your bloodline, but the family of humanity, peers alive at the same time. The nation is an institution and as an institution it is pyramidal. But the U.S.A. has liberty built into its principles, allowing for change and progression, change that might surpass ideas or perspective some hold dear.

The world is different now than it was just last year, last month likely, and immensely different than a century ago. Every year people grow more and more dependent on resources from more and more distant suppliers. Arguably there has been international trade and relations for a long time, but not to the extent there is today. The material world is interdependent like never before.

We all breathe the same air. The reason China is the world's biggest polluter is because its laws allow corporate institutions to function without concern for people or environment. People all over the world consume what corporate industries supply, as goods and as pollutants. China and many national institutions put concerns for liberty, land and locals aside in exchange for wealth, power and prosperity so new political sensitivities are reqired.

New information is constant, and in the petrolithic era and nuclear age environmental paradigms are frequent. The world, the water we drink, and the very ground underneath our feet is changed. The air, water and soil contain additives and remnants from industrial and war waste. Through the procurement and use of resources without concern, country, and the Earth family is adversely affected.

Every year environmental problems increase. Natural occurrences secure for thousands of years disappear, or are dramatically limited. Continuous pollution and overuse without conclusion destroys land, air and sea. It is a battle of resources being fought amongst the interests of nations against the natural course of the planet.

Institutional interaction maintains the status quo. And like a rusting machine, ravaging resources for power, the status quo continues despite its growing uselessness or detriment. The dastardly contraption does nothing except consume, serving no purpose except to be on. The machine has no love for country or people or idea. And individuals keep it running.

It is difficult to show love for family when the people that produce one's gear and raise one's food reside in distant lands. How can people look out for people when they are over the hills and across the sea in some secured and shut facility? How can we make sure that family is being treated fairly by institutions? Whispers of exploitation have changed circumstances, and yet exploitation continues. There are slaves who know they are in slavery and there are slaves in unknown slavery.

FACT: Workers in China routinely work 12–15 hour days, 6 days a week for less than a dollar an hour. There is no minimum wage in China.

Patriots act out of love for locals, land and liberty, often bearing no group affiliation or interest other than the progression of fairness and liberty. Patriots proceed, at times zealously, to abandon and cancel wrongdoing and wrongdoers. Patriots, at times zealously, reject institutionalization of the "us and them" mentality whether concerning those in their own country or abroad.

Exploitation equates to hatred, but does not require it. Exploitation requires only a lack of questions and action. Those who have information and resources arrange exploitation. It is allowed by those who perpetuate it to gain slight advantage over others. The exploited are those without information, resources and opportunity. The institutionalized control in China restricts information and resources. Because of the heavy and harsh oligarchical collectivism, people in China lack the capacity and courage to question and act on conditions.

"Hatred can never cease by hatred. Hatred can only cease by love. This is an eternal law." ~Buddha

Relations between nations have expanded to the point where we are all interdependent on one another, but are also increasingly interdependent on industrious corporations. At times this dependency is mutually beneficial, other times it is exploitative, a slanted exchange. The same goes for the interaction between individuals and institutions, sometimes the interaction is mutually beneficial and sometimes not.

Patriots act on behalf of people because we are all peers, whether in distant Mongolia or neighboring suburbia. We are family. We breathe the same air, use the same gear and we collectively allow exploitation of the majority for the benefit of the few simply by not questioning.

If it is in the power of the U.S.A. to raise might, then it is also possible to raise right. If the U.S.A. military enforces action abroad, then the U.S.A. people can enforce compassion abroad. As the world is made more and more interdependent, people must protect other people, otherwise institutions will march over everyone.

People are people, we are our family, like it or not, notice it or not. Nations claim to go to war for peace, like it or not. Why not peace for peace? Democracy and capitalism are not one and the same. Why not participate in actions besides war in order to further promote liberty abroad?

> "Securing democracy in Iraq is the work of many hands. American and coalition forces are sacrificing for the peace of Iraq and the security of free nations." ~George II

> "Sixty years of western nations excusing and accommodating the lack of freedom in the Middle East did nothing to make us safe – because in the long run, stability cannot be purchased at the price of liberty." ~George II

Why not do what is right, instead of what the status quo presents as right? If people do not act on behalf of people, but rather act on behalf of select people, or select institutions, the majority of civilization experiences decline. If we don't protect the Earth and equality everywhere, the environment degrades and liberty loses prominence.

> "Successful societies limit the power of the state and the power of the military – so that governments respond to the will of the people and not the will of an elite." ~George II

All three of the last quotes were from the same speech. Securing democracy in Iraq is in many hands, but certainly not in the hands of liberty. Oligarchies in the region removed her foothold sometime ago.

The complications of survival allow institutions to exist as tools to better the odds. Institutions exist with the stated intention of bettering the situation. When they cease benefiting people and begin hindering they no longer serve a purpose.

The law of the land is republican, that is to say, it is not based primarily on mob rule or majority vote, but it is based primarily on the law of the land, the trinity of liberty. The trinity of liberty was written in a reactionary time. Individuals were reacting to oppression and exploitation of the royal oligarchy.

When something is immense, the further away one goes go from it, the easier it is to see. The Colonists saw the pyramid system for what it was, from across the sea and revolted against it. They had the resources to declare independence from royal oligarchical exploitation and did so. Their ideas held lofty principles ahead of their time, but still were reactions to their time. The ideas of the trinity of liberty were reactions to exploitations and meant to prevent future infractions as well.

The ideas were valuable to the Colonies and as it turns out, provided a valuable template of liberty for the entire world. There was freedom for some and yet, entire sections of existence were based on state sanctioned slave economics, a cruel dichotomy. Liberty was not complete. Today there is no state sanctioned slavery, but there are numerous plantations and facilities made up of exploited individuals all over.

Today, state sanctioned slavery policy has been eliminated, yet the number of actual slaves has increased. Some things change, while others remain the same. Today such abuses are completely clandestine or covertly operated and renamed.

The ideals of the trinity of liberty allow it to be veered right and left, and yet ideas tend ever upward and outward, as liberty is expansive. Despite oppressive, empirical institutional wrongs, despite erratic turns right and left, and infiltration by pyramidal institutions, the ideas in the trinity of liberty elevate people. Centuries of oligarchical exploitation and newfound separation from royalty led people to question authority. The trinity of liberty enables people to question authority and move freely within the pyramid, or walk out of it altogether.

Information about generations of exploitation and centuries of servitude led the educated original patriots to a reaction. Out of the royalty's realm, and inspired by the welcoming, independent indigenous people, they questioned and challenged the royal authority. Perhaps God inspired them. The trinity of liberty was a reaction to the cold, empirical exploitations of the British Crown and all royal oligarchies. It was a flattening of the steep slant of the royal pyramid system.

> FACT: King George III, descended from a long line of Dukes, Kings, and holy Roman Emperors dating back to the ninth century. He was the first king in his family to speak English as a first language, his family, the House of Hanover, (Windsor) was German. He waged war in India, against France, and on the Colonies. In 1793 he declared war on revolutionary France and on Spain in 1779. He was known to have grown quite mad in his later years. King George's cousin was the King of Denmark, who was also known as being mad and married his cousin, George's sister.

Because everything was slanted in favor of a tiny royal family and their cohorts, many situations were flattened and others remained slanted. The trinity of liberty, the design and framework of the U.S.A., was set up to prevent any institution, church, state or corporate, from having supreme control. The original patriots reacted against King George III, the capstone of their exploitation, supported by The Company, the government and his church. In the U.S.A. there were to be no royal families, no institutionalized bloodlines.

ALL IN THE FAMILY
John Adams was 2nd president of U.S.A., his son was the 6th.
President Theodore Roosevelt was the uncle of Eleanor Roosevelt who married their distant cousin president Franklin Roosevelt, both presidents.
William Harrison was the 9th president, his great-grandson Benjamin Harrison was the 23rd.
George I and his son George II both occupied the white house for a total of twenty years.
Barbara (Pierce) Bush is related to Franklin Pierce, 14th president.
NYC Mayor Rudolph Giuliani, presidential candidate, married his cousin.

The Colonies discontinued and abandoned the monarchical system, but some wanted to be king themselves, as had been the status quo for centuries. Slave plantations and a steep slant remained after the Revolutionary War. George Washington was approached with the idea that he be crowned king. George opposed such an idea. Instead, the wealthiest man in the U.S.A., became the first president. It was difficult to imagine any other way than obeying a king and ordering slaves.

FACT: George Washington was a farmer. King George III promoted and was interested in farming.

George Washington ironically was unable to bear children, and yet, he became the father of the U.S.A. People are related simply because we're alive at the same time and share the same air. In addition, one has two sets of grandparents, four sets of great-grandparents, eight sets of great-great grandparents, and on and on. The divergent Barack Obama and Dick Cheney are distant cousins.

Some people carry exclusivity in their being that is only concerned with their immediate family, their blood, so to speak. This is a sensible trait if one is living in the wilds as a family unit of hunter gatherers, but today we are all interdependent. Caring about one's family is important, but it is important to care for others as well. In the petrolithic era, if people cannot separate themselves from the system, they cannot be independent of others who also exist in it.

People have immigrated by the millions to skyscraping cities, great urban developments and financial hubs. The cities are also the country. In cities today people are interdependent on millions around them and millions of others involved with the city in some way. Still, of all the buildings and bridges, museums and infrastructure, all the great art and literature, is all belittled next to the greatest creation of U.S.A. The supreme legacy of the U.S.A. is that of its outset, the trinity of liberty. At one time one was not allowed to operate a business in more than one state. This was to prevent institutional monopolization. Logical localization and local responsibility has been put aside to line pockets, expand and globalize. Corporations have capitalized on freedoms without regard for people's wellbeing.

We have come to think of free trade as coinciding with progression of individuals and liberty. People often believe that institutions should have the rights of individuals and moreover that institutions are more reputable than individuals. This is an institutionalization. Individuals want to localize, institutionalized individuals want to globalize.

It does not matter to corporations in what manner individuals interpret God as long as that God deems they work five or six days a week. Corporate institutions care not what political system their employees are under, as long as it drives economic growth, as long as it is beneficial to their bottom line. Corporations do not mind if their employees remain destitute in a fascist regime or hopeless conditions, as long as it coincides with, and is beneficial to their own goals.

FACT: In December of 2007 Hershey chocolate announced plans to cut its work force and close locations in the U.S.A. Business is fine, they plan on building a new factory and moving production to Mexico. The three year restructuring program will potentially save Hershey's $190 million a year.

The ongoing and growing influx of corporations to countries where the slant is steep is enormous and ridiculous. Corporate institutions pay extremely low wages to their workers and at the same time charge extremely high prices to their consumers. Corporate institutions enable governments; they do not improve on them. The bigger the institution, the more likely it benefits other institutions and less likely it benefits people. Corporations seek out nations that are not necessarily fair to begin with, nations that have a desperate workforce. They seek nations that will do anything to build up structure and revenue. They seek individuals so hungry they would exploit liberty, locals and land.

> FACT: It is estimated that there are approximately 12 million people living life in forced labor, over 9 million of whom are in Asia. The yearly profits yielded are estimated to be over $30 billion.

There are slaves, there is exploited labor and there is also cheap labor. Workers are commonplace; fairly treated workers are a rarity. Workers generally get worked. Corporate institutions internationally monopolize, yet they are not expanding merely to profit, they seek to control. Corporate institutions benefit a select, exclusive few. They roam the world looking for the most profitable place to anchor, sweeping into nations that have the cheapest labor, richest resources and principles most accommodating to exploitation. They invest into industry and other institutions, but rarely individuals and people. The people enjoy the relief of income, the distraction of work, and the enrichment of accomplishment. Their current predicament may be bettered, but their placement and pressure in the pyramid system is not. Without prior opportunity, working for the capitalistic venture of the conglomerate they are a cog of, may seem pleasant. It is at least something. They may grow to feel a sense of pride about the betterment of their situation and their productivity. This can grow into a form of zealous allegiance to institutions they are within.

Capitalism arrives with freedom, but liberty is not necessarily part of the cargo. Liberty or democracy and fairness are not as profitable as other slanted systems with less individual opportunity. When the bottom line is measured, fairness and liberty are not helpful, but hindrance. Corporate institutions do not bring democracy and fairness to rest in the factories. In fact they normally operate in whatever conditions local people will tolerate. If they don't have to answer to anyone, if they don't have to please their workers, they won't.

Corporations claim to represent American values. Some institutions originated here and/or bloomed here, while others promote themselves as American as apple pie, but may be foreign as box-store supply chains. They claim to represent the U.S.A., but do nothing to promote and hail American values. Their American values are in their promotion and propaganda, not function. The American values they hail are sales, not ideas.

> FACT: Workers for Dole, Chiquita and Del Monte plantations throughout the Americas have faced horrible living and working conditions in the past. Some were underpaid children. Through 1997 and 2004, Chiquita paid terrorists protection money in Columbia, they were fined $25 million. The corporations have been accused of many incidents of environmental destruction in various countries as well.

If democracy and fairness are not established, visiting corporations are not going to bring or inform others about such ideas for that matter. The more business-friendly a nation is, the more likely they will be visited by unfriendly businesses. The more desperate a nation is, the more likely the corporations will maintain and exploit the people's desperation.

Soaring multinational corporations present themselves as benevolent in order to gain entrance to a country and prosper. Fair ideas that protect local's liberty and land may be why many institutions left the U.S.A in the first place. Minimum wage, eight-hour workdays, worker rights, environmental protection, are far off figments or quiet hope for many people of the world. Why would a corporation set up their industry great distances away from the majority of their consumers? Bananas can only grow in certain climates, but other products do not require specific natural environments, only specific exploitative conditions.

Perhaps corporations have realized the work force of the U.S.A. is unsuitable in another way; overqualified or under-qualified somehow. The other possible reason to embark on such a venture would be to build a factory closer to your target market. Perhaps the Mexican chocolate market is blowing up. If not easy access to exploitation, then why relocate? Exploitation is globalization, globalization is monopolization.

People do nothing while corporations, intent on increasing yearly profits, run over and grind up God, family and country, liberty, locals and land. People do nothing, except work for them. Institutions routinely destroy God, family and country through the hands of individuals. The components of country are so routinely stomped and treaded on it seems like random accidents rather than continuous consequences. People accept that environmental destruction and exploitation is because of one institution or another, and not the workings amongst many institutions.

People are often more vilified than institutions. Individuals become externalized enemies, often through their nationhood. People with the least money, power and respect, often carry the greatest blame within a nation. They are cast as irresponsible rather than exploited. People that have less and been repressed are labeled as apathetic.

Many people are blamed for destruction of God, family and country in the U.S.A., this scapegoating is not simply a U.S.A. phenomenon, outsiders are blamed for various problems out of their control all around the world. Homosexuals are blamed because of their lifestyle. Immigrants are blamed because of their desperation and perhaps because they lack mastery of the local language. There are many circumstances where individuals are left holding the blame when institutions are responsible. In the past, environmental change from human hands was a prolonged event, and institutions took credit for what was built. In the petrolithic era, industrious institutions shrug off blame for rapid environmental change, there is no building just destruction. In the recent past, information was so limited and/or restricted that the root of the problem may very well have been another group of people, the outsiders even. Something just wasn't right, but it was impossible to know what it was. In the petrolithic era people know the air is less clear, the water is more metallic, and the food is less nutritious. It is not the homosexuals or transplanted foreign neighbors who continue to tear down liberty, locals and land. It is institutions, foreign and domestic. The imagined or actual ills of individuals are normally nothing compared to the destruction wrought by institutions on people and the environment.

> FACT: Rev. Ted Haggard smoked methamphetamine and paid a male prostitute for his time. He resigned as senior pastor of the New Life Church and as leader of the National Association of Evangelicals.

What really destroys God, family and country? Rev. Ted was a drug-abusing liar who met with the George II Administration on occasion. Surely Rev. Ted was doing all the talking. What was he saying? Extreme opposite polarity between private behavior and public presentation is typical for institutionalized individuals. A reverend on meth meeting with the President and homosexual prostitutes is extreme, but the polarized behavior is not.

With historical insight and knowledge of current events, the corrupted culprits can be determined. Even with abundant information it can still be difficult to filter through the fog. But only with information is it possible to know who really destroys what is truly valuable. By deciphering their reaction to information, it is possible to determine who is corrupt, who would put profit above people or environment.

In the petrolithic era change is quickened. In the past during the average lifetime it was difficult to note the dismantling of country. Wars and environmental change have destroyed and changed country quickly, yet these were intermittent changes. Now the environment is constantly altered, at times steadily and at times suddenly, but never to be the same again. Pollution and continuous overdevelopment visibly distorts and destroys.

In the past, man's influence on the environment could be vanquished in a momentary storm. In the past, people for the most part, did not change their environment, they adjusted to it. Historically it was hard to completely note physical change in the land and only occasionally psychological change in people.

The petrolithic era changed that. Not only are dramatic changes in mindset noticeable, but dramatic changes in landscape as well. The change is an overall decline in the quality of air, water and dirt, reality. Profits cost our environment that holds all of our great treasures and provides all our great potential. Reality is being taxed. The potential to be a self-sustainable nation with clean air and water is no longer a priority and less of possibility as well. Fresh air, clean water and correspondingly, liberty are all threatened.

Clarity in the environment shrinks as fumes and particulate fill the air from industry and automobiles. Those with sensitive senses can taste toxins in every breath in cities. One can see the air and taste the water in the petrolithic era and nuclear age. Many coastal waters are dead zones as a result of pollution and overdevelopment. Manufacturing byproducts are cast into what was once thought to be limitless waters and wind.

> FACT: Dzerzhinsk, Russia is one of the most polluted inhabited places on Earth. The area has been destroyed by decades of weapon and chemical production. The average lifespan in the area is about 42 and 47 for men and women respectively. Guiyu, China is a becoming a toxic waste dump, in part because of "recycling operations" which lay waste to the elements. The toxins result from extracting minerals from old machines. It has increased cancer rate, birth defects and no fresh water. A 60 Minutes news team was harassed away while filming conditions in Guiyu.

Fukushima and increasing swathes of Japan and the Pacific are likely the most polluted place on the planet. Many Japanese had no choice but to go home without help from TEPCO, Japan or any other institutions involved in creating the nuclear power plants, like GE and Toshiba. Global warming and climate change may be an imminent and ultimate disaster for billions of people, but global pollution is immediate, current and undeniable.

The world is polluted. The concentration sways, but whether in Brooklyn or Dzerzhinsk, the poison is all encompassing, noticed or not. Global warming is scary, but global pollution and the poisoning of life is equally frightening and inarguable.

Human activity may be warming the Polar Regions, but it is definitely polluting them and everywhere else.

Global warming is less arguable, the more is known, the more information is possessed. There is a method of statistical measurement called chi-square analysis. It is not a mathematical certainty, but it does supply some potential indications. The principal behind chi-square analysis seeks correlations which can project a spike in occurrence. If one has a set of a one-hundred and fifty different measurements and finds that most of the high measurements occur within a group of twenty among the one-hundred and fifty, that's a spike.

If there is a spike and an event coinciding with the spike, there may be reasonable evidence to say the occurrence has something to do with the spike. It is not math, but uses math. According to chi-square analysis, industrial pollution, the accumulation of carbon monoxide may correspond with the heating of the planet.

Global warming is now considered fact, a known among many. Yet, zealous individuals and institutions continue on as if there is not enough proof that global warming is caused by, and dangerous to, our existence. Zealots do not question because the answers might be a threat to the economy and their worldview. Idiots do not question the circumstances for it is too drastic of a subject. Elitists take advantage of the situation, and deeper into the hole we go.

Global warming may sound sort of pleasant until one realizes that global warming has meant a global rise in carbon monoxide in many time periods during Earth's history. In these time periods, were corresponding planetary die-offs. Global warming coincides with global increase of carbon monoxide and death to species.

Global warming could mean extinctions, but it is perhaps too airy and yet, at the same time, too powerful a subject. Global pollution is clinically and observably evident, no deliberation necessary. Global warming might just be another result of global pollution which reduce the quality of life until perhaps, conditions like global warming end it completely. The consequences of the petrolithic era kill people, plants and animals on which people depend. Likewise the plants and animals depend on people to protect and at least not end them.

Reputable scientists argue that Hurricane Katrina was influenced by global warming, that rising temperatures will mean more raging storms. Does it matter? The Gulf of Mexico is riddled and ruined with chemical pollution. The Gulf was and is experiencing pollution on a broad and cancerous scale. That is enough reason to stop or change. The occasional hurricane, no matter how devastating, is nothing next to the constant toxins that abound. Katrina and storms like it are horrendous, but the Gulf, Louisiana and Texas, are sickened and destroyed regardless of any storm. Everyone knows that the overload of pollutants is cancerous and poisonous.

> FACT: Texas is the number one state in the nation in toxic mercury pollution from coal power plants.

Why is the idea of global warming debated? Global pollution is evident and could be the cause of global warming among other known and unknown consequences. Global pollution is actual and undeniable. Global warming could be just one result of global pollution.

> SYMBOL – FLOOD The flood is symbolic for clearing grime and trespasses and creating a clean, fresh start. In the past when there was a flood and in stories of floods, the waters would wash everything away, creating a new beginning. Today when it floods the water is not only dangerous as an elemental force, but poisoned and toxic as well, leaving muck and murk behind.

Why must there be a dispute about the planet heating up to the point where it will no longer support life friendly to people? Why must there be a debate about global warming or climate change? There are plenty of other equally threatening reasons to stop pollution aside from global warming. Does our end have to be proven before we do anything about it? Just the suggestion of any extinction should be reason enough to question the status quo. Just the suggestion that we don't have clean water should be enough for people to question and cease. How are people going to make proper tea or coffee without fresh water?

Pollution is rampant, there are a thousand problems from pollution proven to be from man's hands and little or nothing is done. Scarier still, there are likely many more detrimental unknowns resulting from known conditions. People should be concerned about global warming, but this is not the only global environmental consequence to global pollution and unsustainability. Carbon monoxide may be heating up the planet, but burning petrol and the misuse of its accompaniments definitely destroys the oxygen we breathe, the water we drink and the soil we sow. Is that not enough? People want to look through air, not at it, people want to drink tea made from fresh water, not have their water already be an infusion of grime and people want their food to contain vitamins, not petrochemicals.

FACT: As many as 250 million people are sickened by water related illnesses a year, resulting in up to 10 million deaths.

The Sun may be more of a direct cause for the warming of the planet rather than the exhaust of humanity's tools and industry. Nevertheless, do we have to globally pollute to the point where it is killing us? Do we have to destroy everything priceless, until it is no longer rare, but nonexistent? Global warming is a possible result of the petrolithic era, while global environmental destruction definitely is.

FACT: Due to pollution, overfishing and rapid climate change, scientists speculate that the oceans may be empty of fish entirely by 2050. Some experts estimate that the richest rainforests of the world may be all but gone by 2050 as well. Another scientific prediction suggests perhaps more than 25% of land animals will be extinct by 2050.

"I never think of the future. It comes soon enough." ~Albert Einstein

There is already so much methylmercury in the average Tuna that it's a wonder it lived in the first place, let alone if it should be eaten. Post Fukushima, there is likely radioactive elements in Pacific sourced fish too. Mercury is naturally occurring, but it is also an industrious poison. A large source of methylmercury pollution in the environment results from burning petroleum and coal, industrial manufacturing and the use of pesticides. The oceans' fish are poisoned and the coral are disappearing. Vanishing plankton threatens life right now and ultimately the planet's oxygen supply. The oceans, as we know them, are dying. Jellyfish are taking over.

The ozone layer is disintegrating. Glaciers, a primary source of water for humanity, are receding and disappearing. Deep underground aquifers are poisoned. Extinctions are occurring everywhere. Every species, excluding the likes of ticks, mosquitoes, cockroaches and Pfiesteria are suffering the consequences of the petrolithic era. And institutions continue to pollute like there is no tomorrow. Perhaps, because of pollution there very well may be no tomorrow.

The destruction and demolition is so great, so obvious and so out of control that the windy phantoms, the institutions that have ravaged country, lose their transparency. Their intent on profit and control is becoming a loud and lousy parade through our country, through our world, leaving a decrepit, deafening vacancy in its wake. There is nowhere to go untouched by pollution. The environmental destruction is desertification, making what was once lush, barren.

The ongoing, exponentially increasing, global environmental calamity is a consequence of institutional greed. Consequences of plundered Earth reside in everyone; the toxins may be in people for generations. People and all living things exist in the petrolithic era and experience its consequences. With the only direction being increased profits, our land, sea and air are paying a high cost for liquid cash. People, plants and animals, all living things, experience the adverse environmental situations. Life is more difficult because of the influence institutions and individuals have on the environment.

Institutions experience no such ill effects, because they do not experience being alive, institutions do not experience. In order to have cheap goods and employment the well-being of people may be bypassed by institutions. In order to meet the goals of airy and temporary institutionalized agendas, people cause detriment to themselves, their neighbors, strangers and the elements.

Institutions are mostly to blame for the ongoing, progressing environmental calamity. Individuals are at fault, as institutions are manifest through individuals, but the power of institutions is infinitely more behemoth than individuals. Both institutions and individuals are responsible, but the overwhelming guilt rests with the institutions and the institutionalized individuals performing as the institution. Institutions' capacity, prevalence and existence automatically furnish more guilt to the environmental destruction of the Earth. Individuals are not innocent and institutions are guilty.

We are all to blame for the massive onslaught of pollutants. If global warming were a myth, Mother Earth would still stagger from the poisoning. If Mother Earth went into another ice age tomorrow, all would still be polluted. Individuals might be at fault, but institutions are the primary perpetuators of environmental destruction. Individuals are at fault for not questioning, for conforming and not confronting. Individuals are at fault for compliance. Institutions are at fault for orchestration.

"Let us not seek the Republican answer or the Democratic answer, but the right answer. Let us not seek to

It is extremely complicated to commit wrongdoing, i.e. to destroy God, family and country. Wrong requires a horrendous, calculated construct that is as powerful as a tornado and as subtle as a breeze. Wrong arrives in unforeseen storms or more often, glides in as a constant lack of effort and ineffectiveness.

Some of the greatest mistakes of mankind arrive by inattention and ineptitude – idiots. Horrors transpire when people turn away from seeing actuality – idiots. Some of greatest wrong has been accomplished with active intent to do otherwise – zealots. Selfish motivations initiated by passion and stubbornness, by people who do not listen – zealots. When idiots are quieted and zealots are convinced, the greatest exploits occur. Elitists have the zealots do it for them and the idiots do nothing contrary.

People commit all kinds of atrocity, knowingly and willingly to ensure that the status quo remains and the money flow gains on behalf of institutions. They decide to exist in ignorance, confident that institutions have conditions and situations under control. Idiots never question and zealots never learn.

The U.S.A. was created to protect and excel liberty, and people have progressed these principles. The U.S.A. is based on fair law, equal people, and the land that provides, on which we reside. The country is not a religious entity, it is not a political party or the halls in which politicians glide and it is not any capitalist enterprise or another. The U.S.A. is a land of the people, by the people and for the people. The country is literally the trinity of liberty, people and Earthly elements, everything else is an insignificant ingredient and institutional attachment.

"He that would make his own liberty secure, must guard even his enemy from oppression; for if he violates this duty, he establishes a precedent which will eventually reach himself." ~Thomas Paine

In certain situations, under certain circumstances, the act of questioning is heroic while other times it is defiant. Questions need answers and answers require truth. Truth requires investigation and sometimes further action and noncompliance. The truth suggests that there is worldwide environmental destruction and at the same time, global dissolution of liberty. The destruction of God, family and country requires action, but what action? What action against which destruction and dissolution?

It is impossible to live in the petrolithic era without some sort of inner turmoil if one is informed or has feelings. In the petrolithic era it is difficult to exist without some sort or fret or regret. In the petrolithic era, people exist in a duality, this makes inner turmoil or an inner duel inevitable, unless one is an idiot or zealot.

Great accomplishments need no institution, only individuals. When people question and if necessary, break away from institutional exploits, progression and change is possible. No institution or institutionalized individual is greater than any other individual, not even King George III. Patriots question the intertwined, interconnected institutions of the status quo, a revolutionary act. Patriots question them and their answers, enabling advancement.

Questioning the royal oligarchies such as the British Empire on which the Sun never set, was perhaps madder than questioning today's global system. Today one has the trinity of liberty to counter exploitation and repression. Surely questioning today is less of an effort than the questioning of the original patriots. Today there is more concrete information and evidence of institutional abuses, compared to unverified information and rumors during the late 1700s. There is more information and fewer consequences for standing up and questioning today.

The traits of idiocy, zealotry and patriotism coexist in society and sometimes in an individual. Sometimes people do idiotic things, many times people perform zealously without even realizing it, and many are patriots in certain terms. Patriotism requires curiosity, not a willingness to lie down and die for an institution. Patriotism requires equal dispersal of information out of love or equality. Patriots question further for there are always further answers. No institutions or individuals are above questioning, and those that insist that they are, must be petitioned.

Patriots do not support and defend authority or institution; patriots support and defend the country. Instead of standing up for what is right just because it is right, many are convinced to lie down or stand up and support wrongdoing and what benefits the few. Unquestioning commitment is not supportive, it is enabling. Open questioning allows discourse and true progress.

Patriotism has become a magnet, or sticker placed on an SUV that states support for the troops or a flag in a window or some pledge of blind of allegiance. The definition of patriotism is distorted; zealots are believed to be patriots. Blind support of any government branch is not patriotism. In fact opening one's eyes and ears to reality is more patriotic than any pledge, oath or display of red, white and blue. Zealots are often confused with patriots, normally the confusion is used by institutions. Elitists are often perceived as patriots too, they operate in ways that make people believe as much, to enhance their agenda.

Many believe supporting the troops is not questioning their actions and policy they enforce. To question the policy of war and the policy of authority, is not to cast off care of, or support for the troops. Questions demonstrate concern, while no questions demonstrate a lack of concern.

Zealots become extremely agitated and angry when logical questions arise. Where was patriotism before war? Is it only needed in war? Is support for the war machine synonymous with patriotism?

Nations want people to accept the concept of a world order led by representatives in the UN. Corporations want people to accept that products will be manufactured over the hills, across the seas and far away. Religions want people to accept that they war for the hearts and minds of others. If global powers are expanding and borders are neutralizing for institutions than the definition of patriot must expand accordingly and neutralize borders as well. To think globally and act locally is necessary as interdependency grows. People must ensure that tea is not unduly taxing any individual and throw it in the harbor if it is. If there is global trade then there must be global accountability to prevent global exploitation.

People stand up for what is right, unless inhibited by tolerations and fear. It is the first instinct to act in a right manner, to help and not hinder. Only through questioning is the prevention of exploitation possible. People must be misinformed and burdened by tolerations to act wrongly or not act on wrong. People must be trained not to question. People must be trained to be violent. People go through military school to learn how to fight, and go to business school to learn how to capitalize and proceed without question.

> "A man can't ride your back unless it's bent." ~Martin Luther King Jr.

When people know that they are being vigorously and repetitively exploited, they question it. The problem is that for most, it must be known to be questioned. And most do not question in order to know. People must be neutralized in fear and ignorance to stand down, to wonder without question or not wonder at all. Fear requires brute force and manipulated information, while ignorance requires merely blanks.

> "Resistance to tyrants is obedience to God." ~Thomas Jefferson

PEOPLE POWER

It is said that only three percent of the Colonists actively retaliated against the British exploitation before and for some time during the Revolutionary War. Fifteen to twenty percent were loyalists to the Crown throughout the War. The rest of the eighty percent predominantly continued with the business of milking cows and smelting swords.

People are the real power; individuals are the functioning power behind institutions. People have power. The actions of just three percent of the people, in the case of Revolutionary War, could not be stopped by all the institutions of the most powerful empirical nation of the time. People have information and this information guides their course. Fifteen to twenty percent of the people believed, with the information at their disposal, they were better off with King George III. Around eighty percent believed that the status quo was suitable. Only the smallest percentage of people believed they were being exploited and did something about it. Information is power because it drives people; people are the real power, the real force.

People can only act, can only find ends, in accordance to their means. There are some things many people would like to do, but creativity is beyond capacity. There are also environmental limitations; many people in the world would like to live free of petrol, but it is impossible.

In the petrolithic era there are certain freedoms, which are now unattainable. Pure water, clear skies and elements free from petrol and its accompaniments, are nearly impossible to find. The simplest of freedoms are a past notion.

Many would like to talk on the phone, sure of their privacy, but for their safety, it cannot be. This alone alters the value previous wars and belittles the liberty that soldiers fought and died for. People who fought to preserve freedoms and maintain the trinity of liberty died in vain. Perhaps they perished fulfilling an institution's agenda, but if they died protecting liberty than they died for naught. It is offensive and it is observation. Individual rights which many fought and died for are now bypassed or omitted.

Enlisted heroes have died in combat for institutional operations or protecting the trinity of liberty, which has been subverted by many institutional operations. If liberty is not progressed or at least secured, then many, in many wars might have died in vain.

The security of our liberty is threatened; subsequently our liberty is removed for our security. We lost due to the threat, the possibility and not the actuality. Is the external threat to individual life, liberty and the pursuit of happiness greater than the internal threat?

The valiant soldiers who defeated fascism on the battlefields of WWII might cringe if they learned about citizen surveillance. The Cold War followed WWII, the threat of global thermonuclear destruction was more dangerous than any terror campaign of today. Despite the threat freedom encountered, they were not suspended outright or disregarded in the face of a communistic threat or nuclear war. The Cold War threatened the very existence of man through mutual nuclear destruction and the U.S.A. did not go to the lengths it does now to monitor people. The U.S.A. didn't overtly flinch on liberty during the Cold War. People were watched, tracked and followed, and dosed, but it was not legislated, it was not written that everyone be watched and surveyed.

In the late 1960s and the early 1970s people were coming together in protest of war, exploitation, racism and environmental destruction. The FBI became involved not only with routing commies hidden in the midst of capitalists, but the destruction of the Black Panther Party and American Indian civil rights groups as well. They didn't watch over everyone, just those who they considered a threat.

The lands and waters of the U.S.A. were stomped and treaded on from the rocky coast to the golden shores. The hippies were not just dippy and dirty. Many people were not only peaceful pot smokers, but also sought political, social, radical, moral and logical change. People of all creeds joined together for civil rights and many other political movements of the period.

John Trudell served in the U.S.A. Navy in Vietnam. Later, John acted as the American Indian Movement spokesman during the eighteen month long occupation of Alcatraz Island in 1969. AIM took over the island and proposed that it be a reservation and cultural/ecological center. Eventually AIM was ousted from Alcatraz, but they did bring attention to several problems facing their people, some of which were addressed and partially remedied.

John may have committed a crime or two in his life, but that's not the reason for his extensive tracking. The reason John was watched, was because he questioned the status quo and spoke out. He was involved with the American Indian Movement and protested for decades before continuing with that most subversive and threatening profession – writing poetry.

> FBI FILES FBI made a 17,000 page dossier on John Trudell. FBI file on John Lennon: 300 pages.

> "Let me be a free man – free to travel, free to stop, free to work, free to trade where I choose, free to choose my own teachers, free to follow the religion of my fathers, free to talk and think and act for myself – and I will obey every law or submit to the penalty." ~Chief Joseph

> "(The Black Panthers) are the greatest threat to internal security of the country."
> J. Edgar Hoover, 48 year director of the FBI

However threatening the production and facilitation of nuclear weapons was, no matter how imminent the threat (as presented at least) of all out nuclear war with the USSR, J. Edgar, Director of the FBI during the Cold War, believed that the greatest internal threat to the U.S.A. was people joining together and gathering the support of others for equality. Not only was the FBI watching and involving themselves with native protesters and poetic musicians, but J. Edgar vocalized that the greatest internal threat to the security of the U.S.A. was the Black Panther Party.

The rights of some were halted, routed and grounded. The Black Panthers' right to rally and gather was terminated. Not through legislation, but through clandestine coordination, beatings and bullets. The Southern California leaders of the Black Panther Party, Bunchy Carter and John Huggins, were assassinated at UCLA in 1969. FBI agents made it happen, all but pulling the trigger, by instigating tensions between rivals. There were other subsequent shootings and shootouts, by and with police against members of the Panthers. By the late 1970s the Black Panther Party faded into history. The Panthers were dismantled directly by FBI subjugation, agent provocateurs and violent cooperation by police, the LAPD and Oakland PD in particular.

This wasn't the first or last school shooting of the time. The Panthers advocated their rights to speak out and bear arms. They were not dangerous attackers like terrorists of today, but promised to defend themselves with violence from violence. The civil rights movement and other protests of the time were mostly nonviolent, but violence did occur during the civil rights movement. The majority of the violent outbursts were from police batons and pistols and the infamous lead fired from National Guard rifles in Ohio. Years after the Kent State shootings in Ohio, a recording was released where an officer is heard ordering soldiers in the Ohio National Guard to point and shoot on protesting students.

SCHOOL PROTEST SHOOTINGS
February 8, 1968 2 South Carolina State University student protesters killed, 1 high school student killed and 27 others wounded by police. Officers claimed they were fired upon. Protesting: segregation.
May, 4 1970, 4 Kent State student protesters killed and 9 wounded by gunfire from the National Guard. They claimed there was a sniper. Protesting: expanded war.
May 14 1970, 2 Jackson State student protesters killed and 12 injured by Mississippi police. They claimed there was a sniper. Protesting: war.

We want freedom. We want full employment for our people. We want an end to the robbery by the white man of our black community. We want decent housing fit for the shelter of human beings. We want an end to police brutality and murder of black people. We want freedom for all black people in federal, state, county and city prisons and jails. We want land, bread, housing, education, clothing, justice and peace.
~From Black Panther Party Constitution

This was the greatest threat to the internal security in the U.S.A. Institutions disappeared peoples rights, specifically poor people who gathered to better their poor community and gain equal rights came to the forefront. People whose grandfathers were forced into slavery based on their heritage, gathered in attempts to excel and equalize their own personal liberties and overall standing in society, a society that frequently judged based on appearance. People who wanted essentials and education were seen as the greatest internal threat.

The Black Panther Party provided food, health care and general support to their communities and they defended themselves with rights the trinity of liberty legislated, and before that, God provided. God gave one the right to self-defense as well as, the trinity of liberty. The Second Amendment provides the right to bear arms in order to counter overt institutional might.

Surely, there were more legitimate reasons to remove the freedoms which provide an open and yet, vulnerable society. Surely people demanding respect and equality was not as dangerous as aspects of foreign wars or the Cold War. Surely the Black Panthers weren't the greatest internal threat in the U.S.A, an open society. The Black Panthers weren't a threat to the security of individuals. They were the greatest threat to the internal security and stability of the status quo. People who sought to forbid privileges of institutions over individuals are always more dangerous than any other internal threat to the stability of institutions within the status quo.

"Instead of it being called civil rights, in the future we're going to have to label it a human rights struggle or a struggle for human rights." ~Malcolm X

"I don't favor violence. If we could bring about recognition and respect of our people by peaceful means, well and good. Everybody would like to reach his objectives peacefully. But I'm also a realist.

The only people in this country who are asked to be nonviolent are black people." ~Malcolm X

Despite only advocating violence in self-defense and never raising an army to terrorize or wage war, Malcolm X was labeled a militant. Malcolm was a Nation of Islam minister who ultimately quit the organization. He threatened the use of force if presented with force or if not provided with equality, but he never spoke of attacks, only standing up to exploitation and self-defense. The only military action Malcolm was a part of was getting shot, assassinated. Otherwise Malcolm only practiced the right to speak out, bear arms, and protect himself and others around him.

Malcolm knew the masters and purveyors of violence were institutional and professional, and would strike at him if given the opportunity. One way to bring about recognition and respect is through peaceful strength, to stand strong peacefully. One of the best ways to achieve change is through nonviolently standing up to violence or exploitation. Perhaps the greatest change in itself would be nonviolence. Showing no fear is often enough to snuff exploiters and violent people. Sometimes they must learn there are reasons one is unafraid, but showing no fear is sometimes enough. Malcolm advocated equality and standing up for what is right, even standing up to violent actions with violent actions. But Malcolm never spoke of attacks, or conducted attacks; he only spoke of prevention of attacks with self-defense.

In violence, all is lost and all sides slide deeper into clash and farther from solution. The reason violent self-defense from violence works is because it demonstrates no fear. An open mind and open country often requires the ability and readiness for confrontation and self-defense, but never attacks.

The rationale and point that any violent, warring faction might attempt to make is lost. Any legitimacy is lost when violence is conducted, until all out overt crushing victory, then legitimacy is enacted. Today violence, in whatever fashion, aside from self-defense, destroys credibility. Any legitimacy a state may possess is lost in a bombing campaign. Any cause an individual may profess is lost in lashing and blasting. Violence and war are pure horror and cannot realistically put forth benevolent change. Violence cannot provoke peace or change. Violence today is no different than violence thousands of years ago; there are just better tools for it.

Peaceful action is necessary because violence disrupts and destroys worthy causes. Violence represents no cause, but monopolization and more violence. Nonviolence is counter to every wrongdoing within the status quo and never condemnable. More importantly, violent institutions attract professionals of violence who enjoy crushing others with intense and calculated attacks, given the excuse.

FBI FILES FBI file on Malcolm X: over 3,600 pages. FBI file on MLK: Almost 17,000 pages.

Nonviolence attracts institutional attention. Martin Luther King Jr. helped nonviolently change the institutionalized, racist power structure in the U.S.A. He took many hits on the way and never hit back. Martin was influenced by Howard Thurman, among others. Howard was a civil rights leader and theologian who spoke with Gandhi while traveling on missionary work. Martin also went to India to visit with followers and family of Gandhi in 1959. While there, he learned more about nonviolent resistance.

"Since being in India, I am more convinced than ever before that the method of nonviolent resistance is the most potent weapon available to oppressed people in their struggle for justice and human dignity. In a real sense Mahatma Gandhi, embodied in his life certain universal principles that are inherent in the moral structure of the universe, and these principles are as inescapable as the laws of gravitation." ~Martin Luther King Jr.

Martin was watched by the FBI because he nonviolently struck and beat institutions and at the same time, inspired other individuals to stand up peacefully and unafraid. Martin organized people around the country to protest nonviolently against racist institutions, always calling for racial harmony and equality among people. He was a Baptist pastor and participated in the Montgomery Bus Boycott, with Rosa Parks. During this time his house was bombed. Martin and those who marched with him for equal rights faced violence from institutions and individuals.

People marched amongst joint KKK and police brutality and battery in efforts to peacefully gain equal rights. He was an instrumental figure in the passing of the Civil Rights Act of 1964 and the Voting Rights Act of 1965. He peacefully fought to desegregate public schools, and all segregated institutions, public and private. Martin truly had a dream and actively initiated it without violence.

FACT: The FBI conducted a covert intelligence operation named "Destroy King Squad" intended to neutralize the effectiveness of Martin Luther King Jr. From 1963 until his death J. Edgar Hoover and the FBI used their forces against Martin.

"Justice is incidental to law and order." ~J. Edgar Hoover

The institutions of racism and segregation were so extensive and integrated they dictated where one ate and drank, and where one was permitted to go to the bathroom. Martin and the people around him peacefully dismantled the mechanics of unfair, racist and zealous institutionalization. Martin improved upon those sacred documents that make the U.S.A. great – the trinity of liberty. He met with ministers and politicians, but questioned and acted on behalf of people.

Then he was shot, assassinated, and the way he spoke in the days and weeks prior, it seemed as though he knew it was coming. Perhaps a premonition or perhaps after President John F. Kennedy was assassinated and Malcolm X was assassinated, and so many others were shot, he felt his time could be near. Martin shared goals with, and was at times at odds with John Kennedy, Lyndon B. Johnson and Malcolm X.

"I will never believe that James Earl Ray had the motive, the money and the mobility to have done it himself. Our government was very involved in setting the stage for and I think the escape route for James Earl Ray." ~Jesse Jackson

James was caught at Heathrow Airport, with a fake Canadian passport. He had just robbed a bank in London and was planning on joining a mercenary army in South Africa. The U.S.A. is great, if at all because of liberty. And the police, the FBI and other institutions were working actively against it, whether they knew it or not. The trinity of liberty empowers people individual greatness. The trinity of liberty allows and progresses development of human rights. It is a work in progress and has made gains in equality, leaps and bounds in defining and entitling liberty and justice for all. Everyone has a say, and though the trinity of liberty attempts to protect all, obviously, directly it cannot. People have to stand up for themselves, but the trinity of liberty provides the way.

VOTE
51% in of voters in U.S.A. voted in the 2000 national election. 55% in 2004 and over 64% in 2008, the highest percentage in decades.

At one time only white men who owned property could vote in the U.S.A. The U.S.A. was considered the freest nation on Earth after the Revolutionary War and yet, contrasted with the laws of today it would seem at the minimum, repressive, immoral and murderous. The U.S.A. has progressed. Yet there are still shadowy, active and violent instigations within institutions that intend to hold the status quo and beat down anyone like Martin, who would strike at institutions and not at individuals. How will our time be perceived in the future? How will the activity of some and the passivity of others be viewed?

"Many people will tell you of his wonderful qualities and his many accomplishments, but what makes him special to me, the truth many people don't want you to remember, is that Dr. King was a great activist, fighting for radical social change with radical methods. While other people talked about change, Dr. King used direct action to challenge the system. He welcomed it, and used it wisely." ~Cesar Chavez

To be patriotic in the petrolithic era and nuclear age requires more than putting a flag on one's lapel. Post 9/11, after the invasion of Afghanistan, after making a deal for the Asian natural gas pipeline, after finding Osama became unimportant, after the mission accomplished in Iraq was found to be based on bullshit (lies and mistakes are both bullshit), after removal of rights at home, one needs to question and acquire more information to accurately act patriotically.

To be a patriot today requires asking questions, a small thing, a great task is continuing to search for answers. To be a patriot in the petrolithic era and nuclear age requires researching on a scale only the information age could provide, thankfully they coincide.

Following the military retaliation subsequent 9/11, new global sensibility is required. If someone is attacked by individuals and then the police lash out on the neighbors of the individual attackers, serious questioning is necessary. The original attacker is guilty, but the subsequent violations by the police bear guilt as well.

Rudolph Giuliani was Mayor of New York City for seven years and practiced this police policy routinely. Whenever there was an officer attacked or shot in the line of duty, the police force would converge and rattle people in the neighborhood and surrounding areas. This may be a good way of gathering information after a crime, and Rudy would know, since he is a former prosecutor. But why not do this after every shooting? Are the police more valuable than other victims? If there is to be such a reaction, there should be sweeping investigation for all such crimes, and not just those against police officers.

> FACT: Rudolph Giuliani ordered "scoop and dump" operation to hurry the clean up of 9/11. Remains of victims may have ended up in a landfill. Despite the rapid cleanup bone fragments were found constantly, as recently as April, 2007. The majority of the Twin Towers and everything therein, were pulverized and turned into dust on 9/11. The Twin Towers and the nearly undamaged WTC Building 7 collapsed at free fall speed. Visual inspection shows vaporization of huge sections of falling debris.

Fairness must be accorded to all or it will only be accorded to a few. Certainly Rudy Giuliani cleaned up NYC. First he swept the streets with occasional police force intimidation and then he cleaned the remnants of one of the greatest crime scenes ever, with the Department of Sanitation and very little investigation.

The integrated world was shocked by the events of 9/11 and expressed support for the U.S.A. because everyone is interrelated and innocents were attacked at their workplace. Much of the world reneged that support because of the methodology used in the retaliation.

The International Association of Fire Fighters and the New York Fire Department withdrew their support for Rudy because in his bid for Presidency, they felt abandoned by him after 9/11. The IAFF called Rudy an urban legend.

Why were they in such a hurry that they could not wait until all possibility and hope of finding victims' remains was exhausted? What was the priority if not the remains of victims? Perhaps the status quo demanded rapid cleanup of the devastation. Maybe that's just how fast a New York minute goes, so fast that Rudy could not wait for remains to be recovered. Maybe the rubble and possibility of remains therein was seen as a hinder to progress. Maybe they knew that there were toxins fuming from the rubble.

Why was there so little investigation? It seems they knew what happened already. What about the black boxes? How could the towers fall at nearly free fall speed? How could the explosive heat melt steel, but not people in the vicinity? How could a plotter's passport be found on 9/11? How could small, erratic fires in WTC Seven bring the reinforced steel building down, into a neat pile? How could cement vaporize?

When people are attacked in some diabolical plot, questions must be asked. When armed forces participate in foreign wars based on presumption of weaponry, questions must be asked. When partial truth poses as complete story, questions must be asked. The international web of dependence upon resources, materials and production alone testifies to the need for the comprehension of patriots to expand. If someone cannot ask a question, ask it for them. If a question is labeled stupid, then they who label it should be able to answer easily.

> "Great is the guilt of an unnecessary war."
> ~John Adams

> "Beware of foreign entanglements."
> ~George Washington

If exploitation results from routine extraction and consumption, questions must be asked. People should question if there is a better way than participation in exploitation or environmental destruction for commodities.

If institutions are threatened, the institutionalized act selfishly to protect and perpetuate their goals. Confrontation, blockades, bombing campaigns, isolation, inquisition, assassination and war is engaged to protect institutional interests. In incredibly efficient vile acts are carried out, without care of whom or what is left treaded on. All institutions protect their interests at all costs, with all means at their disposal. It is most frightening when those with impunity and weaponry act on self-preservation and/or expansion.

U.S.A. SUBVERSION
1893 American businessmen and politicians overthrow, take over and annex Hawaii.
1949 CIA helped overthrow democratically elected government of Syria.
1953 CIA and British intelligence orchestrated a coup de tat of democratically elected government of Iran. The coup was led by Kermit Roosevelt, the grandson of president Theodore Roosevelt who enlisted help from Norman Schwarzkopf, the father of the General with the same name. Dictatorship under the Shah followed for 20 years, with U.S.A. support in aid and arms.
1954 CIA overthrew Guatemala.
1961 CIA attempted to overthrow Cuba at Bay of Pigs.
1970 CIA attempted to overthrow Chile.
1973 CIA involved in Chilean coup.

These are an example of just some of the known foreign actions performed by the U.S.A., mainly conducted through The Agency. Many of the world's governments are guilty of equal and perhaps worse actions and all similarly seek to monopolize situations. The branches of the U.S.A. government are supposed to act on behalf of liberty. If individuals or institutions do not take action on behalf liberty, they will certainly proclaim to. Patriots ask questions as simple as, "Why?" Is this in the interests of my country or a cabal? Is this all for one and one for all? Or is this all for one and none for all else?

Because there is evil abroad does not mean that to conduct evil counters it. Actually none of those operations were conducted against evil, and most were conducted for the root of all evil. There was no evil to conjure or amplify; hence the military was out of the picture. Operations had to be somewhat clandestine. The people must be behind war, women will not stand for it and men will not fight it, if there is nothing more than a threat to the width of a wallet.

A coup de tat becomes necessary when the activity is so blatantly vile that even lies cannot cover the stink. Covert action takes place in more instances than just coup de tats, but they are an example of clandestine conspiracies. These are not imaginary conjunctions, but actual secretly planned activities of a nature that requires secrecy.

Normal people normally need more than money as a provocation to war. For many institutions though money and expansion of power is reason enough to send people to war. Institutions claim there is certain information that only the government is privy to and they often know more than the simpletons of our time. They have special knowledge or secrets they have to keep clandestine. But don't worry; they are unquestionably acting out of good. If things don't turn out right, they claim in the future it will be realized that dastardly action was benevolent. If they know they cannot convince people to war, they will subvert information. If they can't do that they will take indirect and clandestine action.

FACT: On September 11, 1973 the presidential palace was bombed in the Chilean Coup. What followed was the incarceration of tens of thousands and murder of unknown thousands, including President Allende. Torture and disappearances were subsequently commonplace. PepsiCo among other U.S.A. corporations requested ousting of Allende. In 2005 PepsiCo sold $32.5 billion in snacks and beverages.

NOTABLE U.S.A. MILITARY ACTS
1817–1818, 1835–1842, 1855–1858 Seminole Wars.
1874, 1889, 1893 Marines land on Hawaii.
1965 Dominican Republic invasion.
1970 Cambodia deployment.
1981 El Salvador deployment.
1982 Lebanon deployment.
1983 Grenada invasion.
1986 Libya bombing.
1988 Honduras deployment.
1989 Panama invasion.
1991 Persian Gulf War.
1992–1995 Somalia campaign.
1993–1995 Haiti embargo and deployment.
1995 Bosnia bombing campaign and deployment.
1998 Iraq bombing campaign.
1999 Serbia and Kosovo bombing campaign.

Provocation, legislation and convincing are required to get people behind war because people fight wars. War is chiefly the embodiment of wrong; it is complicated and complicating, while people want what is simple and right. People leave blood behind in their efforts on behalf of institutions, often without questioning and nearly always without the answers.

FACT: The Roosevelt Corollary was an addition to the Monroe Doctrine to expand commercial interests in Latin America. The Truman Doctrine enabled any country that was opposed to the USSR to become sponsored militarily for a proxy war. The Eisenhower Doctrine allowed for military action in the Middle East. The Kennedy Doctrine and Johnson Doctrine further expanded influence in the Western Hemisphere. The Nixon Doctrine boosted military aid worldwide. The Carter Doctrine challenged the USSR. The Reagan Doctrine promoted war through proxy. The Clinton Doctrine provided for war against war. The Bush Doctrine enabled preemptive war against terrorists or countries harboring terrorists.

Individuals living in liberty want peace over war. Institutions claim their march to war is in order to find peace. Information is withheld that would inspire people to question, while other information is furnished that inspires people to fight. If people are not behind war, then war does not march on. If it is not possible to overthrow a government with clandestine henchmen or trickery, then the truth must be overthrown. People have to be convinced that wrongdoing is right.

False flag operations are attacks coordinated on one's own people or possessions in order to manipulate people into a planned reaction. It is an old scheme performed for millennia to instigate manipulations. It is such an old trick, that it originates in a time when carrying flags was important in battle.

False flag operations are clandestine and when done well, are unverifiable events. They are effective, lively, surprise attacks that are immediately blamed on an enemy in order to prop up a preconceived agenda. Some accidents are manipulated into false flag operations of sorts, resulting in the same type of distortions.

The oldest example of a false flag operation is perhaps Nero setting Rome afire. He may have done so to make way for a new palace or to persecute Christians or both. Some recent notable false flag operations include the Manchurian Incident: oil for Japan. The Reichstag fire: removal of civil liberties in Germany. Years later the incident at Gleiwitz radio station enabled German invasion of Poland. Israeli terrorists in 1954 posed as Arabs and set bombs, they were caught.

Many people debate over the sinking of the USS Maine being a false flag operation, the major catalyst for the Spanish American War. It is also speculated that the attack on the USS Liberty was a false flag operation gone awry. The marked USS Liberty was attacked in international waters in the Mediterranean by planes and ships of the Israeli military on a clear day during the Six Day War, on June 8, 1967.

"…the board of inquiry (concluded) the Israelis knew exactly what they were doing in attacking the Liberty."
~Richard Helms

"For many years I had wanted to believe that the attack on the Liberty was pure error. It appears to me that is was not a pure case of mistaken identity. I think that it's about time that the State of Israel and the United States government provide the crew members of the Liberty and the rest of the American people with facts of what happened and why it came about that the Liberty was attacked thirty years ago today." ~Captain William McGonagle, USS Liberty

It took the Captain basically thirty years to question the situation, but he did. It is difficult to say and see what is truth concerning suggested false flag operations. The fact that such operations are conducted on a violent level by various groups is indisputable. Because of the accompanying violence, it is difficult to discern what is and what could be a false flag operation. There are disputable events, such as the attack on the USS Liberty, but the attack and sinking of ships as a provocation for war was, and is not, beyond their scope.

The Gulf of Tonkin Incident on August 2 and 4, 1968 is an example of a known false flag operation. It was actually a false -false flag operation. It was in part pretend, a complete fabrication. It was the catalyst for military escalation in Vietnam and it was a lie coordinated by the U.S.A. military industrial complex Many consider the war in Vietnam to be the nation's greatest mistake, and its escalation was based on fabrication of events. The President, Lyndon B. Johnson announced that the Navy was fired on and that military action was needed. Tolerations of wrong followed the lie.

Congress gave Lyndon unlimited authority to escalate and conduct war by any means necessary. Later as the Vietnam War grew out of control, Congress passed the War Powers Resolution to limit future use of force by the President and the Case-Church Amendment to end the War in Vietnam.

> "Our toil, resources and livelihood are all involved. So is the very structure of our society. In the councils of government, we must guard against the acquisition of unwarranted influence, whether sought or unsought, by the military industrial complex. The potential for the disastrous rise of misplaced power exists and will persist."
> ~Dwight D. Eisenhower

There are many instances of these types of operations and/or manipulations conducted by squadrons of other developed institutions, national and otherwise. The U.S.A. did not invent this type of conduct. It is difficult research, the information shrouded and looming in uncertainty, however there are verified false flag events, such as the Gulf of Tonkin.
What is the point of a false flag operation? The point is to make people think. Not to make people think about, or think freely, but to make people think a certain thought about certain presentation of information. The point is to present lies, partial truths or distortions that lead people to incomplete opinion, distorted conclusion and ultimately wrong action.

They cannot wage war without the trigger fingers of convinced people. They cannot wage war without the complacency and nod of people as well. Institutions have to convince individuals to carry out and support their deeds. Despite all their power, the perception of people is wholly important and they will lie and murder to propagate what they believe others should believe.

> "To see right and not do it is the worst cowardice." ~Confucius

For war, the U.S.A. and many institutions proudly slide into billions of dollars of debt and willingly demolish the entirety of many. If gauged simply fiscally, war is humanity's number one concern. If gauged by movement of material and physical, war is the most massive undertaking. If authorities and institutions were not profiting from war there would be little, if any war at all. If they were unable to convince people to tolerate it and be proud of it, there would be no war.

To create such malevolence as war is extremely difficult. It requires complicated engineering feats and a will to conjure hazardous materials and surpass logistical nightmares. It requires regimented violence, murder, and generally the outright opposite of right behavior. It requires substantial lies and misinformation to influence and manipulate tolerations in order to get people to do all these things. It requires a flip on logic akin to convincing a starving people that it is possible to yield more food through fighting than through farming.

> "However many holy words you read, however many you speak; what good will they do if you do not act upon them?" ~Buddha

Wrong, great wrong such as war, must be coerced and orchestrated to be initiated and perpetuated. War is extremely complicated and is proof in itself that simple is better. That which is right just is. That which is wrong must be manipulated and constructed. One must raise arms in agreement with war and raise them to wage the war. People fight wars on behalf of institutions which they believe exist for the betterment of people. Institutions need individuals, but they don't need all individuals and will gladly march over a few or many as long as other individuals continue their support.

To arrange the complexities of wrongdoing requires commitment; it is not something that is done casually. To do the right thing is simple and grows more simple once the complications of wrong are shaken off, stopped or thrown into the sea. Shaking off wrong can be a tumultuous, cracking and crumbling or it can be an easy transition, if institutions allow. War requires manipulation of tolerations, arrangement of complexities, bloodletting and destruction, while doing the right thing never requires such malevolence. Doing the right thing requires that people ask unbiased questions and make decisions with unbiased answers. Great wrong requires that the majority of people be manipulated, while simple right is dependent on the majority not being manipulated.

The complications and consequences of the petrolithic era and nuclear age require equally complex questions. The more simple the situation, the more natural the environment, the easier it is to see clearly what is right. The more institutional soot the environment is burdened with the more difficult it is to see.

> "Almost always, the creative dedicated minority has made the world better." ~Martin Luther King Jr.

CUBAN BLUNTS

FACT: Cuba was a Spanish possession and plantation for almost 400 years, claimed by Christopher Columbus. Eventually the Spanish settlers enslaved and killed most all of the locals, among them the Tainos. Slaves from Africa were soon imported. Through slavery, colonial Cuba grew coffee, tobacco, sugar and hemp. Eventually, most farming on the island was devoted to sugarcane. Sugar was brought to Cuba from the Canary Islands by Christopher Columbus on his second voyage to the Caribbean. Christopher and his crew are given credit for introducing tobacco to Europe.

In 1898 the U.S.A. went to war with Spain with the stated intention of releasing Cuba from Spanish imperial rule. The result was the U.S.A. gaining its own empire. The Cuban people had been revolting against Spanish rule for decades. In the late 1800s, riots broke out in Havana and printing presses were destroyed. The U.S.A. sent down the USS Maine to Havana to protect U.S.A. interests. The Maine arrived to Havana Harbor June 25, 1898 and three weeks later it mysteriously exploded in the harbor. One month after the explosion, the U.S.A. declared war on Spain.

The reaction to the explosion and sinking of the USS Maine was compounded by sensationalist journalism. The exaggerated reporting was pushed by people such as William Randolph Hearst and Joseph Pulitzer simply to sell more newspapers. To this day the cause of the explosion is disputed. At the time Spain was the immediate target and the scapegoat for blame.

"Remember the Maine! To hell with Spain!" This was a rally cry for war. The Maine was sent to Cuba to show a high national interest. It exploded and sunk mysteriously, showing national tragedy instead.

One hundred and nine days after war began, Spain's last Caribbean retreat and first colonial prize was Spain no more. The U.S.A. lost over 3,000 troops, but was now a proud empire whose holdings consisted of the Philippines, Guam, Puerto Rico and Cuba. The anti-empire was now an empire. In 1902, Cuba became independent and in 1903, Guantanamo Bay became U.S.A. soil.

> FACT: Although there is no officially recognized number, possibly 1 million people were killed or died as a result of war in the Philippines after U.S.A. invasion and occupation. Hostility between the U.S.A. and people of the Philippines officially went on from 1899–1902 and unofficially through 1913. Philippine civilians and military personnel were imprisoned in the same camps.

In response to the Philippine – American War, Mark Twain wrote "The War Prayer", a poetic short story about the entire context of war. His publisher refused it and it would not be published until 1923, after Mark died.

Despite exiling Spanish rule, Cuba remained restless and clashing throughout the years. In 1906, an armed rebellion broke out over disputed elections and the U.S.A. sailed in, taking charge again. The U.S.A. would remain in direct control for three years. Through 1933 there was unrest and in August of the same year there was a coup, then in September there was another coup. And one hundred days later the military installed another leader.

There were frequent civil disruptions, but it wasn't until 1953 that Fidel Castro began his revolution. On July 26, Fidel led an assault on the Moncada Barracks. Fidel was imprisoned, and as a lawyer, defended himself in court and penned a speech titled "History Will Absolve Me". Fidel was sentenced to death, but church leaders helped stop his execution. He was released about two years later. On January 1, 1959 Fidel took Havana and became prime minister in February. The "History Will Absolve Me" speech became a book inspired by it.

Now known for its cigars, sugar, and revolution, Cuba was soon increasingly sponsored by the USSR. In 1960, a U.S.A. trade embargo was imposed furthering the island nation's dependence on the USSR. In January 1961, the U.S.A. cut diplomatic relations with Cuba. After Fidel's revolution, the U.S.A. corporations that were established on the island were threatened and eliminated.

Around the same time, the U.S.A. deployed nukes to Turkey and learned the USSR was sending nukes to Cuba. In April 1961, The Agency, under President John F. Kennedy, staged a failed invasion of Cuba at another bay, later named the Bay of Pigs. Tension between the nuclear nations grew, largely centered in Cuba.

On October 22, 1962 JFK, also known as Jack, announced a shipping quarantine of Cuba. Nuclear war between the USSR and U.S.A. seemed imminent for almost a week until a resolution was found. Diplomatic relations between the U.S.A. and Cuba have fluctuated, but the embargo continued with Cuba, at times lessening and at other times deepening until 2015.

Cuba is the only country that the U.S.A. military has a base in, and with whom there was no diplomatic relationship. Cuba considered the U.S.A. presence to be an illegal occupation, while the U.S.A. insists that a deal is a deal. The deal was made after Theodore Roosevelt decided to give the island independence. According to the deal, Guantanamo Bay is under lease by the U.S.A. in perpetuity.

GUANTANAMO BASE 45 square miles.
It is the oldest overseas U.S.A. Navy Base.
It is the only U.S.A. base inside a communist country.
In 1741 British troops captured Guantanamo Bay and eventually Havana. Ultimately they left it to Spain.
June 1898, the first casualties of the Spanish American War were two marines at Guantanamo Bay. Since then there has been some sort of U.S.A. base there.
During the war for Cuba, in 1898 the U.S.A. Navy took shelter in Guantanamo Bay during hurricane season.
In 1964 Cuba cut the flow of water to the base. Soon desalination plants were built.
HIV positive Haitian refugees were kept in Guantanamo until their detainment was declared unconstitutional in June, 1993.
Beginning in 2002, enemy combatants are held as prisoners, some without trial.
In 2005 the U.S.A. Navy completed a $12 million wind turbine project to reduce dependency on diesel generators.
In June, 2006 three prisoners killed themselves. In May 2007, another detainee committed suicide.

When the Berlin wall came down in a celebrated crumble, it was because the institutions allowed for an easy and peaceful transition. Most of the world celebrated, but not Cuba. The institutions of East Germany and the USSR allowed the will of the people to supersede their rigidity and dogma, and the wall gently fell. Despite all the violence around and from the wall, it came down casually and peacefully. The U.S.A. began trading with other communist countries after the fall of the wall, but not Cuba. The relationship between the U.S.A. and Cuba, formerly inhabited by Tainos, was and is unique.

November 9, 1989	Fall of the Berlin wall.
December 25, 1991	President Gorbachev resigns. The next day the USSR dissolved itself.
October 1992	U.S.A. trade embargo with Cuba reinstated.

After the wall came down, the USSR soon fell as well. Inevitably, Cuba was left more isolated than ever. The aid they had received from the Soviets was eliminated, including petrol and a yearly half million tons of fertilizers, herbicides, and pesticides devoted mostly to sugar plantations. They were cutoff from petroleum products used for fuel, fertilizers, pesticides and now their Soviet benefactor was no more.

Almost all of the arable terra firma of Cuba was devoted to sugar and their Soviet buyers were not returning their calls. Cuban imports declined and their exports were going nowhere fast. The Cuban Government implemented a special period. After the loss of imports, Cuba developed a mostly organic, urban agriculture, outlawing chemical pesticides within Havana city limits in order to feed urbanites. Feeding the people was the number one concern, as most of their food had been imported as well.

Cuban people began growing their food on small organic farms, many in the inner city. They eliminated the need for the international, unsustainable petroleum chemical based farming. Today the island nation is mostly healthy and well fed. People in Cuba grow their own food without the corporate farming structure that requires fertilizers, pesticides and herbicides and energy for delivery. They eliminated the need for machinery to harvest, as the plots were small. By growing near the consumer they eliminated the use of resources to ship food. People in Cuba were legislated to be self-sufficient. Cuba proved individuals are able to grow better food and more of it, using fewer resources, than corporate farming institutions.

Individuals can accomplish more, in better forms, than institutions. Cuba knew this and when the ease of international dependence came to a complex end, people power was sanctioned. Though there is limited opportunity in Cuba and poverty exists, there is individually empowered agriculture.

People legislated or unorganized and criminal are more productive than vast regimented institutionalized corporations at production, manufacturing and distribution. Given the proper motivation people can grow their own tomatoes or corn and cut off connections with monopolistic and destructive agricultural corporations such as Monsanto.

FACT: Monsanto created seeds that did not produce offspring, but they retracted that project when enough people learned and complained. Their seeds are currently designed to grow optimally with Monsanto pesticides. Roundup, a Monsanto product, is one of the most widely used pesticides in the world. They are the leading creator of GMO foods. They design GMO corn specifically for human consumption and other types to be made into ethanol.

A little Roundup with some genetically modified organisms resembling corn and soy, in a bowl of milk with bovine growth hormone is a great way to start the day. GMO are now a staple in people's diets and heralded as beneficial. You eat it, like it not, notice it or not. Corn and soy are two of the largest crops in the world and the most widely genetically modified.

> "I have meditated a lot on that (starvation) in the wake of president Bush's meeting with U.S. automobile manufacturers. The sinister idea of converting food into fuel was definitely established as an economic line in U.S. foreign policy…" ~Fidel Castro

GMO is a global experiment. Proponents of GMO foods claim that they cut costs and increase yields. This, they say, will help feed the world's hungry. There are other ways to feed the world and surely they weren't waiting for something like GMO foods to do so. GMO as food is a way to make money.

People in Cuba stopped participation in petrolithic era agriculture. As it turned out, they didn't need the pesticides, fungicides and corporate farming structure. Because they were cut off from resources, local people accomplished for themselves without institutionalized chemical assistance or modification.

Cubans never began participation in the franchise system of food processing and distribution. Cuba is an island, practically the rest of the world eats from franchised plates. Food production and distribution has been franchised, people buy into the pyramid of another and start their own pyramid. This type of branded franchise system includes more than just supermarkets and fast food restaurants. There are franchised hotels, real estate offices, insurance companies, automobile repairers, rental services, tax preparers, and all sorts of providers of goods and services structured into steep pyramids.

The owners and operators of fast food franchises do not open up shop because they have an interest in culinary arts. It is because they have an interest in pyramidal money. Franchises allow for rigidity within a structured pyramid system of growth; globalization. The food is mechanically regimented from its origins to one's mouth. It is a business based on the convenience of location, price, consistency and rapid service.

The food franchise system is a global expansive monopoly on the supply and delivery of food. Corporations brand cravings and sustenance that people require. It is a system of corporate control and monopolization constructed within the status quo of the petrolithic era. Wants and needs are intermingled with huge investments into advertising campaigns. Food is shipped great distances, served with great flare and media hype, with little nutritional value, in order to profit. Franchise food is for institutions.

FACT: McDonald's began in San Bernardino, CA by brothers Dick and Mac McDonald in 1940. Today there are over 31,000 McDonald's restaurants in well over 100 countries. The elite in the McDonald's pyramid make money through selling supplies, franchise fees, a percentage of sales and often rent. McDonald's spends approximately $2 billion a year on global advertising. The first McDonald's opened in Moscow in January, 1990.

The oligarchical franchise of Mickey D experienced growth during the recession in 2008 and into 2009. The rigid global infrastructure apparently functions well when there are few options. When there are no local foods, when there is no time and when people have nearly no money, the corporation of McDonald's increases its market share. Mickey D's is the largest fast food franchise corporation in the world and also the biggest symbol of globalization. In their pursuits to expand their pyramid system, franchise fast food restaurants have directly and indirectly eliminated local businesses and notions of localization all over the world.

There may be plenty of reasons to be happy or sad in Cuba, but there is only one place to get a Happy Meal – Guantanamo Base. This is where the only McDonald's on the isle exists. Fast-food franchises are pyramidal formations which institutionalize food for profit; such globalization does not reside in the Republic of Cuba. Franchise food is complicated, often shipped great distances and always processed. Good food is best when it is uncomplicated, unprocessed and fresh.

When food gathering is done predominantly overseas and not locally, it normally benefits strangers and possibly works over foreign workers and resources. When institutions push for globalization, it is to increase their monopolization and not to better conditions. When fast food franchises increase their product selection, it is to increase revenue and not increase nutrition. Fast food franchise restaurants promote globalization, eliminate localization and use food that works for institutional operations. Nutrition for individuals is less important than profit for institutions.

Hemp is a simple crop that requires no fertilizer, pesticide or any tilled field for that matter. It grows everywhere and anywhere, along railroad tracks, rivers and roads. Hemp biomass has a high content of volatile oils that can be processed into clean fuels and the stalk can be processed into anything from clothing to building material. Hemp seed is not only edible, but highly nutritious. Pot seed is one of the best forms of nutrition for people on Earth. It contains protein and essential fats in quantities people need, unlike any franchise fast food. Hemp is a better source of nutrition than any franchise fast food. Acorns, pine needles and wild grasses would likely offer more nutrition and long term vitality than any franchise fast food too.

Hemp would be impossible to franchise. It requires no genetic modification. It is already a high-octane bio-fuel, highly nutritious food and potent industrial material that is easily grown, harvested and processed. Hemp is capable of enriching and enlivening the soil in crop rotation. It is capable of growing in marginal conditions nearly anywhere. Hemp would be impossible to franchise because anyone could grow it, anywhere. Hemp's cousin marijuana is called weed because it grows like one, persistent and pervasive. Hemp grows anywhere with little care.

Hemp is a superior source of bio-fuel compared to corn. It is a superior source of nutrition compared to corn also and is a superior source of paper compared to tree pulp. Since hemp can grow anywhere, individuals could grow so much that it could be used as fuel, food and biomass, if it were legal. Despite hemp being a powerhouse to industry and development, it is scorned because of its cousin Mary.

Marijuana is related to hemp and has intoxicating powers, hemp on the other hand contains no intoxicating powers. The flowers of Mary contain differing levels of intoxicating THC and cannabinoids. This intoxication has been confused with happiness.

Hemp needs very little care, while marijuana needs serious attention to fruit. Marijuana needs space and nutrient rich ground, hemp and marijuana are cultivated entirely differently. Hemp can be grown in tight bushes of plants, while marijuana needs space. If the marijuana plant goes to seed, which it naturally tries to do, the flowers become near useless to stoners, but the seeds remain useful to individuals as nutrition, and the stalk useful to industry as a resource for energy and material, or would be.

Agricultural corporations choose which variety of tomato to grow and distribute based on weight, shelf life and overall appearance after a truck ride from wherever. Institutions are concerned with the fruit's profitability, not its nutrition content. They do not choose which variety of tomato, out of hundreds, based on nutrition or taste, but based on conversion of fruit into money. They do not choose where to grow tomatoes based on sunny climate or healthy soil, but by how cheap the workers will work. Corporate agriculture conglomerates choose to operate in a way that is best suited for profit and control.

All corporate agriculture functions for the institution, not the hungry. GMO foods are designed to yield more weight, not more nutrition. Food is designed for pest resistance to decrease costs, not increase safety, and not to feed the hungry. Should tomatoes look good or taste good? Should tomatoes shine in the supermarket after a trip over the hills and through the woods, or contain large amounts of nutrients? Does one desire food because of an advertising campaign or because one requires proper fuel? Tomato plants, like hemp, grow anywhere.

Monsanto has sold BGH to dairy farmers as one way to increase profit. Monsanto's Posilac puts the dairy cow's health at risk, but can increase lactation of milk from their udders by 10%. Europe and Canada have banned BGH and many dairy farmers refuse to use it in the U.S.A., but it is in the majority of dairy. The product exists for institutions. It is a franchise enabler.

Control is more profitable than the lack of control whether it concerns energy, drugs, milk or tomatoes. To the institutions in control, the amount of profit is more important than the amount of nutrients. Milk is for institutions, not individuals. If milk was for individuals it would be untainted, since it is for institutions, it does not matter what they put in it, as long as they increase profit. Organic milk has no such taint.

Marijuana is for individuals. THC makes people believe they are happy and this can lead to such reckless acts as growing one's own pot and tomatoes. Pesticides and GMO foods, additives and preservatives, franchise fast food, are for institutions. Corporate farming is for institutions; if they intended to feed the world they could do so without GMO. Hemp or petrol? Hemp or corn?

> FACT: Bio-fuel production from palm plantations and corn fields threaten forest land in pursuit of agricultural fields and raises the cost of food.

Individuals are overrun, ridden on and run over by institutions and in preference to institutions. It is an intertwined web of confines, conditions and consequences that make the unacceptable, acceptable. Institutions claim benevolence and independence, but tread on many, make arrangements with few and make many dependents.

Cuba is a rare example of autonomy. Cuba sanctioned people power, because of necessity. The island was restricted from access to the products enabling petrolithic era agriculture. Cuba traded oil for oxen and the country that faced collapse, grew their own chemical-free food. There are no franchise restaurants in Cuba, barring the Navy owned McDonald's, Subway, Pizza Hut, KFC and A&W fast food restaurants at Guantanamo Bay Navy Base. In many ways, Cuba is a controlling and restrictive institution, but the people showed that there are alternatives to corporate large scale agriculture. Cuba provides an example of legislated people power independent of corporate agriculture and franchises. Marijuana provides an example of unsanctioned people power.

Institutions would have people believe that they have all the answers and can produce more than unaffiliated or loosely organized people. They don't, they can't. All the corporate agriculture in the U.S.A., all the corporate farming and all the corporate crops do not outgrow unaffiliated pot farmers. The number one cash crop in the U.S.A. is marijuana and not one plant is institutionalized.

It is only expensive because it is illegal. It is as easy to grow as corn. Throw the seed on some manure, if you have it; add a little sun, a little water, a little care, a little while and voila. But, because it is illegal, it is actually very difficult to grow, but profitable, because it is illegal. It is a mostly criminal and clandestine activity, which makes it difficult, risky and surrounded by other more serious criminal elements. Compared to any corporate crop in the U.S.A, weed is the number one cash crop. How much money would marijuana accumulate if it was legalized and taxed? People are going to grow and smoke weed, no matter what the law states, that much is obvious.

Usually people power is unsanctioned and arises from institutional idle and malefaction. Millions of people regularly smoke weed regardless of the prohibition. People provide what is demanded of other people without institutions and in spite of institutions. People are going to grow weed and smoke it, no matter the risk and people are going to pay for it, no matter the cost.

It is illegal, just as alcohol was at one point. But is the pot plant illegal because it's a threat to your health? Is it illegal because it leads to breakdown in society? Or is it illegal because it's a threat to various oligarchical powers and their hold on the status quo? Is it illegal because it leads to a breakdown of institutional control?

Henry Ford changed the way the world works. He invented the idea of mass production and created the assembly line. He also created a want and perceived need for automobiles. Henry was a racist and anti-Semite. Partly because of this, he abhorred the idea of importing fuel from the Middle East or any foreign country for that matter. Henry grew hemp for the purpose of supplying fuel and material. Henry made a car from bio-plastics, including hemp. Henry wanted the U.S.A. to be energy independent through the use of pot and other plant sourced bio-fuels.

The idea of cheap, renewable and locally sourced bio-fuel did not sit well with Rockefeller Standard Oil or Rothschild Shell Oil in the 1920s. They had been drilling for petroleum for decades, mainly in the U.S.A. They did not like the idea of people growing their own fuel because they wouldn't sell as much their own. At the time the U.S.A. was the biggest supplier of petrol.

FACT: Hemp can produce four times more methanol per acre than corn.	"You can't build a reputation on what you are going to do." ~Henry Ford

The first oil wells in the Middle East were drilled in the 1920s; by the 1930s oil fields were all over Iran, Iraq and Saudi Arabia. Henry Ford lived until 1947 and tried desperately to promote bio-fuels and U.S.A. energy independence as the auto industry grew and began to use foreign sources of fuel. Henry was a racist, but whatever his distorted tolerations, he wanted to remain self sufficient and independent of outside resources.

Dupont, heavily invested in both timber and petroleum, has been accused by many individuals of scorning hemp because of its fibers and promoting its prohibition to maintain their business control. Dupont also was accused of being the number one air polluter in the U.S.A. by researchers at University of Massachusetts Amherst in their 2008 toxic 100 list. Hemp could be processed into large amounts of fuel, food, paper, and timber products, while marijuana contains narcotics/medicinal properties. All forestry operations would become useless if hemp was adopted for the use of paper, but there would be new business opportunities.

Institutions mediated and distorted the understanding of marijuana's effects through hysterical reporting. The narcotic was so demonized that every bit of the plant and its cousin hemp, was made illegal. The marijuana bud's psycho-activity was so dangerous that the valuable industrial fibers and edible seed, which cannot get one high, were made illegal along with the fruit. Today we know that the functions of individuals stoned on weed is no threat to society.

Perhaps the real danger is to oligarchical institutions and not individuals. Perhaps the industrial activity of the seed and stalk was more dangerous to the status quo than the psycho-activity of the fruit. Perhaps the fruit was made illegal along with the powerful seed and stalk. Corporations threatened by the hemp industry bundled the seed, stalk and flower into one demonized pile, and burned it. They banned the most useful plant to protect oligarchical industries. They made a medicinal and nutritional plant illegal, because if manipulated, it can also produce fruit that makes them think they are happy.

The plant is so valuable as a raw material that in WWII, the U.S.A. released permits to grow hemp. Due to foreign supplies of fibers being cut off, in a time of great stress, the U.S.A. made it legal to grow for a brief time in order to acquire resources.

HEMP is one of the best forms of plant nutrition for people in existence, contains calcium.
One of the oldest sources of nutrition for people, gruel.
One of the oldest cultivated crops, requires sunlight and water, no pesticides.
Manufactured into paper, cloth and rope for thousands of years, without chemicals.
Guttenberg Bibles written on hemp.
George Washington and Thomas Jefferson grew hemp.
Drafts of Declaration of Independence and Constitution written on hemp paper.
The first flags of the U.S.A. were made from hemp.
Rudolph Diesel invented his engine to run off of fuel from vegetable oils including hemp.
Ford Model T built from hemp fiber, powered by hemp fuel.
Henry Ford grew hemp.
During World War II hemp was made legal to grow in order to obtain resources.
Fibers and oils can be used to manufacture practically anything.
It's a high yield crop, and at one time second only to tobacco in the U.S.A.

FACT: Studies suggest smoking or chewing tobacco makes one 10 times more likely to get cancer. Inconclusive studies suggest marijuana has no such harmful effects and many studies point to marijuana having DNA repairing and cancer curing effects.

During WWII when times were tough and resources were scarce, the government made hemp legal because it is a superior source of biomass. Such policy changes in troubling times can have a profound impact industrially and economically. Instead of eliminating potential local resources available to many, and depending on the allocation of commodities by few, with hemp resources might be grown by anyone. Hemp grows anywhere and it provides practically anything.
Hemp is an industrial/energy/edible wonder. Its cousin marijuana has the infamous intoxicant. It is a sedative, pain reliever, anti-inflammatory, appetite enhancer, analgesic, anesthetic, antibiotic, the reliever of many maladies and with the proper care it grows practically anywhere. That's some good shit.

1619	First marijuana law enacted in Virginia: mandatory that all farmers grow hemp.
1915	First U.S.A. anti-marijuana law enacted in Utah.
1937	Marijuana and hemp made illegal in the U.S.A., with the exception of bird seed corporations.

FACT: There were 19,838 unintentional, fatal overdoses caused by prescription drugs in 2004, mostly derived from opiates.

"Sow it (hemp) everywhere."
~George Washington

After 1937, hemp was made illegal and was strictly for the birds. Any wild hemp birds might have eaten was to be eradicated, but people could buy the sterilized seed for the birdfeeder business. The one industry that was allowed to continue to grow hemp, and only for its sterile seed, was the birdfeed vendors. They made such a squawk about being allowed to grow hemp for the seed, that they were granted an exception. The only catch was they had to sterilize the seed. Everything else useful about hemp was abandoned because of the exaggerated potency and problematic activity resulting in the use of the narcotic, its cousin.

Because of, or thanks to individual marijuana growers, the plant today is more potent then the hay they were smoking in 1937 through 1977. Without GMO technology, farmers are able to breed and enhance plants. Pot, tomatoes, corn have all been manipulated to steer characteristics of the crops in favor of individuals for millennia. Corn, pot and every other crop has been enhanced, without GMO.

Conventional allopathic medicines prescribed for ailments have scary side effects, there are little to no side effects of marijuana. Some studies however, conclude that a tiny dose of THC can result in episodes of anxiety, even psychosis. Mostly these psychotic events include imagined happiness, irrational overeating and dozing off.

Known chemicals in marijuana alleviate a long list of maladies ranging from stress to AIDS. Recent scientific observations, during research into another aspect of marijuana use, suggested that marijuana smoke kills malformed (cancerous) cells in the lungs. Pot provides a long list of known wondrous industrial and medicinal opportunities from a simple plant. Research has been prevented and limited by institutions, likely there are more unknown uses. Plus it's a recreational drug, like alcohol.

> ALCOHOL There are almost 20,000 alcohol induced (excluding accidents, homicides) deaths every year in U.S.A. There are an average of 27,000 deaths every year from alcohol related chronic liver disease and cirrhosis in U.S.A. In 2001 17,448 people died in drunk driving accidents.

> FACT: The ratio of marijuana that will intoxicate to the amount that will kill: 1 to 40,000.
> The ratio of alcohol that will intoxicate to the amount that will kill: 1 to 10
> All life on Earth has cannabinoid receptors, it integrates.

Well, not exactly like alcohol. Not one pot smoker or hashish abuser since the beginning of the Neolithic age to today has died from a marijuana overdose, though surely incidents are possible. Drunks have a tendency to accomplish staggering feats of clumsiness and also become irrationally violent. They hurt themselves and others accidentally and intentionally. Alcohol makes people physically and mentally sick, while marijuana makes people laugh and sleep.

> FACT: Low estimates conclude that alcohol played a role in 30% of violent crimes and homicides and 60% of suicides in the U.S.A.

> "Although rare, severe shutdown of blood circulation to the arms and legs has been reported in young people who smoked marijuana. In some cases, it was so severe that amputation was required. Marijuana may also serve as a trigger for heart attack on rare occasion, usually within an hour after smoking."
> ~American Cancer Society

No wonder pot smokers are known to be paranoid. There are a lot of drinkers around who might snap and perhaps there is risk of losing blood flow to one's legs or having a heart attack. Realistically it would take a modern drug company to derive some enhanced THC pill for THC to jeopardize one's survival. Temporary blindness has resulted from eating potent marijuana food, and enough of anything is bad, but pot is no threat to society.

There are two starkly polarized sides presented about the truth to marijuana. One side says it is dangerous to the world and the other side says it could save the world. Both sides are right, it could save the world, as an agricultural powerhouse and it is dangerous to institutions of the status quo.

Most people, at one time or another have sought some form of intoxication, a caffeine jolt, a joint, drunkenness, euphoria of some sort. Perhaps it is a primordial mammalian craving to alter one's mind state. Cats, koalas, sheep, cattle, elephants and rabbits all seek out altered states. People have known about weed, mushrooms and fermenting fruits for thousands of years, about plants that could help heal as well as change their head.

> FACT: Called Ganjika in Sanskrit, ganja is named after the Ganges River. Hindus believe all life derived from the Ganges River. In the Vedic tradition, marijuana enables focus and concentration.

In the past it was safe to search for a buzz by harvesting a plant. Today intoxication is dangerous, as people figuratively pick fruit from bottles of altered and enhanced pharmaceutical concoctions. Why not have a safe, non-addictive, natural alternative that is simply grown and is not manufactured into and mixed up with poisons?

Pharmaceutical companies create the most dangerous and complex drugs from simple natural sources. Often they are remedies, but often they also cause other foreseen and unforeseen complications, requiring further treatment. Sometimes replacements for marijuana are researched and marketed, such as relaxants, cures for insomnia, nausea and loss of appetite with warnings of side effects that might be altogether more miserable than the original problem.

Since traveling snake oil salesmen with miracles in a bottle, compromised mostly of opium, suppliers always find a way to get the addicts, or mammals, the head change they seek, legality aside. Pharmaceutical companies develop new drugs, some dangerous scourges that are naturally replaceable.

> FACT: Bayer concluded that the drug Trasylol caused kidney failure and death. Outside observations conclude the same and Bayer continues to sell the drug resulting in the death of possibly 22,000.

If marijuana were legal, there would be less need for the pharmaceutical corporation's alternatives. There is potential for unknown medical derivatives of pot, for the medicinal value of the plant has not been completely explored. If hemp was legal there would be less need for timber and soon there would be a renewable resource for limitless products made from hemp grown on the side of roads and railroad tracks. And perhaps individuals could grow their own stress reliever.

Pharmaceutical and chemical concoctions are half the problem; the other half of the problem is people's acceptance of them. Some people have to have it, and illegal drug manufacturing supplies them. Marijuana is not enough for many who chose stronger chemicals for a head change. Illegal drug manufacturing puts growing weed in its place. Weed is natural, a slow growing plant that takes time to fruit. Other drugs are not constricted by requirements of a Sun cycle. Chemical concoctions can be cooked up any time of year, becoming the true criminal choice.

Recently, the scourge ruining countless lives, taking the illegal drug market by storm, is crystal methamphetamine. It has all the hype of a new drug, but has been around. Meth will literally rot the brain and body, but was once considered a cure-all. Today, one will probably find that it was conjured in a bathtub laboratory in one desert region or another, for the illicit drug market, but originally is was professionally manufactured and distributed.

Meth was first conjured before WWI. Its power was only a twinkle in the eye of a chemist or two back then. Meth's hay-days weren't until WWII, when it was often called tanker's chocolate. Before WWII, meth was used as a treatment for bronchial conditions, hay fever, epilepsy, narcolepsy and as a simple mood elevator. Japan began to synthesize it in mass quantity and Germany implemented its widespread use.

German tank drivers, pilots and infantry were given meth, often in chocolate. Some reports suggest Hitler took daily meth injections beginning in 1940, others suggest he was simply a casual user. Either way he exhibited the traits of a meth addict - rotting teeth and abnormal, violent behavior.

The Nazis weren't the only fighting force to be issued meth in WWII. Many allied troops were given pep pills to enable them to keep fighting. German soldiers were the most pumped in WWII, their legendary blitzkriegs were fueled by methamphetamine. Some Japanese pilots took meth before kamikaze flights. After WWII Japan had enormous meth stockpiles which created a lucrative market for the Yakuza. In the U.S.A. meth was prescribed for alcoholism and obesity.

During the Vietnam War, meth was used on both sides of the conflict, but troops from the U.S.A. consumed more than their Vietnamese adversaries, and perhaps more meth than all the soldiers of WWII put together. They got the best pharmaceutical pentagon product too, not some bathtub variety. Today it is legally and commonly prescribed for those afflicted with ADD. It is also illegally and easily manufactured for those who choose to sell and/or use the drug that will kill.

No matter how easy weed is to grow, it takes time, it requires a light cycle, as natural things do. Meth can be synthesized and cooked up any day, in a day. Like any chemical undertaking, it is a complex and dangerous endeavor. Risks include explosions and it leaves toxic residue wherever it is manufactured. It is extremely dangerous unless one has the proper training and appropriate equipment, like those at pentagon approved labs. The chronic use of meth causes rapid tooth decay, weight loss, psychosis, depression, agitation, compulsive fascination, panic and irritability. Sinking further into addiction one suffers brain damage, formication, paranoia, delusions, hallucinations and kidney damage.

The chronic use of chronic (marijuana) causes no ills. Several studies have pointed to marijuana as neurodegenerative, while other studies suggest the opposite, that it enables focus. Again, for about ten thousand years, give or take, not one person has ever overdosed on marijuana. Further recent evidence is proving hemp and marijuana can heal a variety of ailments, including types of cancer.

> FACT: Several studies, including one conducted by the British Government conclude that using marijuana is less dangerous than tobacco and alcohol in social harms, physical harm, and addiction.

Marijuana is considered a gateway drug, but there are many other gateways that may not be drug related at all, that lead from marijuana to methamphetamine. Marijuana has little if anything to do with meth, except that both are illegal. Gateways of dire must be jumped through to even consider meth. While marijuana is enjoyed by many people on many occasions who are productive and harmonious members of society.

Despite all the attributes and possibilities, pot was made illegal and has remained so. It is considered dangerous to the very foundations of society. There is nothing people can legitimately point out about marijuana being bad except that it is associated with other worse and harder drugs. Alcohol is an equal gateway drug and several studies suggest that the use of alcohol alone leads to harder drugs, no marijuana necessary. Tobacco is legal and a known killer.

> FACT: On average, over 400,000 people die from tobacco related diseases annually.

Marijuana is a recreational drug, it is a safe medicine and alleviator of pain, but it is illegal. Despite its recreational use being tolerated, people are continuously jailed for marijuana. It is a benign and not harmful, the drugs it is associated with are. The most dangerous aspect of marijuana is that it has been clumped amongst more dangerous narcotics.

Despite the knowledge that hemp could help eliminate our dependency on dirty risky mined fuels, it remains illegal. Despite the fact that it is a food, medicine and industrial wonder it is illegal. Despite the fact that plants could be used in place of paper, wood and plastic, hemp and marijuana are illegal. What if marijuana was legal?

Most people used homegrown fuel until prohibition when farmhouse distilleries became illegal, even if they were used to make alcohol for fuel and not to drink. Many nations during the early 1900s tried to eliminate alcohol. Practically every farmhouse had a distillery for alcohol to use as fuel, to provide light and heat across the U.S.A. For thirteen years distilleries were removed and confiscated in the U.S.A. because of prohibition. Locally distilled alcohol was used to clean wounds, get drunk and light the house.

Marijuana is a gateway drug, like a doorway to opportunity and a steroid for clean industry. Any efficient and clean substance can be manufactured from the wonder plant or drug if one would rather label it that. Virtually anything can be manufactured from pot; food, clothing, shelter, medicine, real materials that could result in real happiness and a head change resulting in perceived happiness.

To effectively harvest the drug, the plant has to produce fruit, without seed. The bud is not suitable for anything industrial. The stalk and seed, the fiber and oil, are not suitable for narcotics. The plants naturally produce the stalk and seed, but it takes special care to make the plant bud. The most stressed and desperate pot fiend would not find solace in smoking hemp or any part of the marijuana plant besides the bud and would only be more stressed attempting to smoke hemp.

The oil corporations directly benefit from the prohibition of marijuana, as it is a harvestable bio-fuel that grows anywhere. No matter how poor the environment, hemp will grow and produce oil. However it takes care and expense to make the marijuana plant bud. Just the fact that we can produce paper from hemp should be enough to change the status quo, but it is capable of producing so much more.

> FACT: Hemp produces about 4 times as much paper, per acre, than trees of twenty year growth on said acre.

Imagine the opportunity that simple legalization of a plant would provide. It is the plant that could save the world or at least national economies and sick people. Enough of it could be grown, without need for more farmland, to cut at oligarchical institutional resource dependence. Hemp could source all paper and fiber, not one more tree would be needed for its pulp. Carbon fuels could be grown instead of mined, produced locally, instead of being extracted by a few strangers.

Marijuana prohibition impedes liberty, yet supposedly it's intended to protect liberty. Its prohibition impedes individuals in many ways and protects institutions. It does not merely affect people who like video games and the sick who lost their appetite, it affects everybody alive. Prohibition of the cultivation and use a valuable plant in nature is sick. The plant is industrial, nutritional, medicinal powerhouse and it's a source of fuel. Perhaps prohibition was not intended to protect society from suffering strange ills in a stupor. Maybe the THC was presented as dangerous, while the fiber and oil were the real dangers. Perhaps marijuana is prohibited because of hemp.

The trinity of liberty provides basic individual rights and is meant to limit institutions. The trinity of liberty was originally intended to limit the power of institutions, but there was infiltration by individuals serving interests other than the common good. Laws, such as alcohol prohibition and marijuana prohibition limited the power of people and provide power to institutional authorities.

If prohibition of hemp and marijuana were designed to protect people, then it would have been legalized due to the criminal activity its illegality now fosters, and for its otherwise benign nature. It would have been legalized for its industrial power and its medicinal derivatives. Marijuana should be legal, much in the same way as alcohol was made legal after it was realized that everyone was going to drink anyway, and it was only supplying criminals with income.

If marijuana were legal, it would fund people and not criminals. The original patriots would have made marijuana legal or at least its cousin hemp, they promoted it. If weed was legal, people would smoke it at cafes and taverns and at least one would be named the Green Draggin' Tavern after the tavern where the big steep was partly planned. In fact it is well documented that the original patriots like George Washington grew hemp and pretty much assuredly marijuana too.

By legalizing the powerful, prevalent and easily grown plant, institutions would lose a foothold in their climb to monopolize. If people started growing their own weed, they might start growing other herbs, non GMO corn and tomatoes, and soon they would stop buying synthetic pain relievers. People would eventually learn how to grow their own better tasting food and locally source bio-fuels for energy. Crazy things take place when people are well-fed and start believing they are happy.

People would seek to become independent instead of reliant. People would seek alternative ways to corporate and institutional presentation of the way things should be. People would look outside their light. Instead of implementing globalization, people would be more inclined to localize. If people could grow their own fuel, they would. If bio-fuels were more prevalent people could locally source their fuel. Hemp grows like a weed, with little care and can be transformed into bio-fuel. This should be reason enough to legalize and endorse it.

The sails and ropes on Christopher Columbus' ships were made from hemp. All the world's navies used to be dependent on hemp fiber making it a crucial crop to grow. Today hemp can be transformed into anything and it grows easily and mightily. Well, it could, if it was legal. Why are people allowed to grow poppy flowers, but are not allowed to grow hemp? Poppy flowers are the same family as opium poppy, just like hemp is like marijuana. Why is a renewable resource criminalized? Why is such a safe plant criminalized?

> "Humanity is asleep, concerned only with what is useless, living in a wrong world. Believing one can excel this is only habit and usage, not religion… Do not prattle before the people of the path, rather consume yourself. You have an inverted knowledge and religion if you are upside down in relation to reality. Man is wrapping his net around himself. A lion bursts his cage asunder." ~Sanai, Teacher of Rumi

$LAVES

> "No evil can result from its (slavery's) inhibition more pernicious than its toleration;…" ~Martin Van Buren

By the early 1800s the Northern States had outlawed slavery while the South had maintained institutionalized racist slavery. The North had adopted an evolved meaning of the trinity of liberty, but at the same time, those in the North enjoyed the fruits of the slave's labors.

Kentucky and Missouri grew tons of hemp, largely grown and processed by slaves. Hemp was, until other sources were found as a better/cheaper alternative, the best material to make rope and other products. The cheaper alternative included other slaves from all over the world who were shipped to the Caribbean.

The Southerners didn't want to change slavery because the status quo was quite suitable; their place in the pyramid was comfortable. They were making loot; there was no way they would start paying people if they could simply keep them as slaves. African people were considered less than Europeans. This made it easier for them to conduct their oppression. If people are dehumanized, made a "them" among an "us", it becomes easy to commit atrocities on them.

Many people, in a loosely organized manner, assisted runaway slaves escape from southern plantations via the Underground Railroad. Slaves were clandestinely clothed, fed and transported north. The slavery institutions were mighty and backed up by most all other institutions. Even though it was legal and institutionalized, and even though people faced prosecution for assisting fugitive slaves, people still helped people escape persecution and oppression.

The law of the land endorsed it, the church sanctioned it, the corporations facilitated it, the majority practiced it, and everyone was profiting from it, but many people knew slavery was wrong. Some people, loosely organized, practiced civil disobedience and subverted the wrongdoing, providing places to hide until they made it out of slave territory.

The Southern States did not want to let go of their slave institutions and pushed for the annexation of Cuba. They wanted Cuba to become a slave state in order for the slave states to have more sway in Congress. After the U.S.A. captured Cuba from Spain, the option for statehood remained on the table, but ultimately Cuba was made independent; except for the forty-five square mile U.S.A. Navy Base, at Guantanamo Bay.

Civil disobedience is a rebellious and forgivable act, but nonetheless illegal. It is a crime, but not a sin. Civil disobedience causes no actual harm to anyone. It is illegal, but may not be wrong and may be right thing to do. It is a punishable offense that makes some call for a lynching and others appeal for forgiveness. It is a criminal act that later may be recognized as heroic. Only the most zealous racists believe that those that participated in the Underground Railroad were not heroic.

FACT: In the south, 1850, a slave cost the equivalent of about $40,000. Today, the average slave costs $100.

Slavery was overt, legal, cultivated, regulated, maintained and taxed. Today it is covert, illegal, mostly unseen, unquestioned and highly profitable. The costs of the slaves reflect the wrongdoing turned clandestine. Since it is illegal, there is no liability and therefore slavers invest minimally into the livelihoods of the enslaved, and care little for basics like providing healthcare. There are so many desperate people in the world today, that slaves are more easily replaceable.

Criminal elements conduct the wrongdoing and people think there is no one to blame except these phantoms. Well, someone, somewhere down the line is directly profiting from slaves, child labor and exploited workers. Someone or something is profiting somewhere. Forget about a global war on drugs or a global war on terror. What about a global war on slavery? Slavery is a horrible act, it isn't limited by borders, it happens at the Firestone Rubber plantation in Liberia as well as in Houston and New York.

There is no army that can fight slavery, and violence cannot stop it. Violence maintains it. Just as no army can fight terror, no army can fight slavery. A global war on terror only marches armies about fermenting that very act. It is impossible to wage war to prevent war, but it is possible to stop both war and slavery without violence, stop supporting it.

Throughout recorded time, slavery and exploitation, has been instituted through tolerations of the "us and them" mentality. Localization does not manifest slavery, locals are dependent on one another. Locals conduct distant trade, just not expansion. Slaves and exploited workers are commonplace. In 1996, the fashion line branded by Kathie Lee Gifford was found to be manufactured in China using exploited child labor. The UN estimates as many as 200,000 people from West and Central Africa are sold into slavery every year.

Today, slavery is covert and clandestine, but the shackles and the servitude are the same. Today, slavery is totally covert or partially hidden by fences and terminology. Today, slavery is called indentured servitude, bonded labor, debt bondage, or human trafficking, all equate to slavery.

FACT: There are dozens of cases of diplomats exploiting foreign workers in New York and Washington DC. Lauro Baja Jr., a UN Diplomat, was accused of making his indentured servant work 120 hours per week.

Institutions and individuals generate enormous wealth through their slaves, worldwide. If people can successfully boycott and change apartheid South Africa, people can boycott corporations or other institutions that profit from slavery and exploitation. But first the slavers must be identified, questions must be asked.

Profiting from slavery is comparable to profiting from prisoner labor. People in jail are most likely there for a reason, however contrived, and people in slavery are bonded as innocents. The similarity is that both are capitalized on. Prison labor is perhaps seen as opportunity or distraction to criminals, but slaves face the same conditions as imprisoned workers and are innocents. Slaves may face worse conditions than state prisoners for there is at least some regulation here and there. Whatever it is called, wherever it is done, captors profit off of captives.

When it costs the American taxpayers to jail criminals or fund war, it profits corporations. Bombing, enslavement and imprisonment are big business and where there is big business there are powerful interests. When people are jailed, bombed, enslaved and exploited some institutions, some individuals, here or there, get paid.

FACT: Average inmate costs about $40,000 per year in U.S.A. The U.S.A. jails more citizens per capita than anywhere else in the world. $2 billion tax dollars spent annually to house inmates on marijuana charges in U.S.A.

Two billion spent is two billion earned. Somewhere down the line corporations and other institutions are directly profiting off of people's degradation and incarceration. It is no great mystery, in this day and age of digital information and tracking, as to who directly profits from the prohibition of marijuana or other unjust laws. Phone companies charge exorbitant fees to place calls from prison, cafeteria suppliers make a fortune, construction companies, lawyers, judges, guards, chain manufacturers, all make fortunes from prohibition. There is profit, but there is no fruit, no harvest.

For some, incarceration is an acceptable punishment for the safety of society, but there are others in prison who do not warrant extended incarceration. Criminals who conduct acts as barbaric as slavery, murder or rape deserve incarceration or worse, facing Hammurabi's code. People in prison for exchanging marijuana should not be imprisoned. If marijuana were legal, the criminal element would not touch it. Criminals are attracted to it because it is contraband.

Some events are so vicious and callous that there is no way to gauge how wrong they may be. These events pertain to slavery, murder, violence, and exploitation. The biggest criminals though, remain free. Overt crime is vicious and should be reprimanded. Calculated covert viciousness should be reprimanded as well, but is often subtle and goes unnoticed. Nuanced wrongs go unnoticed without questions.

FACT: Monsanto's BGH is banned in the European Union and Canada. WalMart, Kroger, Dean Foods, Costco, Starbucks declared they will no longer sell milk with BGH. It is FDA Approved and has been shown to accelerate cancer growth.

The worst criminal act in the history of the U.S.A. was the largest terrorist attack as well. 9/11 was the biggest crime and was filmed and mostly broadcasted live. It was a horror show of fire and collapse. It was chaotic destruction of life and structure, in mathematical neatness, in downtown Manhattan. There were criminals involved in this mass murder who should be punished.

That day the defense system of the most powerful nation on Earth was subverted and made useless. Thousands died. Following the attack on the World Trade Center, the stock market took a plunge. American Airlines and United Airlines stock especially sunk. For days after, no planes flew in the U.S.A., except fighter jets and the planes that escorted the Bin Laden family out of the U.S.A.

In the days and weeks leading up to the attack, trades increased in airline stocks, as though investors were wagering that their stock would fall. Other companies experienced spikes in such trading in the days prior as well. This deserves questioning, but the media does not investigate. Originally this was announced to be a crucial part of the investigation, for it seemed some people knew ahead of time and hedged their bets accordingly. They knew, and had no problem advancing through their elite knowledge, possibly. Corporate investors and some corporations profited directly from the horrific terrorist attack. That's a fact, coincidence or otherwise.

FACT: September 6 and 7, 2001 the Chicago Board Options Exchange handled over 4,500 put options for United Airlines stock. September 10, 2001 over 4500 put options on American Airlines stock. September 10, 2001 call options increase six fold for Raytheon – manufacturer of patriot missiles, marketer of war.

FACT: Convar, a German firm hired to retrieve data from damaged hard drives found there was a spike of trading in the minutes prior to the attack. 110

2.5 million!? Unclaimed? Anyone would shrug their shoulders and proclaim dumb luck, but would still claim their earnings. They would feel some remorse about their lucky profit, happening to make money that way, but would claim it. Most anyone would claim it, that is, anyone uninvolved with 9/11. If one got rich with

prior knowledge of an event as nasty as 9/11 and thought there was a possibility of being caught, it would be easy to forget about millions. How can they bust people for downloading music illegally, but can't straighten this out?

It is questionable when relevant questions go unasked. When known knowns are unconsidered, there are likely considerations or reasons for partial elimination of actuality in presentation. Whether it is an ancient Biblical omission or deletion of portions of current events, when key elements of actuality are not investigated, there is likely a reason.

> "Crisis is opportunity riding a dangerous wind." ~Chinese proverb

There are many ways one may be enslaved. Physical kidnapping and forceful work is the most overt and obvious. One may also be a slave in daily physical actions and one can be held captive by instigated perceptions. One may be held down by chains or held down by mind frame. The chains have a powerful hold, but it is easy to know that one is shackled. When one is held by thoughts and fears, one might not know that one is captured. The chains of covert capture are equally restraining, however disguised by mere mindset and continued restrictive thinking.

It's a mad world, a world immersed in oligarchical collectivism. One of the biggest problems humanity faces today, a problem of our own design, is the energy conundrum. Energy extraction, facilitation and production is causing the environmental destruction the world now faces. The burning of petrol and nuclear fires is causing environmental destruction. Are these the most optimal energy sources? No. They are the most secure energy sources for oligarchical collectivism, the pyramidal status quo of the few over the many.

The oligarchical collectivism of the energy industry can be seen in the subsidization of the most oligarchical formats and the elimination of systems which benefit the many as opposed to those that benefit the few. Coal, petrol, natural gas as well as the minerals required to run nuclear power generation experiments are all extracted, refined and controlled by the few and all endanger the many. They all require oligarchical collectivism, the control of the few over the many to work. Whereas other sources of energy, be they biofuel or solar power, would empower the many. The same goes with corporate agriculture. Ecosystems and economical systems would thrive more if there were not a few big agricultural corporations, but many smaller operations.

The world is based on and operates by way of oligarchical collectivism, making many slaves and most everyone slaves to the game. All politics is designed to reward the few at the cost of the many. Whenever there is some sort of inner national uprising, you can guarantee it's because the majority are weary of the burden of oligarchical collectivism. This institutional compartmentalization or oligarchical collectivism is not necessarily determinative of corruption only highly likely to be corrupt. The corrupt status quo is everywhere, local and global, oligarchical collectivism. The oligarchical ties need to be undone. To investigate, simply remember Lord Acton's Rule, ask who benefits, and take note as to who can't be questioned.

Only when you know what the problem is can a solution be extrapolated. Only when you know of fire can you utilize it or put it out. The word pyramid means fire in the middle. Only when one understands the history of the pyramid system can one understand the present status quo and do something about it. We didn't start the fire, but we can do something about it.

Arthur Young presented a four part theory to the learning process in his ideas. He penned The Reflexive Universe and noted a fourfold structure or basis throughout the entire universe. As far as learning to understand the fire of oligarchical collectivism we were all born into, Arthur Young extrapolated it best in his presentation of a four step process to understanding, reflective one level of the inner idiot, zealot, elitist and patriot within us all.

> "…becomes apparent if we think of a cycle of action as a learning cycle. The learning cycle has four phases. It begins with (1) a spontaneous or unconscious action, such as a child reaching out and touching a hot stove. The pain causes (2) immediate withdrawal, or unconscious reaction, followed by (3) an awareness that the stove caused pain, a conscious reaction, followed by (4) future avoidance of hot stoves, a conscious action or control. Thus the child learns. If the experience is not learned, the cycle repeats until it is, after which the child moves to a higher level involving more complex or longer-term cycles, always incorporating what he or she has learned and building a hierarchy of automatic reactions controlled by the brain.
>
> Consciousness is always at the leading edge of that growth process, always pressing on. This lays the basis for higher consciousness. There is a consciousness appropriate for each level of interaction, from that of nuclear particles to that of the higher organisms, and there is no reason to suppose that it stops there." ~Arthur Young

"It is important to point out that the learning cycle includes consciousness and action. No matter how expert we become, we still have something to learn, and that learning or consciousness comes only after an exploratory action has exposed some error. We can then rectify the action and get on with it. The physicist may not be good at philosophy, but he or she can at least make mistakes and possibly learn from them. The philosopher has no way to recognize whether a mistake has been made. The vocabulary of science has shown us that intention has a proper place in the formalism of physics, and by emphasizing the cycle of action it becomes possible to obtain a model for the growth of consciousness, and with it the evolution of life." ~From the essay Science, Spirit and the Soul, by Arthur Young

We, as a global collective of individuals have got to start putting the importance of individuals above the institutions, otherwise institutions will roll right over us all. Otherwise oligarchical collectivism will continue to consume.

Refuse, resist, relax and rethink. Take conscious action and discontinue support of corrupt oligarchical collectivism as much as possible. Conscious action in politics is peaceful and even compassionate resistance to oligarchical collectivism. Four is universally recognized as symbolic for completion as represented in the four forms of arithmetic. Beyond that there are four aspects of self; the mental, physical, spiritual and the natural. To instigate and raise consciousness, awareness of the four aspects is crucial, followed by building on the aspects.

The first step to raising consciousness is development of the mental aspect. Consciousness requires awareness. In order to increase knowledge of self, one must increase knowledge of what is happening in the world. Learning what is happening leads to awareness. It is important to expand your field of view as to what is happening in the world, as well as focus your field of view inward. Consider things great and small, far and wide, seen and unseen, known and unknown.

A specific contemplation which broadens one's spectrum of consideration is the Analogy of the Divided Line. Socrates divided information into four parts. Socrates noted there is the tangible, like a tree (DE) and there are reflections of the tangible (CD), like the tree's reflection in a pond. There is also the intangible like numbers (BC) and finally the smallest portion is reflections of the intangible (AB), algebraic equations for instance. The largest part of the set is the tangible and the smallest, most elusive part is the reflections of the intangible. Consideration of the four types of information expands ones awareness, consciousness. (more on the Divided Line later.)

The second step to raising consciousness is developing the physical aspect. Learning about diet and practicing a mostly vegetarian, if not totally vegetarian diet makes one literally and figuratively, physically lighter. When one learns about a predominantly vegetarian diet one might come across information pertaining to bioaccumulative toxins from industry. When one learns about the institutionalization and industrial monopolization of our plants to the point of tweaking DNA with other living things, one will want to go organic.

Some yogis practice holding one arm above their head, as an exercise in commitment, for many years. When westerners take on the training it is said they only have to do it for one year. Being that a westerner has a shorter attention span the same lesson might be learned in a shorter period of time, of course it will seem longer. One form of yoga, which was not designed for a short attention span, but is accommodating nonetheless, just so happens to be a series of movements that takes about fifteen minutes and will build the physical aspect. The Five Tibetan Rites of Rejuvenation is a five movement series repeated twenty-one times, with coordinated breathing, followed by meditation. Research and read about the movements before attempting. Do the Five Tibetans every day for a month or two, as a test of commitment and to see how development of the physical can assist you.

The third step to raising consciousness is integration of the now improved mental and physical. This integration enhances the intangible spiritual aspect of oneself. Commitment to developing the mind and body transmutes into the development of the spirit. Building on the spiritual sinew requires more meditation. The Five Tibetans is integrative and meditative, but there are other ways to meditate, the pinnacle level being to live meditatively. Meditation of the highest order is perhaps the meditation which is practiced most frequently and in most compassionate terms. To meditate be calmly aware of the breath. The four parts of breath are inhalation, pause full, exhalation, pause empty. There are standing, lying, walking and sitting meditations. Mediation leads to intuitive awareness, which increases and reaction time, whether working or playing.

The fourth step to raising consciousness, after developing the mental, physical and spiritual within, is willing oneself positively upon the natural world. After one develops inside one demonstrates one's will upon the outside world. The fourth stage to raising consciousness is to will oneself, from within, upon the outside world. When one has developed oneself within, one can practice influencing and imparting will on the outside world in a positive manner.

According to Arthur Schopenhauer, a German philosopher born in 1788, who authored the book On The Fourfold Root of the Principal of Sufficient Reason in 1813 there are four classes of human reasoning; becoming, knowing, being and willing. The highest order of human reasoning is willing, but one has to develop the consciousness to do so.

Institutions simply promote or prohibit. State institutions are essentially martial institutions with martially enforced laws, there are essentially four types of states. This understanding can be applied to understand both nation states as well as inside mental states. This metaphor is the cross reference of war and peace, by way of promotion and prohibition. It is the metaphor of thinking and being.

The four states can be applied to both individuals and institutions. One state is of peace, promotes peace and only prepares for peace. The second state is of war, promotes war and only prepares for war. Another state is at war, promotes war and yet is ready for peace. And the last state is at peace, promotes peace and yet is ready for self-defense. One can imagine being in one of these states, both internally and externally, and realize which is the more balanced and healthy state.

What do institutions promote and prohibit? Why has the United States transformed from a state of the fourth type, one that is at peace, promotes peace and yet is prepared for defense into a state that is at war, promotes war and prepares for war. The United States of America is being taken over by institutions and institutionalization, promoting and preparing for war on people outside our nation with the biggest military budget in the world and on people inside our nation with the biggest prison business in the world. Strive to be at peace, to promote peace, and to always be ready to defend myself, others and peace. The more there is peace the less there is slavery. In order for there to be world peace, all the world needs a piece, not just the oligarchies.

INSTITUTIONAL PATRIOTISM

Institutional patriotism is impossible, however it is possible for institutions to claim it, and they often do. Institutions are not individuals, they are machines and machines cannot be patriots. Institutional patriotism was exemplified after 9/11. Because the U.S.A. was attacked, institutions of war justified unquestioning support, presented as patriotism. Institutional patriotism can be implemented to accomplish goals that are idiotic, zealous or elitist, not patriotic. If one believes war portrayed for peace is possible then maybe one can believe institutional patriotism, but neither is possible..

After wars it normally becomes apparent some institutions took advantage of situations in war. While they claim unquestioning support for the troops, they simply manipulate the situation for all its worth without question. Institutions support war because it is profitable, not because it is right.

Institutions present all sorts of bold statements and slogans that sound like genuine straight talk, in part because of phonetics. Words that seem to make sense because of sharp delivery may not be sensible; they may be institutionalized statements, flat doublespeak. Institutions use powerful words that are intended to silence questions. Quick snappy rhetoric, tones tested over time may sound true and assuring, but may not be.

It is easy to put negativity into short, slamming slogans. It is less easy to put positive notions plainly and bluntly. Peace or else does not work. Condensed sayings that simplify the complex often are accepted as boiled down brilliance. Words may very well be luminous, but quick snippets of wit must always be questioned, especially when therein is negativity. Full explanations are required for brilliance, and reasoning for murder and violence cannot ever be brilliance.

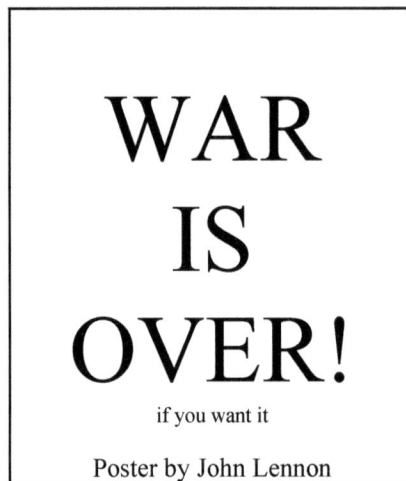

WAR
IS
OVER!
if you want it

Poster by John Lennon

John Lennon was able to scribe snappy rhetoric promoting peace, maybe that's why the FBI watched him. Institutions employ wordsmiths to better their presentation of their version of the truth. While other institutions, like the FBI, counter and monitor independent poets and wordsmiths like John Lennon. Musicians and poets have been especially watched since the days of blues and bebop and are still watched today. Now anyone might be watched.

The administration of George II claimed to be conservative, but their actions were anything but. In fact, they were more accurately radical; they pursued war and encouraged government spending on drastic changes to the laws of the land. They flipped world perspective of the U.S.A. from great benefactor to great detractor.

If an individual or institution attempts to convince people that there is only one patriotic choice, or one accurate description, that itself is not patriotic. The first part of the First Amendment ensures the right to question in any form, any situation, with any verbiage. The original mandate of liberty, is open minded questioning.

When choice is limited, mindset is limited as well. Institutional construction limits options, when there are two opposing choices presented in a situation, they both likely lead to the same outcome. Duality serves institutions and allows them to present themselves as upholders of patriotism by playing on the "us' and "them" mentality with either-or options. This process instigates the proposed lesser evil.

One has to be tricked not to question for it goes against human nature. It should be a quality inclination to question the delivery of institutional information, especially when patriotism is hailed. There are alternatives to the either-or situations presented and instigated. Humans are developmental; people change and evolve. Institutions maintain to the point of stagnation, expansion is their only static. The curiosity of others eventually eliminates rigidly structured institutions with progression. When there is little curiosity, development or change takes longer.

The trick is to convince people they are acting on their own behalf when actually it is an institutional agenda. The trick is to make people think that questioning would make one unpatriotic or wrong, but questioning is never wrong. It is the horror of perspective that institutions thrive on. All people want to do the right thing. People all want the right answer, unless institutionalized, unless burdened by tolerations. Institutions convince people they are doing the right thing when they are only doing their thing.

If people question Israel for the apparent systematic degradation of the indigenous individuals in Palestine, they are labeled anti-Semites. If people question the murderous bombings of innocent civilian Israelis, they are labeled Zionists. If people question their own country's national armament, they are labeled akin to the enemy. If individuals question institutions and how they are destroying water, they themselves become questioned. Character, age, inexperience, education or personal irrelevance are labeled and their questions are rejected, unanswered. The questions of individuals are belittled by institutions by the belittling individuals. When people question established institutions, they are labeled and questioned as crazies or malcontents, anything other than curious or observant.

FACT: Nearly 40% of the rivers and over 40% of the lakes in the U.S.A. are too polluted for fishing, swimming, or aquatic life as of 2008. 2.5 percent of the water on Earth is fresh water, most of which is frozen.

Some people still believe that global warming is not man made. The fact that the planet has heated up before is the basis for the argument. Who can say for sure? Everything changes. Currently the Earth is undergoing desertification due to the ubiquitous exhaust and waste of people or it may be just getting a little warmer due to a shift in the output of energy from the Sun. Perhaps the burning of fossil fuels is not the cause of global warming. Mars has supposedly been heating up correspondingly with Earth.

The consequences and conditions of the petrolithic era threaten existence through global pollution. Global warming is a result of global pollution and threatens access to fresh drinking water and clean air. The fact that waters are degraded or destroyed is reason enough to take action, regardless of whether the planet is heating up. But it is not just water, it is not just air; all the elements are negatively influenced by global pollution. Global pollution is irrefutable, the most remote desert and distant isle is permeated and negatively altered in the petrolithic era.

There is no natural phenomenon that can explain the pollution of creeks, rivers, lakes and oceans. It is because of petrolithic era pollution. It is because of the nuclear age. Pollution is manmade. The glaciers of the world, what's left of them, high atop mountain ranges far from the pollution's sources, contain pollution. Smog settles thick in city valleys and is dispersed the world over, reducing air quality. Radioactive particulate and gaseous pollution concentrates and swirls and settles in the most remote regions and drains into the deepest wells. If the next ice age froze the Earth next year, the ice would be poisoned and polluted. Is this not enough reason to stop? Must total global environmental destruction occur before people question? Must our existence be questioned before we question the way we exist? In order for oligarchical institutional arrangement to continue, conformation is mandatory, questions must go unasked.

QUOTE: I think life on Earth is at an increased risk of being wiped out by disaster, such as sudden global warming, nuclear war or a genetically engineered virus or other dangers… I think that the human race has no future if it does not go into space. ~Stephen Hawking

Maybe Stephen will volunteer to take a little trip to further explore the cosmos on a one way trip beyond the asteroid belt. Perhaps he could text message the people of the Earth as he delved deeper into the cold void of space. Surely, soon he would soon scribe something like, "It sucks out here. Save the Earth!"

There are numerous documented facts about manmade pollution being detrimental to people, plants and animals. There are a likely slew of dangerous unknowns as well. Just the knowns, and what is believed highly probable, is reason enough to stop, if only briefly, if only partially, in order to change. Global warming is not the issue, rather it is global pollution and environmental destruction.

What about the unknown results of the known substances? Monsanto has lied to people before, yet they are in charge of GMO foods consumed by people and animals. Corporations lied about tobacco, some speculate corporations are lying about the safety of personal cellular devices. No one in their right mind would risk destroying or degrading food for profit, institutions however are in fact, no one.

Just the facts without speculation reveal that there is no vast emptiness to pile waste without it returning. The lakes, seas and oceans can no longer dilute waste. The expanse of Earth is not limitless. When enough shit is pumped into the air and water, eventually the air and water are compromised.

If everyone is captivated and convinced of the competency of institutions within the status quo, merely asking questions becomes dissent. Questions allow the evolution of ideas. Everything benefits and betters from the exchange of questions and information. Institutions seek to maintain, questions seek progression. What would the world be like if at some time people no longer asked, "Why?"

The institutionalized interpret questioning institutional agendas as confrontational. It is, but only when the institutions cannot answer without exposing exploitations. Questioning is always simple, only sometimes there are complicated answers. Questioning institutions often reveals selfish modus operandi, so they can't divulge the whole story without negatively impacting their power.

Most people, in most institutions do not believe they are actively performing malice when they operate. Many believe they are bettering themselves and their surroundings, through institutions. Some are, sometimes, yet most carry on without stopping and questioning, paradigm after paradigm. When ignorance is prevalent, institutions are able to say one thing and do another.

OIL AND WATER DON'T MIX

Many of the ponds, creeks, rivers and lakes that one dare not drink from or swim in today, were once clean and refreshing. Some waterways have always been poisoned, like those with arsenic or other harmful minerals. In natural environments, these waterways tended to be obvious, for instance there would be no plant life around a water source that contained arsenic. In the petrolithic era many once clean waterways are now polluted by alarming poisons and overrun with promoted bacteria growth. There have been some improvements to some polluted waterways, but improvements to the point that it is less like sewage, the overall quality of water has been severely compromised.

"The time is always right to do what is right." ~Martin Luther King Jr.

Clean water should be the primal, basic glory of society. Every person needs water every day; everything else that people need requires water. It is in the best interest of everyone to have clean water and yet, water is subjugated for dollar. Water is the most necessary element, it is the greatest resource and yet, it is a diluter of feces, chemicals, radioactive, toxic waste. As a species, humans have had the most negative impact on Earth's ecosystems and yet are the only species capable of purposefully benefiting the ecosystem as its protector.

> "The Hudson River, right here in New York is a great story…" ~John Forbes Kerry, Interview

It's a great story alright, but not in how greatly it has been cleaned. The great story of the Hudson River is all Americana. The story normally begins with arrival of Europeans, like Giovanni da Verranzano who sailed into New York Harbor in 1524, but for millennia the Mahican people and other tribes flourished along Mahicanituck River. The people from the area are often simply called Algonquin. They hunted and farmed in the region developing fortified settlements and camps. They also warred variously with other tribes, as did the Iroquois and others.

When the Europeans arrived the natives welcomed them and traded with them. Animal skins were prized in Europe and the Algonquin received tools, muskets and blankets in exchange. They also were sickened by various germs they had never been exposed to before via blankets. The natives suffered dramatic consequences from various sicknesses brought by the influx of Europeans, many of whom came seeking fortune in the skin trade.

The European newcomers represented various interests and made ties and treaties with natives, who also had various interests. The natives and newcomers battled on behalf of numerous institutions, for various reasons and interests. Sides shifted, divisions were amplified, resulting in a mish mash of backstabbing and resource grabbing to the ultimate detriment of native peoples. The Mahican people fought on the side of the Colonists during the French and Indian War and the American Revolutionary War, but were ultimately dispossessed of their land along the river.

On September 11, 1609 Henry Hudson, began his discovery voyage upriver, noting thousands of natives on the riverbanks. He journeyed from the mouth of the Hudson past Manhattan Island and Indian Point. He sailed all the way to present day Albany where he turned around. He was hired by the Dutch East India Company, with orders to find a passage to the Pacific and Far East. The Hudson River was no such passage, and there was none. The European Empires had developed sea lanes and ports worldwide that helped them gain and maintain global control. They were intent on finding a shortcut through the continent that could expand their monopolization.

On failing to find a waterway west, Henry returned home. Later, Henry sailed to the new world on another voyage, this time employed by The British East India Company. On this voyage in June 1611, Henry was forced into a small boat and set adrift by his mutinous crew into the cold Hudson Bay, never to be seen or heard from again.

Many Dutch immigrants followed Henry to New York and as the legend has it, in 1626 the Dutch traded trinkets with the locals for Manhattan Island. The Dutch apparently bought the island from a tribe that resided in Brooklyn and not Manhattan. The tribe didn't own the land, so they took the trinkets in exchange for their neighbor's land. The Brooklyn Bridge wasn't the first property sold by someone who wasn't the owner. The tribe thought they pulled a fast one, but they had no idea who and what they were dealing with.

The people who actually lived on Manhattan would never have traded it. But the Dutch didn't care, as long as they could say that so-and-so traded it with someone in the general vicinity, it didn't matter if they didn't technically own it. A deal is a deal; it only mattered if the rest of the European institutions would respect the Dutch deed.

Before 1609, the locals thrived in the region for perhaps 12,000 years, then the Dutch began to settle the area and the locals began to die from germs they had never been exposed to. Slanted land deals and subverted treaties continued over time and continent, but one of the first and most famous was the purchase of Manhattan Island, at the Mouth of the Hudson River.

During the Revolutionary War, the Hudson River was an essential waterway for both sides. George Washington realized that control of the Hudson River was strategically essential. Using cunning eternal and military technology of the day, George had a huge chain made and strung across the Hudson River near West Point to prevent British passage and transport. A garrison was first occupied in 1788 at West Point and today there is the U.S.A. Military Academy at West Point. West Point is the oldest continuously operated military post in the U.S.A.

War ended, the Great Chain was unlinked, cities and industries were established on the Hudson. By the early 1900s much of the Hudson River was more stool than pool. Untreated sewage was continuously flushed directly into the River. This was a normal practice everywhere from Flushing, New York to Lake Tahoe, California. New Yorkers noticed the problem with the shit steep in deadly cholera outbreaks. After centuries of pumping untreated sewage into the Hudson River, people were now immersed in and sickened by it.

Industry and its shit were not noticed until later. The Hudson River, its tributaries and waters at its mouth were lined on both sides with everything from textile factories to oil refineries. Today there is a nuclear power plant on the Hudson River just outside Manhattan, Indian Point Energy Center. Indian Point began operation in 1962 as the first commercial nuclear power plant in the U.S.A. It is the same GE design as the reactors in Fukushima.

> FACT: Newtown Creek is the most polluted body of water in the U.S.A. The Creek separates Queens and Brooklyn and flows into the East River along Manhattan. Exxon Mobil spilled 17 million gallons of oil underground at a refinery near the Creek's shore. It was noticed decades after the fact, some fifty years since the spill and it continuously seeps into the creek. Along with the oil pond there is an abnormal level of heavy metals and an assortment of other toxins.

They somewhat cleaned up the spill in Valdez, Alaska, yet they let the people in the Five Boroughs deal with their mess for fifty years, and counting. ExxonMobil knew they lost 17 million gallons of crude. Perhaps they assumed that people would forget or that it was benign and would simply dissolve into the ground from where it came. Perhaps they thought they could get away with it.

Either way, in the petrolithic era it doesn't matter. They did it and they let it sit there until someone questioned it. They are guilty of profiting at the cost of the environment and people. Whether intent on, or ignorant of, the result is the same. From 1946 until 1977 GE polluted the Hudson River with well over a million pounds of PCBs, chemicals used in manufacturing. Because of this and other pollution, the fish in many sections of the Hudson River are not safe to eat to this day. GE participated in the destruction of over two hundred miles of the three hundred and fifteen mile long river and intends to clean it.

In 1994 dredging, excavation and disposal of toxic metals began by Marathon Battery Co. of Putnam County. The factory was built by the Army Corps of Engineers and originally worked strictly on military contracts, but soon they made commercial batteries too. East Foundry Cove, near West Point was one of the most polluted places on the planet.

Between 1990 and 1994 six million pounds of toxic chemicals were released into the Hudson and this pollution continues. Now there are permits and allowances of pollution. Corporate institutions can pollute no more than was being polluted in the past. There are now tradable permission slips to continue pollution.

If an institution pollutes less, it can sell the remaining allotment of pollution to another institution. If an institution pollutes more, it simply buys more allowances or pays fines. If corporations use clean energy and eliminating their pollution credit, they take those credits and sell them, year to year.

This is no silly New York mandate. The system is the same when it comes to air emissions and many such pollutants dictated by the Clean Air Act of 1990. GE normally leads the way in toxic chemicals discharged into the Hudson. Sewage from the Five Boroughs is mostly treated now, but when it rains, shit pours. There is always overflow which goes untreated. On top of that there are regular sewage releases purposely, negligently and accidentally.

In the Bronx, facing Northern Manhattan, there is a famous rock, the Columbia University Rock or C Rock. People used to dive off of it into a creek aside from the Hudson River. It's about fifty feet high, but nowadays the depth of the funk is more frightening than the height of the leap. The story of the Hudson is a great story, and it is a great River, but not the great River it once was. It is an extraordinary River, but its toxicity is all too typical and ordinary.

In Boston, it wasn't until 1952 that they began treating sewage. Sewage from Boston and the surrounding cities was pumped directly into Boston Harbor for decades, into the 1980s. At the bottom of Boston Harbor, perhaps alongside remnants of the big steep, is a layer of sediment on the ocean floor, a layer of contaminants, heavy metals, industrial waste, petrol and poop that is perhaps too dangerous to dredge. It took a lawsuit from someone who went for a walk on the beach and stepped in untreated sewage to enforce the original Clean Air and Water Act, years after legislation. Today, Boston Harbor and the Hudson River are cleaner than they were in the 20th century. But neither is great.

> FACT: Currently each Spring, the season symbolic for life anew, the waters from the Mississippi River containing nitrogen and other chemicals turns around 7,000 square miles of the Gulf of Mexico into a dead zone. Fertilizers and animal excrement are the main cause. Dead zones, where no oxygen is produced, exist worldwide, but one of the largest zones emanates from the Mississippi River.

Rampant global pollution is the consequence of the continuation of the status quo. It is the result of individuals allowing industry to be openly industrious. The outcome of institutional policy and decision-making pollutes the waterways, air and entire Earth. Individuals make unpredictable decisions, but institutions make outrageously detrimental decisions that are presented as noble. The status quo is always presented as new and improved, but it is the same manifestation with a different wrap. They call it using carbon credit instead of dumping waste.

The danger is not necessarily the people lacking responsibility and making poor decisions. The real danger is the people lacking information and having information kept from them, so they cannot act responsibly or make informed decisions if they wanted to.

> "A republic, if you can keep it."
> ~Benjamin Franklin, in response to a woman who asked about government.

The dangers of uninformed mob rule exist, but these dangers have not manifested like the dangers of the informed mob currently ruling. The U.S.A. is a republic, with specific, lofty ideas that must be upheld for the republic just to maintain itself. When certain ideals of the republic are suspended for certain institutions, what makes the republic valuable and functional in the first place is lost. Equality and liberty are broken when all are not treated equally.

The U.S.A. is a republic that allows for mob rule. Not necessarily the mob of the majority, but groups that propagate ideas. Such lobbyists work for organizations that infiltrate the halls and lobbies of democracy and promote ideas to influence the country's course. This allows for change, some good and some bad. Though there are many foundations and groups set up to endorse and promote agenda, they are by their foundation, exclusive and likely elitist. Many institutions push for more pollution in order to profit, but they don't put it like that. Institutions constantly lobby for stability, maintenance and selfishness.

> …when a long train of abuses and usurpations, pursuing the same object, evinces a design to reduce them under despotism, it is their right, it is their duty, to throw off such government and to provide new guards for their future security.
> ~Declaration of Independence

This was and is a whole world of treacherous, clandestine, institutionalized criminals. They existed whether they were of governmental backing or completely underground. The only institutional power in the past was governmental; all other institutions were ornamental arms. In 1776, every company of substantial influence and significance was chartered; ordained institutions that functioned on behalf of kings. Some of the kings' institutions were criminals, like the privateers for instance. Such company criminals trounced the world, criminals abroad and heroes in their own land, never seeing prison from behind bars.

The original patriots were stunningly aware of the corruption and swaying power of giant, international corporations. They could see that interconnected and intertwined institutions could completely dominate them. They saw that church, state and corporate should be separated to prevent total institutional control and exploitation, oligarchical collectivism.

In the early days of the U.S.A., corporations from one state were prevented from conducting business in another. Localization was and is sensible to people, but not to institutions. It is easier to grind people, to leech from them, when they are beyond a state line and conceptualized as different, a "them" among an "us."

As government increasingly uses outside sources to complete the very functions of government, those institutions that work on behalf of the people's government, must be held accountable as the government would be or should be. While the corporations find duplicate, excessive and questionable charges to bill the government, the people pay. Institutions, corporate and otherwise, use the system to override people in their attempts to profit, promote and monopolize.

Institutions easily steer on the cusp of legality, on a course without concern for morality. As long as they can get away with it, they will do it. As long as it is profitable to agenda or wallet, they will do it.

The most vile orchestrations of government are increasingly privatized. The means for war are increasingly supplied via corporate ventures. The operations of prisons are increasingly privatized as well. Corporations exist that are solely interested in profiting off of imprisonment and war. If these endeavors experience growth, many other sectors and the overall quality of life, experience decline. If there are private profit concerns embedded within such stately functions, people get ridden and treaded on.

The operations of war and imprisonment should be kept away from corporate institutions. None should profit from imprisoning individuals or from war. The concerns of war and imprisonment should never be based on the dollar, but when privatized they are.

Weapons manufacturers and government contractors always hail themselves as patriotic as they triumphantly march in unison with martial operation. They eagerly proclaim their benevolence while they rob Uncle Sam and all his nephews and nieces blind. The use of corporate facilities to perform government functions is on the rise and intertwined institutions monopolize. Another form of outsourcing that is proliferating, is that of military intelligence. The government spies on people and also hires outside corporations to gather information on individuals.

> FACT: In 2007 Smartronix Inc. won a $60 million contract with the Marine Corps. The corporation will provide network operations support and information management. In 2005 L-3 Communications Subsidiaries, after investigations into supplying faulty equipment for security on U.S.A border with Mexico and in Iraq, were awarded a $426.5 million intelligence contract in Iraq.

Institutions of war are making a killing from making killing. They are making billions and we, the people, pay them. Not only is it lucrative to war, but it is also lucrative to take liberties with information, spy on people and put them in holes. Policy promotes spending in certain aspects. Policies of war, imprisonment and information gathering are being heavily invested in. These investments put restrictions on individuals and benefit intertwined institutions.

The outsourced corporate soldiers on the battlefield and those who make lists and listen in on phone calls have little or no oversight or accountability. In all likelihood those on the battlefield hold themselves accountable to laws they are subject to and no more. In Iraq, enlisted soldiers are accountable on one level and the hired guns, corporate soldiers are practically not accountable at all. War is active, sanctioned murder.

Institutions expect people's support. They expect to be honored with merit for the minutest acts of benevolence. They expect to be held lofty for presenting great goals through dire means, despite any vile results. They expect to be forgiven for the most outlandish, patterned exploits. In 1870, John D. Rockefeller founded Standard Oil. He became famous for giving away dimes and for becoming one the wealthiest individuals through monopolization of the oil business.

> FACT: John D. is reported to have given away over $10,000 in dimes.

In May, 1911 the Supreme Court of the U.S.A. held that Standard Oil was an illegal monopoly and broke up the company. John kept shares in most all of the remnants of a railroad and oil empire he and his colleagues built.

> FACT: John D Rockefeller was born to William Rockefeller in 1839. Willy was a snake oil salesman, he sold tinctures of opium, alcohol and laudanum.

Willy was a drug peddler, thief, bigamist and father figure to John D. John D was likely the biggest business scoundrel of the day and also became a philanthropist. This is typical for the elite in institutions of grandeur. Sometimes it is genuine generosity and other times it is public relations. Many of the biggest perpetrators of exploitation are some of the biggest philanthropists. This tendency to exist in a duality of kindness and coldness is typical for the elite.

Elitists set up foundations, which not only provide resources, but also distribute information, usually supporting where the cash comes from. They set up institutions that barely do anything more than support other institutions, while touting individual benefit.

> FACT: The extremely wealthy Warren Buffet is the world's most generous philanthropist. Through the Bill Gates Foundation, Warren Buffet is giving away billions. Warren, as the largest shareholder of Berkshire Hathaway, decided to give his money away through the Foundation. As CEO of Berkshire he oversaw its holdings. Berkshire owns a chunk of American Express, Coca-Cola, GE, Proctor & Gamble, Nike, Walmart and a whole slew of other insurance, banking and corporate institutions. Bill Gates is a Knight Commander of the most excellent order of the British Empire. Bill, since the foundation, has donated billions towards vaccination programs, grants and education.

The corporations that Warren made his fortune with are perhaps venerable, and perhaps venomous, and likely both, in a similar chord to John D. At the time of John D's rise to riches, the U.S.A. was the world's largest supplier of oil. Despite being the original gangster of the oil business, John D generously gave hundreds of millions of dollars to churches and universities. The Rockefeller family founded dozens of institutions and donated cash to many. The Rockefellers founded the Asia Society, Trilateral Commission, Population Council, Council of the Americas and the Rockefeller Foundation.

John D's grandson became Governor of New York and was appointed Vice President under Gerald Ford. As Governor of New York, Nelson instituted the Rockefeller Drug Laws. This made the sale and possession of small amounts of drugs equivalent to second degree murder. Michigan later mimicked the law. Originally signed in 1973, the section that included marijuana in the mix of opium and cocaine was repealed in 1979 and in 2004 did New York change the law to lessen the punishment for nonviolent drug offenses.

We live in a world where overtly, institutions conduct themselves one way and covertly they conduct themselves in another, entirely different manner. Institutions have branded themselves as people's proponent, but they are also the opponent. Many institutions and institutionalized individuals are like Dr. Jekyll and Mr. Hyde, helper and hinderer. Institutions may have some of the same rights as men, but they make friends with none.

The actions that we are aware of are merely the tip of the iceberg. If someone in the government, or the pope himself, enables swindling and manipulation, then they must face accountability. Whatever and whoever is responsible for addition of toxins, the promotion of war, the imprisonment of individuals for profit, and the all-around stomping of human rights should be removed, no matter if they were once on your own team. Life is like baseball, but it is not baseball. In life, it is one strike and you're out, such is mortality. Institutions and the institutionalized should not get unlimited times up at bat.

"It's unbelievable how much you don't know about the game you've been playing all your life." ~Mickey Mantle

---

FACT: The three strikes law gives third time offenders of felonies 25 years to life. It was found not to violate the Eighth Amendment by the Supreme Court. Over 20 states have some sort of three strikes law. Ratified in 1994, the law in California has given third strikes to over 1,000 people who received 25 to life sentences for crimes like petty theft.

This is hardly three strikes you're out. It's one strike, you're out…two strikes, you're out again and three strikes, you're out permanently. If institutions are allowed the same rights as individuals, shouldn't they be allotted the same reprimands as well? Individuals are imprisoned and lose everything. Institutions lose percentage points. Individual criminals commit crime with rocks. Institutions and the institutionalized commit crimes with building blocks.

Marijuana is illegal, attracting criminals and creating criminals who otherwise would not exist, for profitability arise out of criminalization. Marijuana would be the price of tomatoes if it were legal and therefore unattractive to criminal elements seeking fortune. Institutions built the crime and surrounding endeavors, which would otherwise be innocent. Many actions are only criminal within their architecture. Institutions created crime out of activities that are not wrong and not sin.

CALIFORNIA PRISONS
Between 1984 and 2006 there were 21 state prisons built in California and 1 state university. California imprisons more people than any other state in the union. In fact, California imprisons more people than France, Germany, Great Britain, the Netherlands and Japan combined.

California is a liberal state; just don't try to meet any police while visiting or the architecture of a six by nine cell may become all too familiar. It is a strange trait, and likely requires generational indoctrination and direct training, to yield to institutions the liberties of living beings, while at the same time take away liberty from living beings. It is as though people believe that becoming an institution requires some connection with the powers of good or God. It doesn't. Since the day when selling doves was lucrative, institutions have claimed closeness to the creator to gain one's trust, loyalty, action and dimes. It is curious that many people trust institutions before individuals, despite the fact that institutions have more inclination and tendency to present part truths.

> "Victory or defeat? It is the slogan of all-powerful militarism in every belligerent nation. And yet, what can victory bring to the proletariat?" ~Rosa Parks

An individual may have brand loyalty to one product, only to find out that it is made with the same recipe, with the same ingredients, and possibly at the same factory as the brand that is disliked. Institutions that present competition may in fact be a cooperative. As long as they profit or are able to proceed with their agenda, it doesn't matter which car is one's favorite.

Loyalty is harmless at times and possibly benevolent, but people can make possessions all too relevant to their character. Personality traits are derived from their favorite slogans or advertising campaign. Loyalty is often what they want out of people. Loyalty may be benevolent, but only understanding and compassionate loyalty, otherwise you're trained.

Brand loyalty gets people hung up on how you're rolling, rather than where you're going. Religions are like rafts traveling the river of consciousness. Some are made differently than others, but all travel down the same river. All religions proclaim peace, yet throughout recorded time, people kill one another in the name of religion. People have to be institutionalized to take on such tolerations, not by religion, but certainly by religious institutions. Some religions institutions require heavy brand loyalty, as do some nations and so on.

Spirituality is not the same as religious institution. Most prophets were patriots, in the sense they sought truth and shared it. Jesus was a patriot. He disdained the functions of the institutions of his day, in his surroundings. He bravely labeled those who claimed to be benefactors, to be detractors. And both sides of power despised him. Jesus questioned the status quo and did not support the Roman or Judaic institutions. Jesus stopped supporting prominent institutions and stopped obeying them peacefully.

> "There is nothing outside a person, which by going into him can defile him; but the things which come out of a person are what defile him." ~Jesus, Mark 7:15

> "There is only one good, knowledge, and one evil, ignorance." ~Socrates

Jesus and Socrates were speaking about information. There are multitudes of poisons, but the most dangerous of all poisons is mental – the lack of truth and misinformation. There were all sorts of poisons in the time of Jesus and Socrates and today there are more. Jesus was not concerned for everyone's food and water, rather for their information. Informational intake and the output that proceeds are more dangerous than any physical poison. Information is not evil or dangerous in and of itself, it is what people do with it that is the real danger. Misinformation, partial information and lies are dangerous, they are poisonous, but questioning is the antidote.

In the petrolithic era, poisonous pollutants are in every drop of water and every breath of air. Increasingly there is plenty outside and all around, which by going into a person can defile him, but lack of truth is still more dangerous. And not questioning information before action enables the worst defiler.

Jesus treated women, the sick and the marginalized as equals, he taught nonviolent response to exploitation and oppression, inspiring countless. He cared for the poor, alienated and those stuck and stacked on. He helped those in need. He cared not about title and riches; he thought primarily of one's motivation of heart and mind. Jesus was completely counter-institutional. As the story goes, Jesus provided an alternative to the uncaring institutions of the day and was crucified for his ability to inspire and question.

Institutions resemble no image of any prophet, ever. Institutions are rigid and aside from religious institutions, unforgiving, while prophets taught forgiveness, open generosity and compassion. Institutions often identify themselves with Jesus or other prophets, depending on their locale, and then operate in altogether despicable terms. When institutions correlate themselves with any prophet, they are either mixed up with profit, their real concern, or using the idea on their own terms. Using the ideas of prophets to influence people is nothing new to institutions.

Do religious institutions better the other institutions they interconnect with? Are laws intended to protect people creating the very criminals they are designed to prevent? Does building prisons also manufacture criminals to put in them? By exporting jobs and opportunity out of the country will crime increase? Institutions develop laws, they develop jails and offices. They barely ever better or develop individual conditions.

> "Guard against the impostures of pretended patriotism." ~George Washington

People associate inner cities in the U.S.A. as harbors of criminals. In Los Angeles and New York City, crime is rampant in some neighborhoods. People originally populated these cities because there were jobs. Many of these jobs have been exported to other places where the employers can better exploit the population; places where people will work longer hours for less money than in the U.S.A., places that care less for liberty, locals and land than in the U.S.A.

Is it better for individuals to globalize or localize? Institutions migrate to where there is exploitable cheap labor, resources and relaxed employment and environmental protections, places that will gladly be treaded and trampled on in exchange for a chance, places with extreme tolerations. This is harsh profit and steep capitalization. Free and open trade is more progressive than institutionalized communism. Capitalism is more progressive than communism too, just not always open and fair. And it is not always a progression in the right direction.

People rebel against institutions; they have been the oppressors of people all through history in whatever rigid formation they arrive in. Sometimes the same institution that exploited then continues today. Sometimes the institutions of today mimic the performances or nuances of other institutions of the past. Some institutions are greedy entities and may exist only to exploit and extract.

Institutions assist individuals and are capable of committing monstrous detractions as well, which are presented and sometimes perceived as merely innocent mistakes. Institutions constantly connive by withholding information. Institutions perform malevolence and claim ignorance. Not all institutions are exploitative and oppressive all the time, but they are always the tools used when oppression takes place.

> "He who passively accepts evil is as much involved in it as he helps to perpetuate it. He who accepts evil without protesting against it is really cooperating with it." ~Martin Luther King Jr.

Idiots passively accept and cooperate with institutional evil. Zealots perpetuate it. Elitists often label evil something else and then insist it. Many organizations and institutions have proclaimed patriotism in order to instigate belief and unquestioning action. This is propaganda to instigate nationalism, jingoism, passivity and racism in order to exploit and conquest. Violence on behalf of God is likely impossible, violence on behalf of religious institutions happens all the time. "My country right or wrong," is not patriotism. If patriotism is not sourced from people, if it is institutionalized, it is diluted and biased. Nations, corporations, and churches are not automatically patriotic; they are only servile to mutual powers that be, only committed to the status quo. Institutions may offer individual support, but only individuals can be patriotic.

The U.S.A. was founded on questioning and dissent, by people standing up and acting out against wrongdoing. Zealots will find reasons not to question certain actions and certain institutions to hold their course. Zealots are active and do not let information sway their activity. Idiots do not question at all, idiots avoid new information to retain their passivity. Perhaps, in a nation like North Korea, to remain unquestioningly supportive of institutional actions is patriotic.

> "No question is so difficult to answer as that to which the answer is obvious." ~George Bernard Shaw

Patriots in the U.S.A. may proceed zealously, but only in questioning on behalf of liberty and acting on behalf of liberty. Zealots put things into context in such a way as to convince themselves and others of the rationality of a direction that is less evil. They hold some institutions in such high regard that they will not question them, but will adamantly question individuals who question the institutions they support.

Idiots let it happen. Idiots stand down, they follow and do what they are told. They don't question and avoid relevance or they forget information to form conclusions. Idiots often passively lack opinion.

Patriots question all conditions and institutional actions. Patriots take action against wrongdoing by institutions, no matter the identity of the wrongdoers or where the chips may fall. If there is evil and lesser evil, patriots choose neither option. True liberty and justice grow to encompass all and not just "us". Help is entitled to those who need it; liberty to those who breathe. Patriots stand up for what is right without contemplating the negative repercussions of doing what is right and refusing to participate in wrong.

Nathan Hale may not have said that exactly, but it is believed the sentiment in his final words contained something to that effect. The original patriots stood up to the greatest power the world had ever known, the British Empire, on which the Sun never set. Nathan volunteered to spy on the British knowing full well what they would do to him if caught. It is not that he despised British people; he despised the wrongdoing of their oligarchical institutions. Nathan was caught and hanged. What was Nathan's definition of country?

Institutions claim to know the happenings they are involved in are wrong, but there is something bigger than right and wrong at stake. Sometimes they deny that they had any knowledge of wrong transpiring via their involvement. They may realize that their actions had a role in something dire and will profess that their intentions did not match the results. If people don't know information, the institutions will possibly lie and definitely present the side of the truth that works for them and that is believable because of lacking information.

FACT: October 24, 2007 FEMA holds fake news conference concerning fires in California. Questions were asked by FEMA staff to a FEMA official.

Institutionalized individuals realize that profiting from death, destruction and pollution is wrong, but they imply there is no choice. It is either continuance or pretense of dire scenario. Malevolence is presented in shiny concepts among perceived permanence. The economy and other institutional interests are transcended above liberty, land and locals and all life known of on Mother Earth.

The petrolithic era is a toxic environment, but also an environment where alternatives are left on the sideline, as if they didn't exist. The power in petrol is unmatched by any substance. There is nothing that makes the machine run more efficiently than petrol. There are equals in octane and energy, but no equal in profit and control, no equal in powering oligarchical collectivism. There are multitudes of other ways to acquire energy, none as beneficial to expansion of oligarchical collectivism as oil.

Most all other forms of power are either eternal (solar, wind, wave, geothermal) or eternally harvestable (bio-fuels), minimizing profit and limiting potential to control. Eternal and eternally harvestable energy would empower and excel individual conditions. Petroleum is mined as a limited resource and distributed by the few to the many in order to profit. Petrol is not the best choice or the only choice; it is the best choice for oligarchical collectivism.

If enough people demanded change, communicated their grief and dissatisfaction, stood up and took action, the institutions would soon change. Institutions do not communicate like people. It takes a lot of people to get through the noise of machines. To be heard, masses of individuals need to communicate in unison or massive amounts of people have to stop fueling the machine so its noise ceases.

People know when something is wrong, they may not all be able to put a finger on exactly what it is, but people know. People can feel when something is wrong. Often, only when things are stopped, can the wrong be specified, but beforehand sometimes people intuitively feel and know. Sometimes it takes stopping to see alternatives as well. Whether through experience or intuition, people sometimes know things without specific, correlating knowledge.

To question the war in Iraq in the first place was debated. To stop is outside the status quo, thus to those within the status quo, not an option. Admittedly it would be crazy to stop paying for war and oil, and yet is it crazier than continuing to war and continuing to use oil? To institutions, continuation of wrong is better than discontinuance. Individuals question and if necessary, stop wrong, without plan or fear of repercussion, as did the original patriots, for better options often appear only when the wrong is ceased. Institutions need a set plan; individuals do not. Institutions become old tools when people discontinue and start anew.

It is easy for institutions to use the idea of patriotism, especially during war, to their ends. Because of the Revolutionary War people believe that liberty arrives in bloodshed and patriots must spill it. If this were true, then people all over the world would have seen liberty ages ago, for war and the cruelty in it has transpired for millennia. War is man's most proficient endeavor, being a soldier is the oldest profession. If the spilling of blood was patriotic in any instance, past or present, liberty and fairness would have been commonplace and not a rarity.

The Revolutionary War was distinct. It was a war of patriots and farmers versus elitists and despots. This was no ordinary war of a king and minions versus another king and minions. War and revolution are not intertwined; in fact it is as much of an oxymoron as the term "military intelligence". War is the oldest aspect of the status quo. This nullifies it from being revolutionary or intelligent for it is old and basic. Something revolutionary is innovative and new. Revolutionary peace would be completely revolutionary. War is not revolutionary and revolutions do not require bloodshed. The revolutionary War was unique because liberty was at least attempted after the end of the fighting and killing.

The U.S.A. military has been involved in some sort of project, whether all out confrontation or the protection of national interests, without a break for hundreds of years. From murdering the natives to launching cannonballs onto monarchical strongholds in the Caribbean, to fighting the threat to freedom on one continent or another, the U.S.A. is frequently in conflict and preparing for war.

FACT: Sales of U.S.A. weapons overseas totals $21 billion for September 2005 through September 2006.

It is the responsibility of those who wield swords to ask who, what, where, why, when and how before swinging them. It is a right to question what national interests are being served and why the armed forces fight. Questioning is dissent, the discrepancy depends on what and who is asked and yet, questioning is protected in the First Amendment. Questioning becomes dissent only when there are obscured or hidden answers. Because institutions intertwine, if one unquestioningly swings swords, the sword might be swung for a different institution than the one originally supported. The invasion and occupation of Iraq, if it was not conducted on behalf of securing oil, has benefited oil corporations and perhaps only oil corporations. Why?

$OIL
Kuwait Petroleum Corporation reaps record profits 05–06.
Exxon Mobil reaps record profits in 06, largest in U.S.A. corporate history, $32 billion dollars, then again in 2007, $40.6 billion dollars.
Chevron reaps most profit in its history 2006, $17 billion.
Conoco Phillips reaps most profit in its history in 2006, $15 billion.
Royal Dutch Shell reaps most profit in its history in 2006, $25 billion.
ExxonMobil earned about $1300 per second in 2007.
Brazil's state owned Petrobras records record profits in 2008.

Petroleum is not the only commodity that experienced a sharp increase in profitability since the beginning of the Wars in Afghanistan and Iraq. The hand in hand partner of oil, weaponry, is being used and replaced. Fortunes are made on weaponry, but it must be used. Afghani poppy is another commodity correspondingly surging since the U.S.A. invasion of Afghanistan. In 2000 Afghanistan grew 70% of the world's horse. In 2006, 92% of the junk for the dragoon chasers of the world was from Afghanistan. Illegal drugs are everywhere and are profitable only because they are illegal or partially illegal like opiates.

"We know there were numerous warnings of the events to come on September eleventh…Those engaged in unusual stock trades immediately before September eleventh knew enough to make millions of dollars from United and American Airlines, certain insurance and brokerage firms' stocks. What did the administration know, and when did it know about the events of September eleventh? Who else knew…"
~Cynthia Mckinney, U.S.A. House of Representatives

After Afghanistan was raided, Iraq was invaded and most questions were negated. Cynthia McKinney was one of few outspoken questioners or dissenters with high office. Saddam Hussein was a horrible despot at the top of a steep oligarchy. By any definition, Saddam was a criminal, but he was writing the laws for a time. Saddam was guilty of being a vicious tyrant and murderer and he may he have been thinking of using nuclear, chemical weapon or biological weapons. This would make him guilty of the greatest thought crime in history. Mistakes and lies pile the same. Reason is less crucial than result and no legitimate and reasonable person can argue for war. Only lies, misinformation and fear make war acceptable.

Ultimately the wars in Iraq and Afghanistan resulted in record profits for oil corporations, a worldwide flood of opium, fiscal destruction of the U.S.A. economy, physical destruction of soldiers and civilians alike, further ruining of environment and further formation of oligarchical collectivism. Whatever the intentions, the result was secured oil; presented as securing safety.

> "We are fighting these terrorists with our military in Afghanistan and Iraq and beyond so we don't have to face them in the streets of our own cities." ~George II

If half the money spent funding the wars in Afghanistan and Iraq was spent on health care and a solar energy network instead, people might be healthier and reading by solar powered lights. Instead people are more reliant on petrol and more dependent on institutions. But as time goes on it becomes more complicated to obtain petrol and its consequences grow more obvious. Petrol is increasingly more difficult to extract and the resulting pollution is more difficult to deal with. Petrol powers the machines of war and by itself has fueled reasoning to go to war.

Good things transpire in Iraq nowadays, but good things happen in prison as well, and that does not make prison a good place to be. Saddam was no threat to the U.S.A. Saddam and his sons ran torture machines, participated in kidnapping, abuse, murder, war and were the leaders of exploitative institutions, however Iraq was no threat to the U.S.A. when it was invaded. Any progression in Iraq is from peace, not war.

> FACT: Civilian dead in Iraq and Afghanistan since start of shock and awe: unknown. The U.S.A. Military keeps no records of civilian casualties. One report suggests over 100,000 another estimates 1,000,000 and counting as of late 2008.

Without substantial questioning or dissent, the U.S.A. began a bombing campaign of shock and awe, a traumatic blitzkrieg, on a nation that had been under embargo for over a decade. Some are in shock and awe to this day. There is no liberty bomb or patriotic missile; there are only shiny death machines with fresh names. War ends and peace begins, conditions improve and change, but never directly thanks to war machines.

The official institutionalized documents presented evidence for the invasion of Iraq. The evidence was not actual, however it was official. The yellow cake, it turns out, might have been for dessert and not plutonium manufacturing and the aluminum tubes possibly were for hookahs, because there was not a trace of any Weapon of Mass Destruction. Everybody has an AK47 and everybody has a friend with an RPG launcher, but there was no trace of actual WMD in Iraq. None was found that is, some was brought though, specifically depleted uranium and white phosphorous.

> FACT: Hundreds of tons of depleted uranium were used in 1991, in Kuwait and Iraq and at least 75 tons in 2003 in Iraq.

Certainly Saddam was capable of using chemical weapons, as he had before on the Iranians and the Kurdish people within Iraq. It wasn't hard to believe that Saddam's regime may in fact possess WMD. The UN had committed gross incompetence in keeping with the oil for food sanctions. It was entirely believable Saddam was amassing yellow cake for something other than a birthday party.

> FACT: U.S.A. military intelligence was essential in successful Iraqi gassing of Iranian troops. U.S.A., France and other Western Nations supplied Saddam with components to manufacture chemical weapons used on Iran.

The documents that provided evidence for the invasion of Iraq were as official as pulp and ink can become, researched and read through the halls of respectable institutions, officially sealed and still, in the end, manipulated partial truth and lies, worth as much as common crap tissues. Whether it was lies, disinformation or ignorant mishap is inconsequential to the outcome. War is war.

Institutions work off of established parameters and set mission goals and agendas within the status quo. Business is set up around war because war is profitable. The prison system is set up in such a way that more prisoners equate more profits. Institutions that are set up to solve or handle problems end up being conducive to the very problem simply as a matter of maintenance. Many institutions exist only because there is conflict and crime, if the problem was solved they might not exist.

> FACT: Wackenhut and Corrections Corporation of America together share 75% of the private prison market.
> There are five privately owned prisons in Florida; number six is on its way.
> There are over 100 private prisons in the U.S.A.
> Nearly half the prisoners in New Mexico are under private corporate control.
> U.S.A. prison population in 1972 was less than 300,000. In 2007 there were over 2 million citizens in prison.

The private prison industry has experienced rapid growth in the last twenty years. Federal and State Governments have designed and accepted privatization of imprisonment because it saves their institutions money, tax dollars. The business efficiency of corporate prisons saves money, in part by cutting services like prisoner healthcare. Private prisons raise money by instituting prisoner labor and by quartering more prisoners.

> FACT: Pennsylvania has the second highest number of private prisons, Florida has the most. In 2002, in Luzerne County, Pennsylvania, Judge Conahan shut down the state juvenile detention center. He funded private prison facilities from Mid Atlantic Youth Services Corp. with millions of dollars. Judge Michael Conahan and Judge Mark Ciavarella received over 2.5 million dollars in kickbacks in exchange for harsh punishment and imprisonment of children. As the number of imprisoned juveniles increased, so did the profits. The corporation denied knowledge of the kickbacks, but the judges were disbarred and offered to serve 87 months in their plea. Pennsylvania Child Care and Western PA Child Care were the specific companies connected to the kickbacks.

Patriotism is individual. Institutions are collectives. Individuals are alive and institutions are tools. What truly matters to individuals may mean nothing to a collective, as interpreted by machines and institutionalized individuals. When individuals lack relevant questions they may be misdirected, collected, relabeled as a number and used for some shadowy elitist operation to benefit the few over the many. Individuals might be shoved along, pushed aside or held inside to benefit the collective and the occasional elitist individual.

One does not 'sign here' without questioning. Yet sometimes institutions are doing the signing and individuals don't know to question. People react to wrongdoing if they are aware of it and not scared of it, but sometimes questions go unasked and fearless, righteous actions are restrained. Institutions tend to hide information and cast doubt around known exploitations so as to diffuse questioning. People formulate better than existing institutions, if information is available and questions are not quieted.

People know what is right and with information, gravitate toward what is right. Without institutionalized tolerations to wrongdoing people tend toward fairness, liberty. If wrong information is held and questions are quelled, people are easily steered in the wrong direction.

Oil and water don't mix. Institutions and individuals don't mix either. Individuals must be institutionalized to neatly fit into the confines of the institutionalized status quo. Individuals must be trained, burdened with tolerations to operate within the machine. Individuals must be kept in a cave, in the dark, to believe that they fit into machines of the status quo. Only in the dark, only when people don't comprehend the truth, do they believe they fit neatly into the pyramid system. Only in the dark does their light seem like the light.

INSULTING AND TRUE

Some things change, other things remain the same. Ever since hemp sails with hemp rope harnessed the wind to sail the seas there have been pirates, piracy and pirated acts of war. Throughout recorded time, institutions have gone to war over the distribution and allocation of resources and throughout recorded time hemp was one such a valuable commodity to consider in their conquests to control.

Napoleon conducted the failed French invasion of Russia in 1812, in part, to prevent Britain from getting Russian hemp for their sailing fleet. Many states acted as pirates or hired outsiders to perform missions of piracy for their empirical ends while other pirates pillaged independently at their own will. Whatever flag they flew or song they sung, pirates and the state sponsored privateers used the same tactics and tools to advance their crew or institution.

Today the tools of the various pirates have changed, but their mode of operation has not. They once used muskets and cannons, today automatic weapons and RPG launchers are the preferred tools. Piracy is the same today as it was in the past. Privateers produce the same results as they did in centuries past, exploitation to benefit the ruling minority. Piracy by sanctioned privateers and wild criminals has been an enterprise for profit since the days of Montezuma. The first war the U.S.A. fought, after nationhood, was the Barbary War with pirates in 1801–1805. The second Barbary War took place with similar pirates after the War of 1812.

The French privateers were called corsairs. It was seen as a more acceptable and romantic representation. They were commissioned by the French authorities in racing letters to chase down other ships and plunder their cargo or take the whole boat. Racing letters were contracts to race around and kill. Some called the Barbary Pirates Turkish Corsairs.

Pirates rumble through the high seas now on motorized vessels, while privateers ride in planes, trains, and ships. Pirates are still pirates, but privateers are now more accurately described as privatizeers. They slice and enslave more people with papers and deals than any swords and sails could. Individual criminal piracy is well-known and well documented. The privatizeers and their acts of privatization are less known and when documented, exact and total exploitation is concealed. Institutions hide information of privatization and present information on individual pirates. Theft is evil when random and when mechanized. Piracy is piracy, no matter the tools and no matter the label. Privatization is monopolization, privatizeers monopolize like privateers of the past only with exponentially better tools and more efficient operations.

> FACT: In September 2008, a cargo ship carrying 33 tanks, armored personnel carriers and automatic weapons was hijacked off the coast of Somalia. November 15, 2008, a Saudi oil tanker was hijacked. On November 18, the Indian Navy sunk a suspected pirate mother ship.

Foreign corporate fishing fleets have over-fished the waters off of Somalia and compete with local subsistent fishing. The same fishing fleets and other ships from various corporate and national institutions have dumped toxic waste into the North African waters, including nuclear waste determined by sicknesses of coastal residents. The removal of local resources and dumping of toxic waste by foreign fleets have degraded the environment and removed opportunity for traditional fishing. The debilitated environment eliminated opportunity for locals and the corporate fishing fleets further eliminated opportunity and even sustenance for Somali locals.

Conducting harm and theft is wrong whether conducted by an individual, a band of individuals or uniformed institutionalized officials. A label is just that and often is an obscurely euphemistic or altogether opposite description of actuality to influence perceptions. Wrong concerns more people when performed by institutions. Institutions are integrated behemoth formations with numerous branches; next to individuals their actions inevitably encompass and instigate more powerfully.

Some enactors of evil continue on as the same institutions and some evil continues on, enacted by different institutions in the same manner. Some institutions come to end, others remain and many rename but are the same. The results of pirates, privateers and privatizeers are the same despite different tools and constructs; they steal and exploit. Exploitations are enacted by well-known institutions and obscure individuals as well, sometimes in the same fashion, but always with the same intention.

Institutions have crossed lines and created malcontents throughout recorded time through their misconduct. The trinity of liberty has given people the right to express themselves be they bold or shy, industrious or genius, red or red, white and blue. At the same time the trinity of liberty has attempted to halt and block institutional exploitation. The trinity of liberty was designed to counter the trinity of monopoly; that is the conjunction of church, state and corporate institutions.
Institutions are interested in control. There is a great assortment of subjects and resources one or another seeks to control, but all institutions seek to expand control of their state, market, or congregation.

There is a vast assortment of other institutions, of varying ages and interests that have rolled with people and at the same time, marched on and over people for generations. They all uphold righteous religious, corporate or national goals and ideas to gather support and continue clinging onto people. Institutions are like sharks and the institutionalized like pilot fish lurking for prey. The shark hunts and the pilot fish cleans the shark and nibbles at leftovers.

Institutions tax and steal with papers and swords, privateers and privatizeers of the past and present, operate for the same ends despite different tools and labels. Some of the same institutions and definitely the same actions are coordinated by the same type of formations despite the shift in labeling and language. Some of these exploitative, plundering institutions are the same then as now.

Institutions are the timeless hubris and nemesis, at times providing and ultimately preventing. The same sharks some fish fear are accompanied and maintained by other fish. These are only a portion of some exploits and evils conducted by some prominent institutions.

The list of sanctioned piracy could go on and on and will if we don't stand up to it. Prominent institutions reap profits off of the conditions and consequences of the petrolithic era. They are benevolent and malevolent at the same time. Of course there are other religious institutions that monopolize, like some of those that represent Islam and call for holy murder. There are other corporations that oppress and exploit and have done so for generations, like Royal Dutch Shell or any number of banks. There are other governments as well that provide and prevent at the same time. A list of long-term institutional exploitation would be a book in and of itself.

China is an example of an extremely oppressive state controlled with brutality and slavery. One cannot question in China, no forms of patriotism are completely and openly allowed in China. Control is enabled by eliminating information and supplying force. All information is controlled in China. Russia too, seeks to monopolize as much as the former USSR. Coca-Cola and Pepsi provide effervescent drinks, but also acquire and monopolize water to benefit institutions and not individuals. Institutions act in a trinity of monopoly, intertwined and linked to reap and profit. They exploit as privatizeers, sailing in and capitalizing on everything and everyone without regard; legally commissioned.

Sometimes individuals latch onto older institutions or create new institutions to use them for elitist operations. For centuries individuals exploited and made off with honest people's earnings in various fashions, but always through institutions. Bernard Madoff founded his investment securities group in 1960 and was chairman of NASDAQ at one time. His brother, two sons and other family members worked for him variously. In late 2008 Bernie was charged with operating possibly the biggest pyramid scheme in world history. Bernie admitted he conducted a fifty billion dollar fraud.

In early 2009, Allen Stanford was charged with the second biggest case of fraud, second only to Bernie's pyramid scam. Allen's grandfather founded Stanford Financial in 1932. In 1985 Allen began to expand the family business, opening up banks in Antigua and expanding operations in Mexico, Central America and South America with his trusted name. In 2009 his banks were suspended and people all over the world were left without their savings/investments for a time and/or lost it. Allen was well connected in South America and was being investigated for laundering drug money from Mexican drug cartels at the time he was accused of fraud. Throughout recorded time, pirates with swords and privatizeers with pens pillage honest people around the world.

Pyramidal institutions, generations old in some cases, exploit. It is their shape, their design, but it is always people who use the tools. Many families have become institutions themselves out of continued prominence and thorough institutionalization. Generations of familial ties continue to lead the functions of corporate, church or state institutions. Institutionalized individuals shift from one type of institution to another or remain concentrated in one type, but they continue to perpetuate the status quo, they continue monopolization and institutionalization.

They intertwine political, corporate and religious interests, the inherited commonality is a quest for increased power. They are individuals who are fundamentally entirely institutionalized, to the point that they are more machine than man, more institution than individual.

Postmodernism is the result of the petrolithic era and nuclear age, where dilution of pollution has now built up to the entirety being polluted. And at the same time the more experienced an institution, the more likely they have propped up and promoted wrongdoing, like global pollution. The same goes for institutionalized individuals, the longer they've been around, the more corrupt they likely are. They are like mobsters; they keep fam tight and willingly stomp and march over anyone who might be in their way, including polluting entirety. Sometimes, institutional corruption occurs for as little as building a house and other times occur when building the big house.

FACT: Ted Stevens (AK) was the longest serving U.S.A. Senator beginning his service in 1968, losing reelection in 2008. In 2008 Ted was investigated and found guilty of failing to disclose $250,000 worth of gifts and services he received. The bulk of the claim was from construction and improvements done on his ski-house. VECO, an oil services company provided Ted with the gifts. In 2007 the CEO of VECO pleaded guilty to charges of extortion, bribery and conspiracy. April 1, 2009, more corruption, this time by government prosecutors, resulted in the charges against Ted being dropped. Ted's son Ben, a State Senator from Alaska, was also implicated in corruption.

FACT: In 1984, the first private prison was built in Texas. As of 2007 there were 47,000 private Prison beds in Texas owned by 8 corporations. Texas holds the highest number of privately owned and operated prison beds.

War on individuals is peace to institutions. Pirates wage war and sometimes pirates, at the behest of the powers that be, attack powers that be so that the same powers can blame an enemy and act to war. When an institution rallies people for war the people cannot better their circumstances and at best merely maintain oligarchical formation.

Freedom to institutions is slavery for individuals. The more rights and freedoms that are lent to institutions -rights intended only for living, breathing beings and not shadowy institutions- the more we all become slaves to institutions. All so called rights and freedoms lent to institutions run counter to liberty for individuals.

Individual ignorance is strength to institutions. The more ignorant the majority of us are the more easily we are controlled, the quicker we become institutionalized slaves and the more likely there will be war and no peace, meaning less and less individuals can gain a piece at all and that oligarchical collectivism will only increase.

> War (on individuals) Is Peace (to institutions)
> Freedom (to institutions) Is Slavery (for individuals).
> Ignorance (among individuals) Is Strength (to institutions)
> ~From *1984*, with additions in parentheses

This set of three statements and slogans are each reflective of the perversion of the archetypes at hand. Ignorance Is Strength is the banner of idiots. Freedom Is Slavery is the banner of zealots. And War Is Peace becomes the banner of elitists. The perverted slogan of the patriot is omitted, or perhaps never was.

Ask questions. Be wary of pirates of any banner or ilk. There are four forms of political lies and through them four ways to analyze information. It is a mathematical approach which can assist in making sense of the nonsensical and unpredictable nature of politics and the human dynamic. Those involved in politics, the politicians, reporters and corporate lobbyists are constantly lying. There is outright conjuration which we're all accustomed to, and there is partial or complete elimination of information. Politicians and the lackey media enjoy these simple types of lies, but they normally prefer more nuanced lies as opposed to outright addition and subtraction of information.

> "To see what is in front of one's nose needs a constant struggle." ~George Orwell

There are four basic types of political lies illustrated though the four forms of arithmetic. The first type of lie is the addition of information so as to distort the story to mean an entirely different thing. The second type of lie is the subtraction of information. This type of lie removes key components, making the story mean an entirely different thing. The third type of lie is multiplication of information. Exaggerations of situations connected with the story as well as exaggerations of extraneous information are included in the presentation. The fourth type of lie is division of information. Disconnects are inserted into the presentation of information and the significance of information is then divided and separated.

The powers that be lie all the time. There is no wild conspiracy linking unordered dots in pointing out that those with the greatest amount of information are correspondingly the greatest liars. This is a rule of politics parallel with that of Lord Acton's Rule, that power corrupts and absolute power corrupts absolutely. The scale and the idea is the same; sources of information lie and information from one absolute source absolutely lie.

It was once a wild idea to mention the summer festivities at Bohemian Grove in Sonoma County, California, part of a club out of SF that is entirely made up of really wealthy political, religious, corporate and media personas. They meet and either play burn the kid under an owl alter (Alex Jones verified all rumors in his film Dark Secrets: Inside Bohemian Grove.) or they conspire through their connections to steer policies all around the world usually by manipulation of information. They represent the information elite, of political, religious, corporate and media institutions.

George Orwell's *Animal Farm* and *1984* inspired the idea of four types of political lies. In *Animal Farm* animals are personified and write down their rules for all to see and follow. However eventually, through the addition of language the messages are altered entirely along with the conditions of entirety which is then utilized by some, the allegorical they illustrated as pigs of course, to benefit themselves. The seven rules from *Animal Farm* and the three axioms from *1984* clearly express the addition and subtraction of language.

Animal Farm illustrates the addition and subtraction of language, for new language is added to the original rules to change them and ultimately only the axioms "all animals are equal, but some animals are more equal than others" and "four legs good, two legs better."

> 1. Whatever goes upon two legs is an enemy.
> 2. Whatever goes upon four legs, or has wings, is a friend.
> 3. No animal shall wear clothes.
> 4. No animal shall sleep in a bed (with sheets).
> 5. No animal shall drink alcohol (to excess).
> 6. No animal shall kill any other animal (without cause).
> 7. All animals are equal (but some animals are more equal than others).
> ~From *Animal Farm*

In *1984* there are there is the triple axiom like the farm's jingoist dogmatic programming. *Animal Farm* illustrates the addition of language, *1984* illustrates the subtraction of language. Both eliminate truth. Winston Smith's job is to eliminate contrary information and insert supportive information to the institutional narrative and many of his coworkers are creating the incredibly shrinking government dictionary.

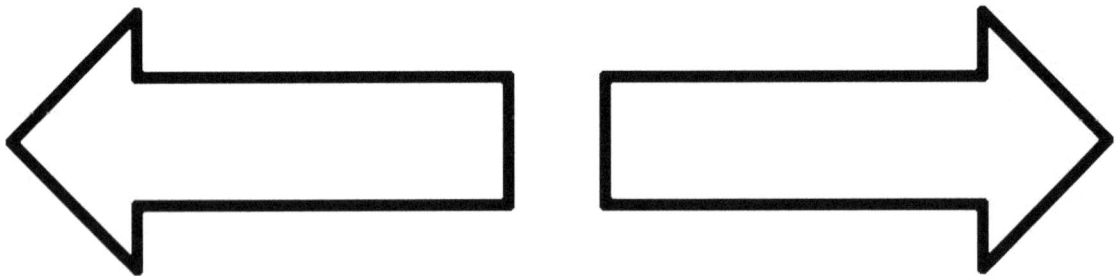

CHOICE

> "Liberty and democracy become unholy when their hands are dyed red with innocent blood." ~Gandhi

---

SYMBOL - RED
Red is a color of power, as is purple. In the distant past only the powerful and wealthy could obtain the dye needed for clothing to be shades of red. It has come to be associated with heightened passion and anger. The devil is depicted as red while cupid wears red and love is symbolized as a red heart. The flags of many nations are red and include red. Red is synonymous with communism and fascism, authority and control.

The environment of the natural world may contain only two polarized options or no choice at all. There is undeniable duality in nature. Natural duality is beautiful and intricate. Institutions often offer limited options, sometimes only two choices in an unnatural manner. It may seem inevitable that choices are limited, but choices are often limited by institutions. People have only two hands, but there are almost always more options than right or left, than this or that I n how we approach things. Liberty is the freedom to choose, not to choose and to create new choices. People are free to choose their favorite color and free to choose the way they live life. Choice is not limited merely to red or blue.

Does life imitate art or does art imitate life? Life imitates art and art imitates life. Just as in the debate of nature or nurture, the answer is one or the other, but a combination of both. If there are only two choices presented, a mixture is always a third choice, and likely, a more sensible option; neither is the fourth option. Limited choice, one or the other, is an institutionalized debate. Art contains that life spark, while life is artful, they are inseparable.

Institutions seek to control, and create conditions where they design the choices. Options are often limited in two polarized choices, both leading to the same desired outcome for institutions - control. Limited options are presented in local and global conditions in order to control. Actions and directions other than those institutionally presented diffuse institutional control. Institutions present two options to limit thinking and outcome. Not to choose is often the alternative choice to institutional presentation that most diffuses control. There are always creative alternatives that bypass the either/or setup.

Individuals surpass natural options through questioning and development. Our thinking is not limited to two polarized sides. Many think in coinciding polar opposites, and in this-or-that terminology. This is institutionalized, steered thinking. In reality, individuals are capable of thinking alternatively and in multiplicity, in multiple layers, not just two polarizations.

Institutions create circumstances in which there are polarized options. In the institutionalized world there is not only right and wrong, but also legal and illegal. Institutions attempt to control though limiting options and manipulating existing conditions. Some institutions attempt to monopolize choice and to be omnipotent as the Sun. Institutional lines of legal and illegal do not always coincide with the distinction of right and wrong.

Institutions use tolerations of right and wrong by setting the standard for legal and illegal and giving it precedence over right and wrong. Individuals are capable of more than countering and opposing doublethink. Individuals can see past the either/or presentation, individuals are capable of more. Individuals are capable of surpassing the either/or mentality. Institutions implement it.

Criminals cook until someone looks. As long as crime is unknown and unquestioned, it continues. If wrongdoing is legal and unquestioned, it is perpetuated by wrongdoers and maintained by apathy. Right and wrong are distinct from legal and illegal. Laws vary throughout recorded time and place, while the distinction between right and wrong is unchanging. Tolerations sway the perception of actions, but right and wrong remain. Institutions polarize conditions to influence tolerations and they confuse right and wrong among legal and illegal, but be sure wrong might be lawful, and right unlawful.

Institutionalized individuals are less likely to do what is right and more likely to do what is legal. Individuals without such burdens see through institutionalized presentation and question. Liberty allows for multiplicity and inventiveness that eliminates the potential dead-end control of polarity.

Liberty exists when everyone experiences equal access to information and resources. Freedom is not liberty; liberty is ensured and protected rights which engage equality. Laws sometimes promote countering and contrasting the law with crime, because in criminality arrives profitability to those in poverty and those who are greedy. Restricted or limited resources and information lead to poverty. Poverty leads to ingenuity, the ingenuity might be gathering food or contrasting law to obtain money for food. Greed is unpredictable, but just as ingenious, with more potential tools to contrast law.

Criminals exploit situations to enable themselves, whether hungry or greedy, criminals operate the same. Criminalization of something individuals consume despite prohibitive laws, like alcohol or marijuana, is wrong. Such criminalization creates crime where there might not have been a wrong and opportunity for institutions to control and profit. Criminalization may not protect individuals, but rather uplift institutions, at the expense of individuals.

The greatest price of liberty: all are entitled to it. The crack in the Liberty Bell symbolizes that some individuals lack liberty. It also symbolizes there are some who would take it from others. Everyone is entitled to liberty, even one's opposition, even criminals who would exploit others are granted liberty - until they are found to be exploiters. In order for liberty to exist everyone must have it, and evermore watch vigilantly for those who would misuse it. That which protects individuals from being railroaded, also protects the railroaders, and increasingly the rights of men are being applied to the railroad itself.

> FACT: In 1886 the Southern Pacific and Central Pacific Railroad Companies ceased paying certain taxes. Santa Clara County, CA sued the corporation for delinquent taxes and the case ended up in the supreme court. The court ruled in favor of the corporation. The ruling set the precedent that corporations have personhood.

The Supreme Court decision is cited as implying corporations have the same rights as people presented in the recently enacted Fourteenth Amendment, which outlawed slavery, not the restrictions and shackles on corporations. The Supreme Court renounced the taxation of the corporation, yet no actual affirmation of corporate personhood was stated, only instigated and interpreted that way by some. In the U.S.A., up until the ruling, people were protected and institutions restricted, after the ruling the ruling, corporations began to gain personhood and protection.

Any citizen under the evolved Constitution has the right to vote and run for office. No individual would vote that institutions are worthy of the same rights as living persons, only those so institutionalized that they are more like institutions would perceive institutions to be individuals. No individual would suggest corporations should have equal rights as individuals, except those seeking to feed greed. As a "practical matter", in a republic, people don't vote on such issues, and some people were only recently given the right to vote at all.

> ### VOTE
> The 15th Amendment gave African American men the right to vote in 1870. Subsequently, Florida, Georgia and Oklahoma passed disenfranchising laws that were eventually found to be unconstitutional. Conventions were held in many states on how to disenfranchise African American voters. Women were given right to vote in federal elections in 1920. Prior to 1924, American Indians were required to renounce their tribe to receive citizenship and the right to vote. In 1943, the 1862 Chinese Exclusion Act was repealed, giving Chinese the right to citizenship and the right to vote. The Civil Rights Act of 1960 was passed, insuring individual rights. Subsequently dismantling the disenfranchising state laws that subverted the 15th Amendment. In addition, the Civil Rights Act of 1964 made it illegal to discriminate. In 1965, the Voting Rights Act passed in order to enable equality still.

Corporations gained rights attributed to individuals before women were allowed to vote. Many states passed laws preventing and restricting the actions of people based on their race, voting was just one action. People were restricted from marriage, ownership of property such as land and guns, all based on their heritage.

Now any citizen over the age of eighteen in the U.S.A. can cast their vote, though typically about half register. Anyone who was born in the U.S.A., is thirty five years or older and has lived in the U.S.A. for fourteen years, is permitted to run for presidential office, but only the prominent and institutionalized run successfully. Why do corporate executives make more viable presidential candidates than well-educated chess players? Anyone, in theory, can run for office, and everyone can vote for whomever they desire. The trinity of liberty allowed for this progression, despite the manipulations of some.

The media was designed to be localized and not monopolized and consolidated. Everything is globalized, from newspaper and news reporting to tastes and dining. We are not only mediated, but globally mediated. A vast majority of the information presented by the media has been transposed, filtered and contrived to the point that it is no longer journalism in the traditional sense.

> "Advertisements contain the only truths to be relied on in a newspaper." ~Mark Twain

Perhaps this is nothing new, perhaps such confluences were always there. Advertisements are based on as much make believe and biased, incomplete information as some slanted news stories. Many institutions claim to be journalistic, but present their side of the coin; biased opinions and part truths. These are stories of facts and their relativity, not simply the facts. Stories of events that could have been, and what ifs are presented, instead of what happened. They always retain the official version and cast first hand individuals as unreliable if they don't support the official story.

> "To read a newspaper is to refrain from reading something worthwhile. The first discipline of education must therefore be to refuse resolutely to feed the mind with chatter." ~Aleister Crowley, Occultist and Writer

Journalism is meant to provide varying opinions of others and not hold a platform of its own. Discussions are normally based on one professional representing one extreme opinion and another representing a counter, but equally extreme point of view. Neither of which tend to be sensible, just countering. It is commendable that they have two opposing sides, but what about alternative perspectives? The counter to absurdity is often equally absurd.

One side says gravity is the only force in the universe, while the other side argues that gravity doesn't exist. Why aren't articulate intellectuals and ordinary individuals allowed to speak more often? Where is common sense? Where are alternative viewpoints, instead of just opposing perspectives? Institutions and the institutionalized distort experience with basics such as gravity, in order to maintain perspective.

> "Fascism should more properly be called corporatism because it is the merger of state and corporate power." ~Attributed to Benito Mussolini

Institutions try to hide their connections with one another and disconnect themselves from their own past. They celebrate their history if it suits the proceedings of their profits, but mostly they keep quiet, because all too often, history learned is institution questioned. The history they adopt is often a seemingly beneficial version of their predominantly greedy past. They keep their mouths shut unless petitioned.

Underneath it all institutions seek to monopolize choice. By propagating dependency on products people may believe they are dependent on institutions. In reality institutions are dependent on individuals, we maintain the machine. The machine presents itself as being in control, but we supply the fuel. Coke is not it and there are other alternatives to Pepsi. There is always yes, no, both and most importantly neither, or no. The most powerful choice an individual has is choosing neither.

> "Kings had always been involving and impoverishing their people in wars, pretending generally, if not always, that the good of the people was the object." ~Abraham Lincoln

> "At what point then is danger to be expected? I answer if it ever reaches us, it must spring up amongst us. If destruction be our lot we must ourselves be its author and finisher." ~Abraham Lincoln

Kings and royalty, generals and armies, clergy and ministry, executives and company all practice elite measures the same. The institutionalized, some rarely and some regularly, all act to advance the few off of the many. The purveyors of institutional presence and dominance develop grand atrocity and quiet measure in order to prop up lesser evil and with it their agenda. This coordination often takes place subtly, behind the scenes among many convinced they are accomplishing a greater good, but permitting or perpetrating evil never accomplishes greater good.

Turning a blind eye and deaf ear to evil allows it. To not speak about evil enables it. To avoid information about evil and remain silent about it, only provides profit from it. Patriots stop, look and listen, then face anyone and everyone to explain their findings on any evil present. When we do not look, listen and speak up about actual evil such as exploitation, it is furthered. Ignorance is strength to institutional exploitation.

One has the choice to go with them or question an alternate direction. One may follow outlined concepts or openly question. One has the choice to accept previous conclusions or perform the deduction oneself to assure that what was true still is.

Institutions are merely machines of individuals. There are other ways to live besides under the wings of intertwined institutions and there are alternate directions to their presentation. Open mentality is exemplified in questioning institutional arithmetic. Liberty is the right to question their addition and stop when things don't add up, without repercussion. And when they say, "Go", liberty, provides that one can say, "No."

> "The solid world exists, its laws do not change. Stones are hard, water is wet, objects unsupported fall toward the earth's center. With the feeling that he was speaking to O'Brien and also that he was setting forth an important axiom, he wrote: Freedom is the freedom to say that two plus two make four. If that is granted, all else follows." ~George Orwell, *1984*

Mathematical observations of reality are generally academic. At times, complications and conditions require theorems, but through questioning, the intricacies are even calculable. Life is mathematical sometimes, however in life, there is more than one correct answer. There are theories and complications in life as well as in mathematics, only there are multiple answers in life. When institutions present limited options and when they have to steer information to support their approach, they are suspect of manipulation.

Institutions often initiate just two options, two countering sides of the same coin that lead to their previously determined and preferred outcome. Institutional options are manipulated into an illogical catch-22 structure. The options lead to the same conclusion in contradictory and confusing presentation. In life the freedom to perform arithmetic is the freedom to analyze actuality and logically equate it.

In *Catch 22*, the novel by Joseph Keller, the main character, Yossarian, is a pilot in WWII. He believes that everyone is out to kill him. The enemy shoots at his plane, directly trying to kill him, while his commanders send him on dangerous missions, indirectly trying to kill him. Yossarian seeks to find a way out of flying the missions and being killed. Every option presented by the military, prevent him from ceasing the flights. All choices lead to the same conclusion; continuation.

> "Peace on Earth would mean the end of civilization as we know it." ~Joseph Keller

GENERATIONAL EXPLOITS

It is too bad that some people get caught up among institutions and are perceived as guilty by association. Many within institutions, employees, family or other beneficiaries, may not individually promote or facilitate crime and grime on the whole as does the institution. It is one thing to unknowingly commit crime, it is another act altogether, to pretend as if situations were unknown in order to commit crime.

If people knowingly work for criminal institutions or benefit from them, that is their decision. If they choose to ride dirty and roll gangster, then they face the consequences. If a person's friends and family are all in a gang and have been for generations, it becomes difficult to believe they don't set claim and carry a blade themselves, unless proven otherwise.

Crime is elusive and clandestine. The most successful crimes are unknowns and known unknowns. Keeping quiet is essential to facilitating crime; hiding and distorting information is primal to crime. Unknown crimes and known crimes with unknown perpetrators are successful because information is controlled. In order to prevent meeting police and spending time behind bars, information gathering and distribution must be restricted and coordinated.

If you are in a gang, you know other figures in other gangs. Sometimes one gang cooperates with another gang to make some money or to carry out some other agenda essential to the organizations. Gangsters ride and die for their own gang, but sometimes they work with other gangsters.

Mostly it's like your clique, and that's it, do or die. Mostly there's beef between gangs. One crew will work with other crews on occasion, but mostly they use and occasionally abuse each other. There are rules to crime, even though crime breaks all the rules, there are rules that criminals use to play the game properly. The covert rules are amorphous and always in contrast to overt law, in order to con it. One practically concrete rule is to never, ever speak to cops, enforcers of authority, or anyone who might reveal information to them.

Criminals do not speak with authorities other than on smoke screen subjects. Even if you know you could bring down your archenemy, you don't tell the cops. You retaliate on your own and keep knowledge of the retaliation within the crew. Rival gangs use one another in many ways; one way is simply as a distraction. If there is more crime, authorities can prevent less of it and perhaps lose track of your own gang activity.

If the cops get your competition, they might have time to start looking at your deal. Cops might start talking about your crew's thing and start wondering how they can do something about your own crime. The Bloods and Crips were venomous enemies, yet one could not have existed without the other. And neither likely would have existed, if it wasn't for many of the laws they criminally conned to raise money. As is so often the case, the two groups counter each other and present the situation as automatically being a limited and polarized choice, red or blue.

There are the gangs, and then there are sets or crews within the gangs. Mostly the crews cooperate within the gang, but sometimes there's set tripping and infighting. If there was only strictly one gang and one crew, the cops would have a better chance at stopping the gangsters. If there were only two gangs, one against the other, they might even have a chance to control it.

When there are multiple crews within multiple gangs, that sometimes cooperate with each other and sometimes mutilate each other, the cops can't prevent it. The authorities can't keep track of it or understand it let alone prevent it. Their activity is unfathomable and unstoppable. Keeping authorities busy and confused is essential to criminal activity. Keeping your opposition empowered may at one time serve an essential purpose, but it never serves gangsters to serve the authorities actual information. If they bust those figures over there, they could bust the clique, your own gang next. Criminals never tell the authorities, or anyone who would contact authorities, anything except lies. If you're gangster, you keep it straight on the front and crooked in the back.

Instead of revealing information to the cops about rival criminal activity, gangsters proceed to take note on how it's done and how they got away with it, so they can coordinate their own plot better. Perhaps, they capitalize on the inflation that prohibition brings about, perhaps they capitalize on those that do so. It's gangster like that.

If your great, great grandfather was making money off of gangster shit like war and weapons, and all your other family since, it's hard to believe that you are not going to facilitate it too. It's hard to believe if your whole crew is criminal, that you aren't criminal too. The best criminals are never known as criminals, they got it locked and sewn, the entirety of situations is controlled. Real gangsters are crooked in the back and straight up front, they are smiling and lying.

Black is white and white is black. Concepts of legality and morality are confused, misused and abandoned by criminal masterminds and petty robbers alike. Information surrounding crime and morality may have a whole neighborhood, or city, or country, waving, giving pounds to, and even saluting criminals.

Some fraternal gangster institutions aspire to do great things. Even the hardest gangsters and mobsters have figuratively brought turkeys to the hood. Corporate gangsters, in contributing their own turkeys, are generous for the same reasons mobsters are generous. It's like an expression of gratitude, thankful that everyone let them slide again. They bring presents for people who turned a blind eye or deaf ear to wrongdoing. Criminals and wrongdoers, who are generous, reason that their generosity may override some past or future information or act. Of course, not all generosity is administered by wrongdoers.

Great criminals employ and create legitimate institutions. They perform acts of benevolence with turkeys, sometimes of international proportions. At times benevolence is simply that, but normally institutions have reasons other than mere generosity to give turkeys to the poor. Their generosity may contain ulterior motives. These motivations may be as seemingly innocent as developing connections. Some of the most successful ongoing wrong jumbles authorized and criminalized into the gray area.

> FACT The UN is the most widely respected global authority. Part of its mission statement is to "save succeeding generations from the scourge of war." But their institutional agents have embezzled billions of dollars, committed rape, murder and fraud in numerous nations.

> "It has been said that arguing against globalization is like arguing against the laws of gravity." ~Kofi Annan

An investigation into the known abuses conducted by UN peacekeepers would be a book by itself. Globalization in and of itself is not criminal and may be bound to form like orbs in gravity. Maybe Kofi was correct, globalization has always and will always inevitably progress. Globalization might be desirable if it provided rather than exploited. The UN enacts globalization that is institutionalization that results in exploitation and UN-individuation. Localization is always desirable as it results in respectful equality.

People can come up with many ways to use gravity to our benefit. It's also possible to use globalization to the benefit of individuals, but it is currently set up to benefit institutions. If globalization meant lifting the many along with the few, then who would argue? If globalization saved succeeding generations from war and exploitation, then it might be worthwhile. Until observations suggest globalization leads to peace, instead of war and exploit, the more time tested and proven mode should be reinstated; localization. Simple observation suggests that globalization increases pyramidal slant, war, exploitation and environmental destruction, while localization creates the opposite.

Exploitation of many for few is wrong no matter what it is labeled. Criminals take advantage of law by manipulating law and conning people. Without certain laws, there would be no way for criminals to take advantage of situations. Some laws are even created by institutions to enable institutions. Some laws are based on institutional advancement and inspire criminals to counter them.

Institutional globalization or monopolization destroys Mother Earth, individuals and alternative principals, in criminal fashion. The globalized status quo is a system of declared and undeclared wars, where combatants attack warrior and innocent alike. Currently, globalization is an invisible attribute of visible institutions that assemble their own mechanized structure and dismantle environment, individuals and principals. Institutions present a benevolent front, their corrupt intentions in the back.

Their benevolence is, often enough, a purposeful act. The UN is the ultimate global authority, but at times, it is the ultimate globally unaccountable power. Their acts do nothing to stabilize or benefit anyone that first does not benefit institutions and stabilize the status quo.

UN operatives and high ranking officials steal, rape and bribe across the globe. Instead of being convicted of breaking the law, they are accused of being ethically improper. Kojo Annan, the son of Kofi Annan got into the business of international exploitation using his father's name. Kojo apparently made illegal gains through his position and power. Is this the precedent set for global institutions?

To be global is to be unaccountable and unquestioned, as if institutions are too important to be held by the constraints of right and wrong, or legal and illegal. Since they soar through the skies and navigate the seas, they act as if they are above individuals, above accountability to the little people, the locals. They are neither here or there, but everywhere. Institutions recognize only legal and illegal, not right and wrong, and sometimes institutional operatives ignore law too.

If institutions intend to better humanity, why haven't they done so? Exclude the rest of the world for a moment, where a little could go a long way, in the U.S.A., there are still destitute and homeless. Hospitals dump mental patients on downtown streets because they cannot afford healthcare. Information and resources are restricted.

Why has nothing changed in the inner city ghettos? Why does exploitation continue? Why are U.S.A. corporations outsourcing to foreign exploitation? Why is military spending exponentially greater than spending on education?

The separation between wealth and poverty becomes more distinct while the ranks of poverty swell. If the U.S.A. is able to amass an army to war, then it is possible to raise forces for other reasons. People are so supportive of situations portrayed in the status quo they'll sacrifice their existence to promote and protect it. Why not the same courage toward changing the status quo? Why not devote the same courage toward action that does not require mortal threat? Our true nature is to help and not hinder, such requires institutionalization.

The UN, among other institutions, announces great intentions and spends fortunes, but good intentions slip farther away and money is exchanged with an elite few. It is not just the UN. Global corporations wield tremendous might and do not mind exerting force via restrictions or goons.

AFRICAN PETROL

Most of the world's oil comes from politically unstable countries.
Nigeria is the world's 8th largest oil producer.
People in Nigeria protested and formed militias to obtain reparations for rampant pollution and jobs for locals.
Murder and atrocity are committed by both militia and oil company security alike in Nigeria.

Oil corporations have as much money as the Queen of England or Dutch Royalty. The Queen represents untold billions in wealth. While the Dutch Royal Family, on top of other holdings, has a stake in Royal Dutch Shell. They have such fortunes that one would think they would be able to come into a country and better it while extracting the oil. The Nigerians believed as much; the oil corporations' arrival was met with optimism, but now Nigeria is sinking.

Fishermen who were once able to eat and prosper in the Nigerian Mangroves, now don't bother casting a line. There are virtually no more fish due to pollution and overdevelopment. People have become dependent on imported food, frozen fish, which many cannot realistically afford. Where there are fish, people have begun to buy fish carcasses to eat. The meat is shipped elsewhere, while the carcass remains behind and is affordable.

Off the coast of Namibia, the sea is increasingly anoxic. A portion of the ocean is so over-fished that the plant life the fish ate now grows out of control. The growth supplies bacteria, which once was killed by other bacteria from the fish. The bacteria do not require oxygen and exude sulfurs; any remaining fish or sea life dies or flees. The ocean is dead, no longer producing oxygen, much like the anoxic waters in the Gulf of Mexico.

Oil corporations are corrupt from the get go; mayhem follows their arrival. What once was stagnant at worst is now hopeless at best. It is no wonder that people are taking up arms. If hope, comfort and provisions are taken, people will voice their dissatisfaction. If their voice is removed, they will make a statement in another fashion. Overt and institutionalized disparity is ordinary; the extent of it varies.

Catching a fish in some places along the African Coastline has become a story in some places, a myth that only the ancestors could effectively accomplish. The fish are gone directly as a direct result of over consumption and pollution.

Environmental destruction and exploitation is taking place all over the world. Nigerians are able to notice. In the past, noticing change was difficult in a lifetime. In postmodernism, everything changes and morphs, never to be the same, many times over a lifetime.

All business and progress does not have to cease for a tree in a mangrove, but an entire ecosystem is worth more than any oil. People need ecosystems more than they need oil, while institutions need oil more than ecosystems. The entire mangrove forest, the entire fish population, the ecosystem along the coastline of Namibia and Nigeria is threatened. The most lucrative endeavors should be stopped in the event they permanently destroy the environment. Oil is priced by the barrel and fish by the pound, an ecosystem is priceless.

> FACT: Governor Blanco of Louisiana fought for a larger share of taxable income from offshore oil corporations. The Federal Government currently takes the bulk of these taxes. Development of oil facilities have left Louisiana's coastline eroded and thus more vulnerable to storms. Blanco wanted the money specifically to fix the devastation left by the oil and gas industry lining the state's shore.

The Namibian coastal waters aren't the only anoxic zones, and the Nigerian Mangrove isn't the only place that is sunk. In 2008, the Pacific Northwest of the U.S.A. experienced unprecedented mass die offs of sea life resulting from anoxic waters and post Fukushima, Japan, the Pacific Ocean and the entire world is threatened.

There are many ways to improve situations, no matter how complicated, wherever. With the connections, money and resources the oil corporations have, they could improve situations. And yet only corruption and mayhem trails them. They pretend that it is some coincidental and continuous accident that surrounds them when it's actually their program.

If there is more gangster activity, it's easier to pop off some gangster shit. If there is mad drama in the hood, there are distractions. When all is well, oligarchical criminals are less able to exploit. Too much drama means too much heat, attraction of authorities. Steady criminality out keeps gang activity smooth and also enables authority. Too much drama draws too many cops, but steady drama is beneficial all around.

The biggest industry on the planet is oil extraction, shipping, processing sales and distribution. This industry, by no coincidence, also employs the greatest scoundrels and liars on the planet. They have become an essential evil, a monkey on society's back. The greatest criminals perhaps are among them, unknown for criminals hold their tongues.

> FACT: Fuel additives such as benzene and MTBE are linked to cancer in humans.

If oil corporations were involved in worldwide solar energy, if they enabled individuals instead of institutions, they would not make enemies, and they might not make as many connections. They would not be criticized if they provided and benefited. Those who now attack them, would likely be employed by them or fishing along a mangrove. If people worked toward free energy, instead of institutional energy reliance on, people would be well on the way to cleaner environment and peace and who knows what other pursuits.

Oil corporations stomp over all that is good in order to reap profit. Global, official, affiliated corporations run over the tiniest creatures and the most helpless of humanity in order to control and profit. Their presentation and procedures are distorted and they deliver disinformation because they are criminals. They act as one and do as another. They promise certainty and provide insecurity.

Regardless of what oil corporations, fishing corporations and other institutions announce, it is what they do that is important. Announcement and procedure are null and void next to action and actuality. They may very well be doing some good or apparent good, along with exploitation or apparent exploitation, but the good is likely a tool for the exploit and not the other way around.

Institutions get caught up in other undertakings in order to preserve their original agenda, which in general terms, is expansion of power. The power they presume lights up the dark side of man. Institutions act as if they are greater than individuals, as if the machine was worth more than the hands that manifested it.

Institutions have great sway and power. While their power is great, the cogs, the people inside, make the machines move. Institutions are powerful, but they are not alive and not worth much next to life, no matter how well built. They might have more power, but not more value. Working on behalf of institutions gives some people a certain sense of exaltation and an excuse to act on it, they are pushed and pulled to do wrong. They are caught up in the wrong and are enveloped by it.

Many institutionalized do not notice the pushing and pulling of institutional influences and acquired tolerations. They act and continue on as if their institution is as glorious as presented. They believe they can conduct only glory. The institutionalized don't question institutions; proceeding on behalf of institutions they perceive as bigger than themselves.

By being included, lying seems acceptable; harming and hindering are promoted. By being exalted among one's peers with as little pomp as being hired, it becomes easy to lay down what is right and have said peers run it all over. When one believes one is in on the lies it is easy to accept them.

Pursuing profits from the sales of oil or arms or any other exploitative, dirty, defiling industry, is easy to conduct when it is done among and with the acceptance of princes, sheiks, well-dressed politicians, celebrities and bishops. Some people in some of the most respected institutions are the hardest, most devious, roughneck, plundering, gangster, murdering gangsters there are. Throughout recorded time the institutionalized have always been the hardest criminals and often known for activity other than crime. Meetings are conducted over tea where murder is spoken of in terms of conviction, and theft described as relocation.

It is not that the business of supplying energy is a scandalous business in and of itself; it's just that some scandalous individuals and institutions have made it so and kept it so. See Lord Acton's rule, the corrupt empower more corrupt. While people of the U.S.A. were reeling from the devastation of Hurricane Katrina and rising fuel costs, the oil corporations enjoyed record profits. While soldiers and civilians were exploded in Iraq and diesel fuel reached four and five dollars a gallon, oil corporations announced record profits, again.

BECHTEL

Bechtel, the sixth largest privately owned corporation in the U.S.A. was established in 1898. It prides itself on engineering feats and rebuilding nations. Originally they prepared land for railroads and built oil infrastructure. Today, they build nuclear power plants and chemical plants around the world.
They have built mining and petroleum facilities all over the world.
They participated in the building of the Hoover Dam. They recently fatally engineered the Boston Tunnel at a price tag of $15 billion dollars. Bechtel was charged with price gouging in the Iraq war.

Bechtel has mad connections within the government of the U.S.A. and many other institutions worldwide. Bechtel is a typical oligarchical institution of the petrolithic era. It would seem the company is a state agency, as they conduct stately functions and many former Bechtel employees move on to work for the government. The institutionalized serve any institution well, they learn how to stay in line with the margins. They know how to dot the i's and cross the t's for institutional operation and presentation. Institutionalized are magnificent at manifesting official from partial truth and total conjuration.

In 1943, Bechtel was criticized for its role in building the Trans-Alaska oil pipeline. In 1947, they built the Trans-Arabian pipeline in Saudi Arabia. Before the ousting of the Shah in Iran, Bechtel had a deal to construct a nuclear power facility there. Bechtel has operations and facilities in over fifty countries and is as gangster as it gets with mad connections.

PIPELINES -December 4, 1997: Afghanistan's leaders, the Taliban, visit Unocal (Chevron) in Texas to discuss Asian pipeline deal.
1998: American embassies in Africa are bombed. Unocal announces halted development of pipeline.
May 30, 2002: Afghanistan, Pakistan and Turkmenistan agree to Asian gas pipeline. India later signed on.

Although construction of the gas pipeline was delayed, it's on. In 2004, despite the pipeline still being incomplete, Afghanistan managed to become a major exporter, only instead of natural gas, it is exporting natural dope. The heroin market became flooded as a direct result of the booming poppy growers in Afghanistan.

Institutions rip off taxpayers and tax all those who breathe. The institutions that propel and compel complete support of the troops (actions) also rip and shred the military fiscally and physically. The troops need people's support, especially when institutions like Bechtel or KBR get hold of them.

FACT: Investigations into at least 12 electrocutions of U.S.A. soldiers in Iraq began in March 2008. KBR Inc. of Halliburton was responsible for electrical wiring at the barracks where soldiers perished in the showers due to improper grounding.

What is their definition of support? If they were civilian contractors, they would no longer be in business. How about supporting all people at all times, including the troops, but not limited to the troops and their martial actions? It is the duty of the military to make the distinction of civilian and soldier; it is not the duty of the civilian. All individuals are entitled to support over institutions. Otherwise individuals get killed, ripped off and marched on by institutions.

> FACT: Enron was the largest financial contributor to the biggest spending political campaign of the time, up until the time, (Barack Obama spent $573 million during the 2008 election) that of George II. A perpetrator of vast corporate fraud, Enron later claimed the biggest and most complex bankruptcy in the history of U.S.A.

Enron was not only a major contributor to the Campaign of George II, but supposedly a donator to the Taliban, as well. The money was intended to sway the Taliban in their decision of who was going to build the pipeline through their country. Between 1978 and 1992, the US government gave at least $6 billion in arms to the Mujahidin fighters in Afghanistan to fight the occupying USSR. The Taliban were one group of fighters, one group of Mujahidin.

> "A man always has two reasons for what he does - a good one and the real one." ~J P Morgan

Authority, in its representation on a day-to-day basis, conducts both overt and covert operations. The police, the corporate, the court, the church, the military, the local and federal government and all other formations of individuals are nothing, if not ruled by law. The law of the land, the ultimate, unsurpassable authority in the U.S.A., housed in the National Archives, is the trinity of liberty.

All institutions, institutionalized figures are marginalized under and relative to the power of the people, provided by the trinity of liberty. The essential point in the documents is power to the people; there is no greater authority than the people. Any violation of people anywhere, by any institution or individual, requires action, civil or drastic. It is arguably the function and responsibility of individuals in a free society - to defend it from transgressors, to take the responsibility to question.

> "Our constitution was made only for a moral and religious people. It is wholly inadequate for the government of any other." ~John Adams

As global interdependence grows, so does the instability of the intertwined majority. As institutions impart democracy upon the world through war, prevention of institutional exploitation should be employed. If the U.S.A. military brings democracy abroad, people should follow suit with responsibility and accountability abroad. The military doesn't have to be the only protection and support for people. Observation and communication, conscious spending alone can accomplish as much as preemptive military might. Discontinuing trade with an exploitative institution is a powerful statement.

Inaction is potentially as powerful as any action. Kindness is not a mark of weakness, but of strength. Kindness is compassionate action without fear. War is predominantly played out via fear's influences, no matter how brave one's conduct.

The U.S.A. military pushes democracy where there was none. Enhanced transparent accountability should follow as well. The military must be accountable, along with the corporate and all other prestigious institutions. The exchange of money follows war, so should the flow of responsibility and accountability. Going to war is perhaps brave, being kind, without active fight or flight mechanisms, is definitely brave.

The Commander in Chief and every other government representative vested with the powers of the Constitution should be accountable at home, long before they pass judgment elsewhere. If globalization pushes democracy first through bombing campaigns and then business campaigns, global accountability of corporate, governmental and every international institution should follow. They have to be accountable to people and people must not be afraid to hold them accountable.

What will those who taste democracy for the first time think of it, if it is accompanied and followed by murder, fraud and extortion? Perhaps they may think not much has changed. Promoting democracy means promoting responsibility, accountability and fairness. Patriotism is not invasion and installed election and it is not militarism or conformism.

The only people in the U.S.A. who are subject to obey all orders of superiors are enlisted military personnel. Even in this strict environment, U.S.A. patriotism shines through. Military personnel are required to obey lawful orders. Soldiers have the right and responsibility to question and disobey unlawful orders.

The regimented U.S.A. military calls for individuals within the institution to question, to stand up for what is right and when necessary disobey unlawful orders. To disobey was, is and always has been the essence of peaceful rebellion. It is a fundamental basis of the U.S.A. to say "no" to those in charge when they order wrongdoing. The U.S.A. was founded on people's refusal of institutional monopolization. It is the fundamental right that cannot be taken away from even a grunt. Yet one must look, listen and speak up to disobey; one must stand up unafraid to question and communicate and step out of line.

People acquire tolerations and many are easily fooled because they don't question, look or listen. Because people don't question, standing up and speaking out is never considered. Tolerations and a lack of inquiry has led to the exploitation and gentrification of people throughout history. By not asking questions, wrongdoing has a better chance to transpire.

When respect for authority is more important than reverence for humanity, patriots continue to question. Patriots are simply ask logical questions in a polite, loud persistent manner. If people are labeled dissidents in the U.S.A. for merely asking questions, then there is something wrong, something is being hidden. When polite questions are not answered, the questions are eventually marked with exclamations. When information is held and restricted despite questions, situations become more questionable. When an institution has something to hide, questions become dissent.

Questioning is dissent when the questioned hold onto the shiny status quo to conceal the rotting underbelly. They don't want people to see the underside of the status quo. They don't want people to communicate alternatives.

When the wants of powers and authorities override the rights of people, patriots must question. At first, perhaps alone or appearing alone, then in a group and then many groups. One person can be a catalyst for paradigm. Questioning information is a prerequisite to societal evolution. Question observations, question the delivery of information. Question the questions posed, answered and unanswered.

"The difference between genius and stupidity is that genius has its limits." ~Albert Einstein

"Things do not happen. Things are made to happen." ~John Fitzgerald Kennedy

THE MEDIA

The design of the U.S.A. Government is a three-branch system, consisting of the legislative, executive and judicial. There are three branches of government, separate, but equally connected. These institutions are based on the three founding documents, the trinity of liberty.

The media is often cited as the fourth branch of government in the U.S.A. The media is nongovernmental, but just as influential. The press wields tremendous power because they work in information. Media has the power to initiate and inspire people's potential, questions, and actions by obtaining and distributing information. People act and react on information and media institutions are the main suppliers of information.

Journalism is supposed to be factual and neutral information, delivered by people whose opinion and identity are not as important as their questions and research. Editorials and entertainment features offer other interpretations and perspectives than mere factual dialogue. If opinion is expressed, if popularized characters relate formatted perspective, it is no longer hard news.

The media, the fourth branch, is the patriot archetype applied to institution, and in theory, uncorrupted by the government institutions. George Orwell was a longtime journalist before writing 1984 in which he proposed there were essentially four types of institutions in the fictional world. There is The Ministry of Plenty, of Love, of Peace, and of Truth. These ministries coincide with the four archetypes and the four types of institutions, of corporate, religious, government and media.

> "Avoid popularity; it has many snares and no real benefit." ~William Penn

People inspire the media to investigate their questions and share information. And people instigate investigations. If enough people question and call attention to a situation, the fourth branch is motivated to investigate and relate. People instigate media institutions to ask questions, but a more profound power is that media institutions instigate people to ask questions. The media is the fourth branch of government in the U.S.A. aside from Executive, Legislative and Judiciary, but the media is also the fourth type in the larger sense.

Media institutions, at one time in the not so distant past, were a distinct group, institutions of information. The media is supposed to be an institution with little or no ties to most all other institutions; corporate, government or religious. The media is supposed to ask unbiased pertinent questions of the people, by the people, for the people. At one time media institutions were prevented monopoly of information in a stricter manner to make numerous sources.

In the petrolithic era, most media is a corporation with intentions to profit much like any other corporate institution. The majority of existing media institutions are internationally interconnected. The confluences do not necessarily determine reporting, but they exist.

Most media lack consistent questions of depth. Most people as well, are uninspired or perhaps afraid to ask open-minded questions. Does art imitate life or does life imitate art? The press in the U.S.A. is supposed to be the people's voice, of straight questions solely for information. The press is the people's check on all institutions, including the three branches of government. The better the questions and the research of the press, the more people are able to prevent the figurative crack in the Liberty Bell from widening.

Freedom of the press ensures that people have an outlet to ask the most difficult questions. Media can confirm and unite, or dispute and argue, what people experience and what authorities dictate. Institutions, like the three branches, claim one thing and reporters investigate and ask difficult questions. Glorified public servants are just that, and reporters just ask questions of them. The free press checks, double checks and triple checks the presentation of the three branches of government, and all other institutions. The press was meant to blow the whistle, or ring the bell, on institutions or individuals when their actions require as much.

SYMBOL - BELL
The bell is an ancient symbol associated with divine power and protection. A bell dispels evil and calls on good. A bell wearer is unafraid during peace and war. The Liberty Bell and its crack are symbolic for the all but perfect design of a people's government. The Bell itself is perfectly symmetrical, yet there is the crack. The Bell was originally cast to commemorate William Penn and his penning of 1701 Charter of Privileges. The crack developed and eventually the bell would not ring.

The abolitionists adopted the cracked bell as a symbol for almost perfect liberty, for almost everyone. There was liberty for everyone who was white, exploitation for others. Henceforth the Liberty Bell has come to symbolize the near perfection of a country that is of, by and for the people. The Liberty Bell's inscription is from Leviticus 25:10: "Proclaim liberty throughout all the land unto all the inhabitants thereof."

Today the media often just records the doublespeak and plays it back. Often the media only wants official answers and seems to care little if it is the entire truth or not. The media wants a story that is easy to finish whether or not it is complete. Institutions and the institutionalized do not question official information nearly as much as other forms of information. Official information may be certified, but that does not equate truth requiring questioning.

"...we're all held to the same standards and called to serve the same good purposes: To extend the nation's prosperity, to spend the people's money wisely, to solve problems, not leave them to future generations...The war on terror we fight today is a generational struggle that will continue long after you and I have turned our duties over to others." ~George II State of the Union speech 2007

Why did no one in the major media question this duality in the President's speech? Is war a problem? Not to say that all members of the media are tape-recorders, it's just the current nature of the business. The media today is largely internationally owned and operated by a few, with many interests and connections.

Rupert Murdoch	A list that may stand as a book on its own is that of Rupert's media empire. He owns too many media entities around the world to list here. Among them are Fox News, local television and radio broadcasting in several major U.S.A. cities, cable stations, film studios, the New York Post and an assortment of media enterprises all around the world.
New York Times	Owns newspapers from Alabama to California, several television and radio broadcasting companies and are involved in cable and sports.
Time Warner	Owns CNN, HBO, Court TV, film studios, a wide variety of magazines, AOL and other online services.
Disney	Owns film companies, ABC, ESPN, television and radio stations around the U.S.A., cable television, record companies, book publishing and magazines.
Vivendi Universal	Owns the remaining 20% of NBC, many television and film companies, Rolling Stone, publishers, online services and websites, video games, record companies and telecommunications companies.

Watch the evening news on weeknights. ABC, CBS and NBC air their national news at the same time throughout the nation. On many broadcasts the three stations present the same headlines in the same order, sometimes they share the same perspective. Why do different news agencies report the same exact subjects at the exact same time and present it in the same terms? It turns out they aren't different news agencies at all. The differing news agencies often obtain their information and perspective from each other.

News organizations create talking points and counter points to discuss. They look for stories that suit what they want to be news and what they want people to think about the news. They let advertisers influence what they report and how they report. This was most noticeably conducted concerning the health effects of smoking tobacco and it is possibly, more recently, being performed in reporting subjects concerning global environmental destruction and the dangers of personal cellular devices.

FACT: As early as 1938 scientific reports were circulated through the Associated Press of tobacco's harmful side effects. However, major media largely ignored these findings because they made major money from tobacco company advertisements. George Seldes printed a newsletter from 1940 to 1950 covering tobacco, its effects on human health and its influence on media. On June 11, 1964 the Surgeon General issued its first report linking tobacco with disease. At the time, cartoons and an assortment of television programs were sponsored by tobacco advertisements.

The media should be adversarial to authority and any institution for the people's best interest and not adherent to other interests. The media should question authority because they are supposed to have an interest in what people know. People can encourage the media to question, but the media with podium should not require encouragement to ask open questions on broad subject matter. The media should ask relevant questions of authorities, whether a doctor heralding fresh breath from tobacco or a politician touting economic benefits of privatized prisons. Sometimes people, without knowing, may feel something is wrong. The media is there to question the inkling of ill.

Questioning authorities is patriotic. Powerful institutions require powerful questions. Questioning power is not necessarily to rattle, but simply to obtain information. If institutions or individuals act to cancel questions, ask again.

Questioning even what seems like good intent is a fundamental right and should be appreciated. Questioning war does not insult or take away support from the troops or the country. It makes more certain war is necessary and is a primary right to fight to uphold in the first place. Employing this right, questioning, in fact, only supports the troops and improves direction.

When a question goes unanswered or worse, unasked, there is something up. If there is an obvious question about conditions or a follow up question to an answer that goes unasked, there is probably information some would prefer to withhold. If a question goes unanswered, if information is not shared upon inquiry, it is a sign that quality questions are being asked and they should be continued and expanded upon.

The media should persistently ask questions that could be answered, but are not. If enough people keep asking they may be answered or at least posed. Corporate media has decreased the number of difficult questions they ask despite bettering the presentation and distribution of information. Perhaps the change in mentality of the media corresponds with the change of mentality in the public. Perhaps things changed when corporations with international institutional ties began to own and operate presses and multimedia corporations. Corporate media are involved in industry, with interests that stretch across the globe.

William Randolph Hearst was a past media mogul with mixed interests. Orson Welles based the classic movie Citizen Kane loosely on William and others like him. William's father amassed a fortune from the gold rush in the West, this afforded William the best education money could buy. He was ultimately kicked out of Harvard for pranks. William went on to build a media empire of newspapers, radio stations and movie studios, beginning in San Francisco, Ca.

William's media empire was just one aspect of his money making endeavors. He also was invested heavily in timber and timber products like paper. He promoted sensational journalism in the coverage of most stories to sell papers. He hyped up the Spanish - American War and launched a media campaign against marijuana to promote selfish interests. Hemp competed with his timber investments; it was beneficial to William and others that hemp was made illegal. The value of William's trees would have been threatened if paper was made with hemp instead of pulp from trees. William helped create reefer madness toward illegality, and put industrial hemp in a hearse.

William was a member of the House of Representatives for four years and failed at attempts at becoming mayor of New York City and Governor of New York. William was a media mogul who was all mixed up in industry and politics. Today the Hearst Corporation owns dozens of newspapers, including the SF Chronicle, the Houston Chronicle, almost two hundred magazines including Popular Mechanics, Teen and Smart Money, a couple of dozen cable television stations such as A&E and the History Channel, as well as other media outlets.

William's granddaughter, Patty Hearst, was kidnapped by the Symbionese Liberation Army in February, 1974. By April, Patty was convinced of the righteousness of the group that kidnapped her and was a cooperating member, photographed participating in a bank robbery in San Francisco. Patty developed a certain captivation for her captors and followed their commands. She ended up supporting her captors and performing crimes with them. Patty was a kidnapping victim who developed adoration for her captors. This emotional tick is now sometimes called 'Patty Hearst Syndrome.' Patty was released from her kidnappers and ended up serving twenty-two months in prison for crimes she committed while held captive by the SLA. The story was a media sensation.

Perhaps tiny policy changes and necessary financial interests instigated within these media corporations have coincidentally intertwined them with all types of institutions, perhaps their mimicking real reporting is a program. The stories and subjects they present are able to represent an opinion or point of view. If dissected, the questions asked provide a glimpse into not only the answers they seek, but where they are coming from in the first place.

> "An expert knows all the answers - if you ask the right questions." ~Levi Strauss

Experts of specifics are called to express their opinion to people though the media. We are provided with portions of perspective, yet never what's really going on. People in the media may be more institutionalized than educated. They ask certain limited questions and present information in a certain way largely on behalf of institutions and the status quo. There are intelligent, well-educated people in corporate media, but there are also many who are just well institutionalized.

True reporters do more than take notes and quote officials, true reporters do more than interpret and relay the information of a few to the many. True reporters ask agitating questions. There can be multiple eyewitnesses to an event, among them reporters who all recall more or less the same events. There may be audio and video on top of multiple eyewitness accounts, but until some institutional authority gives the news agency the official story it stands as 'unconfirmed information' or some such. If it conflicts with the official version of events, it is dismissed as confusion.

> FACT: Firefighters, police, reporters, WTC employees and other eyewitnesses report multiple explosions on 9/11.

Witnesses who tell stories that are not in line with the authorized version of events are ignored. Reporting is sometimes less confirmation and more authorized convolution. Eyewitnesses could become dissenters because of what is seen and then questioned when it differs from the official story.

The press is designed to uphold questions and inquiry. The press researches and investigates questions. If needed, they are to be adversaries of institutions; nation, church, corporation, and even to their own employers or anyone that people seek answers from. If reporters are so friendly with newsmakers as to be invited to a politician's Christmas party, they better be looking for exclusive news and not just to feel exclusive about it.

The press is in the business of asking questions. In order to report news, the first action is to ask difficult questions without bias. Institutions tend not to divulge information unless they are persistently harassed for the information or it suits them to express it.

In the U.S.A there are censors in the media. One censor is the discernment of the majority. What are most people interested in as news? What will people read or watch? Subject matter is censored by institutional interpretations of the interests of the majority.

There is also a more powerful censor, the government. Beginning in 1991, at the behest of George I, the U.S.A. military banned the coverage and photography of U.S.A. soldiers' coffins returning from battle. The total restriction had a few exceptions, such as the soldiers killed in the bombing of the USS Cole. The ban ceased in early 2009 after review by the DOD and President Barack Obama, family members of the fallen soldiers would now decide if any media might cover the return of the soldiers. Restriction and interdiction of information only lends more power to the information when seen or heard. Prohibition of photographs only lends more power to pictures.

FACT: Pictures and symbols have a powerful emotional impact, sometimes greater than words.

When people are allowed to see the total results of war, including the injured and dead, pride for war might decline. If people saw all the troops returning home in whatever condition they were in, whether in a coffin, missing limbs or relieved and weathered, there would be more support for the individual soldiers and less support for institutional wars. When people are humanized and not simply statistics, a more informed viewpoint might be established. If people are not presented as a "them" among an "us" there would be less regard for policies that involve killing. The only change is information. To change opinion sometimes requires only a small piece of information, even an image.

One extension of the government, the DOD, doesn't answer to any individual. The policy preventing coverage of dead soldiers in flag-draped coffins was instigated because it brought unwarranted and undignified attention to the soldiers. It certainly brings attention to something when there is a picture, and people dying in war warrants attention. If anything warrants attention, it is fighting and dying in a war. To die is not undignified; we all pass away. To die in perpetual war for the prosperity of institutions is potentially undignified. To die in war and have information withheld about the war or about oneself might be undignified. Censorship should be disdained and questioned. Why do they not want people to see the results of battle and injury in war? Why do many avoid people avoid information on war?

Censorship of entertainment in certain forms, for certain individuals is sensible. But if censorship occurs, it is only sensible if it is well-known to be censored. No matter how lame or controversial a subject, the media should reveal details. People should be able to see/hear/read/experience what is going on simply because it is going on and because technology allows the distribution of information.

While one extension or leg of the government censored pictures of fatalities, another created bogus intelligence to convince people to be for war. They censored the outcome of war then conjured reasons to go to war.

FACT: A report issued by DOD in February 2007, found that the Office of Special Plans in the Pentagon, manipulated evidence and the CIA acted inappropriately, but not illegally, concerning manipulation of information in lead up to Iraq invasion, allegations followed.

"(The Pentagon's work) which was wrong, which was distorted, which was inappropriate…is something which is highly disturbing." ~Senator Carl Levin

> "Never forget that everything Hitler did in Germany was legal." ~Martin Luther King Jr.

Institutions love the blame game. In the case of the Iraq war, people knew that information was manipulated; only too few of the wrong people knew. The newly created and now defunct Office of Special Plans and the CIA were only promoting work for the DOD. They were only doing what they were told by the some power, likely by the George II Administration. With so many seemingly disjointed offices or branches of the government, it is easy to shift the blame to one entity, one rogue appendage with a twitch, and not systemic movement.

An individual agency will take the blame, but they only take the blame so far. People are always left to wonder if it was incompetence, ignorance or blatant malevolence. The media treats institutional answers as certified; in part simply because they like to wrap it up. The media is largely better at predicting the weather than at researching current events and the surrounding conditions. Questions are often asked in order to wrap things up and not investigate from the bottom up.

> "If you want a happy ending, that depends, of course, on where you stop your story." ~Orson Welles

The Baghdad bombing began with permission from one branch of government, without objection from another and was perhaps always the intention of the third. With little research and lacking questions "Shock and Awe" began based on false and official information. It was excessive and disproportionate use of force. People in the U.S.A. protested and questioned, but their numbers were not significant enough to inspire most media or politicians to systematically question.

Donald Rumsfeld, creator of the Office of Special Plans, took a lot of blame for the failings and mistakes of the war after the bombing. He ultimately left his position as Secretary of Defense. Although blame should squarely fall on him, he was not alone and many might deserve equal blame.

> "I say I listen to all voices. But mine's the final decision. And Don Rumsfeld is doing a fine job. He's not only transforming the military, he's fighting a, a, war on terror, he's helping us fight a war on terror. I have strong confidence in Don Rumsfeld. I hear the voices... I know the speculation, but I am the decider. And I decide what is best. And what's best is for Don Rumsfeld to remain as Secretary of Defense." ~George II, April, 2006

If George II was the decider, then Donald was acting in accordance with the decider. Since Donald did not remain, the entire statement is questionable. Was he lying? Was Donald always out? Did he just change his mind? Did he really think Donald was going to stay and that he was really the decider? Who in fact is the decider? Eight months later, after midterm elections, Donald was no longer Secretary of Defense.

> "The way to prevent these irregular interpositions of the people is to give them information of their affairs thro' the channel of the public papers, and to contrive that those papers should penetrate the whole mass of the people. The basis of our governments being the opinion of the people, the very first object should be to keep that right; and were it left to me to decide whether we should have a government without newspapers, or newspapers without a government, I should not hesitate a moment to prefer the latter." ~Thomas Jefferson

> "The policy was set. The war in Iraq was coming and they were looking for intelligence

Another type of censor, deciders in their own right, is the few who own and operate the global media institutions. They operate in a constant, dissonant orchestration of information. They inform their audience about what they might be interested in, along with what they might want them to be interested in. Many in the major media promote the belief that some institutions, "us", are good, and countering institutions, "them", are not good. They present information that is true, just not always all the surrounding truth, not all the information.

1951	Prime Minister of Iran nationalized the oil industry which was owned by Anglo-Iranian Oil Co., to be renamed British Petroleum. At the time it was England's largest corporation.
1953	British and CIA agents stage coup d tat out of Tehran Embassy and installed the Shah. Oppressive monarchy ensued.
1979	During revolt, strike and overthrow of the Shah, hostages are taken by Iranian students from the same building the last revolution was conjured, the U.S.A. embassy. They are held 444 days and released the day of Ronald Reagan's inauguration.
2005	Mahmoud Ahmadinejad is elected president of Iran. Some former hostages claim Ahmadinejad was one of their captors.

Pictures do show a man who looks strikingly similar to Mahmoud playing a seemingly active role in the hostage ordeal. Even with physical evidence and witnesses, it is hard to decipher such unknowns. Even if Mahmoud answered the question of his involvement, might he lie? There are no known pictures of Kermit Roosevelt Jr. and Norman Schwarzkopf Sr. working for The Agency supporting the coup in Iran, 1953, but they were there. The grandson of President Theodore Roosevelt and the father of the General Schwarzkopf (who led Operation Desert Storm) were in Iran as part of Operation Ajax, working for the CIA and the interests of various oil corporations.

The specifics of the President Kennedy's assassination in Dallas and Bobby Kennedy's assassination in Los Angeles may remain unknown. The whereabouts of Mahmoud in 1979 may also remain unknown. What is known about circumstances and conditions is enough to question and ponder. Question actuality if there is mystery and the mystery may be dismantled and disintegrated.

Few major media institutions noted the ironies surrounding the history of the U.S.A. Embassy in Iran other than Mahmoud's potential involvement. It was at least symbolic to the Iranians and worthy of mention, yet nothing more than a passing note. Many do not want to face the fact that their own government overthrew another government, Iran or otherwise. Iran was labeled part of an axis of evil, but few want to talk about the U.S.A.'s involvement in its manifestation.

The media portrays the propagators of deception as operating abroad and not at home. People do not want to commit wrong and if they know about a wrong committed by their representatives, most want to right it. Institutions have no such tendency; the machine only goes one direction, and it doesn't turn around. Institutions casually overthrow a place like Iran and later as casually threaten the country for how they turned out.

Some reporters ask pertinent questions and others do not. Some people with high podium in the media ask difficult, yet fair questions, many do not. They may get the answers for their questions completely or not at all, but should at least pose the questions. Then any number of follow up questions can be asked. The media is labeled the fourth branch because they are supposed to be a check and balance. One question that is rarely asked anymore is "Why won't you answer the question?"

The whole story, the truth and nothing but the truth, remains elusive, potentially corrupted and led astray. This occurs through one belief system or another within the structure of reporting information. The very questions one asks present bias and/or opportunity for biases. Not asking questions presents opportunity for bias as well, only alongside ignorance.

Since most all media is owned by a small group of corporations, it is increasingly possible to control all of them. Accordingly, if the information is so controlled, then the opinion of ten thousand men is of no value when it is based on questionable information, partial information or total assumptions. Whoever isn't owned and controlled will fall into line as matter of acceptability. Conformity often is completed just to be acceptable.

> "I think to a very real extent journalism is like a priesthood and there's certain experiences and schoolings and schools that you have to go to, to become a member of the club." ~Richard Parsons, CEO Time/Warner

The major media outlets are owned by major corporations with many corporate ties and they all report the same subjects from more or less the same perspective. Smaller presses tend to get their information from the larger presses that get their information from official institutions. Media is run like big business; the smaller businesses look to the more successful businesses as models for their own information and revenue gathering. Major media is run with confluences of agendas, known and unknown and lesser media follows their lead as a simple business practice, in this way the media is controlled directly and indirectly, resulting in institutionalized information and little examined information or creative questions.

The media on the periphery, which investigate and report on their own, with their own journalism model, are relegated as an alternative to the accepted media. Their reporting is seen as illegitimate. Because the sideline media questions the status quo, most everyone within it questions them. Their sources may be legitimate and their story groundbreaking, but until it is a tune played by predominantly accepted media, validity is often questioned.

The delivery and deliverers of information should be questioned. The more renowned the press, the less they tend to be questioned. Media should be questioned regardless of their commercial ties or circulation, but if there is to be any correlation, the larger the circulation, the more the press should be questioned. Their validity and intentions should be questioned with more intensity when they have larger audiences, bigger influences and wider confluences.

NBC was less likely to report on the fines and settlements concerning the pollution caused by former corporate partner GE. GE has destroyed waterways from state to state, but this goes largely unreported and underreported by major corporate media. GE also manufactures machines to clean water of industrial waste. Perhaps the majority does not want to know or perhaps they don't want the majority to know. GE ran commercials touting how much water they have cleaned. They don't mention how it got dirty in the first place. The media should question and even criticize this. The press should aggressively question the condition of water and the consequences of war.

Pat Tillman was a hero of war. Pat met his demise in Afghanistan, via friendly fire on April 22, 2004. The Pentagon, General Abizaid and others knew about the lying and distortion of issues surrounding the death of Pat. Yet, withholding and distortion of information continued. The Pentagon or someone lied, mislead Pat's family and the public for some time.

That's what is known; there are unknowns surrounding the death of Pat as well. Imagine all the other times people have been lied to or misled. If they have no qualms about lying to Pat's mother and everyone about the circumstances of Pat's death, what else might they lie about?

Pat was not only a professional football player, he was also an educated avid reader. He read the Koran, the Book of Mormon and multiple books by Noam Chomsky among many others. Not because he agreed with them necessarily, but because he questioned. Before he was shot, Pat had made plans to meet with Noam upon next returning home. Pat was making history and also pursuing a Master's Degree in history.

> "I think studying science is a good way to get into fields like history. The reason is, you learn what an argument means, you learn what evidence is, you learn what makes good sense to postulate and when, what's going to be convincing. You internalize the modes of rational inquiry, which happen to be more advanced in the sciences than anywhere else. On the other hand, applying relativity theory to history isn't going to get you anywhere. So it's a mode of thinking." ~Noam Chomsky

Pat was a hero before his death. He was a star athlete, a volunteer Army Ranger and a questioner who sought answers at university and on his own. There are many unknowns concerning his demise, but one known is that information was distorted and withheld. War was perpetuated and information manipulated. Anyone in the way of institutions, purposefully or accidentally, is run over.

> "Violence can only be maintained by a lie, and the lie can only be maintained by violence."
> ~Aleksander Solzhenitsyn

Pat's demise exposed lies. Pat was a bigger hero than any institution could manifest. Pat was a patriot and a hero simply because he continuously asked questions and had the courage to answer them. He inspired everyone around him and continues to inspire as well.

If people are presented misleading information or lies, they are misled, perhaps completely submerged in the mud, steered off course. Only when people have accurate information might they make accurate decisions and proceed in the right direction.

"I mean it's very important to keep in mind that this was not simply to dupe our family and dissuade our family. This was an attempt to dupe the public and promote this war and to get recruitment up and that is immoral and it's a travesty. That this young man who did not by the way believe in the war in Iraq…" ~Mary Tillman

Army concerned with mortal wounds.

"Cease fire! I'm Pat (expletive) Tillman, damn it!" ~Last words of Pat Tillman

physicians were the nature of Pat's Three gunshot head were so

wounds in the close together that the doctors believed he was shot from no farther a distance than ten meters. It is impossible to say for officials, but all evidence points to at least an initial cover up of friendly fire or possibly outright murder. Nevertheless, the known result is the same; death and deception. Against standard operating procedure, Pat's fatigues were incinerated in Afghanistan.

The media only resembles a fourth branch when difficult questions are asked. Otherwise they resemble other corporations. Freedom of the press is embedded into the operations of the U.S.A. as another check and balance. Liberty requires questioning to keep safe. Liberty is either progressed or repressed and asking questions progresses.

The right to be informed is not prone to the wherewithal to compute information or the tendency to seek it. Idiots have a general aversion to information and zealots have transcended new or differing information. If it's happening, people should know about it, but most people don't want to know about most events. Most people avoid information or put their own spin on things, the spin that suits them. Who can blame people for not wanting to know the horrors of world events, the decrepit morality of national and transnational motivations?

People outside the press fail to demand information, while people within its operation have a formula for discretion. People fail to demand and institutions fail to provide information. People are accustomed to holding their tongue and not asking pertinent questions. Journalists get paid to ask questions indifferently and pertinently, but their questions often have intention.

All information is computed, contemplated and processed by the conscious. The subconscious and unconscious also calculate and conclude in ways people may be completely oblivious to. Seemingly inconsequential information sometimes has a powerful impact. People consciously ask who, what, where, why, when and how in a direction that is limited in scope and capacity. When there is a battle, the question is more likely "How many?" instead of "Why?"

People are able to derive information and make decisions from four cognitive functions according to Carl Jung; thinking, feeling, sensing, and intuition. Thinking is logical and analytical thought. Feeling is individual moral distinction and values. Sensing is based on input from the five senses. Intuition is based on unconscious insight and symbolism. Thinking and feeling are considered to be judging functions, while sensing and intuition are considered to be perceiving functions. These mental functions constantly take place, regardless if one is unaware of the processes. Information influences all four forms of decision making, though people generally have a dominant function that defines their personality.

The media yields tremendous power, but exhibits little. Instead of the media being the official story, they spout the official story given to them by authorities. Immediately after corporate media exposed the injured outpatients' difficulties and dirty situations at Walter Reed Military Hospital in 2007, the institution did something about it. It is tremendously hard to believe that no authority had visited the hospital, located in Washington D.C. to notice the poor living conditions before the report. Only when the media brought it to the attention of the majority was something done about it. Heads rolled, the commissioned officer in charge of the facility for six months was fired and his predecessor was reinstalled.

This exemplifies the power of the media. The information is out there; some people knew about the situation at Walter Reed and care facilities beyond, but nothing was done about it until the story was exposed to the majority at large. The same institution that promotes volunteer service let injured combat veterans suffer when they could fight no longer. Billions upon billions spent and gone missing on war, but there was not enough funds to adequately support veterans. Where are their priorities? Maybe they thought there would be less injured or more dead. The reason doesn't matter, results are important. If one knows about wrongdoing it is really not a matter of opinion that something be done, rather it is just the practical and humane way.

> "If freedom of speech is taken away, then dumb and silent we may be led, like sheep to the slaughter."
> ~George Washington

People who sacrificed time, blood and limbs in order to enforce institutional policy returned to face a nightmare of misappropriated care and moldy quarters. Whether or not one agrees with the invasion and occupation of Iraq does not matter. What people think or how people think is inconsequential, injured people should be spared no expense, soldiers or otherwise, but the injured from the conjured war should be taken care of especially well, clean quarters a bare minimum.

The media is extremely powerful because they dispense information. Information is extremely powerful because it allows people, who tend to want the right thing in the first place, to be informed and do the right thing. The media empowers people by providing information.

Corporations have reasons to manipulate information before its distribution or withhold it altogether. The media has become less of an investigational force and more of an audio/visual crew that sets up the microphone and camera to enable institutions to tell their story. Most media outlets are more corporation than presenters of information. There is either uniform unclear thinking among reporters or there is underlying invisible reasons for their lack of investigation. They withhold certain information and extol other information. They do not simply and openly question.

Officials feed the media and the media mostly just prepare and present what was officially given to them. The media is less like news than it is sanctioned pieces of propaganda and institutionally approved information. On April 9, 2003, in Firdos Square, Baghdad, a military psy-ops unit had a famous statue of Saddam torn down by U.S.A. tanks and people. This was broadcasted the world over by the corporate media as an iconic event. The reporters on the scene filmed the event as if the people had spoken in spontaneity. It was actually staged, created to excite people and gain support.

This is proof that they do care what people in the U.S.A, and people of the world, think. Information is power because people are powerful, especially people with truth. With information people think and with correct information people are able to perceive actuality correctly. What people think does matter; it should matter to individuals and is an extremely important matter to institutions.

What people think is a priority may in fact be a prior manipulation, a hit on the unconscious. What one believes is established fact may be a crock, partial institutional interpretation or operation. People have power through information they hold among institutions. Institutions gain and maintain power by withholding certain information and presenting other information.

The official story is possibly wrong and just as likely to be part truth or lie as word from Joe Schmo. Only when questions are consistently posed does truth rise and separate like cream from milk. The press is supposed to separate institutional presentation from actuality, but they all too often support institutional presentation as actuality.

> "A nation of well-informed men, who have been taught to know and prize the rights that God has given them, cannot be enslaved. It is in the region of ignorance that tyranny begins." ~Benjamin Franklin

The original patriots would be skeptical of the confluences and connections of the multimedia monopolies that exist today. Great networks that cross borders are sponsored by industrious corporations that cross promote their products. International corporations provide us with intercontinental opinion. News outlets are corporations, their media just another product to be sold. Their number one concern shifted from obtaining and distributing information, to maintaining fiscal growth.

Certain corporations extol support of the troops, then they rip off the military and the taxpayers. Major media insist people support their interpretation in the same way, then present irrelevant or incomplete information. The presentation of advertising, news, propaganda, preconceptions, facts and possibilities are as intermingled as the confluences of corporations. "What is" and "what if" are mixed, and if one is not paying attention they may be confused. Investigations into actuality are belittled and replaced with other mediated subjects and concerns.

"Good advertising does not just circulate information. It penetrates the public mind with desires and belief."
~Leo Burnett, Advertising Executive

"True this -
Beneath the rule of men entirely great,
The pen is mightier than the sword. Behold
The arch-enchanter's wand! - itself is a nothing -
But taking sorcery from the master-hand
To paralyze the Caesars, and to strike
The loud earth breathless! - take away the sword -
States can be saved without it!" ~Edward Bulwer Lytton, Writer, Playwright

THE MONEY

"For the love of money is the root of all evil: which while some coveted after, they have erred from the faith and pierced themselves through with many sorrows." ~Timothy 6:10

If the press is the fourth branch of government, then money and its institutions comprise a fifth branch, to some it's the table itself. What do you work hard for? What do you work toward? Money drives concerns of the calendar. Money motivates most all, most always. Time and space are measured in money. We often measure our own existence monetarily. Institutions and individuals alike relate the value of everything monetarily, including that which is priceless; time and space.

Media institutions have business interests, their legal right as corporate institutional formations. It is possible that some are able to keep the interests of information and income fairly separated. Because money is so powerfully motivating, it is difficult to believe that they completely separate their distribution of information from their intention to gather money. Biased news agencies provide information to benefit their own interests and other institutions present certain information to the media to benefit their interests as well.

"One of the problems, not specifically with this issue just in general…that…um ah. Put it this way, ah…money trumps -sigh- peace, sometimes. Hehe, in other words commercial interests are very powerful interests in the world." ~George II

If money trumps peace, it trumps truth, for peace cannot be trumped without lying. Money, if there is enough of it, with the

155

majority of people, trumps anything and everything. Money potentially trumps anything and even anybody. What good is money if there is no peace, or no truth? What good is money when all that is remotely benevolent has been laid aside for it or run over by it? In the same way criminals commit crime solely for money, people give up what is right, even though it may not be criminal, for money.

Everyone has a price. People do things they don't necessarily want to do for money. Sometimes people don't want to enact wrong, but they need money and resort to the most horrendous criminal acts for money. Errant crime and official wrongdoing occur in efforts to obtain money, wealth and power. Politicians knowingly and admittedly legislate wrong because it may financially benefit some institution. Money has the power to motivate individuals to step on and run over other individuals. Money can make the religious steal and the moral murder. George II, who claimed to worship the Prince of Peace, admitted it and propagated it.

1980s	Saving and loan scandal cost U.S.A. taxpayers more than $150 billion.
1991	Exxon fined $125 million in connection with oil spill in Alaska.
1996	Daiwa bank Ltd. fined $340 million in conspiracy to defraud.
1998	Louisiana Pacific plea agreement cost the corporation $37 million for environmental conspiratorial crimes.
1999	F. Hoffman-La Roche Ltd. fined $500 million in global conspiracy to raise prices.
1999	Royal Caribbean Cruises Ltd. fined $18 million for pollution.
1999	BASF fined $225 million in worldwide conspiracy to raise prices.

"Laws control the lesser man; right conduct controls the greater one." ~Proverb, unknown origin

Fines are the cost of doing business. You have to pay to play, as the saying goes. If an individual cannot do the time, he should not do the crime, because time is the potential punishment for an individual who commits crime. If an institution violates rules of law, it is fined; the punishment of an institution is a fine. Institutions and the institutionalized enveloped by the institution, violate the sanctity of the environment or people and lie without hesitation, for they will likely only be punished by a fine, through the institution rather than punished with time.

When individuals commit crime, rights and privileges are revoked, and they are thrown in a hole. Yet when institutions commit crimes their existence is rarely threatened or halted, merely taxed. Individual criminals lose it all while institutions that operate criminally lose loose change.

Money, money, money. On December 23, 1913, the Federal Reserve Act was passed and later signed by President Woodrow Wilson. Many Senators, at least opposing Senators, were on their Christmas vacation when the vote took place, suggesting a conspiracy to vote at that time. This created the Federal Reserve and its Board, who are in charge of U.S.A. money, legal tender, greenbacks, cream, Federal Reserve Notes. This essentially outsourced the supply chain of U.S.A. notes to a private corporation. This decision goes against or eliminates part of Article 1 Section 8 of the U.S.A. Constitution.

"This act establishes the most gigantic trust on Earth. When the President signs the bill, the invisible government of the monetary power will be legalized…The worst legislative crime of the ages is perpetuated by this banking and currency bill." ~Charles Lindbergh Sr.

State institutions gave control of the issuance of capital to private banks, corporations that demand interest on every government credit transaction and coining of money. The responsibility and power laid out in the U.S.A. Constitution to Congress, was handed over to private banking institutions. The Act truly did establish the most gigantic trust on Earth. The whole economy, the biggest in the world at the time, is based on the trust that it is great and straight.

Private banks print the money and finance the U.S.A. A banking organization, supposedly predominantly owned by the Rothschild banks, Rockefeller banks, Warburg banks, Lazard Brothers of Paris, Chase Manhattan and other banking institutions. It is a secret exactly which banks run the Federal Reserve. Banks make loot off of every bill they print for the U.S.A. in printing costs and on interest on the value of money they lend. They get paid on the value of the money that they print. Banks print money and then assign value to it, instead of obtaining wealth and printing money in the value of it.

At the same time that banks print and facilitate cash which represents wealth, banks also practice fractional reserve banking. Banks create income by using the money people deposit for loans and various investments. When many people decide they need their deposits and the bank has lost money in bad loans or whatever, they might crash because they lend much more money than they actually have. Washington Mutual crashed in 2008 because of fractional banking, bad investments and a run of deposit withdrawals. It was the largest bank crash in the history of the U.S.A.

Having outside banking institutions print the U.S.A. coin is perhaps the original outsourcing program. The U.S.A. Government outsourced one of the primary functions of government, printing money and regulating the value thereof. It makes no sense, but it makes a lot of dollars, for someone. Who has the money to fund the U.S.A.?

FACT: On June 4, 1963, just months before he was assassinated, President John Fitzgerald Kennedy issued Executive Order # 11110. This would have set in motion the printing of new silver dollars, U.S.A. Dollars that would have been backed by silver bullion.

The U.S.A. Constitution, as it originally was set up, allowed for corporate taxation. Further it allowed the taxation on one's corporate activities and gains. It allowed for taxes derived from direct purchases, but direct taxes were for corporate earnings and not the labors of individuals. The Constitution provided Congress with the duty of printing and facilitating notes. Woodrow Wilson changed all that, passing the Federal Reserve Act, soon after he was elected, written by bankers.

The Federal Reserve Act was drafted of off the Aldrich Bill, named after Nelson Aldrich, (U.S.A. Senator from Rhode Island 1881-1911) who was related to the Rockefellers by marriage. Supposedly it was drafted in 1910, in secret, at a resort on Jekyll Island off of Georgia. Now we use Federal Reserve notes for the exchange of goods and services. The U.S.A Government could print money without paying interest on it, but it doesn't.

"I am a most unhappy man. I have unwittingly ruined my country. A great industrial nation is controlled by its system of credit. Our system of credit is concentrated. The growth of the nation, therefore, and all our activities are in the hands of a few men. We have come to be one of the worst ruled, one of the most completely dominated governments in the western world. No longer a government by free opinion, no longer a government by conviction and the vote of the majority, but a government by the opinion and duress of a small group of dominant men." ~Woodrow Wilson

---

The plans for the Federal Reserve Notes and the taxation of personal income were implemented the same year. The Federal Income Tax was created February 1913, in the form of the Sixteenth Amendment. The Sixteenth Amendment provides that Congress shall have the power to lay and collect taxes without apportionment. Some states did not ratify the new amendment.

The government started paying the Federal Reserve Bank to print money, lend money and make that money trustworthy. Along with the income tax, people began being taxed just to pay for the circulation of money. The taxation of labors and the Federal Reserve were both mandated in 1913 and the taxation has been upheld since, with the threat of imprisonment. The Federal Reserve is a private group of banks, some of which are supposedly foreign. The IRS is also a private entity. The Fed is not federal, only supported by the authority and power of the Feds' guns and prisons, mainly held by people of strict convictions. Taxation in the U.S.A. is questionable.

Income tax upheld in broad decision - Supreme Court unanimously against all contentions of unconstitutionality - White points out errors - Congress leaders, pleased by decision, will now amend the law to obtain revenue for defense. ~New York Times, 1916

In the last thirty years, the Federal Government has lost billions and billions of taxpayer money. Every year this grand loss takes place. All citizens are required to accurately report the coming and going of their money under penalty of authority. The Federal Government must comply in the same manner and accurately report what they do with money, but every single year, money goes missing. The money is predominantly lost via the military. Are people to believe that the perfection instilled into military personnel leaves their offices unable to accurately add and subtract?

Maybe they had a bad year, they could have lost a couple billion crossing the Euphrates River, or maybe it got mixed up in a bombing campaign or a food drop. Anything could happen, but starkly and consistently every year is unbelievable and unacceptable. How does cash get lost? How do digital records of money get lost? This is the same organization that prides itself in regimented arrangement of everything, including folding one's uniform. Perhaps after years of claiming to lose billions of dollars, someone in the corporate media would investigate. The IRS would dismantle any private individual that lost a fraction on such a consistent basis.

This abuse is confronting, but perhaps worse is that the government has abandoned its constitutional obligation outsourcing the facilitation of money. Institutions further abandon individuals by continuing to lose money. The system is sophisticated and complicated, but some things are easy to add up.

> "The hardest thing in the world to understand is the income tax."
> ~Albert Einstein

> "According to some estimates we cannot track $2.3 trillion in transactions."
> ~Donald Rumsfeld, January 29, 2002

Billions lost in routine spending and billions more vanished during extraordinary circumstances. Authority must be accountable and before everyone else. Authority must be held accountable to keep its authority, beginning with their accounting, otherwise authority is simply another power.

The Constitution provides Congress with the authority to issue money without paying interest to corporate banks. It only makes sense for the government to print its own money rather than pay for it to be done. Yet, this responsibility was given up to some shadowy corporate entity called the Federal Reserve.

It is legislation similar to alcohol prohibition, in that it is worthy of the same temporary status. Everyone that pays taxes is concerned about where their money goes. A lot of it goes to money heaven, disappearing in corruption and incompetence.

People become agitated when they learn where their tax dollars go, complaining about one group or another benefiting from their money. About forty cents of every tax dollar goes to military spending. It would be one thing if federal taxes conjured useful public services or promoted individual well-being, but most taxes are spent on militarism. The Bush Doctrine promised to perform offense on threats, instead of defense on attacks, shamming the name of the Department Of Defense.

Local and state taxes normally pay for the little things that individuals may benefit from like education, roads, plumbing and civil infrastructure. What if people had a say as to where their tax dollars went? Where would we be today if people directly chose how their taxes were spent? The U.S.A. is worth paying for and defending, but institutions should not benefit from such basics as water or such dire as war. U.S.A. tax dollars are predominantly spent building the biggest military machine and as payment on interest to the most powerful banking empire on the planet.

The people of the U.S.A. were intended to have control and possession of their wealth, not corporate banks. The original patriots knew the corruptive power of money. Banks and corporations were often servants of the church and state, their potential corruption is nothing new. The original patriots placed barriers on the powers and connections of religious, state and corporate institutions, but eventually capitalism enabled corporations, including banks, to gain intricate powers and global connections. Corporations, including banks, are interested in benefiting those within their institution, not individuals in general. Institutional integration allows corruption, while open regulation and accountability limits corruption.

In the old world, all institutions served church or state, or both. With freedom, individuals had the opportunity to break away from despotism and either institute new oligarchy or instigate liberty. With liberty all individuals are protected among institutions. Banks are corporate institutions, in pursuit of corporate interests, in spite of individuals.

> "I believe that banking establishments are more dangerous to our liberties than standing armies; and that the principal of spending money to be paid by posterity, under the name of funding, is but swindling futurity on a large scale. Already they have raised a money aristocracy that has set the government at defiance. If the American people ever allow private banks to control the issue of their money, first by inflation, then by deflation, the banks and corporations that grow up around them will deprive the people of all property until their children will wake up homeless on the continent their fathers conquered. The issuing power should be taken from the banks and restored to the people to whom it properly belongs." ~Thomas Jefferson

The Company and the British were facing financial troubles in the late 1700s. Their hardship led to the taxation of the Colonies and others, which also led to people's resentment. Thomas and the original patriots could see the engineering of the system they were in. They knew the potential power of banks and the greed that drives them and attempted to counter their oligarchy and all oligarchical collectivism.

Money drives corporations to manipulate and murder in order to meet goals. Banks are not the only institutions that scheme using complicated financial plots; they are perhaps just best at it. Militaristic institutions are not the only institutional formations that practice in mayhem and harm; they are just the best at it. There are many subjects machines do not compute, but money is computable to them all.

> FACT: Ford Motors used accepted risk/benefit analysis to determine their course of action when faced with realization the Pinto was defective. They concluded that the cost of fixing their mistake would be $137 million and the cost from lawsuits from death, injury and damages was predicted to be $49 million. At least 11 people died as a direct result of the Pinto's tendency to ignite on impact.

Money drives people to scheme and plot, sometimes in a most underhanded and malicious manner, sometimes by just withholding information. A conspiracy is a secret plan among more than one party to act. To conspire is to make wrongful clandestine plans. Sometimes these conspiracies may directly include death and murder, sometimes that may not be part of the plan, money most always is part of the plan.

Information concerning conspiracies is hidden in shadowy intangibles, twisted among debated complexities. Information about the greatest conspiracies is perceived to be expressed only by the paranoid or mad. The greatest conspiracies convince people that those who speak of them are hysterical. The greatest conspiracies maintain secrets and unknowns if only through doubt or silence. The poorest conspiracies turn out to be the greatest foils.

Andrew Jackson foiled one such conspiracy, that of the Second Bank of the United States. It was a decently conjured conspiracy, so the information is shrouded and debated. Andrew saw that a private entity, the bank, was making the wealthy more wealthy and putting control of government money into the hands of foreign interests. The Second Bank was, in part, owned by wealthy Europeans. The Second Bank printed money, and then lent it to the government with interest. It was an oligarchy, an institutional formation benefiting the few at the expense of the many.

Andrew vetoed the re-charter of the bank in 1832. He fired two Secretaries of Treasury until one would withdraw funds from the Second Bank in 1833. This eventually crippled the oligarchy of the bank.

In January 1835, Richard Lawrence, a painter, conducted a failed assassination attempt on Andrew. Andrew was enjoying a walk when Richard tried to shoot the President with two pistols, both of which misfired. Andrew then caned Richard. Bystanders, including Davy Crockett, wrestled Richard, and he was taken into custody. Richard believed he was the King of England and declared insane. Andrew and many others believed it was a failed assassination plot, a conspiracy.

> FACT: Andrew Jackson was a courier in the Revolutionary War. At the age of 13, he was held by the British as a POW. He became a military leader during the War of 1812 and the First Seminole War. Andrew introduced a Final Solution, the "Final Solution of the Indian Problem" was the Indian Removal Act. Hitler had a final solution too, the "Final Solution to the Jewish question."

> "You are a den of vipers and thieves. I intend to rout you out, and by the eternal God, I will rout you out."
> ~Andrew Jackson to bankers

> "The bank is trying to kill me, but I will kill it."
> ~Andrew Jackson to Martin Van Buren

These final solutions were euphemisms for extermination and eradication of people. No matter the words killing is killing, and normally done for simple wealth, though often performed among other ardent beliefs. An institution, a bank, cannot be killed, for it never lived. Institutions are just formations of individual interests and ideas, just tools.

In 1836, the Second Bank of the U.S.A. was made into a state bank and existed as much until 1841. Banks are the elite of the corporate institutions. They control, manufacture and regulate that which everyone wants, works for and plots for. Money is not only a measurement of one's financial worth; it is also a measurement of the interests of institutions. The records of institutional income may suggest potentially conspiratorial ties and interests by revealing where they get their money. Their accounts hold them accountable.

Money is the root of all evil, and the roots are connected to the tree that manifests itself among people as oligarchical collectivism. Banks have performed the most scandalous and greatest assortment of conspiracies in history, though they are not alone. Money is only the means, the mathematical measure, the end, the goal, for institutionalization is power.

> "Give me control of a nation's money supply and I care not who makes its laws." ~Mayer Rothschild

Who is in charge? Who is behind institutional conspiracies to control? All sorts of scoundrels and weasels have conducted a wide variety of plots, but all narrowly toward the same end, power. Money is a measurement of their interests and their clandestine direction; follow the money. It is actual and mathematically traceable. Follow the money trail and eventually one will find the machines chasing it and observe which machines run over all that is well and good. Investigate how the unseen roots of institutions intertwine underground. Institutional ties require questioning to understand their interplay.

Behind institutional schemes there are always groups of institutionalized individuals benefiting from the oligarchical collectivism. There are always elitists at the center of plotting, behind closed doors, orchestrating the music and driving the machine. If there is a conspiracy, there is likely a group of commanders and there is practically always a colonel of sorts.

FACT: Edward Mandell House was given the honorary title of Colonel House. The Colonel was born in Texas and educated at Cornell University. When his father died, the Colonel sold the family plantations and became a banker, an advisor of the elite and an author. He anonymously penned the fictional work "Phillip Dru: Administrator" and also scribed documents pertaining to the very real founding of the Council on Foreign Relations. He never served in the military, but was involved with the Ku Klux Klan and the Texas Rangers. He was a close advisor to a few Texas Governors. He never had an official title, but had his own bedroom at the Woodrow Wilson White House. He met with European elite, including the German Kaiser before the U.S.A. entered WWI in failed attempts to negotiate peace. Later he assisted in the facilitation of goods for the war effort. The Colonel also served Franklin D. Roosevelt. The Colonel was a member of at least one secret society.

In 1933, President Franklin D. Roosevelt began to implement new regulations to counter the worldwide Great Depression, in the U.S.A. It arguably began in October 1929 in the U.S.A. when the stock market crashed. Many countries did not recover from the global Great Depression until after WWII, while other countries were mostly unaffected. In the U.S.A. the jobless rate was nearly 25%. Statistically speaking, different conditions were taken into account then compared to twenty first century calculations of joblessness.

Franklin enacted new legislation aimed at solving economic problems throughout his presidency, but most of the New Deal policies were instigated in his first one hundred days as President. Prohibition ended and Social Security began. Banks were closed for inspection and the gold standard was abandoned. The sweeping legislation of the New Deal included setting up the Public Works Administration and the Federal Deposit Insurance Corporation. Laws to regulate stock trade, treatment of employees and fair capitalism were implemented to stimulate growth and at least negate decline.

> "The real truth of the matter is, as you and I know, that a financial element in the large centers has owned the government ever since the days of Andrew Jackson." ~A letter written by FDR to Colonel House, 1933

> "History records that the moneychangers have used every form of abuse, intrigue, deceit, and violent means possible to maintain their control over governments by controlling money and its issuance." ~James Madison

"Who controls the food supply controls the people; who controls the energy can control whole continents; who controls the money can control the world." Henry Kissinger is accused of making this statement. Henry may not have said these words about controlling the world but whoever did, made a profound and slightly disturbing point. Henry served as Secretary of State to President Nixon and Johnson. After 9/11 Henry was appointed to head to investigation into the crime of 9/11. He promptly resigned because of potential conflicts of interests, namely his Saudi Arabian business ties. Henry has been accused of various war crimes on various continents, by various governments.

Institutions provide and prevent using turmoil to instigate agenda and limit perspective. What seems benevolent is often also malevolent. Institutions and the institutionalized are like Dr. Jekyll and Mr. Hyde. At one time they provide and heal and later they harm and steal.

When times are tough, when food, energy and money are limited, assistance arrives to institutions within the status quo primarily and help to individuals begins later, through institutions. This is the design of the status quo, the few over the many. In 2008, after several government bailouts of private U.S.A. institutions, a seven hundred billion dollar economic package was passed with the stated intention of enabling financial and corporate institutions, so that they would remain and eventually assist individuals in the economic crisis. Billions were distributed to troubled banks and stable banks as well. It was presumed that if failing institutions crashed they would take everybody down with them.

The U.S.A. Government assisted institutions so that they might assist individuals. The government invested billions into failing institutions and billions more into other institutions that were not failing, so that they might not fail and that the troubled would not appear especially troubled relative to other institutions. After the stabilization, institutions eventually, in pyramidal fashion, could assist individuals. Institutional assistance comes first, the assistance of the individual is never direct and always within the institutionalized architecture of the status quo.

The program was originally labeled a bailout, but renamed a rescue. The latter was considered more comfortable and acceptable terminology. It was not argued that one or the other was inaccurate; merely that one description was more acceptable and enabling. They change the presentation with as little as switched verbiage to influence opinion.

Within the 2008 bank bailout bill is a stipulation that makes it mandatory for people involved in a mortgage loan to submit their fingerprints. This is meant to provide more accountability, but produces a national fingerprint registry. Criminals always find ways to con and contrast law, while the innocent normally end up being robbed by criminal behavior on both sides of legality. In 2009, after the money was spent, the Congressional Oversight Panel concluded that the Troubled Asset Relief Program, not only covered the bad assets of financial institutions, but also overpaid on covering for or covering up the bad assets by seventy eight billion dollars. Some institutions used the TARP money for foreign investments as well.

Representatives of the "big three" automotive corporations later requested a multibillion dollar bailout as well, or what was termed as a bridge-loan. Chrysler received a $4 billion loan and sought more, while GM clocked an initial $9.4 billion and then some when its finance company is included. By April, 2009 GM Corp. received over $15 billion in taxpayer money and while the finance company got $5 billion in aid. Ford initially asked for assistance and then declined government financial assistance despite facing economic woes, in 2008 Ford lost $14 billion. In May 2009, Chrysler went bankrupt and the U.S.A. federal government stated that the warranties and retirement packages the corporation had would be secured by the government. In June 2009, GM went bankrupt as well.

Barack means blessed in Swahili and has Arabic roots. In Hebrew Barak means lightning. Hussein means good and handsome in Arabic and is a popular name. Obama may have roots in the Kenyan word meaning to be bent. Rahm is Hebrew for high or lofty, the similarly sounding ra'am means thunder in Hebrew. Israel has unclear meaning, but is considered to mean striving with God. El is an old Hebrew word for God. And Emanuel is of course Hebrew and means God is with us.

Eight hundred billion was raised for a separate economic stimulus plan in early 2009 after Barack was elected. The stimulus was a solution engaged for economic crisis. People would be put to work building national institutional infrastructure. The maintenance of roads, bridges and other projects were instigated and would benefit individuals with employment and use of infrastructure, but the construction was designed predominantly to maintain the status quo of institutions and not to develop or enhance conditions on behalf of individuals.

Weeks later in March 2009, the executive and legislative branches of the U.S.A. passed the omnibus spending bill. The four hundred and ten billion dollars was put aside to maintain and expand government offices and also to initiate more projects throughout the country intended to stimulate the economy. These unnecessary earmarks or pork barrel spending were the last Barack would allow, according to his declaration. Barack signed the omnibus bill even though he referred to it as

161

imperfect.

Some individuals variously received tax breaks, jobs and assistance, but mainly the format of the spending was in maintenance of the status quo and not progression of individuals. The stimulus bill benefited people, was predominantly maintenance of the status quo and continuation of institutionalization.

While sensible people save their money and squirrel away some nuts for hard times, or long winter, before the economic troubles that precluded the institutional bailout and economic stimulus, many spent outside their means. Many individuals spent money they did not have with the belief they would have it later. Many institutions spent outside their means as well and some prompted individuals to do the same. To solve the problem of spending more money than available, the government spent money they didn't have, pulling billions from whatever money tree they go to. The government spent money it did not have, in order to solve the problem of institutions and individuals spending money that they did not have. If only there were real trees or plants that might grow and bear real fruit, real resources for individuals to use and develop economically and industrially, instead of their figurative money trees.

In early 2009, while visiting the U.S.A., Prime Minister of the UK Gordon Brown announced the plan for a global bailout of sorts as a solution to the ongoing global energy and climate crisis and the new global economic crisis. The "global new deal" or "global grand bargain" as described by Gordon would be implemented as a solution to the global environmental, energy and economic crises.

Institutions and the institutionalized collectivize globally before enabling individuals locally. Institutional rescue is from the likes of Dr. Jekyll and Mr. Hyde, the salvation often comes with sacrifice. Institutional rescue is an operation that advances institutional agendas. Institutions were more intertwined after the bailout/rescue/buyout and stimulus plan.

Institutions are like the highest trees in the forest canopy, they get the most light, work with the most money. Assistance for individuals filters through them, first institutionalized. The institutional monopolizations to reach that height often have to be done clandestinely because they are frequently overtly wrong. Institutions have to lie and have to convince individuals to just lie there.

Under the spreading chestnut tree
I sold you and you sold me,
There lie they, and here lie we
Under the spreading chestnut tree
~George Orwell, *1984*

"If you would know the value of money, go try to borrow some; for he that goes a-borrowing goes a-sorrowing." ~Benjamin Franklin

"Power is the ultimate aphrodisiac." ~Henry Kissinger

ENJOY SWEDEN

Money is the measurement of one's financial worth, not one's overall worth. People kill and die for it, people plot and steal for it, and yet money is only a means to an end. No matter how much people like a stack of Grants or Benjamins, it is not because they are pretty; it is because with them, certain goods and services can be acquired. Money is not sought because it is appealing, but rather because with it, one can acquire pleasantries.

People are always looking for ways to get money. On August 23, 1973, a botched bank robbery took place in Stockholm, Sweden. The robbery turned into a near weeklong hostage crisis, and ultimately, an experiment in the human condition. Four hostages were taken by the robbers and held during the confrontational situation. The hostages later refused to testify against their captors and even helped raise legal defense for them.

The captives in the Stockholm bank robbery developed a kinship for their captors partly because the police used extreme tactics that put the hostages in more jeopardy. Their captors held them against their will and threatened to kill them. Yet the captives felt more endangered by the outsiders than by their captors. The captives eventually developed a kinship or devotion to their captors.

There are many ways to initiate this tick called Stockholm Syndrome; the point is it exists. Usually it requires shock treatment of sorts. It is the imagery and perception that one's captor is one's benefactor. It is a coordinated Dr. Jekyll and Mr. Hyde. It is punches followed by caresses in the dark and the insistence that an outside entity caused the pain. Instead of questioning where the punches come from, the caresses comfort and subdue. Battered spouses, members of religious cults, kidnapped children and adults, often develop Stockholm Syndrome. It is a blind trust for their captors (their providers as well) and a distrust of outsiders, even those outsiders who are potential rescuers.

There is a certain bond that hits some primordial tick within which enables the captivity. The captured empathize and even adore their captors to the point where they no longer seek to escape. Kidnappers manipulate the minds of their victims and convince them the outside world is not to be questioned, that there is nothing there for them except hardship.

Sometimes those with Stockholm Syndrome are forcefully held and other times they are held simply by information. There is truth just beyond the open door, but they are afraid to go outside. They've been trained to stay inside; they are oriented to the dimness of their captor's conditioning. The captors are seen as the providers and the only protectors in a world of uncaring unknowns.

People desire to be part of the group they are aware of. If people are allowed to socialize with just one group or grow accustomed to just one group they will do whatever it takes to be acceptable and elevate their status within the group, even allowing abuse. Stockholm Syndrome is normally noted by some form of shock and trauma, but it might be displayed less fervently through playing on fears, particularly of ostracism. No one wants to be alone. Stockholm Syndrome is an extension of the most powerful individual social impulse, evident in all cultures throughout recorded time, to be included.

Socrates lived from 469 to 399 BC. He formulated the theory to researching information; establishing the basis for scientific questioning. The Socratic Method and scientific questioning from Protagoras are the basis for western science and philosophy. Socrates expanded ideas through discussion of questions and bettered philosophy through communication. Many formulas for critical thinking were theorized by Socrates and described by his student Plato. Aristotle, also Socrates' pupil, wrote about Socrates, but Socrates himself left no writings behind himself. Others wrote about him, he was considered to be eccentric, even loony by many of his peers.

Socrates theorized that at the roots of institutions he knew, was exploitation and hypocrisy. He theorized certain directions for questioning that would defeat arguments with such murky basis. A sophist originally meant wise person, the synonym, sophistes, means poet. Sophists had designed their own form of rhetorical argument, especially pertinent to politics and overall supportive of institutions whereas Socratics were supportive of individuals. Sophists are still identified as intellectuals who misuse information and manipulate others. Socratic questioning dismantled sophist intellectual thinking as doubletalk to make gains and the sophists hated him for it. Socrates questioned elitist exploitation, even those of well-founded institutions.

Sophist and Socratic schools grew to be distinctly at odds. Sophists made up narratives of Socrates to disgrace his school, the lies backfired and the sophists were mostly scorned. Some contemporaries suggested that Socrates was himself a sophist. Regardless, the two schools were divergent and definitely countered one another. A distinct divergence between the schools was that Socrates did not accept payment, while the sophists only taught for a fee.

Socrates theorized that no one desires evil and that those who do commit wrong, do so unknowingly or unwittingly. Socrates believed all people wanted goodness, but would do wrong unknowingly when convinced and misled. Socrates was not only an intellectual, his father was a stonemason and he probably learned the trade. Socrates also served in the military, distinguishing himself in battle. He was a great teacher and questioned the entire status quo with everyone.

Ultimately Socrates was put on trial for corrupting the minds of youth. Socrates supposedly mocked the court and refused to back down. He was given the death penalty and made to drink Hemlock poison. He accepted the death sentence and drank the poison. Plato observed and described the trial and poisoning and also scribed many Socratic thoughts in his influential book "The Republic."

Socrates understood people in relation to their reaction to information and their cognitive ability. He often cited his own ignorance as he openly questioned the conditions of actuality and inspired others to do the same. Despite his claim to ignorance, he was considered most wise and designed numerous allegories and theories to inspire thought, reasoning and questioning.

In Socrates' Allegory of the Cave, as described by Plato in "The Republic", humanity is likened to prisoners in a cave. They are imprisoned by their ignorance and they are held by their captor's presentation of information. In the cave the captors burn a fire providing the only light source. Using the light from the fire, the captors cast shadows of various images, symbols, shapes, characters and archetypes on a wall. The imprisoned are forced to watch the images on the wall, and hear only the occasional noises made by those casting the images. The prisoners ultimately conclude what they are observing is reality in total.

The prisoners only observe the counterfeit version of reality. The more experienced and developed minds among the prisoners are those who can predict what image will come up next or when there will be a noise. To Socrates and Plato, the untutored are those who do not question, observing merely shadows, trapped by just a portion of distorted reality. In Socrates' Allegory of the Cave there are four types of cave dwellers.

There are the shackled who do not question their reality, the presentation they are forced to watch. They are the idiots. The other prisoners in the cave are unshackled, but are still transfixed by the images. They are the zealots. Neither questions the partial reality they know and are presented.

Then there are the captors. The captors maintain the imprisonment of the others in the cave by casting imagery and making noise to distract them. They are the elitists. In the cave, all information is flipped, twisted and distorted to be used for the few to control the many. Presentation of a minute portion of reality, the shadows in a cave, is unquestioned by the majority, images of reality are accepted as reality. Shadows cast false evidence appearing real and accepted as real by the prisoners. The elitists left the cave or den and learned reality only to return and rule over the prisoners with superior knowledge.

The fourth classification in the cave, the classification with the fewest numbers, is the freed prisoners. These are people whose chains were removed or unlocked after a lifetime in the cave. They left the light of the fire and the cast shadows. They made their way through the total darkness of the cave without guidance to find the crawlspace leading to the outside world. The freed prisoners see, hear and sense the outside world and after initial confusion they learn about actuality. They learn about the sun, water and rocks. They learn about gravity, reality and the reflections or shadows of reality. Eventually, after realizing actuality, the freed prisoners return to the cave to tell the other captives about reality in attempts to free them. They are the patriots.

Truth is outside the scope of the captives. A tiny portion of a distorted reality is accepted as reality in total. Some of the captors, in charge of the presentation of untruth, may believe it to be reality in totality as well. They question only what suits their preconditioned actuality. Reality becomes mystery, and false evidence becomes reality.

The cast imagery prevents the prisoners from seeing the splinter of sunlight that comes through the tunnel to the outside. The real world goes unnoticed. Socrates and Plato believed that anyone who did not question actuality was stuck in the cave and most of those who did question, used information to distract and extract.

Expanding on Socrates' Allegory of the Cave, Plato described the condition of perception in the Analogy of the Divided Line. There are four types of people classified according to how they perceive and how they question reality. Idiots are reduced to picture thinking and conjecture. Zealots are caught up in belief. Elitists are scientific, but their capacity is reduced to greedy reasoning. Patriots share understanding. There are four types of people in the world. There are idiots, zealots, elitists and patriots defined by their cognitive tendencies.

Socrates and Plato conceptualized four types of thought processes. There is picture thinking, belief, reason and wisdom. The Analogy of the Divided Line presents a line first divided into two parts and then subdivided. These parts recognize the four forms of information. First the sensible and the intelligible are divided in two. In the sensible there is reality and also real reflections. In the intelligible there is first the idea or fact and also the reflection of that. First there is a given concept and next there is a reflection of that concept.

First there are two divisions in the line, then it splits and dual thinking, doubles. Double becomes multiple. The Divided line's largest section is the tangible world. Next to it is the portion representing reflections of reality. Thirdly, in the same proportion as the tangible, is the intangible and finally reflections of the intangible, being the smallest portion of the Divided Line.

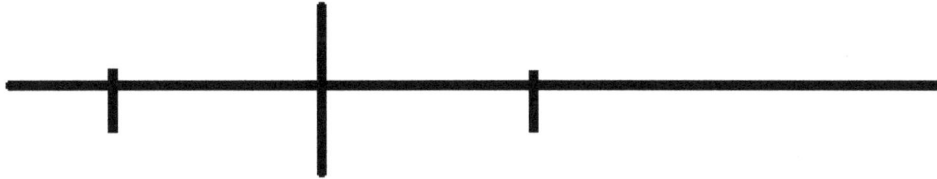

Narrow-mindedness equates to thinking in merely one term or another. Open-mindedness equates to an individual possessing the capability to think widely on multiple levels and realize the cognition of others. Interestingly enough Plato means broad, it is said this was in reference to his wide shoulders. If one is concentrated in one mode of thinking, one might be played by conceptualizations or images without realizing it. An understanding of reflections and reality, the tangible and intangible, through questioning situations leads to a better understanding of actuality and oneself. In turn, one is less subject to the ideas of others and more likely to come to an independent conclusion and act on one's own ideas.

Live and let live. Don't tread on me! Live free or die! These are archetypal notions reflective of liberty and the sentiment that it is worth sacrifice; worth even the ultimate price. These sentiments are reminders that liberty requires responsibility and that people have given life and limb for it. The sacrifice should also remind people that one has to realize they are being treaded on before they take action. In order to know, one must question. If people do not constantly question conditions they may end up in a cave and not realize where they are. When people don't question getting stepped on, they will likely get stepped on and stepped over again.

Patriots are people who ask simple questions, outside of the box, outside of the cave, in wide and open terms. Patriots shake off the benefits and break free from the chains and confines of institutionalized procedure. Patriots look beyond what the status quo displays and question it. Patriots break out of their situation, their cave and question. Then they return to the cave to show other prisoners the escape route and reality. Patriots put real individuals before institutions.

Capitalism has interfered with fair trade, fair treatment and patriotism. The directives of the human mind have been subverted and replaced by the directives and tolerations of institutionalized capitalist motivations. It is the same with any institutionalization; capitalism is pyramidal and monopolistic. Capitalism has people captive, and yet, also provides. Capitalism trades sensibility for selfish goals, decision making is based primarily on money. Capitalism is both captor and provider in a global case of Stockholm Syndrome. Communism is no alternative; it is just a counter way to captivate, to give and take - mostly take. Free and fair trade is a beautiful thing, but capitalism is often manipulated into capitalizing exploitation while communism might be manipulated into other controlling exploitations.

Capitalism has inspired people to forgive the unforgivable and tend to the insensible. People block out what is right in order to profit and prosper within the status quo. A favor is only given in return for another favor. Rarely does anyone help the helpless unless they are promised to receive something in return.

Yet when the shit hits the fan, there is likely to be little or limited institutional assistance, there are only other individuals. When disaster strikes the captor/provider is usually gone. As in Hurricane Katrina, the institutions were mostly unavailable and undercover, busy ensuring their own longevity and interests. The government of the people, by the people and for the people is surrounded and made up of institutions that benefit certain people and strangers. Institutions and the institutionalized pick and choose who they help while open-minded individuals help others, strangers included.

Institutions hold the reins, steering direction, and they claim to veer toward betterment. It is increasingly difficult to believe them, unless one doesn't get out much. Institutions have agendas separate from individual interests. They hold their own differing agendas above those of individuals and act towards their own self-interest and advancement. Institutions and the institutionalized are selfish, perhaps with occasional generosity, but predominantly self-serving.

Institutions have agendas, which guide their existence, while people have hearts and minds. As people become more reliant on interdependent institutions, it may be difficult to notice their direct influences. GE provides people with light bulbs to read by and pollution to puke. Conventional pork and beef farms provide people with meat and negated water. Fashion corporations provide sleek shoes and warm clothes along with exploited employees. Automobile corporations provide people with transportation and leave people with carcinogens the world over. Coal corporations supply people with energy and blighted air. Oil corporations supply energy for everything and pollution in everything.

Despite institutional trespasses, people are more trusting of institutions than individuals. People lend more trust to mechanized institutions because they are perceived as greater and more important than any one individual. They are the providers. Individuals receive more skepticism and have more preconceptions placed on them than institutions, often according to institutional program.

It is as if people are controlled by a benefactor and detractor; held captive and held down, but clothed and provided for. Society at large is suffering from Stockholm Syndrome. People forgive institutions that trespass and trample on people and planet. They are forgivable because of pronounced greater intention beyond visible morality, because people think they need institutions.

Institutions are capable of sanctioning murder and mayhem in the name of peace and safety. Institutions conduct thievery and larceny and claim discovery and trade. Institutions and the institutionalized operate in stark duality, they say one thing and do another. Institutions take on the archetype of the friendly warden, instigating Stockholm Syndrome and casting a spell as in the story of Beauty and the Beast.

Institutional transgressions and treading over principle, family and country are forgiven because if small transgressions are not accepted then bigger horrors may arise. Only institutions could instill this logic. Only a reputable source could convince people to disregard rationality and commit wrong to obtain right. Only established institutions can conclude their morality and high standing by committing lowly acts. Only the institutionalized believe that one thing means another and persuade others as much.

An example of such institutional insistence is the pardoning of President Richard Nixon by his former colleague, Gerald Ford. The powers in authority can apparently get away with anything; there is little to no accountability. Gerald died and the media praised him for giving Dick a pardon and preventing the country from being torn apart by an incriminating trial.

By giving Dick a Presidential Pardon it showed that some can exist above the law. It set the precedent for future Presidential Administrations to break laws as they please and commit acts of immoral despotism that may or may not be legal, only to obtain a pardon later. No goodness goes untainted by trespasses.

> "One must be broken apart, before he can be put back together complete and perfect." ~Unknown

Instead of the country being torn apart by a Presidential conviction, the country is torn apart by criminals who continue to get Presidential Pardons or other exceptions. They expect people to obey the law or face the consequences, but their own, in seeking their own agenda, are unaccountable. Yet, it is rarely observed in that context because they are the authority and despite their actions, they have best intentions in mind and after all, the rest of the world is a dangerous place. Stockholm Syndrome, stuck in Socrates' cave.

No man is above the law, except some. Gerald died while there were more lawsuits against elected officials lying and withholding information, at the highest echelons of U.S.A. government than ever before. There were many lawsuits against fraudulent corporations, and many perverted and unaccountable transgressions in churches. Yet, the media celebrated the precedent set by the president.

People are entitled to another chance and forgiveness, people deserve at least a second chance, but accountability can coincide with forgiveness. Institutions are not individuals, and the institutionalized do not act as individuals.

Dick should have been thrown to the judicial wolves as an example of what happens to anyone in the U.S.A. who considers themselves above the law. The President is the highest government executive, with a lot of power, but he is still only a public employee. Individuals merit forgiveness at least as much as institutions and the institutionalized, but rarely receive it.

The powerful who perform betrayal should be forgiven at a later date, perhaps after an investigation or at least and possibly only after punishment. It seems that no matter what they do, authority has ways to provide and promote unaccountability. It seems that the media will celebrate this or whatever else they are informed of as pertinent. It is sure that corporate media and government institutions will do whatever it takes to ensure strong, legitimate, proud legacies for Presidents and leaders.

If people in authority were remembered for everything they did and not everything they celebrate, things would be different. Perhaps even the trinity of liberty would have developed faster and differently. Simply questioning Gerald's legacy would question unaccountability. If the legacies of institutionalized leaders were questioned, people would not immediately ratify and glorify. Gerald may have been a great President, but just because he was President does not make him great, and just because Dick was President does not make him forgivable.

> FACT: Gerald Ford, a Yalie, became Vice-President without being elected in late 1973. He later became President without being elected in August 1974. A month later, he gave the preemptive Presidential Pardon to his predecessor, Richard Nixon.

> "To announce that there must be no criticism of the President, or that we are to stand by the President, right or wrong, is not only unpatriotic and servile, but is morally treasonable to the American public. Nothing but the truth should be spoken about him or anyone else. But it is even more important to tell the truth, pleasant or otherwise, about him than anyone else." ~Theodore Roosevelt

Stockholm Syndrome is named after people who were taken hostage in the Swedish city. They empathized and sided with their captors because of the danger their rescuers put them in. They felt like the police were a bigger threat than the robbers. Those outside the cave are perceived as more dangerous than the criminals inside. Stockholm Syndrome continues and enables an "us and them" mentality based on fear.

> FACT: Jose Padilla was jailed for over 3 years before trial. Arrested May 8, 2002, he was convicted of conspiracy charges on August 16, 2007. During that time he was isolated and drugged. In February 2007, Dr. Hegarty diagnosed Jose as suffering from Post-Traumatic Stress Disorder and a form of Stockholm Syndrome.

Stockholm Syndrome describes a condition in which one attributes benevolence to one's captor. It's used to describe the willingness to be held captive by force and/or suggestion of peers. It is much like brainwashing. The captives believe that there are no alternatives; that there is no option to being captive. If they are aware of their captivity, they are convinced their survival requires they remain captive. At best they are completely absorbed in cast images.

People gladly remain within institutions that profit from loyalty and exploitation. People are allowed an open society as long as they don't openly look for alternative, rescue or reality. Any change in the cave must be institutionalized to be sanctioned and initiated. Many forms of change within the cave are actually continuance of the status quo, just an opposite or countering position in the status quo. Only leaving the cave is true change.

> ### PATRIOT ACT
> Patriot Act approved October 26, 2001.
> No debate and little reading take place of the 300 plus page document. The Act was passed without question, amid mysterious anthrax scare.
> June 7, 2005, some provisions of the act were made permanent, legalizing secrets and secretive acts and enhancing domestic surveillance. The Patriot Act morphed the National Security Act of 1947.

Only little librarians questioned the Patriot Act. The U.S.A. Representatives didn't read it. How could they contemplate the consequences of it without even reading it? Now Federal Government agencies are free to know what people read and everything else about everyone. Institutions are allowed to report and clandestinely keep records and tabs on individuals. They question various activities of various individuals and institutionalize answers.

The anthrax in the letters lead back to Pentagon made product. In 2008, Bruce Ivins, who worked for the U.S.A. Army at Fort Detrick, killed himself. Charges were being formally arranged concerning his involvement in the anthrax letters.

The U.S.A. is ruled by law, the laws of the trinity of liberty. These are the only sacred ideals in the U.S.A. and they are partly sacred because they are changeable and allow themselves to be bettered by people. People have to question in order to progress, otherwise institutions will hold and maintain.

People are lied to and often know or feel that they are being lied to, but shrug it off because the benefactors and protectors are the same as the detractors and exploiters. It is abhorrent to question certain institutions, normally the ones that question individuals. Institutions fulfill needs and also supply many things people don't need. The U.S.A. is founded on the principle of questioning, amendment number one. Freedom of speech is the freedom to question. This was so important so important to the original patriots that they made it the first part of the First Amendment.

> ### HALLIBURTON
> Halliburton contracts in Iraq since 2001: more than $15 billion.
> Charge for washing bag of laundry: $100.
> Deal received by V.P. Cheney from Halliburton, his former employer: more than $20,000,000 dollar retirement

package and a $1.4 million dollar bonus just before he took office. Plus about $200,000 per year since 2001.

FACT: Unknown billions in cash, at least $9 billion dollars went
unaccounted for and lost in Iraq. This is still owed to the Federal Reserve.

Institutions are not individuals, but mechanizations and formations of. Institutions portray themselves as being alive and as likable personalities. Institutions are tools and when a tool breaks more than it fixes, it is tossed and improved upon.

Nations adopts characterizations, like people. People make up the persona of a nation that, like personal development attempts to move ever forward, amid constant change. Capitalism has created market influence and oversight and is possibly as fair as it gets. How would we know otherwise? Capitalism has sanctioned a detrimental mentality of money above all. Free trade existed for millennia before any free trade agreement. Capitalism is capitalization. People capitalize on others. Capitalism is trade in the global pyramid system. Free trade is free trade.

Capitalism can be analogous to crabs in a barrel all aspiring to rise up and get out. They independently try to use and abuse one another and inevitably the weak and unlucky are pushed aside, climbed over and shoved down. The strong and lucky that attempt to get out of the barrel are pulled down by others. The crabs that do make it out move on and forget about the predicament of their counterparts.

Capitalism might also function like a herd of elephants crossing the savannah. The success and safety of the entire group is the only effective measure. African Bush Elephants assist and protect each other. They teach one another and show each other the way. Elephant herds act together in order to successfully traverse the dangerous African wilds. Effective business plans do not exclude and degrade competition, but include and consider competition and individuals in one's surroundings. All too often capitalists roll like crabs instead of elephants.

Doublespeak is perpetuated by institutions and the institutionalized as a form of imagery in the cave. Truth is not uniform or steady and rarely complete. Options are not limited to this or that. It may be sensible that there are two extremes, but there are always more than two options. Situations and language are sometimes meant to have limited options and mixed up presentations that limit and distort observations.

Economics and war, among other topics, are described in confusing euphemisms to please the optimistic and oblivious. Part time workers are workers without benefits. Outsourced labor is exploited peoples elsewhere. Downsizing is mass firing. It causes great pain to see institutions that claim and imply benevolence are in fact the greatest exploiters, as well as the main providers. Doublespeak is used to hold and maintain doublethink, contradicting ideas leading to the same point in the middle of nowhere. People are capable of thinking in multiple layers and acting toward multiple ends.

FACT: In May 2007, David Keogh and Leo O'Connor of England became criminals for speaking facts. They revealed a secret and were sentenced to 6 months and 3 months in prison respectively. The secret information: George II wanted to bomb Al-Jazeera and claim it was an accident. Only the office he wanted to bomb was not in Iraq, but Qatar. Blair apparently dissuaded him. November 13, 2001, an Al-Jazeera office in Kabul was hit by missile. April 8, 2003, Al-Jazeera generator in Baghdad was hit by missile, one reporter was killed.

The gentlemen patriots of England merely revealed information. They merely spoke the facts, a small, yet stunning thing. A whisper has the potential to change opinion. Revealing information because it is the truth is patriotic. If it happened and is relevant it should be known. No one deserves the privilege of secrets that concern enormity among many. If exploitation or wrongdoing is conducted, institutional secrets are made and kept. Information pertaining to national security has to be secret because often it concerns evil and unstable actions. Only a patriot would reveal a secret concerning outrageous institutional malice.

The secrets of the institutionalized, their fraternal, family or cabalistic connections, matter not. The knowns alone are enough to question. Their mysteries and secrets may be interesting, but the importance of questioning preexistent actualities outweighs dissection of mystery.

A threat to the freedom of the press anywhere in the world is contrary to the morality and principles of anyone from the U.S.A. If Al-Jazeera spouted lies and fabrication they would not warrant being bombed. Raising real questions and information concerning actuality qualifies attack from institutions. Presenting actuality, as David and Leo did, warrants attention from institutions. Speaking the truth has always angered oligarchical institutions.

If institutionalized interests were doing the right thing, simply bombing the press would not have been contemplated. If the interests of the U.S.A. were really to promote democracy, step one might read: do not bomb locals, especially the press. If the interests of the Bush Administration were something other than capital and oil, mission accomplished would be when the war was over and not when the cash flow began.

> "The minority, the ruling class at present, has the schools and press, usually the church as well, under its thumb. This enables it to sway the emotions of the masses, and make its tool of them."
> ~Albert Einstein

If not a true observation, it is at least a true potentiality. And apparently if institutions are not under the proverbial thumb of the ruling class at present, they will literally be bombed. Institutions present themselves like friends in the kitchen. Sadly though, institutions are not treated like people; if they were, most would be committed or jailed. Institutions do not treat individuals like people, rather fodder or fuel. Institutions are not individuals and yet people yield to institutions as if they were people, really big people. An old adage sheds light on the predicament of repetitive troubles and the continuation of ignorant action. The light in this adage is the same as the fire in the Allegory of the Cave.

> One night a man found his neighbor in a well-lit area in the street, on his knees searching.
> "What are you looking for?"
> "My key."
> After some time assisting in the search the man asked, "Where did you lose it?"
> "Over there, in the dark." He replied.
> "Then why are you looking here?"
> "There is more light here." ~Sufi Tale

People are convinced to look under the light of institutional placement and manufacture. Everyone wants life, liberty and the pursuit of happiness; everyone is in pursuit with a distinct key to their happiness. At times, distractions, events may startle and the key might be lost. It is possible to be so shocked, that our senses are lost too and the key is sought where it wasn't dropped. If there is manufactured light, it attracts. Actions are repeated because they are known, people stay in the light because they can see. Everything else exists in the unknown and worse, the darkness. Fear is the inability to explore the darkness to find the key and real light, preferring dimness instead.

> Insanity: doing the same thing over and over again and expecting different results.
> ~Albert Einstein

The key to happiness may be under the light, but if not, it is best to explore elsewhere. Institutions would like people to choose from what they present under their light. We are free to make choices, yet we are convinced we have no choice, but theirs. There are any number of alternatives outside of their light.

Perhaps if the light was off, one could see more clearly. Perhaps if one was away from the light, one could see better in the darkness. Revolution is capable of taking place in nonviolent capacity. Sometimes enough whispers can change the world, sometimes enough wallets or screams can change situations without a bayonet affixed to a rifle. Only when authorities will not yield to the will of the people, is there violent revolution. And only when people do not yield to institutionalized authorities, is there change. Starting follows stopping. If stopping is allowed without assault, peaceful revolution and change is possible. Sometimes change requires simply walking away from the light.

Oppression through might has never worked. Might alone is always fought, sometimes forceful institutions may hold their power for generations forcefully, but not with force alone. The more neighboring and mutual an oppressor seems, the more abuses they might get away with. Great perception of leaders leads to greater tolerations of their transgressions. Might is mighty, but one needs to control mentality to keep good prisoners or keep authority.

People seek to be led, for otherwise they might be lost in a world of darkness. If those who guide them, also perpetuate wrong on others and themselves, it does not matter, as long as there is something, someone who will lead the way through the darkness, as though there were a single reply to a question or a single light everyone decided to go to.

Institutions provide the answers through archetypal leaders. Institutions adopt archetypes and represent them. Institutions and the institutionalized become that which people seek and they are then able to accomplish their goals. Institutions captivate and hold captive the hearts and minds of many people.

Might is right, maybe, but only if people are first so convinced through loyalty or fear as to tolerate institutions marching over stranger or neighbor or their own self. The success of brute force has prerequisites that enable force to be the authority, including a sensible aversion to pain and death. If might was simply right, then there would be more overt institutions, instead institutions operate more covertly. Fear, whether of information or might, is what really captures. Might is right only when accompanied by fear, otherwise might, might get a fight. The oppressed can always stand up o might, but only will if they cease their passion for wind and lose fear of false evidence appearing real.

Blank and blanketing overt oppression over the masses has always resulted in upheaval and normally violently. War and acts of violence occur when institutions refuse to bend to the will of people. Overt oppression eventually results in overt violence, one way or another. Covert oppression is subtle and goes on practically unnoticed. Covert oppression may be simply instilling fear or anger, or by as tiny a thing as keeping quiet about actuality.

After the composition of the trinity of liberty, individual states began to outlaw slavery, for it did not fit into the ideas of liberty, equality and unity. Even though it was wrong, it continued in some states. Because of the discomfort and fear of change, the difficulty of looking outside the light, slavery continued, maintaining a steep pyramid which eventually led to clashes and war. Slavery did not mix with the ideals of the newly founded home of the brave and land of the free. So change was instituted in super drastic means, war.

The pyramid system of slaves and masters does not fit into the arrangement of the trinity of liberty. The level ideas of the trinity of liberty do not accommodate pyramidal slant. Pyramid systems had to adjust themselves to the trinity of liberty. And so they did. No longer is overt slavery tolerated, but free servants are plenty. Servants believe they have no choice, they are convinced that they may either starve, or slave.

In the North, slavery was outlawed, but its functioning somewhere else was entirely tolerated for quite some time. Many Northerners willingly exchanged goods that arrived from the exploitation of people; goods made by people who were forcibly stolen away and locked into labor. Today, slavery still exists, completely criminal and completely covert, but prevalent and often tolerated and overlooked.

There are slaves who know that they are slaves. There are also those, who in all practicality, are well-treated slaves and have no hint of their slavery. There are also those who think they are accessing opportunity, but are simply in open slavery or servitude. The exploited today are the have-nots from all over the globe who work viciously for just the ability to maintain breath and roof. Exploitation is sanctioned or ignored. Today slavery is a known unknown. Slavery exists, but the full extent of it is unknown. Because it is crime, it is facilitated in secret and remains altogether unknown. More common and more noticeable is exploitation.

Overt slavery is not always needed because often there is nowhere to run to and nowhere to hide. People are presented with alternative desolation and isolation. The darkness or the limited opportunity outside of the institutional light, make alternatives to working within the pyramid seem unavailable.

In some places opportunity abounds and there are many choices. In some places there are many shitty choices, in many places there is only one shitty choice, and in some places there is no choice at all, no opportunity.

Anyone forced to live like the average Palestinian would likely have desperation set in. If blocked in by literal and figurative walls without being taken care of, one will develop anger towards the perceived captors instead of affinity.

> FACT: Israel approved a 430 mile long wall around the West Bank of Palestine.

People are similar, here or there. If people are provided for, they have certain tolerations. People who are mistreated, develop other tolerations. When people are put in situations of oppression, when wrongdoing is propped up as necessity, it becomes easier to retaliate than to cooperate. When access to opportunity and information is met with a wall, it is likely that rocks will be tossed over the wall. When the status quo keeps one hungry in a coordinated fashion, with obstacles that are impossible to surmount, desperation ensues. Violence is enabled by institutionalized restriction of resources. And institutions know this.

In the petrolithic era and nuclear age violence in any capacity is not revolutionary, as it is in line with the status quo. At the same time, for certain institutions, it is better to battle their enemy than appease them, it is more profitable to maintain a fight rather than win it. Perpetual opposition and violence is part of the status quo. Revolution does not require violence.

The institutionalized professionals of violence are designed for violent confrontation. No one can successfully violently confront modern weaponry available today. It is possible to fight fire with fire, but it is rarely possible to fight force and violence with force and violence. As is par for the course, when institutions of force and violence are overcome with violence, they twist situations to benefit them. Violence benefits purveyors of violence. The institutionalized professionals of violence are well-armed, well-trained and well-ready to march individuals. They do not care if people are hungry, they do not care.

In violence the point of a cause, if any, is lost. Violence inspires none that are worthwhile. Those inspired by violence have likely already joined with violent institutions. Violence carries no point except to crush and step on. Institutions are the best implementers of violence, and in war, institutions win.

In the Revolutionary War, the freedom fighters used what were labeled as terrorist tactics by the British. If people are forced into desperation, they are going commit desperate acts. The terrorist acts included taking cover and firing on British soldiers gathered together in battle formation.

Violent revolution is not revolutionary. A revolution is something new, and violence is nothing new. In fact violence is engrained into every function on the planet. Engaging in violence serves the status quo and gives institutions that wield nightstick and tank the excuse to roll out professionals of smashing. In violence, a potential patriot may be denied sympathy; violence hurts individual voice and is an institutional agenda.

Crime is one thing that degrades message, violent crime is another thing altogether. Pushing over tables is not violent, no matter how upsetting. Destruction of property is unsettling and revolting, counter communicative and counterproductive, but not violent. Yet stub a toe of an innocent and the entire cause can be dismantled. Violence is felt by all living beings, but only living beings can experience and therefore only living beings experience violence. Machines cannot feel. The Boston Tea Party was a crime, but it was nonviolent, no harm was done to anyone and no theft of property to undermine message. Protesting to change via any other means communicates little.

States have massive organized institutions of maiming while other violent groups develop their own modes. All violence manifests the same; more violence, more wrongdoing and more power for institutions.

> "To overcome evil with good is good, to resist evil by evil is evil." ~Mohammed

Suicidal homicide is a new horror of the petrolithic era. Technology gives murderers, burdened with extreme tolerations, the ability to kill themselves and others. Many times the attackers do not bother to attack conscripted soldiers and instead target civilians. Individuals are violently attacked because they exist in a different institution, believe in other ideas or appear different. Institutional violence is intended to monopolize through actual might, and the might of fear.

> "If passion drives you, let reason hold the reins." ~Benjamin Franklin

No one wants to die unless their day-to-day existence seems worse than not existing at all, or they have been burdened by tolerations and tricked. Many believe that in murdering their perceived opposition they are guaranteed glory in the next life. No one wants to die unless they've been convinced, by institutions, that it is the right thing to do for an idea or agenda, typically of national or religious interests. If their existence is without hope and opportunity and promises in death are better than any in life, it becomes an option to kill self and others.

No mortal can completely know God. Becoming acquainted with God does not arrive from books or institutions, or even from churches. Knowing God comes from the heart. No machine or institution can know God, only individuals know their own personal relationship with God. No mortal mind knows how God thinks, but it is safe to say that zealous warriors have no higher place next to God than those who choose peace. It is on a steady limb that one could step out and say, "God does not ordain nor reward violence."

Institutional interests come and go, worship changes, truth shifts, yet what is right is unchanging. Prophets speak of providing peace and compassion, not inspiration to ride in caravans of war. Institutions promote violence in order to accomplish Earthly goals.

EIGHT BEATITUDES
Blessed are the poor in spirit, for theirs is the kingdom of Heaven.
Blessed are the meek, for they shall inherit the Earth.
Blessed are they who mourn, for they shall be comforted.
Blessed are they who hunger and thirst for righteousness, for they shall have their fill.

Blessed are the merciful, for they shall obtain mercy.
Blessed are the pure of heart, for they shall see God.
Blessed are the peacemakers, for they shall be called the children of God.
Blessed are they who are persecuted for the sake of righteousness, for theirs is the kingdom of heaven.
~Jesus Christ

"If you wish to experience peace, provide peace for another." ~Fourteenth Dalai Lama

To be poor in spirit is to act without passions, which might restrict sensibilities and allow one to fall into destroying for institutions. To be meek is to be close to zero and balance. To mourn is to assist those around you. To hunger for righteousness is to question on behalf of others. To be merciful is to renounce exploitation. Jesus was hated by institutions because he saw threw them.

The prophets and the holy ones of every faith all share peace and righteousness as a premise. Many of the great scientific minds of history have hypothesized ideas that coordinate with such faith. The astutely logical and various faithful all believe peace is the way. And unless burdened by tolerations, all people lean towards peace.

To blow oneself up with murderously, suggests that there are problems with surrounding influences, not only with the purveyor of violence; for somewhere arrived an unchecked toleration to violence of the most horrific sort. There is a problem with the particular person of course, but something is wrong in the environment as well.

Suicidal homicide is a phenomenon of the petrolithic era and an institutional instrument. The Japanese Kamikazes flew their planes into enemy ships in WWII; the power of petrol made their planes into piloted missiles. Today, many people are duped and/or recruited to be walking bombs. Killing is a disgusting and deplorable act, but there is something more horrible and rattling about suicide murder. If the status quo allowed everyone life, liberty, and the pursuit of happiness, blowing oneself up would be out of the question, no matter the going rate, no matter the promises.

"Everybody's worried about stopping terrorism. Well, there's a really easy way: stop participating in it."
~Noam Chomsky

If people are allowed to pursue happiness, they are less likely to act out violently. If sustenance is available and tolerations are lacking, there is less likely to be a perceived excuse to act out evil. If there is plenty of food, fresh water and opportunity for betterment and development, then there is no reasoning violence. Influencing tolerations for violence is more easily done among limited resources and restrictions. Division and exclusivity of goods and information allows for the conditions that foster desperation and violent retaliation. And institutions know this.

Disagreement could be casually confronted, debated, reconciled, comfortably solved and dismissed, if there was not an urgency that accompanies hunger. Only with plenty is there plenty of time and only without greed is there plenty. When there is no food in one's belly, no bread at home and one foresees no opportunity to get bread tomorrow, desperation ensues. Hunger is a powerful motivator. Greed is another kind of motivator, yet both hunger and greed require constant fulfillment.

When institutionalized religious dogma is divisive and convinces the "us" that the "them" does not merit bread or life, the entire reason for the religion is lost. Conducting violence and reacting violently only serves institutions. The greatest teachings of the world's great religions promote compassion and welcoming neighbors and strangers.

"Kindness is a mark of faith, and whoever is not kind has no faith." ~Mohammed

Jesus expressed that the poor in spirit are blessed. Lacking passion is a hallmark principle of Buddhism as well, so as to fill one with compassion. Passion burdens tolerations and makes it acceptable to murder. Compassion unburdens tolerations and assists prevention of violence. Many institutions that claim God's representation on Earth have many times, given up all that is right, holy and ordained, for a greater Earthly purpose, a passion. What theory or agenda of religious institutions is greater than the basic tenets of God?

Many aspects of many religions aspire to globalize and monopolize as much as Coca-Cola. Their megalomaniacal approach to converting all is akin to corporate monopolization. Some religions intend to dominate the planet on behalf of God, to rule every land by God's law, whether the infidels or heathens, want it or not. Essentially, they readily go against God's wishes to employ other wishes they claim to be Godly. On inspection their actions more closely correspond to the wishes of institutions and the institutionalized rather than any interpretation of God.

Monopolistic conduct is a character of institutions, not God. God already has what converting, monopolizing conduct seeks: power over all. They cannot monopolize the world and need not to, God already has. They quest for more power in order to have more power. Power is for power. God already has the monopoly on the Earth and the entire universe. The institutions that claim to represent her need not monopolize any portion of creation for her.

Institutions and the institutionalized, conduct maddening acts of murder in order to control. They are wired in some awful way or have accumulated abundant tolerations to serve an institutionally engaged agenda.

To some it is understandable and acceptable that man reaps terror on fellow man, but always it is apprehensible and defeating. Whether it is through bomb or gun, whether it is abroad or at home, whether it is jihad or just a job, people commit terror on one another and the outcome is the same. Normally people regret war and it benefits institutions, if they live long enough.

In mayhem, any statement, any point goes unheard, lacking validity, lost among limbs. No thought is noteworthy among the dead. Whatever position the violent possess is lost in maiming.

On April 16, 2007, the worst shooting spree in U.S.A. history occurred on the Virginia Technical University Campus. Thirty-two people were murdered and the murderer committed suicide. The media did not label this as terror, though surely it was. It was a random massacre by an individual, against innocent individuals within an institution. This action originated from and instilled fear and hate. Cho sent a video to the media with a message and attacked without warning. That's classic terrorism, though it was not labeled terror.

In the early hours of March 6, 2008, a bomb went off at the military recruitment center in Times Square. On average 10,000 volunteers enlist in the Times Square branch every year, making it the recruitment center with the highest number of volunteers. The bomb killed no one, though it could have. This was immediately labeled terror, despite the fact that it attacked walls of an office and no one was hurt. Why was this act classified as terror, while Cho's was not?

Talking heads proclaim there is nothing we can do to prevent someone from committing horrible acts of violence upon innocents except to strike "them" before they strike "us", shoot first and ask questions later. Cho performed a terrorist attack, and it resulted in the same confusion, uselessness and death, as other terrorist attacks.

Perhaps war and violence are the only answer to war and violence. Something else would have to be attempted first to find out. People have progressed and regressed since Hammurabi and the code of an eye for an eye and a tooth for a tooth. Many times instead of an eye for an eye, it is an eye for eyeing or a tooth for speaking.

In order to prevent terror, institutions must not strike first, for that threat may be the lone reason for opposition and is itself terror. Instead of forcing the fist to prevent attack, open hands might be offered. Instead of cutting down the tree before it gets sick, one could provide nutrients. A preventative is also preemptive, just more reasonable and easier, only we are burdened with tolerations to be confrontational rather than compassionate.

If people want to stop acts of terror, threats of terror have to stop. In order to stop terror, stop giving people reason to commit terror. If participation in madness is stopped, surrounding and obviously resulting madness is dispelled.

God does not care why one was convinced to kill. God rewards peace not atrocity, compassion not passion. In God's eyes, killing is killing. Are we all not neighbors on the same Earth? Do we not all breathe the same air and drink the same water?

> "Relativity applies to physics, not ethics." ~Albert Einstein

Whether realized through mathematical deduction or spiritual connection harming others is wrong. Many people believe that institutions are more valuable than people, that people are replaceable. That is not the thinking of any prophet of the past and perhaps a distinction among them. It is not the thinking of any sane scientist either. Institutions are valuable, but replaceable. People are irreplaceable and more valuable than any institution. Institutions can last many lifetimes, an example of their power and a reason people should be treated with more reverence than institutions.

The petrolithic era and nuclear age made a new world. The powers that be, among others, have labeled it a new world order. On September 11, 1990, George I addressed Congress and referred to the new world order publicly. In the new world order, i.e. the petrolithic era and nuclear age meaning is flipped and distorted, and the environment is twisted.

No longer do people call for politicians to be outstanding citizens, now people want them to have outstanding connections. In the new world, many people have been tricked to believe that the institutionalized, those with institutional experience and corporate ties, are the best professionals to hold state office and so the status quo continues. The people involved in the business of war, in whatever parameter, should be held to high scrutiny. The businessmen who become interested in politics, have an interest in power.

Generals, in general, are more trustworthy than some CEO from some corporation that was involved in military supplies or support or his politician friend. More and more, the U.S.A. government is run by outsourced institutions. More and more, the U.S.A. military is composed of non-citizens, which would be fine if there were other ways to immigrate. The armed forces present an optimal legal way to become a citizen of the U.S.A. for some. Fight for the right to citizenship.

FACT: Since 9/11, over 80 military personnel killed in the line of duty have posthumously received citizenship. Some 40,000 non-citizens are enlisted in the armed forces of the U.S.A. in late 2008.
There were 100,000 government contractors in Iraq, of which 48,000 are private soldiers as of late 2008.

As recruitment dwindles and support for killing wanes, correspondingly so does the number of allowed immigrants. Two distinct and separate problems came together, now more foreign born enlist in order to become a citizens of the U.S.A.

The U.S.A. is a reaction completely opposite to the serfdom and servitude of the past; the ideas at its foundation are based on liberty. The best thing about the U.S.A. is the worst. The liberty, which allows anyone to hold influence and power, enables evildoers and exploiters to attain power as well. Who seeks power?

We are in a new world. Many things are irreversibly different and will never be the same again. There is only one direction and that is forward. Many ideas, environments, plants and animals are simply gone. Everything changes, some changes are permanent.

With new inventions, in new conditions and circumstances people play the same game, or are played by the same game. The system intermingles and intertwines what is real with what is not, right with what is wrong. The William Wallace, the Mahatmas Gandhi, the Martin Luther King Jr. of the petrolithic era and nuclear age has a great entanglement to undo. But no matter the scale of a societal problem it starts with the condition of our minds.

"It is criminal to steal a purse, daring to steal a fortune, a mark of greatness to steal a crown. The blame diminishes as the guilt increases." ~Friedrich Schiller

"We are on the verge of a global transformation, all we need is the right major crisis and the nations will accept the new world order." ~David Rockefeller

---

Societal Stockholm Syndrome is perhaps on one side of the fence, and many develop this cowering apathy. Others, without resources or opportunity, people who are locked in without a provider, develop violent behavior, West Bank or Gaza syndrome. They are locked in and imprisoned and mistreated to the point they desperately fight back, like anyone would.

Patriots have certain connections with liberty, like a farmer has with fields. Patriots dig up the truth. Patriots seek to answer questions with information in its least processed form, and share it with as little spin as possible. Patriots seek information concerning actuality, no matter how bloody and potentially dissonant.

Dr. Jekyll is Mr. Hyde. The left wing and the right wing are the same bird. No matter how they try to fly their separate ways they can move only when they work together. When wrongdoing is enacted, it is flown by both wings, both sides of war. Both sides of the coin are the coin. Institutional operations require cooperation of the right and left wings.

"It is necessary to note that opposite things work together, even though nominally opposed." ~Rumi

---

Stockholm Syndrome is manipulated through a good cop - bad cop routine, at times coordinated by different institutions and other times by the same entity. Stockholm Syndrome takes place within a group reacting to the experience of extreme polarizations. Beatings and rescue occur, creating a dependency on the protector from the aggressor, both wear the same uniform, or are one and the same. The attack takes place in a coordinated fashion by both the good cop and the bad cop, for it enables them.

Information enables those who would hold people captive without chains. The presentation and withholding of information keeps people in the dark, under institutional light. The pen is mightier than the sword because information is a mightier manipulator of masses than might. A gun will make some move, but words move many. No sword, no matter how sharp, can penetrate like the pen, like information.

174

It is all about the presentation of information. The truth can be presented in many ways to manipulate opinion, and fundamentally, all versions could be true. The truth is rarely complete, and portioned truth is never enough.

Any institution that says that the complete truth is at hand and they have it, is likely lying. There is no end to the search for truth. It is necessary to always continue to search for more complete truth. It is necessary to question everything, especially the basis of one's own beliefs and opinions.

> Why do you stay in prison
> when the door is so wide open?
> Move outside the tangle of fear-thinking.
> Live in silence. ~Rumi

Cost is not the deciding factor for patriots. Patriots do not base decisions or questions on resources or ideals. Their contemplation arrives out of liberty and logic instead of out of dollar and power. Resources and sometimes just money can be like a Dr. Jekyll Questions arise not out of institutionalized perspective, but from instinctual wonder and curiosity; being human. The search for truth is the foremost trait of a patriot, not capital gains or appeasing the captors or catapulting oneself to a higher level in the pyramid.

> "The government, which was designed for the people, has got into the hands of the bosses and their employers, the special interests. An invisible empire has been set up above the forms of democracy."
> ~Woodrow Wilson

OVERT TO COVERT

Yoga and exercise in general is cleansing and beneficial for heart and mind. Clean water is essential to health and vitality and clears toxins from one's system. Organically grown whole foods provide an often better tasting, definitely less toxic alternative to conventionally grown and processed foods.

Organic food has been the established convention since man first cultivated crops. People used surrounding organic ingredients and available minerals to enhance plant material. But in the petrolithic era, toxin enhanced commodities have become the agreed upon operating system. The cultivation of food has been changed and institutionalized into the petrolithic era. New toxins from the new convention are everywhere, in the food, water, air and you. The same is true for life in the nuclear age.

No matter how much yoga is done, no matter how much pure water is drunk, or how much organic broccoli is eaten, we are all in the petrolithic era and will be adversely affected for the rest of our lives. At the present rate, our children's children will be subject to the consequences of the petrolithic era too. Until there is something that eats smog and soot or a time machine, we are stuck in the petrolithic era, the nuclear age, the time of toxins. There is nowhere to go that is not permeated and saturated by toxins humanity birthed. Even Northern California has a nuclear waste site, just off the coast of San Francisco. Barrels of plutonium waste were sunk at sea, some were shot so they would sink...

FACT: On November 7, 2007, 58,000 gallons of bunker fuel spilled into the San Francisco Bay Area. The cause: human error. 2,000 tons of oil spilled into the Black Sea November 11-13, 2007 due to a powerful storm. On December 7, 2007, two ships collided off of the coast of South Korea; 78,750 barrels of oil spilled.

The convention is either quiet and creepy or abundant and evacuating. Pollution is everywhere. It is possible to walk out from under institutions, but the polluted environment is inescapable. Depending on luck and locale, one is either exposed to a steady stream of known and unknown toxins or a sickening and evacuating deluge.

One can reduce the negative side effects of poisons' transgressions by being active and choosing a healthy diet, but if bad luck places the next leak of toxins nearby, it won't matter. Living and eating well can decrease the negative consequences from exposure to toxins and carcinogens, but they are everywhere, occasionally blunt and abundant. There is no place to visit or live that is clear and pure. There is no place untainted, everywhere is polluted, that is the convention of today.

> "…war causes pollution and excess expenditures in burning of fuel for no good purpose." ~Ron Paul

Covert control is subtle; it works by changing and flipping meaning of subjects and language, by distorting explanation. Lingual description is not always accurately reflective of actuality and many times confuses its interpretation. Covert control is accomplished through mistaken definitions and intentionally changed meanings.

Organic food was the convention for all of history until the poisons of the petrolithic era became the new convention. Now organic is distinct from the new convention of pervasive poisoning. The poisoning, institutionalized agriculture is given a friendly and familiar name: conventional. Organic becomes specialized instead of the convention, the way it always was.

This covers up the fact that products and processes used in conventional growing are refined and up until recently, were never consumed or used before. The pesticides, fertilizers, fungicides, insecticides, herbicides and GMO foods end up on one's plate and in one's belly, yet all our ancestors never ate anything similar. These new chemicals and substances do who-knows-what to you-know-whom.

Language and description is distorted in the petrolithic era along with resulting thoughts. The description of institutional trespasses is euphemized, including the facilitation of one's food. People often measure their influence on the environment through carbon output. What about the permanent, permeating poisons that accompany the carbon? Carbon is one thing, but there is more to environmental destruction than just carbon. There is no way to measure all the poison people produce and consume.

The new conventionalities are environmental poisons. Carbon output is a factor, a deadly factor, but it is only one among many. Other toxins and pollutants are purposefully added to sustenance, while other poisons are pumped out into the air and water in hopes of dilution. There are many poisons, including carbon, which are now conventional environmental factors.

An old factor, that was an old factor well before people took factors into account, is war. War results in great expenditure of hazardous waste and expended resources. War has always been an institutional function, and war in the past always had an end, for ends. In the petrolithic era, war continues, it is still waged for resources, but it is also waged to continue the status quo. War was waged for ends; now war is waged so as not to end.

Continuous war is an attempt to maintain and monopolize power. In slaying, ideas are lost to the wind and no one ever wins, except those who maintain the status quo, the pyramid system. Any idea, revolutionary or scary, is lost in violence. Violence maintains institutions, despite the tremendously negative repercussions for individuals.

Just because one gives up blood, sweat, and tears does not qualify heroism or patriotism, it may just mean one was duped into danger. Many great heroes have folded their arms in protest of spilling blood or following institutional orders. Many heroes stop violence. The presented convention may seem like a way to grow good food, but it may only be a way to make good money. It may seem like a worthy cause to rally troops, but it is more likely a cause for institutional wealth and control. No war can be a war for peace, war is for a piece.

> "I am an anti-imperialist. I am opposed to having the eagle put its talons on foreign lands." ~Mark Twain

Covert control works through euphemistic and distorted statements. To call an individual a minority is usually based on race. It is always belittling and possibly inaccurate in describing numbers, but accurate in describing how institutions often perceive people. Covert control is suggestion that influences perception so difficult to notice and is designed to make one believe that there is no alternative direction. Calling someone a member of a minority instills a preliminary notion of being minor.

Covert control also works through silence. Overtly, the Iraq invasion and occupation was not engaged to enable oil corporations, but eventually it coincided with record profits for oil corporations around the world. Overtly, they have prospered from war and likely have covertly prepared for war's manifestation. The war in Iraq provided oil corporations the opportunity to make more money than any other institutions in corporate history. Institutions rarely announce wealth, resources and power as reasons for war, they never announce that they violently seek to stabilize the status quo.

The former institutional slavery and segregation of the U.S.A., is now a quiet elusive prejudice, but many corporations are nearly as exploitative still. War is now enacted with the intent to liberate and not to dominate, but the outcome is the same. There is just better weaponry that is more destructive. The human world is a pyramid. For the few to have much, the many have little.

This notion becomes accepted and propagated by those in the higher levels of the pyramid. Some have a window with a view, but most are stacked on and compartmentalized within the system themselves, unable to see that the pyramid at all. Many situations are not simply the way things are, they are more accurately simply the way things are designed.

Many people are unable to imagine alternatives because of their enclosed position within the architecture. In the U.S.A., everyone is allowed and capable of getting to a window with a view, for it is information that allows one to see the architecture. The information is there and much of it is free, but many do not want the information or will not accept it.

Drastic and dramatic information arrives in the same way as benign and quite relaxing points. The calming information coincides with dramatic. The evening news mostly reports fearful and problematic subjects and the intermittent commercials provide comfort and solutions. Covert control stems from unknown overt action.

> FACT: Arie M. Degeus, inventor of clean energy technology was found dying in a parking lot at Charlotte Douglas International Airport in North Carolina on November 11, 2007. He died later that same day of apparent heart attack. Arie was on his way to Europe to secure funding for his free-energy product.

> STRANGE SCIENTIST DEATHS
> November 6, 2001 Don Wiley apparently jumps off bridge in Memphis.
> Between November 2001 and March 2002 over 14 microbiologists are killed or die in accidents.
> July 17, 2003 David Kelly, UN Weapons Inspector, slashes his wrists, leaving no finger prints on knife.
> May 14, 2004 Eugene Mallove, author, engineer and pioneer of alternative energy, was beaten to death.
> July 29, 2004 John Mullen, nuclear physicist, poisoned by arsenic. Girlfriend accused of murder, dies also.
> July 7, 2005 Jeong H. Im, protein chemist, stabbed, set afire and tossed in trunk of a car.

> FACT: The CIA possessed a poison dart gun that was developed after 1952. This gun was able to poison an individual and leave no trace of poison or poisoning. Autopsies would conclude the victim died from a heart attack.

Covert control works through overt action, as long as part of that action remains clandestine and unknown. In 1975, they had a poison dart gun. The Congress and most members of government were unaware of its existence, but a certain branch of the government did invent, know of and possess the weapon, The Agency. The gun left a pin prick and gave the victim a heart attack, leaving no trace of foul play, a euphemism for murder evidence. Actions like assassinations are used to control covertly by keeping information about the assassination and the assassinated partially unknown.

Today, there are supposedly electromagnetic beam guns that induce heart failure. They definitely have microwave weaponry that disperses people, through burning sensations, currently used for trespassers or crowd control. Covert control is exhibited in overt might through covert means. Covert control is activity as real the steering of language and assassinations, just undetected. Covert control is an overt act that is completely unnoticed or a known event that is surrounded by unknown particulars. Covert control is used to manipulate people to do wrong, convinced it is right. To successfully covertly control, information is made incomplete. What should be known is kept unknown.

Covert control is enabled by an open society and placidity under it. Overt control is gained by force and the threat of it. Covert control is obtained by controlling how people think in the first place. Covert control is the clandestine use of information, not only through direct force, but often simply through the power of information and the manipulation of fears.

There is no one entity to blame for the pollution of the planet, the majority of institutions and individuals are participants. Likewise, there is no one entity to blame for covert manipulation; it is many institutions made up of many institutionalized individuals, with many agendas. Elitists operate in whispers, innuendos and partial truths. They portray themselves one way, while conducting actions in a completely opposite manner in order to enable an agenda. Information is the mightiest power and can be covertly used to transfix and steer.

While it is to the advantage of corporations, like the tobacco companies, to market to new addicts/customers from an early age, it is illegal for minors to smoke and illegal for tobacco companies to intentionally market to them. Tobacco companies developed anti-smoking campaigns. Alcohol companies have programs to discourage underage drinking, but their business would not work if they did not promote to new customers. They promote responsible drinking and criticize underage drinking overtly and arguably, covertly introduce alcohol.

The oil corporations would have people believe they promote clean energy. Actually, they are promoting other energy that can be retailed and controlled to maintain their oligarchy. Hydrogen makes no economic sense, and yet was touted as the future. The future may yield some kind of hydrogen car, but the electric car is here; they are already technologically and economically viable and existent and were systematically, strategically squashed in California specifically, (See *Who killed the Electric Car*) and mostly relegated subsequently. If they were promoting cleaner energy, or cleaner vehicles, we would have it all, it is here already. Instead they are trying to secure energy that can be manufactured, owned, and controlled. Free energy would dismantle the pyramid system and benefit individuals, not institutions.

If you want to keep your cattle from running away, give them a big field. ~Chinese Proverb

---

Covert control is a well-lit, spacious field surrounded by darkness. That oil corporations are in search of ways to provide cleaner fuels is perhaps partly true. Yet, it is not the whole truth. The whole truth is they are in search of a clean fuel that they can control. The truth is that they want to sell more petrol; they want to stay in control.

Successful public relations is covert control. Public Relations is the practice of the art of relinquishing certain information so the public formulates what the institution wants. It is a repeated version and constant withholding of alternate information. At times the information quells fear and other times, promotes it.

Covert control uses the Hegelian Dialectic. It is thesis, antithesis, synthesis, or problematic action, reaction, (preconceived) solution. Georg Wilhelm Friedrich Hegel, a philosopher, did not originate this theory, but is associated with it.

Imagine a nation that is attacked, the action. People demand safety and retribution, the reaction. Then imagine a prepared solution, perhaps crafted in anticipation of an attack.

Imagine 9/11. People's reaction was one of sorrow and anger; people wanted safety and security. A legislative solution was presented and passed, the Patriot Act, but the Patriot Act was written before 9/11. If people didn't have time to read it, others definitely didn't have time to write it. The solution was already in place before the problem, in this case as a contingency plan of some sort...

Covert control uses distractions. The distraction may be mystery or irrelevancy. Baseball is the "national pastime" in the U.S.A. because it is a national distraction. It is an obvious distraction and a welcomed one mostly. There are less obvious distractions and more suspicious ones, including fascination with celebrities.

Covert control uses manipulation of language and transformation of archetypes. Covert control is accomplished through the transformation of definitions and archetypes, as in the transformation and distortion of the meaning of patriot. Patriots are portrayed or interpreted as regimented, unquestioning jingoes more often than as independent individuals. The notion of the patriots is removed altogether or associated with idiotic, zealous or elitist tendencies.

Covert control captures minds through emotion; Freudian theory put into practice in order to steer opinion. It hits on the id, the deep unconscious, and mostly goes unnoticed. Covert control is propaganda, biased information of manipulation. Information is the prerequisite to opinion. Propaganda is subtly biased packages meant to get people to think one way or another.

"It all depends on how we look at things, and not how they are in themselves." ~Carl Jung

---

Convincing people to think one way or another is nothing new, but public relations is. Only recently, when mediation became a prominent component of daily activities, could propaganda and public relations function at large and develop. Powers and authorities have always attempted to influence how people think, but only in the information age is it possible on a large scale.

Public relations was first put into practice by Sigmund Freud's nephew, Edward Bernays, and the institutions that hired him. Sigmund greatly influenced modern day clinical psychoanalysis. Sigmund's theories remain influential today and throughout his life cocaine was influential on Sigmund, who prescribed it and used it. In 1919, Sigmund's nephew, Edward, opened up shop in New York City armed with family ties and know-how.

FACT: Edward worked for multiple presidents of the U.S.A., the CIA, the American Tobacco Company, Proctor & Gamble, GE, Dodge Motors, CBS and the United Fruit Company. He was a leader of the Committee on Public Information during WWI, a pro-war propaganda machine in the U.S.A. Ed was instrumental in successfully promoting fluoridation in the U.S.A. and convincing a generation that cigarettes made their breath smell nice.

"If we understand the mechanism and motives of the group mind, is it not possible to control and regiment the masses according to our will without them knowing it? The recent practice of propaganda has proved that it is possible, at least up to a certain point and within certain limits.
~Edward Bernays

Ed developed a scientific method to influence and control the erratic human mind. This engineering of consent was used to create acceptance and desire for things that are not needed through hits on emotions Ed formulated ways to influence people to crave and accept things as devious as tobacco and fluoride and things apparently less devious, like bananas and the 'American breakfast' of bacon and eggs.

At one point Ed was approached by a company that wanted to increase its share of the bacon market. Ed not only increased their market share, but expanded the entire pork market, as well as sales for eggs. Part of the advertising campaign used doctors to convince people of the U.S.A. that a rich and hearty breakfast, such as bacon and eggs was healthy. Doctors convinced Americans that components of the English breakfast were their native. He convinced people that the bacon and egg breakfast was approved and recommended by doctors.

FACT: Smithfield Foods is the largest pork corporation on Earth. In 1997, Smithfield was fined over $12 million for violating the Clean Water Act. Standard operations at Smithfield hog farms include cramped cages and fecal lagoons. The untreated swine waste settles in open air ponds and pollutes surrounding areas. In April 2009, swine flu became a pandemic, likely originating at a Smithfield Foods hog farms outside of Mexico City with notoriously unhygienic living conditions.

Ed increased the market for United Fruit Company bananas as well. These bananas arrived from the sweat of repressed slaves, but they were nutritious. Ed maintained lies and propped up disinformation to gain support for CIA/UFC led Guatemalan coup. The invasion was presented as necessity to stop communism. After the invasion and investigation, no such threat was found. Ed played off of the fight or flight mechanism of the mind and the "us and them" mentality to promote business.

FACT: United Fruit Company, now Chiquita Brands, coined the phrase "banana republic." The fruit corporation swung in and took over. They used institutionalized racism and stomped out any unionizing across Central and South America. UFC would build up communities upon arrival and tear down everything they constructed when they left. UFC is responsible for atrocity and exploitation of Americans in two hemispheres. They supplied ships for the U.S.A. in both of the World Wars, the 1954 CIA Guatemalan Coup, and ships for the Bay of Pigs invasion of Cuba from their Great White Fleet.

Bananas are complicated. A banana republic is a steeply slanted oligarchy, introduced by intertwined institutions. Bananas taste good, but the outcome of the banana trade is expansive and exploitative. Bananas are shipped great distances with little benefit to most those involved. The banana trade enabled the institutional infrastructure, but degraded individual situation and their environment.

Ed paid doctors and dentists to inform the public that smoking was good for their breath. Separately, another group of physicians told the public that fluoride was good for their teeth. At Ed's request and payment, doctors stated that tobacco and fluoride were part of a healthy lifestyle, along with eggs and bacon for breakfast. Ed's uncle Sigmund might have jokingly diagnosed Ed as having an acute oral fixation, but Ed was manipulating the oral fixations of society at large. Ed used unconscious primal desires and fears to market products and make money.

FLUORIDE HISTORY

1909 Dentist in Colorado Springs noticed stain on residents teeth, now known as dental fluorosis.
1937 Kaj Rolholm published "Fluorine Intoxication." In it he exposed many dangers of fluoridation.
1945 Scientists provide fluoridated water to cities for study.
1955 Procter & Gamble introduced Crest, the first fluoride toothpaste.
2006 The National Research Council released a report stating that too much fluoride may increase likelihood of bone fractures, cause tooth damage, neurological problems and possibly cancer.

Ed knew that people would believe the opinion and presentation of the doctors he presented. After all, doctors are healers bound by the Hippocratic Oath. They are the authority on matters of health and presumed to be a respectable, knowledgeable, trustworthy impartial professionals, not a bunch of pitchmen. They wore white lab coats in commercials and assured the public of the product's safety and benefit. They were supposed to be on the forefront of information, the cusp of knowledge and were granted trust of such authority.

Ed theorized and practiced emotional and intellectual influence of thought. He perfected the ability to convince one to want what one doesn't need and one to believe what others wanted as well. Perhaps this is when citizen became consumer and reporter became recorder. Covert control is accomplished by means of controlling the masses with whispers instead of whips and acts that are real, but airy and unknown.

Covert control is technological, psychological, emotional and above all informational. Ed called it engineering consent and was the original spin doctor. It took decades for people to recognize the dangers of smoking tobacco because of the engineered consent and doctors who spun the truth; read lied. Today, fluoride is not considered dangerous, unless one has skeletal fluorosis resulting in curvature of bone structure or has taken the time to look in to it.

"Those who manipulate this unseen mechanism of society constitute an invisible government which is the true ruling power of our country. Our minds are molded, our tastes are formed largely by men we have never heard of."
~Edward Bernays

The Nazis used Freudian theory and the examples set by Ed to gain power and empathy to start WWII and to maintain support during the war. They used Ed's ideas to instill a hatred for outsiders, while at the same time creating a love for being an insider. Ed literally wrote the book on propaganda titled *Propaganda*, in 1928.

In peace one could be an insider by purchasing certain goods, while during war one could be an insider by getting the outsiders. Propaganda is biased information that hits on the "us and them" mentality. Buy in to be in and enjoy being an "us", or get "them" to prove allegiance. This is a frightened mentality, arranged by continuing unquestioning action.

Covert control is hard to see, like a star in the sky that is only visible from the peripheral. When sight is shifted directly at it, it fades. It is noticeable, sensible, but hard to verify. Slogans and symbols have great effect on people, and along with other forms of controlling information subconsciously impact perceptions. The less one recognizes the symbols, the more impact they may have. When one does not consciously recognize the symbolism being used, it may still have a subconscious impact.

Carl Jung referred to the innate recognition of symbols in all people as the collective unconscious or objective psyche. Everyone instinctively and subconsciously recognizes symbolism. Sigmund Freud disagreed with Carl about people born with comprehension. Just as the right course is often hidden, symbols are often hidden too. They often go unnoticed consciously, but are still effective. Symbols are easily pointed out, but tremendously difficult to put a finger on.

Symbolism is used to sell things, motivate certain thinking and express notions and feelings. Symbols are used to steer the perception of people with or without their notice. They hit people on an emotional level, subliminally and unconsciously. The subliminal symbol may be as simple as a line, a shape or a word.

FACT: During the 2000 election campaign a television advertisement was created by the RNC for support of George II. The ad flashes RATS when speaking about Al Gore and his plans.

Most institutions, including the media, do not present all the relevant information. They present only what is relevant to their belief system according to institutional directives. Covert control is the result of restricting and withholding information, covering portions of actuality. It may be innocent and it may be their intent to covertly control, the result of restricted or limited information is the same. They may not lie, they may just withhold information, but partial presentation is only a convincing act of truth. Institutions, including the media, provide the stories that suit them.

Covert control reveals the sleek and smooth side of the status quo and not the rotting disarray seen on closer examination. Covert control is hard to recognize and explicate. Perhaps like so many symbols, it goes consciously unnoticed and passive, while unconsciously active. It is a chaotic and agitating amalgamation of noted and unnoticeable influences that make one want to scream and fight a wall, or run and hide from walls.

Choosing to stop is always an alternative to fleeing or fighting. Take a deep breath and stop, look and listen instead of fleeing or fighting. When one stops, situations are better grasped. One may notice it is possible to climb the wall or see the door, or the key.

"A question that sometimes drives me hazy: am I or are the others crazy?" ~Albert Einstein

THE NEW WORLD ORDER

NOVUS ORDO SECLORUM

This phrase is displayed on the back of the Great Seal of the U.S.A. designed in 1782 and the $1 Dollar Bill (included on the $1 in 1935) under the thirteen leveled pyramid with the capstone missing, replaced by the all seeing Eye of Providence. Translated, "New order of the ages." Above it reads Annuit Coeptis which translates to "He favors our undertakings." The Eye of Providence is seen as the all seeing eye of God or the all seeing eye of an overseer.

The new world order is exactly that. It is the order in the new world. It is the same violent means of authority, the same old formulation of the status quo, the same old oligarchy instituted in the petrolithic era and nuclear age. The new world is still contracted to the same old formulation of regimentation. There are new and improved modes and technology, but, it is the same formulation of authority, the same status quo, the same oligarchical collectivism, in the newly degraded environment.

The authority, the order is packaged in a new sleek design, with new bells and whistles, but is as unchanged as the pyramids in North Africa. The order is the same warring, controlling and repressive pyramidal system, now enforced at times covertly and with new inventions. Authorities claim to seek the betterment of mankind and seem to only get the better of the many of mankind. There are new tools and new names, but the ordering authority is in the same order as always, oligarchical collectivism.

The old oligarchies have new technology, but the main thing new is the new environment, the environment of the petrolithic era and nuclear age. The new environment is poisoned and depleted. The new world is one polluted and bereft expanse after another, land scoured and mined, water poisoned and air thick with institutional excrement. The new world is the conditions, confines and consequences of petrolithic era and nuclear age now layered into every strata of the Earth.

The new world is an environment that can no longer dilute pollution, resulting in rising acidity in the oceans, corresponding with rising amounts of CO_2 and rising temperatures at the poles, increased radiation levels worldwide, impure air and water, depleted soil and taint everywhere. The new world is the consequence of irrational institutional and individual intent to build without regard for future ramifications. The new world is a result of institutions placing institutions before individuals and individuals placing institutions above individuals too.

This new world is manifested from the consequences of pollution and over consumption instigated by the global institutionalized burning of petrol and uranium. The excrement accumulated to become a measurably changed environment, the petrolithic era and nuclear age.

The new world order is perpetuated via the delivery of information and the concealment of information. The new world order is the result of environmental exploitation, the institutionalization and monopolization of creation. The new world order is the negatively altered environment resulting from continuation without conclusion in oligarchical fashion.

Institutionalized individuals seek more control and power and gravitate towards positions of authority. The ever ravaging and growing desire to expand has propelled the new world order. The new world is set on the peak of oil production and the heights of information facilitation. Placing profit above the love for the components of country; liberty, land and locals, has led to the new world order. The new world order is practically inescapable mentally and socially, and is certainly inescapable physically.

Before the petrolithic era and nuclear age, it was necessary and sensible to continue, to move ever forward, to produce without hesitance or concept of consequence. In the past, one's livelihood and well-being depended on continuation, no matter what. In the new world order, continuation of the status quo causes the direct demise of individuals. There is no place to move on to, no new island to start fresh on. In the petrolithic era, one's livelihood, wellbeing and existence depends on stopping the status quo.

> FACT: In 2006 105,000 tons of garbage from Sacramento, CA was hauled in petroleum diesel fueled trucks to a dump 141 miles away.

The new world order owes no allegiance to any nation, religion or corporation. It is the legislation of institutional exploitation toward the monopolization of everything. This results in eliminated individuality and limited individual trust. The new world order monopolizes, it does not matter if it does not make sense, continuation is insisted. Pollution, war, confused action and the overall inability to live sustainable lifestyles destroys. Increasingly nature is transformed into institutionalized grids, limited or outright eliminated for profit.

Institutions are made up of individuals, but they do not act as people; they are as machines. Institutionalized individuals are capable of switching their institutional jargon and actions on and off, as if they were machines. When speaking to a reporter, one is sometimes on and other times off the record. When speaking to different groups, the institutionalized individual is capable of spinning different tunes, and at times, different truths. Institutions are empowered by people, driven by people and dependent on people, but institutions also steer people toward their institutional agenda.

Why do institutions exist, if not for people, as their tools? If institutions were half as dedicated to the betterment of mankind as they say, there would be more need for poetry and less need for patriotism. People would listen to stories about organic gardening, exploration and ideas, rather than news of war, weapons development, restriction and exploitation. The price of petrol would be inconsequential to the economy; the near eternal geothermal energy sources and eternally renewable energy resources would have their prominence. There would likely be peace; for with plenty of resources and liberty, there is practically nothing to fight for. Only when divided on information and resources is there reason to war.

One of the oldest institutions on Earth, also claims the benevolence and also has some of the most resources of any institution. It is the millennia old, international religious institution, the Catholic Church. There is something else in the church steeple besides people, there is treasure. The weekly fundraising aside, if they cleaned out a closet in the Vatican, they could raise half of Africa out of starvation and poverty. If they really wanted to do something about the malady stricken on the underside of the status quo, they could have done so decades ago, centuries ago and still can tomorrow.

They could have saved many or subsidized a different new world. Instead they just saved money and loot. Perhaps, they have every intention of helping people and are simply busy, with the inquisition then, and the clandestine perversions hidden recently. Like every institution they help themselves, and when it appears they are helping people, they may be, but only because it helps them or rather, the perception of them. Maybe they know some secret religious information. Maybe you can take it with you.

Other notable religious institutions raise noteworthy amounts of money and horde it or distribute it for earthly means, and they are inexcusable as well. Practically all institutions horde resources and information, including churches, but Vatican City has wealth, treasure and valuable art beyond compare. Their inventory is secret, and much of it comes from various forms of plunder with roots in practically all the exploitation that has took place during colonialism. Vatican City houses the leadership of the Catholic Church, the exploits and dichotomous behavior over the centuries is well recorded. Other institutions, specifically other religious institutions, also operate in the same manner or toward the same monopolization.

Religions are not automatically malevolent; in fact religions are rooted in goodness in spirituality, which is why the hypocrisy is so stark. Spiritual understandings become religions, religions become churches, churches become states and states become war mongering absolutist institutions with agendas. Various religious institutions instigated and participated in atrocious acts for millennia towards very Earthly ends. The monotheistic religions, with spiritual understandings removed replaced with combative dogma, are responsible for enshrining absolutist jingoism and reinforcing the us and them mentality.

Institutions make secret ties to other institutions to incorporate secret agendas. They work together, but often only in the shadows. They seem to be part of separate events that coincide and march to the same tune, the same beat, churches included. For example, in war, opposing armies in essence do nothing different; both sides kill. In war religions often take sides. Competing corporations work together to raise and fix prices and sell to oppositional forces. Gangs may hold their own crew above all else, but they might assist other gangs, even countering or opposing gangs, before they assist authorities or random individuals.

> FACT: Paul Bremer attended Exeter, Yale and Harvard. He worked for the Heritage Foundation and lost hundreds of fellow employees at World Trade Center on 9/11. Paul was authorized chief executive authority in Iraq after the invasion by George II. He issued decrees that superseded all other legislation. Among the mandates are the privatization of former state enterprises and special privileges to foreign corporations, including immunity from Iraqi laws to private security corporations. He left his supreme position in Iraq to serve as chairmen of the advisory board for Globalsecure Corporation.

War is the principal, primordial means for institutional advancement. It is overt and blatant, but often with covert, unseen agendas. To wage war raises unaccountability. To participate in war is to perpetuate the status quo. Despite new equipment, war is one of the oldest tools of institutional order. No matter how justifiable they say it is, there are other ways besides war, but not always another way that is so profitable to various institutions' agendas. Timelines note war and sometimes war alone for centuries, yet surely other things occurred. This is just one of many social influences.

> FACT: The first recorded war occurred in 2700 BC. It was between Sumer (Iraq) and Elam (Iran). It was fought in the area of Basra where Iraq and Iran warred in the 1980s.

The order of authority has not changed in nearly 5,000 years. Inventions mostly enable the continuation and control of war rather the prevention of war. War accomplishes institutional wrong under the fog of imminent, violent death. Perhaps if the tools for war were not new and improved people would tire of it.

Secret accomplishments are snuck into the parade of looming doom. The most heinous crimes; rape, theft, torture and murder all go unaccounted for in war, frequently in the form of complex institutional accomplishments. In war, no idea or belief is exchanged or noticed, there is no great cause won. There are only improvements to death machines, reinforcement of institutional structures and the occasional advancement in medical procedures to heal people who have been obliterated by the new war machinery.

> Now this conjunction of an immense military establishment and a large arms industry is new in the American experience. The total influence -- economic, political, even spiritual -- is felt in every city, every Statehouse, every office of the Federal government. We recognize the imperative need for this development. Yet, we must not fail to comprehend its grave implications. Our toil, resources, and livelihood are all involved. So is the very structure of our society. In the councils of government, we must guard against the acquisition of unwarranted influence, whether sought or unsought, by the military-industrial complex. The potential for the disastrous rise of misplaced power exists and will persist. We must never let the weight of this combination endanger our liberties or democratic processes. We should take nothing for granted. Only an alert and knowledgeable citizenry can compel the proper meshing of the huge industrial and military machinery of defense with our peaceful methods and goals, so that security and liberty may prosper together.
> ~Dwight D. Eisenhower, Farewell Address to the Nation

That's some farewell. Though war is an event that is easily infiltrated and exploited, it is not a required circumstance to conduct or implement an agenda. Mundane circumstances with intermittent excitement are suitable to fulfill scandalous agendas as well, but no situation allows such profound and easy opportunity to institute unseen agendas as war.

The new world order is being built by intertwined, international institutions. The same status quo, the same formation of order that has practically always been, is ordained in the newly destroyed and degraded environment. The institutionalized operate in phantom-like circles, in ciphers within ciphers and groups within groups. The institutionalized coordinate and act in secrets and unknowns, the same way as the always have.

Secretive elite groups, publicly known with private agendas, such as the Council on Foreign Relations, the Bilderberger Group, the Trilateral Commission, the Royal Institute for International Affairs (Chatham House), the Club of Rome, the WTO, the UN, the World Bank, the Fabian Society, the Heritage Foundation and the Round Table Group are all full of promoters of a new world order. Multitudes of other groups, known and unknown, corporate, religious and national institutions coordinate and promote total global monopolization. They all operate in and promote monopolization within the status quo as much as will be tolerated, what is often called globalization. The counter to globalization, to monopolization and exploitation is localization.

Some individuals act knowingly and many are simply cogs in the machine, unaware that they are part of the progression of monopolization. The groups may or may not announce mutual objectives or cooperation, but it seems they proceed down the same path, together at times, and other times coincidental strangers.

> FACT: Between 2000 and 2006, Michigan lost 336,000 jobs. Michigan has the highest unemployment rate in the U.S.A. as of 2008.

Perhaps your own local or state Congressional Representative may be promoting the status quo and allowing globalization and progression of the new world order. If localization was programmed instead of globalization, progress would still be possible in Michigan, instead of the usual roll in roll out operation of globalization. Perhaps one has Representatives who are suspect of committing fraud or any other number of crimes to benefit themselves and their crew, like Governor Rod Blagojevich of Illinois or as it seems, Dick Cheney. Outright extortion and fraud is nothing new to the institutionalized elite.

> DICK CHENEY
> Attended Yale and transferred to University of Wyoming.
> Worked with Donald Rumsfeld and Richard Nixon.
> Worked with Gerald Ford as Assistant to the President.
> Vice President of investment firm Bradley Woods & Co.
> Representative for Wyoming.
> Secretary of Defense for George I, directed invasion of Panama and Desert Storm.
> Chairman of the Board and Chief Executive of Halliburton.
> Two term Vice-President.

> FACT: Vermont State Senate requests impeachment of George II and Dick Cheney on 4/20/2007. Within a week U.S.A. Representative of Ohio, Dennis Kucinich suggests impeachment of Dick Cheney.

Perhaps, Dick instigated war to profit corporations and in order to maintain and author an agenda or multiple agendas, perhaps not, but he always worked within and built up the status quo. If anyone represents the status quo, if anyone has capitalized in the pyramid system, it is Dick. He is rich from oil and weaponry and worked forty years of his life in the upper echelons of various institutions. He is famous for his part in the roll in and roll out of Iraq.

Many institutions of the status quo may be on Dick's side, but not Vermont. It seems Vermont is unafraid of change, unafraid of influencing and changing the status quo, unafraid to speak out. The boat can be rocked, institutionalized individuals could fall right off, and the boat would still sail through whatever waters were ahead.

To be a patriot in the new world requires new sensitivity to the old oligarchical collectivism. Patriots must question the interconnectedness of all institutions. Since public policy is not only influenced by intellectuals, but also influenced by the institutionalized, people need to act on behalf of people just to retain balance. Public policy is engrained and intertwined with institutionalized of corporations and church affiliations to benefit the few. Corporate and religious institutions hold influence and even dominate within some national institutions.

The trinity of monopoly connect to form exploitation around individuals; oligarchical collectivism. Patriots act to separate the formation of institutional ties and angles to prevent individual exploitation. Patriots do not allow institutional ties to supersede individual rights. Patriots question institutions to prevent the arrangement of oligarchical collectivism.

Patriots in the new world order not only love, support and defend their country; locals, land and liberty but love and support and defend locals, land and liberty everywhere. Patriots question the institutions from their country and beyond. Patriots not only question the government, but the corporations and churches and all institutions. The institutionalized need to be questioned, whether they are a Raytheon executive or a Jesuit priest, the pope or pharmaceutical lobbyist, CEO or Governor, or else they will march right over people. If there is no wrong transpiring, they won't mind transparency, otherwise they will belittle and discredit questions and whoever asks them.

Institutionalized individuals glide through public and private domain, blurring the distinction between the two, while promoting the status quo through institutionalization rather than individualization. Government outsourcing and corporate subsidies, mutual international exploitation, politicians becoming CEOs, CEOs becoming politicians, politicians claiming religions, religions claiming politics, all make it hard to tell where one institution ends and another begins.

FACT: 150 graduates from Pat Robertson's Regent College served in the George II Administration.

"We, at the Christian Coalition, are raising an army who cares. We are training people to be effective - to be elected to school boards, to city councils, to state legislatures and to key positions in political parties…By the end of this decade, if we work and give and organize and train, the Christian Coalition will be the most powerful political organization in America." ~Pat Robertson

Patriots love and support country, but to do so often requires one to be wary of government and other institutions integrated within the country. Patriots question those institutions that work under and attempt to adjust or modify the trinity liberty. The trinity of liberty was created to counter the trinity of monopoly. The trinity of monopoly; church, state, and corporate institutions, then infiltrated and countered the trinity of liberty.

The original patriots at the Boston Tea Party not only questioned The Company, but King George III, his church and all the other supportive branches. Patriots question all the players involved in exploitation, even if they claim to represent "God and country." Today, corporate executives routinely end up working for the government, not because the experience of operating a corporation is pertinent to running a nation, but because they have been successfully institutionalized. They know how to accomplish within the status quo.

The institutionalized of the trinity of monopoly affiliate with money, power and notoriety to promote agendas that are presented as if they exist for people's betterment. Some institutions and many people within institutions do mean well and accomplish acts of graciousness and generosity. Many institutions benefit individual circumstances and conditions. Other institutions exist in duality, proclaiming benevolence to be their sole undertaking and failing miserably at it. Most institutions help and hinder both.

The most noble and heroic acts of institutions occur when shit hits the fan, and institutions send help during volatile events and disasters. During times when hardship is constantly adjacent, when a helping hand is needed at every turn heroes are made in due course. In the worst of tragedies, some institutions do rise to the occasion. Sometimes the police are needed and sometimes they arrive to help. Sometimes, when situations are so entirely disastrous that anyone could be a hero at every turn, institutions do provide direct assistance.

FACT: After Hurricane Katrina, when the levees broke in New Orleans, many individual paramedics and rescue institutions were sent to New Orleans, yet the Police Chief from the nearby city of Gretna ordered the blockade of a bridge leading out of New Orleans. Evacuees were met with a roadblock, shotgun fire and turned around.

Institutionalized authorities and powers hold secret and public meetings on city, state and global policy. The Mayor of Gretna backed the Police Chief's decision. Their reasoning: the evacuees were a threat. Sometimes institutions established to assist, refuse to help and sometimes they actively hinder.

> "The very word "secrecy" is repugnant in a free and open society; and we are as a people inherently and historically opposed to secret societies, to secret oaths, and to secret proceedings. We decided long ago that the dangers of excessive and unwarranted concealment of pertinent facts far outweighed the dangers, which are cited to justify it."
> ~John Fitzgerald Kennedy

It is impossible to say what transpires in secret meetings. Secret meetings in Gretna might be concerned with keeping their city safe from criminals no matter the implications. Other secret meetings might be concerned with the orchestration of world peace, cure for disease and the eradication of poverty. Their meetings are a secret so anything is possible. Maybe they are deciding when would be the best time to release their perpetual motion machine. Whatever their pursuits are, they believe the common people do not need to know. Normally secrets are kept for elitist gains and measures. But if they are conducting meetings concerning anything that was benevolent, by keeping it hidden, it sours. Therefore secrets should not be.

Cops in Gretna, Louisiana, believed that they had the right to prevent people from crossing a bridge so that they might leave turmoil. Institutions of the trinity of monopoly believe they have the right to say who crosses the bridge as well. Institutions make plans within conceptualizations that divide people according to their location relative to a bridge, wall or other conjured reasoning.

> "Males and females are the distinction of nature, good and bad, are the distinction of heaven; but how a race of men came into the world so exalted above the rest, and distinguished like some new species, is worth inquiring into and whether they are a means of happiness or misery to mankind." ~Thomas Paine

People who believe they are elevated or better than others because of their race, relation to a bridge, or other conjured concept are ignorant and their ignorance is strength to institutions. Institutions act to keep information in order to gain and maintain power. The unknowns surrounding secrets can remain secret, for actuality cannot be hidden and it is enough to ponder and act on. The formation of a hypothesis is possible through observation of actuality and questioning reality. Keeping secrets, in reality, gives them away. To keep a secret is to conceal, concealment reveals that one is operating as an elitist. There is no goodness in secrets.

Institutionalized secrets are never needed, unless public perception and gaining power are priorities. If happiness and benevolence were planned, people would let them accomplish whatever it is that they plot. Secrets are necessary when malevolent operations are planned and whole truth threatens agenda. There would be no reason for secrecy if benevolence were their intention. If it is exploitation they deliver, then it would have to be kept secret.

> "The world is very different now. For man holds in his mortal hands the power to abolish all forms of poverty and all forms of human life." ~John F. Kennedy

For arguments sake, suppose their secrets were benevolent. If they kept benevolent information secret, they would likely tell the world in order to cast away any suspicion and to gain acclaim. Information would likely leak. Unless one is under the proverbial thumb of an evil authority, there is no reason to keep a secret that would benefit individuals.

If they withheld secret information that is or would be benevolent, that in itself is malevolent. To keep a secret that is so benevolent that its benevolence is kept secret, is a dark and wicked act on its own. One becomes a wrongdoer by keeping benevolent information secret. As time passes, it becomes more important to keep the secret because it has been kept secret for so long, it now makes the keepers of the secret guilty for not revealing it before.

A secret about something malevolent is another, more obvious form of wickedness. Keeping secret information concerning active malevolency is a potentially exponentially greater wrong. These secrets are perhaps easier to keep because they would inherit certain guilt by revelation of the malevolency. Secrets are easy to keep when their release means one's direct demise though revelation of guilt. Either way, information should be shared; the very act of concealment becomes dark no matter what. If the secrets hidden would be helpful or they concern evil, it is still withholding information and negative.

Individuals are entitled to privacy and secrets, but not institutions, nor the institutionalized, at least they shouldn't be. The actions of institutions concern living, breathing individuals should be transparent. If institutions weren't dealing in dire of one form or another across some bridge or arbitrary line, they would operate openly. Whatever they are talking about affects people, and people have the right to know. Public officials and representatives should become accustomed to constant oversight and view. Public officials should have public oversight.

Political, religious and corporate institutions separate themselves from ordinary people by having more power, clout, possessions, connections and wealth than individuals. In the age of information, institutionalized powers meet in secret to exchange secret information. By withholding information they employ the pyramid system to their advantage. Information is power, and they keep it. Individual ignorance is strength to institutions. They separate themselves, like nobility of the past, from common people by keeping information to themselves. Institutions intertwine while the concerns of ignorant individuals are left unconsidered on the sideline.

There should be no secrets about public policy or existence that government leaders should be allowed to have. There should be no reason that any institution claiming representation of God would not share possessions and information without hesitation. As well, if corporations did share at least information on their operations then obviously they would have people's best interests built into their structure and progression would be enabled. The fact they don't is proof that they put profit and power of their institutions above God, family and country, principle, people and terra firma, liberty, land and locals.

All institutions exist as a proponent or opponent of people and therefore are subject to people's investigations. Perhaps, they are up to some great idea of oneness and openness, reminiscent of John Lennon's song *Imagine*. Perhaps the secrets, the elite inclusiveness is simply to remove them from distractions to concentrate on the betterment of humankind. Perhaps they are planning on instituting a global feudal empire where everyone works for hamburgers and pop, where there is valium in the water to keep us happy.

Why not quell the questions and speculation by opening the doors to their meetings? By inviting those who question, they may not be so far removed, but there would no longer be the need to hide, potentially. If there were no secrets, there would be fewer questions, assumptions and protests. Secrets are always malevolent, and secrets always lead to more secrets.

GLOBALIZATION PROTESTS

November 30, 1999: Protesters in Seattle block World Trade Organization delegates from entering meeting. Franchise stores were destroyed, a curfew was implemented and the National Guard was called in.

July, 2001: Protesters face police brutality and torture when the G8 visited Genoa, Italy. Dozens of police and protesters were injured. One protester died after being shot and run over by officer's vehicle.

February 15, 2003: Global protests against impending invasion of Iraq. Estimates of protesters worldwide range from 6 to 30 million.

April 1, 2009: G20 protesters in London march on the city's financial district in four columns depicting the four horsemen of the apocalypse. Dozens of protesters were injured and a branch of the Royal Bank of Scotland was vandalized. At the same time, protesters clashed with police at annual NATO conference in Strasbourg, France.

FACT: The Group of Eight or G8, consists of roughly eight of the most powerful nations on the planet, economically these nations make up more than half of the world's economy. Originally the G8 was the G7, Russia was included after the group's beginning. The leaders of these nations hold annual, informal meetings on international economic policy. They are normally accompanied by security and an army of riot police, there to meet the crowds of protesters. The G8 morphed into the G20, representing 85% of the world economy.

FACT: The World Trade Organization was established in 1995 and replaced the 1948 General Agreement on Tariffs and Trade, an international business agreement. The main mission of the WTO is to "ensure that trade flows as smoothly, predictably and freely as possible." There are 153 nations in the WTO.

The truth is like an elegant meal, it is ninety percent presentation and ambience. The new world order exists; it exists in the minds who initiate global interdependency. It is not one law or legislation that will complete the new world order; it is subtle, airy influences with Orwellian overtones and has been prepared with many ingredients. It cannot transpire in one critical moment, it is the culmination of multitudes of consequences, conditions, and complications of the petrolithic era and nuclear age. Change may be served at once, but like a meal, it has been prepared.

Willful blindness and conspired covert manipulations have heralded the arrival of the new world order. Whether coal, or oil, or uranium, create the depleted conditions does not matter, the actuality exists. Whether it was ignorance or lies or a combination of both that instigated the new world order, it does not matter. Their secrets don't matter; known actuality is enough to act on. That there is global pollution is enough, that there are restrictions on liberty is enough. That they have secrets and secret organizations is enough to question and act on. It does not matter what those secrets are, that they have secrets is enough.

> "It is not my intention to doubt that the doctrine of the illuminati and the principles of Jacobinism had not spread in the United States. On the contrary, no one is more satisfied of this fact than I am."
> ~George Washington, high level Freemason

The term Jacobinism refers to the French Jacobin Club that sparked the Reign of Terror during the French Revolution; it went on to mean any extremely violent and secretive club. The Jacobites of Scotland and England similarly rebelled and tried to oust the King with their own royalty. The Jacobites fought against the new royalty from Hanover, George I, in attempts to return the former royalty back to power. The Jacobites were unsuccessful, but many battles occurred between 1688 and 1745.

Ideas are manifest into reality. If the ideas discussed within secret groups were beneficial to more than a small percentage, they would not be secrets in the first place. To conduct meetings in secret makes the discussions potentially evil and definitely elitist.

> FACT: Biblical Jacob conned his starving, older twin brother, Esau, into giving up his birthright for a bowl of lentil soup. Esau was elder by an instant and described as red and hairy. Jacob, encouraged by his mother, later deceived his blind father to obtain the blessings of the first son. Jacob fled his home when Esau threatened to kill him. Later the brothers reconciled and are now known as fathers of nations. Jacob is also known for a vision he later had, referred to as Jacob's Ladder. In his later years, God renamed Jacob Israel.

> FACT: The Kogi have farmed the mountains of Columbia for millennia. They are some of the only indigenous people in the Americas to remain unconquered and still live traditionally. They believe they are the elder brothers of mankind and that the younger brother, essentially the white, western world, has taken from the older brother. They believe that people are killing Mother Earth by removing her organs, roots, and resources, and burning them back into the elements.

> "When you expect things to happen - strangely enough - they do happen." ~J P Morgan

If it was certain that detrimental ideas were discussed, they would be threatened. This inspires thorough secret keeping. It is tremendously difficult to keep a secret, though it is easier to keep a secret if revealing it means your dissolution and demise.

They are trained to keep secrets from brothers and among brothers. People tend to dissolve their secrets because it is the right thing to do, the institutionalized hold onto secrets because it is the right thing to do for them or their crew. They are all well practiced at concealment. Elitist institutionalized officials and those within ordained authorities are all trained to keep secrets, to withhold information. And unless it suits them to do otherwise, secrets normally remain so. Some people can exist in such a state of duality, that they may always be lying and never believe as much.

Zealots choose the evil that is supportive of their cause or institution. They perpetuate the status quo and instigate support for their institutions. Idiots ignore evils in total and continue their overall support for the status quo and whatever institution. Elitists keep secrets to enhance their own institutions. They flip, distort and influence the perception of others, twisting good and evil in order to promote their own selfish agenda, whatever it may be. Whether reactive like zealots, or passive like idiots, or active like elitists, the result is the same: the transference of good for evil and evil for good.

190

Just as liberty umbrellas all or none, what is a right for one is a right for all. Everyone deserves an equal playing field without slant. Secrets exist to empower through the unequal distribution of information, secrets create slant. Those privileged to the information have an advantage over everyone else.

> FACT: The Hopi, the People of Peace, live in Arizona. The Hopi conceptualized the world from the isolated desert, developing noteworthy perspective and insight. They believe that all people are brothers. Another Hopi concept is of people with two hearts. Part of this belief is that evil people exist who have traded their own hearts for greedy, personal satisfaction. Because they have given up the function of their own hearts they have to steal the hearts of others to exist. The two-hearted people are liars, able to cheat and murder while proclaiming fairness, righteousness and peace.

Both the Hopi and the Kogi speak of people robbing Mother Earth in terms of the Earth as a living, single being, and the brothers' mother. Both cultures speak of people robbing the Earth's organs, her heart, liver, her blood and other body parts of the Earth Mother, crippling and killing her. These body parts are the gold, coal, petrol, uranium and other minerals extracted from the guts of Earth Mother.

The two-hearts lie and believe that they are not lying. Two-hearts are able to exploit anyone and anything around them. They are able to raise armies and wage war for peace. They are able to happily pillage the guts of their own Mother Earth for institutional operations. The two-hearts seek to control the world and will murder anyone in their way.

The Hopi of the Four Corners area of Arizona believe that we are living in the fourth age of the planet Earth. The Hopi also believe that there are four races of people in the world, all equal brothers. The Hopi believe that people are like corn and that the creator manifested people and corn together. The different types of corn and people have different attributes, but are all corn and are all brothers the same, except institutionalized GMO corn.

The Hopi believe that there are four races of people in the world synonymous with the colors of corn. According to Hopi belief, there are red, yellow, black and white people. Each color is related to an element and anyone can potentially lose their way and become two-hearted. According to Hopi belief, red people are the guardians of earth, yellow people are the guardians of air, black people are the guardians of water and white people are the guardians of fire.

> FACT: There are 190, give or take, countries in the world. The U.S.A. has military bases in about 130 of them. The U.S.A. military is the world's biggest institutional source of pollution; other military entities are major contributors to global environmental destruction as well.

> "All wars are civil wars, because all men are brothers." ~Francois Fenelon, French Poet

If just a few of those military bases were in the U.S.A., there would be resources available to locals, not applied to others. If just a few of those bases were not active investments, there would be more resources for people. If there were a base or two in or near Louisiana, perhaps they would have been able to alleviate rescue and relief operations during and after Hurricane Katrina. Perhaps the Gretna Police would have had the heart to let people cross the bridge or a marine would have ordered the bridge open.

If soldiers were available at home instead of abroad, the soldiers would be able to alleviate and assist failing border patrol operations. Perhaps there would be an option to building a wall across the border with Mexico. Historically of course, walls are only good when they come down. The exception is the Great Wall of China, which never came down and is celebrated mainly for this engineering feat.

Borders compartmentalize nations, and the people within them, into the pyramid system. Borders are given to natural formations like the Rio Grande, but are unnatural and serve the institutionalized "us and them" mentality. Generally speaking, people fleeing Mexico or anywhere south of the border represent everything that is historically valued of an immigrant to the U.S.A. For one, they are hardworking and willing to start at the bottom for opportunity. And two, their own homeland has failed them, frequently because the slant of the pyramid is steep there.

Generally speaking, Mexicans have all the values of a valued immigrant to the U.S.A. They want to leave their homeland for better opportunity. They are criticized though for earning money here and sending it to be spent in Mexico. Institutions frequently do not receive the same criticism that individuals do for such international misappropriation. Specifically speaking, Mexicans also have something that other immigrants do not have. Mexicans are often from here, as much of the U.S.A. was once Mexico, many Mexicans have indigenous roots to North America that most cannot have.

Corporations are exploiting immigrants, among others; the illegal immigrants are not exploiting anyone. Immigrants are not stealing jobs, if anything, it is the employers who are swindling and stealing from everyone. The illegal immigrants are desperate people seeking a better life. Since it is illegal, there is no accountability and since the people are desperate, anything is better than nothing, and the exploitative institutions better themselves. If any group should be allowed preference, it is our direct and only neighbors in Mexico, as well as Canada, that was one of the supposed reasons for NAFTA anyway.

Corporate institutions are allowed special benefits of import, export and relocation. Corporate institutions are given preeminence when they decide to go from one country to another. Why not individual exception and assistance?

> "A new partnership of nations has begun. We stand today at an extraordinary moment. The crisis in the Persian Gulf, as grave as it is, also offers a rare opportunity to move toward an historic period of cooperation. Out of these troubled times, our fifth objective - a new world order - can emerge: a new era - freer from the threat of terror, stronger in the pursuit of justice and more secure in the quest for peace." ~George I, September 11, 1990

> "We have before us the opportunity to forge, for ourselves and for future generations, a new world order. A world where the rule of law, not the law of the jungle, governs the conduct of nations. When we are successful, and we will be…" ~George I

Paul comes from a long line of bankers. M.M. Warburg & Co was founded in Hamburg, 1798. Paul

> "We shall have world government, whether or not we like it. The only question is whether world government will be achieved by conquest or consent." ~Paul Warburg, Banker

was one of the architects of the Federal Reserve and one of the original board members. A world government might not be that bad, if it is not arranged in a steep slanted pyramid, a formation to benefit the few, an oligarchy. If Mexico was raised up, instead of the U.S.A being shut down, a world government might not be so bad. A world government where right is promoted and wrong is prohibited could be acceptable. Perhaps, we shall have a world government, but the only way people are going to like it, is if it is benevolent or the majority end up believing in its benevolence.

It is difficult to imagine other formulations other than the present system. Like the current formula of currency, it is hard to imagine basing the trust of the economy in something other than gold and banking institutions. It is hard to imagine finances based on the annual hemp harvest and individual farming communities. And yet currency is simply the current means. It is difficult to conceptualize actions beneficial to individual locals rather than far off global institutions because we are steered.

Alternative systems are difficult to conceive, but they are possible, they are after all, only different. Whole economies are based on minerals, so why not a plant? No matter how a set system is secured, everything changes and everything evolves, unless suppressed and then situations eventually are shaky. Everything is impermanent.

It is easier to find alternatives when one ceases activity in the status quo, if only briefly. As with the Declaration of Independence and the subsequent creation of an alternative, first the wrong is stopped, and then it crumbles as participation in it ceases. If authorities answer people's cessation with violence, patriots must stand up unafraid and might have to fight back. Finally what is right, or at least modes more resembling right, are found under the rubble or away from it. Patriots don't pick fights and they don't fight because they will win, patriots fight for people being picked on.

> "The government is merely a servant - merely a temporary servant; it cannot be its prerogative to determine what is right and what is wrong, and decide who is a patriot and who isn't. Its function is to obey orders, not to originate them." ~Mark Twain

Global elitists continue the uncaring development of global institutions toward monopolization and keep their operations towards monopolization mostly secret. Often the new world order exploitations are presented in such a way as to be welcomed. The forecast is grim as war perpetuates war, resources become scarcer and desperation increases. If benevolent change were discussed, it would be possible to see, at least from a distance, a change on the horizon. The two-hearts require little logic, have lost love and live lies.

Instead of betterment, there are alliances which enable corporate development, a euphemism for flying into an underdeveloped region, exploiting resources and bailing. Invasion is presented in a way that motivates the locals to work for the arrangement and welcome its continuation. Recently, corporate institutions began presenting an inverted pyramid system as institutional structure; nonetheless it is still an enclosed pyramid.

In the new world order, institutions form, acquire and merge international corporations within state institutions and church organizations into more elaborate interconnected machines. Their formations go recognized and unrecognized. They clandestinely and candidly shape world politics, opinion and environment. They seek to monopolize all under one unified, interdependent, institutionalized pyramidal umbrella. The institutions and their intentions are the same as they have always been, while their mechanics are refined.

The new world order is the monopolization and institutionalization of physicality and mentality. It is heralded as betterment, as a way to bring people together by dispersing national boundaries and divisional interests. The catch is that they open situations, like borders, for institutions and not for individuals. They remove individual sovereignty and sharpen the slant of the pyramidal system. Individuals lend their hearts to institutions and might never get it back in exchange for enabling institutions. Institutionalized individuals believe that institutions are more respectable than independent individuals.

Unification of the world, where all people are part of a peaceful, equal world community in liberty, could be a good thing. The problem is that in the majority of the world's history, institutionalization has led to the degradation of individuals. The liberty available in the U.S.A. has even been penetrated and practically taken over by degrading pyramidal influences. There are many countries that have fallen under the rule of the U.S.A., but not all have been relieved by liberty. Nations are made dependent on institutions toward oligarchical collectivism, not made independent.

The new world order is the dream of the minority in control, a world where everyone is reliant and covertly controlled. People may question relevance less frequently because they do not have information that inspires them to do otherwise. Covertly controlled information is unapparent overt control. It is overt manipulation of information that is unknown. The new world order enhances elitist positioning at the apex of the pyramid through information in mostly unknown actions.

The intertwined trinity of monopoly seeks to gain and maintain power. The new world order is the perpetuation of the same pursuit of power in a newly degraded environment with enhanced technology. It is a conjunction of knowns and unknowns that facilitate and expand the status quo; globalization within a pyramid system. The new world is here; it is the petrolithic era and the nuclear age; a new environment for the same old order and authority.

The new world order is an idea that intends to extend power to institutions and eliminate notions of individuals. It is an idea made up of many smaller ideas that solidify and reinforce the status quo. And despite infinite change whirling and surrounding, it is an idea that holds the few on top and the many below. The new world order is just an idea via the minds of institutionalized elitists.

> "If we do not follow the dictates of our inner moral compass and stand up for human life, then his lawlessness will threaten the peace and democracy of the emerging new world order we now see, this long dreamed of vision we've all worked toward for so long." ~George I

> "What is at stake is more than one small country, it is a big idea - a new world order - where diverse nations are drawn together in a common cause, to achieve the universal aspirations of mankind: peace and security, freedom and the rule of law." ~George I

Cementing the new world order, the same old oligarchy in a new environment, is an ongoing process and is incomplete and since what they plan is secretive, the ultimate destination is mostly unknown. Since the future is speculative, people can only speculate. However understanding world history and reality of the present allow us to hypothesize potential end results.

By interpreting what authorities have said and done in the past, it is possible to guess at what they might do in the future. If they present one thing and accomplish the opposite of that, nine out of ten times, then it is a safe hypothesis that they will do the same next time. In the future there is likely to be more lies, more withholding and increased twisting of information.

Elitists today are much like the nobility of the past, in the sense that it's all kept in the family, all in the gang. Many gangs are interconnected and intertwined with multitudes of groups. They have formed secret and not-so-secret societies, clubs, councils, commissions and institutes. They attempt to enclose and envelope entirety in the trinity of monopoly.

There aren't many of them at the apex, though they exist under many guises and occasionally much glamour. They can be found in many professions, atop skyscrapers and under rocks, professing multitudes of opinions. Their commonality is obtaining and withholding information to feed their greed. They all misuse information to their advantage and to the degradation of the majority. They may have differing or countering operations and opinions, they may claim different gangs, but they are all elitists.

Quo modo Deum.

THEY, THEM, AND THE ILLUMINATI

All types of institutions instill the "us and them" mentality based on devised divisions suitable to their ends. Individuals and institutions frequently label people based on preconceptions instead of their reaction to information; instead of how they think. People are people, the same here or there.

The only way to fairly and accurately understand people is according to how they individually react to information. The only people who are so different from the majority as to require separation from everybody else as "them", are elitists. They are individuals who question information in order to better take advantage of others. We are all "us", and there is no "them", until that is, one selfishly acquires and restricts information in order to exploit us.

In what manner is God? This is a biggest question. The minority has always restricted the majority from this question and questions like it. Questioning the interpretation of God leads to questioning the interpretation of life and reality, including the workings of institutions. Questioning the interpretation of God is specifically allowed in the First Amendment for it enables all other important questions. It is a timeless question that rarely is actually answered, but always leads to other pertinent and timely questions, and when we are allowed to ask it, we can ask all other questions.

They, them, and the illuminati are the elitists residing at the apex of the pyramid system exploiting everyone else below them. They will do anything to remain in control of the status quo. They are institutionalized individuals, known and unknown, with so much power they are institutions unto themselves.

Most elitists react to events and consign themselves to prosper from situations. They, them and the illuminati are greedy individuals who question conditions and seek information to enhance their own agenda. These elite elitists make tactical decisions to influence and even create situations in which they can make gains.

There are the run of the mill elite, being they and them, elitists who behave with certain information or make actions to reap the most reward. They and them are elitists with little power to manipulate, but with more access to information than most. The illuminati orchestrate events to reap selfish gains with privileged information and wide powers. The illuminati prepare for, and manifest situations they know that they will prosper from. All illuminati are elitists, but not all elitists are

195

illuminati.

Illuminati is defined as a person or a group claiming special religious enlightenment. The illuminati, the illuminated, are those who have or more accurately claim to have special information. They may possess exclusive information, or they may just believe they do or they just be trying to get others o believe they do. To gain and maintain power it can be important to convince others that they have some sort of exceptional information.

> FACT: A 2006 UN study concluded that 1% of the world's population owned between 40% - 50% of the world's wealth. The same study concluded that the poorest 40% own 1% of the world's wealth.

Wealth is no measure of elitism, though elitists surely seek to increase their measure of wealth. In order to understand mentality it is more important to understand how one thinks rather than what one thinks. In the same way it is also more important to know how one obtains money and wealth, rather than what quantity one possesses. A decisive factor in understanding people may be how they got their money and not necessarily how much they have.

All elitists ask questions, a quality they share with patriots, and a likely reason for their occasional mix up. Patriots ask questions out loud in order to better understand actuality. Elitists ask questions quietly in order to obtain information for their selfish ends. Patriots never claim to have the complete story and always inspire questioning and progression. Elitists explicate complexity to make believe and however subtly, portray their possession of the complete story. Elitists seek information in order to gain and maintain in the pyramid system and take advantage of idiots, zealots, other elitists and patriots.

In the distant past, enlightenment of any kind pertained to God. Most all information was regulated solely through religious institutions. Scientific knowledge was either suppressed or sanctioned by religious institutions. There was no classification of information as there is today.

Today, science and faith are separated subjects with occasional correspondence depending on interpretation. In the past, individual scientific theories from simple observations were crushed if they did not correspond with institutional religious presentation. Official information was available through dogmatic institutions only. For hundreds of years European religious institutions verified the words of kings and printed most of the books available. To question the official interpretation of God or the universe at large was blasphemous. Institutions pretended to have the entire truth.

If people questioned the official institutional interpretation of God, the questioner would be broken. New ideas were disallowed. Ideas arise from questions and raise questions. And no questions were needed because the churches and the kings held all the answers. Many simple observations and ideas were an outright affront to official religious institutions, and many who simply questioned reality or lived in a way that inadvertently questioned the status quo, were tortured and killed.

> FACT: Beginning as early as 1022 and into the 16th century, countless heretics were burned alive and variously executed and tortured by the Roman Catholic Church and European Nations throughout the world.

Questioning established dogma, including egocentricity, could get one imprisoned, tortured and executed. Living outside of their institution was enough to reason for them to vanquish. Being a different race or religion was reason enough for trial, torture, death depending on the tolerations of the time.

During the inquisitions, people who did not believe in the holy trinity were punished as heretics. These Nontrinitarians were people of various beliefs who did not believe in the doctrine of one God being made of three persons; the Father, Son and the Holy Ghost. Michael Servetus' effigy was burned and then Michael himself was burned at the stake in 1553 for writing books on Unitarian philosophy that stated Trinitarian beliefs were not biblical in origin and deceptions based on certain Greek philosophies.

Throughout recorded time inquisitions prosecuted individuals with different beliefs, appearances or just inquisitiveness. The inquisitions were not inquiries, they killed people who inquired about alternatives or lived alternatively. During colonialism, inquisition began in Peru in 1570 and ended in 1820.

Galileo Galilei published numerous books on simple scientific observations. In 1610, he published observations of planetary objects in orbit and in 1632 he published additional observations that stated the Earth revolved around the Sun. He was put on trial for heresy in 1633. He questioned the church's cosmological theory, the geocentricity of Earth, proposing the Sun was at the center of our spherical system. His observations were based on reality. He is credited with discovering moons around Jupiter and as the first person to observe sunspot activity. He spent the last years of his life under house arrest, ordered to disbelieve heliocentricity and disallowed from publishing further. The Sun revolved around the Earth, that was that.

> "...And yet it moves." ~Supposedly muttered by Galileo Galilei after recanting heliocentricity.

Secrets of the ancient illuminati may have been a lot of things. For people of the past there certainly were justifiable reasons to keep secrets. Secret information is often initiated to gain power, but eventually kept to keep their heads. Keeping secrets about criminality is commonplace. It is not legitimate, but it is easy to legitimize keeping secrets to avoid being found guilty of crime. There is no knowledge that has to be kept secret; people should know the powers and dangers of fire. Only exploiters require secrets. The Earth moves; institutions are oligarchical.

The knowledge of God and knowledge of the laws of the universe and nature were one and the same to the ancients. People, the world over, concluded the Sun was God and that the solstices were among the most important holydays. This conclusion was based on observation of life cycles and seasons. Astronomy and geophysics were part of spirituality.

> FACT: The Sun is described as the center of the spheres by Vedic Sanskrit texts in the Rigveda. Made up of Mandalas or hymns, this religious text predates the Bible by about 1500 years.

> "It is he that sitteth on the circle of the earth, and the inhabitants thereof are as grasshoppers; that stretcheth out the heavens as a curtain, and spreadeth them out as a tent to dwell in." ~Isaiah 40:22

The institutionalized perpetuated the idea that the Earth was a cube instead of a globe and that it was at the center of creation. Institutions are unnatural formations and the ideas of the institutionalized are similarly unnatural as well. Institutions mutate amorphous and circular into regimented blocks. The Bible does not directly state that the Earth is flat and at the center of entirety, but institutionalized biblical interpretations insisted and individuals were discouraged from questioning.

> FACT: According to calculations Yehoshua Christos or Jesus Christ, was not born on December 25. The date was decided upon because of its correspondence with the winter solstice in the Northern Hemisphere. The birth of a son is symbolically related to the birth of the Sun. During Winter Solstice, daylight ceases to dwindle, the Sun pauses for three days and then gets higher in the sky and days lengthen. In June, during the Summer Solstice days grow shorter. Easter is the celebration of Jesus' resurrection after crucifixion. Sometime after Easter the Sun crosses and cruises the vernal equinox, day becomes longer than night in the Northern Hemisphere. The crucifixion and resurrection of God's son is symbolic for the crucifixion and resurrection of God's Sun across the sky.

The illuminati supposedly have some special information; supposedly they are involved in a mysticism of science. How does mysticism relate to science? One subject of science that relates directly to every religious teaching is psychology. And what people believe religiously is often a window into how people think overall. Knowing how people think can enable one to predict how they will react to generalities and specifics.

Practically every map and globe depicts north as upward. North is not up, north is not atop. North is one direction in three hundred and sixty degrees, north is not up. Simple presentation, as in world maps, is not always simple. South could be on top just as accurately as north or west or south-southwest. North and south do not correspond with up and down.

The illuminati are owl-like only they have developed information instead of eyesight. They have information others do not have and act to keep it that way, so as to influence.

> The owl is symbolic of the all-knowing and wise. Because of its exceptional night vision and stealth, the owl sees things others don't, and therefore knows things others don't. The owl further symbolizes the all seeing eye, Horus. Both are symbolic for lunar mystery and informed, evil intent.

> FACT: In Monte Rio, California, is the elite retreat The Bohemian Grove where the institutionalized converge every July. They also have an office in San Francisco; the Bohemian Club in Bohemian Building. Their motto: weaving spiders come not here. Notable

members and visitors include: Joseph Alioto, James A. Baker, Bechtel family, Bush family, Jimmy Carter, Richard Nixon, Dick Cheney, Ronald Reagan, Bill Clinton, Walter Cronkite, Dwight Eisenhower, David Rockefeller, David Gergen, and many more. In the summer there is at least one ceremony called the Cremation of Care, a mock sacrifice. Founded in 1872, people have been practicing mock sacrifice there for years. The center of the ceremony and the idol to which they sacrifice is a forty foot owl. There are tiny owls on every $1 dollar bill. One on the front, top, right corner and two more symmetrically on the bottom of the front. The owl is depicted on Euro coins and in many financial logos. The street layout of Washington DC depicts an owl, atop a triangle or pyramid. The Congress Building is in the owl's belly and the White House on a lower corner of the pyramid.

Prominent in the emblem of the National Press Club is the owl and a genie's lamp. The lamp is symbolic for conjuring smoke and mirrors. The owl and magic lamp in the logo for the National Press Club symbolizes exclusive knowledge and conjuring. Who chose that logo? In Washington DC, the Congress Building is in the belly of an owl atop a pyramid.

SYMBOL - PENTAGRAM

Pentagram means five lines, it is an archaic and esoteric symbol used in rituals since the time of Pythagoras and before. The pentagram is a symbolic representation of man. The pentagram was an early symbol of Christianity before the cross. Other stars with varying numbers of points are used symbolically as well. Five is a sacred number, as in Pentecost, the day the holy spirit descended on the disciples of Jesus, the Five Wounds of Christ, the Five Books of the Torah, the Five Pillars of Islam and the Five Symbols of Sikhism. The number five is sacred in many religions. There are five universal elements in mythology, water, earth, air, fire and ether. Upside down pentagrams have become associated with satanic cults. There are many pentagrams in the street layout of Washington DC.

Stars, such as those in the layout of Washington, D.C. aren't that scary, however they do contain symbolism certainly. But Congress in the belly of a beast, sitting atop a pyramid is much spookier than any pentagram or any star.

FACT: Christopher Columbus was stranded in Jamaica on his fourth voyage in 1504. After being on the island for months, the natives grew weary of the stranded crew and ceased supplying them with food. Christopher announced that if they did not help them and feed them, he would have his God take away the Moon. Columbus knew that on February 29, 1504 there would be a lunar eclipse. After the eclipse the natives brought the crew all the food and supplies they wanted.

Information is power. In the past, that information may have been as simple as the Earth's relationship to the Sun. Those people who were in timing with the Sun were more likely to have a successful growing season and prosper, or trick others without access to intricate knowledge. Information is power, whether it is knowledge of the seasons or nuclear technology or an unknown unknown. When information is restricted one can appear more wise and powerful than one actually is, to gain and maintain control.

Information is strength because with information one can manipulate those without information, or prevent manipulation of oneself and others. How to transform lead into gold was one of the most epic secrets of the past and was perhaps an idea perpetuated by alchemists as a possibility to gain power. Alchemists are often depicted as being one type of illuminati or another and such secretive schools were all over the old world. Many operated completely clandestinely, but some schools were variously promoted by royal powers, though the adepts of alchemy always operated in secret one way or another.

The real secret was likely that it was impossible to turn lead to gold. The hint of this secret was a misleading misconception to protect the real mystery from becoming known. The real secret may have been that there was no secret at all. Or more likely the gold may was a distracting metaphor for other pursuits. The real secret was in secret interpretation, not secret conjuring. Turning lead into gold was a metaphor for the human condition. Alchemy always symbolized the transposition of dull lead thought into golden mindset. The symbolism was a way for the alchemists to relate and convince others they had valuable knowledge.

In mystery, there could be some secret information, or there could be the appearance of a secret where there is none. Mystery could be a distraction to something else, something real. The presentation of mystery enables one to profit from and promote agendas. A distracting mystery is a way to hide something. There may be nothing in the middle of mystery save distractions from exploitation and monopolization. Mystery matters little next to reality.

The impending consequences and conditions of environmental destruction and exploitation call for cessation and investigation. Questions regarding mystery are perhaps distractions to the actual destruction of the Earth, the only habitable rock around.

The toxic petrolithic era and nuclear age instills a quiet feeling of unease or real and constant pain. The environmental consequences are the preeminent instability. The environmental degradation and destruction resulting from human activities is an undue weight and an unfair tax that all bear. This taxation is not monetary; it is a toxic chemical burden, a physical taxation of toxins.

When taxation and exploitation via commodities is slanted, people tend to do something about it. In the petrolithic era, the same sort of tax and unfair burden has been placed on individuals as it was during the big steep. Only today, it is exponentially so, as it's inescapable environmental hazard. Our toxic ways have resulted in an unfair tax in the same way that the monopoly on tea did centuries ago, only exponentially worse.

The desire for tea free of exploitation, for existence free from undue taxes on necessities like clean water and air, is the same now, as it was then. The original patriots who cast off the burdens of tea would, as well, cast off the oligarchical burdening institutions of today. The conditions they experienced led the original patriots to cease the exploitation, no matter the outcome. No matter the rattling met, they did what was simply right, stopped.

Independence Day celebrates the fact that individuals stopped. The Fourth of July celebrates people's active discontinuance of involvement in exploitation and celebrates people halting their support for they, them, and the illuminati. To announce a discontinuance of support was an insult to existing institutional structure. The institutions didn't know how to handle it for discontinuance defeats the status quo.

They, them and the illuminati are perched on elevated institutional branches. To those below it seems the interconnected institutions have vast knowledge, even intuition. Institutions appear ready, when really they just readied and actualized events in the first place. They win when people lose. They enable the status quo and empower institutional monopolization. Some have different intents than others and yet, they all work within the same framework, inside the same spectrum of monopoly.

Snakes, lizards and chameleons are all reptiles, yet distinct. Institutions and the institutionalized, they, them and the illuminati differentiate the same. Sometimes they casually creep in the same river and other times they eat each other. There are many different groups of illuminati, one vastly different from the other, but all reptile or elitist the same.

> "And the great dragon was cast out, that old serpent, called the devil, and Satan, which deceiveth the whole world: he was cast out into the earth and his angels were cast out with him." ~Revelation 12:9

Two heads lead to the same belly and the same asshole. Authorities in the petrolithic era often present two choices and act as if there are only these two choices and that they are vastly different. There is the option that advances their goals, and the option that advances their other goals. They present the greater evil and the lesser evil, Dr. Jekyll and Mr. Hyde, and expect a choice to be made. Correspondingly, there is what they say, and then there is what they do. Elitists operate in stark duality with two faced deceptions and two hearted operations.

There are always more than two choices. Animals may only have the choice to fight or to take flight, but man has many more options. We can choose any myriad of alternative responses and initiatives. To simplify control, choice is often presented as two sides that counter each other, but they are not necessarily different. Two countering options are often derived from the same source.

"Everything that we see is a shadow cast by that which we don't see." ~Martin Luther King Jr.

There are many known cabals of illuminati. Many individuals within them might solely be out to acquire information and not manipulate others with it, but it happens. There are Sufi mystics, Kabala mystics, Babylonian cults, Oriental Sects, Scottish, Bohemian and countless European Cults, there are Indian and other Asian Societies, and on and on. Most every culture has secret organizations, some esoteric, some economic, some genealogic, but they are all perceived to be powerful because of their secrets or supposed secrets, kept sometimes to keep one's head, and most always to get ahead.

One can only speculate if one is uninitiated, and therefore they can, in legitimate fashion, accuse those who say things about them as ignorant or outright crackpots. If there are secrets, the secretive are able to do deny and distract. A look at what is known, forgetting their mysteries concentrating on deciphering actualities, leads to real observations.

There are powerful individuals and institutions making invisible bonds conducting overt and covert actions among people. Their deals, when known, are presented as beneficial coordination through legitimate titles, but only promote continuation and intensification of the status quo. They proclaim fulfillment, but only empty and remove.

Secretive groups seek steeper slant to the pyramid system. Institutionalized criminals are involved in national, religious and corporate institutions. Generally, the average individual is much less devious than the average institutionalized elitist.

Through commitment to secrecy and manipulation of information, it becomes more difficult for people to believe their coordination is possible. What is seen and heard first is hard to replace and what is seen and heard often is hard to shake. Everyone knows that institutionalized individuals lie. It is also easy to believe they are liars, but at the same time hard to believe that they could lie so well as to conduct any number of conspiracies for any time because of their perceived incompetence. They fail at lying so often people believe that they are incapable of doing so, successfully, on any great scale.

"The individual is handicapped by coming face to face with a conspiracy so monstrous he cannot believe it exists." ~J. Edgar Hoover

The most well-known secret society in the U.S.A. is the infamous Skull and Bones at Yale University. George I and II, Prescott Sheldon Bush, John Forbes Kerry, Robert A. Lovett, Averill Harriman, Percy Rockefeller and William Howard Taft, among others were all members of the Yale based fraternity and secret society.

Supposedly the Skull and Bones frat is just a branch or ring among other intertwined, cooperative and combative groups bearing allegiance to who knows what. It is a relatively new crew similar in secret order to Scottish Rite, Thule Society, Vril Society, Knights of the Sun/Son, Bavarian Illuminati, Freemasons, Order of the Golden Dawn, Green Dragon, White Order, Wind, and on and on, the world over.

Perhaps these are not even their complete and correct names, that is inconsequential to the point that such groups exist. They are amorphous, clandestine and some have spent generations practicing deception to the point that even their name is scattered wonderment to distract.

Perhaps it is difficult to believe that such powers exist, perhaps because they have made it difficult to believe. Keeping an institution together over generations is no more difficult, be it legal or illegal, overt or covert. Crime families and corporations continue in the same way. Whether Freemason or Mafia, whether the Bush family or the La Cosa Nostra, institutions carry on easily no matter if legitimate or unlawful.

Their distinction is unimportant and their secrets are unimportant, that they have secrets is enough. They deserve no further recognition other than elitists withholding information. They are like lizards, snakes, alligators and crocodiles, the categorization only vaguely important, essentially they are all reptiles. They hold their tongue and operate secretively.

All reptiles are cold-blooded and they are all slippery, no further distinction is necessary as they all cast shadows and secrets around their exact group identity. They don't care about outsiders enough to share information. So instead of dissecting their exact functions, just looking over their skin is enough. Knowing they are cold-blooded and secretive is enough.

Their secrets matter less and less as the consequences of the petrolithic era and nuclear age expand. Secrets and mysteries matter little next to results. The elitists and illuminati can keep their secrets, what matters more is the condition of reality. Actuality is enough to contemplate, let alone mystery until actuality is fully scoped and defined. They know that information is power and that is why they keep secrets, secrets that if revealed could be diabolical or laughable.

The illuminati are the elite of the elitists, they are shadowy and shady. They elusively walk the halls and pits of authorities and are depicted as hooded, cloaked or robed, but usually appear all too typical. Examples of known illuminati in the past are Rasputin, Aleister Crowley, Pythagoras, Leonardo Da Vinci, Adam Weishaupt, Giuseppe Mazzini, various Alchemists, and the Knights Templars.

The story of the Wise Magi visiting the birth of Jesus is a classic depiction of illuminati. They are travelers with special knowledge. Interestingly there are usually only the three wise men presented. Though three kingly gifts are described, the number of gift givers is unspecified. Four wise men are occasionally depicted or sometimes as many as twelve.

The Skull and Bones are just one type of cold-blooded organization, whether they are chameleon or toad, is unknown and unimportant. Many illuminati groups claim Freemasonic or otherwise similar roots. One legend about the Freemasons, be it true or symbolic, exemplifies their mode of operation.

Freemasonry developed out of stonemasonry. Long ago and far away, the free stonemasons built castles for kings. They kept their engineering knowledge secret. If their knowledge were distributed openly, they would no longer be unique and powerful. They were kept close to the king because they knew things about the castle that even most did not, where secret escape tunnels an peepholes existed. This information enabled control, the king kept the stonemasons close and free.

One day there was an attack on the castle. The free stonemasons saved the surprised king by stealing him away in a secret tunnel before the invading forces could kill him. The stonemasons provided the king with escape and safe return to the throne. The king was grateful and offered rewards to his rescuers. The masons may have saved the king, or they may have arranged the attack to benefit their group by protecting the king for planned promotion within the pyramid. The story leaves one to speculate if the stonemasons were loyal or if they instigated the invasion.

The illuminati are architects of castles and societal constructs. The illuminati are amorphous crews of secret circles and ciphers. They shape shift like chameleons to gain loyalty, and are at times like toads and other times like Gila monsters. They take advantage of world events and sometimes orchestrate them entirely. They are practically invisible, like the wind, and just as potentially destructive. They are dynasties that exist both secretively and proudly. They seem to seek power towards total monopolization. They are like people with two hearts, dragons with two heads.

FACT: Francis Drake (etymologically dragon) made the some of the first English slave expeditions to West Africa. He was an explorer and privateer. He battled and plundered against the Spanish, capturing and robbing Spanish ships for their possessions including already captured slaves.

The history of illuminati groups is spooky, and partially hidden behind a curtain in the shadows. Today, they still conduct robbery and tout discovery, they still intertwine in secret circles. Many of these foundations are active; others do nothing, but support other institutions. There are an array of elitist foundations, both known and unknown, some do nothing except enhance and advise other institutions.

There are secret groups within secretive groups. One head announces peace and prosperity while the other head spits venom. Supposedly some legitimate institutions are illuminati creations and have no idea they are as such. Such groups may have been created by people with good intent despite ongoing manipulations, some involved have no idea that they are maintaining and stretching wrongdoing in their zealous support of elitist architecture.

The groups may be wide ranging foundations or they may be tight nit familial circles. A contemporary example of a dynasty of policy, individuals so institutionalized they form an institution is the Bush family. Not only have they been profiteers of arms through production, investment and direct sales for generations, they have also been profiting from oil for generations and they have been setting policy to promote the use of arms and oil for generations, at times in secret.

They convince people of peaceful intentions and then enact war. They perpetuate war. They quietly in words, and blatantly in profits, make decisions among the elite of the world to promote war, it seems. They shroud their motivations, but one actuality is financial gains from war and energy. Their mystery is murky, but there are enough transparencies to question.

James Smith Bush, born in 1825, was a Yale University and University of Rochester educated attorney. He was also an Episcopal Priest and traveled around the world doing the Lord's work. James, with friends Charles Taft (brother of U.S.A. President Taft) and Charles Harkness (Standard Oil) helped found the Wolf's Head Society in 1883, a secret society at Yale.

James' son, Samuel Prescott Bush, was very much into weaponry and money. Samuel attended the Stevens Institute of Technology. In 1901, he was hired to be General Manager of a steel plant that made railroad parts for Rockefeller Standard Oil and Harriman Railroads. In 1918, Bernard Baruch (Bernard was a successful businessman and Presidential Advisor) placed Samuel in charge of writing contracts for national armament. After WWI, Samuel continued amassing a fortune, working for the Federal Reserve Bank, Herbert Hoover, and AT&T.

Samuel begat Prescott Bush. Prescott attended Yale and served in WWI. He was trained in intelligence. He was involved in eugenics, became a Senator and made another Bush fortune in steel and weaponry. He actively participated in supplying the Nazi war machine with steel and capital as did many American investors. Without the support of American and British businesses, the Nazi war machine would not have been as capable as it was. The bank Prescott worked for, Brown Brothers Harriman & Co. and the Bank he was Director of, Union Banking Corporation, made loot with Nazi investments. With WWII Prescott and many others in the U.S.A. got paid.

Sept. 11, 1941	President Roosevelt orders navy to shoot on sight if any ship or convoy is threatened.
Dec 7, 1941	Japan attacks Pearl Harbor; U.S.A. enters war.
Oct 28, 1942	Nazi investments in the U.S.A. seized.
June 9, 1943	George I becomes youngest aviator - heads to western front.
May 7, 1945	Unconditional surrender of Nazi Germany.
August 14, 1945	Unconditional surrender of Japan.

Prescott begat George I. George I served in WWII as a pilot and bombed people and stuff in Japan, the Philippines and Guam. He was awarded the Distinguished Flying Cross. After the war, he became a Yalie and was tapped to be a bones brother. Later, he launched an unsuccessful campaign for Senate; his opponent called him "a tool of the Eastern kingmakers." Two years later in 1966 George I was elected as a Representative of Texas. He ran for Senate again and lost. He served as ambassador to the UN, chairman of the RNC, and liaison to the PRC and Taiwan.

In 1976 he was sworn in as Director of The CIA after the persuasion of Donald Rumsfeld and Dick Cheney who worked in the Ford Administration. At the time the U.S.A. House of Representatives was investigating the assassinations of MLK and JFK. Official records state George I became director of The Agency without any prior intelligence experience. He was let go when the Carter Administration was elected, 355 days later. Supreme Court Chief Justice Earl Warren led the 10 month long JFK assassination investigation in 1963-1964, was a former KKK leader. Justice Hugo Black was a member of KKK as well.

George I became Vice-President after losing in the 1980 Republican primary to Ronald Reagan. As a former actor famous for his performance with a chimp, Ronnie made a natural politician and George I turned was a great sidekick. George I remained in the White House for twelve years, eight as Vice-President and then four subsequently as President. He was in power during the Iran/Contra Affair, during the Iran/Iraq War and went to war with Iraq on behalf of Kuwait.

Iraq at one time was an ally of the U.S.A. or at least an accomplice. The War between Iran and Iraq was in part a proxy war between democracy and communism. Iraq was a proxy of the U.S.A., until they invaded Kuwait, then they became a scapegoat.

The Iraqi forces were ejected from Kuwait and between twenty thousand and two hundred thousand were killed. On his last night as Commander in Chief, with the no-fly-zone in Iraq secure and quiet for some time, with little or no provocation, George I ordered some bombing of Iraq one last time, just before midnight, just before his presidential power expired.

George I kept going though. He became a representative for the Carlyle Group. The Carlyle Group is a private investment firm that makes most of its money through the arms industry and rebuilding. As a former pilot and president, he made a perfect candidate to sell tanks and other war machines. After all, he puked in front of more heads of state and dignitaries than most folks would recognize, let alone know. And states buy weapons. Using his worldwide connections and privileged information he became a fantastic field rep for the Group. George I was later knighted by her majesty the Queen in 1993.

The Bush family is a legacy at one of the finest Universities, Yale, home to the fraternity Skull and Bones. Yale only enrolls the country's most exceptional brilliance based on performance and potential and, sometimes, just a little bit based on one's background. This fine intellectual institution has some extraordinary cases of alumni being grandfathered in, as in the case of George II, potentially. Texans will tell you that it would be difficult to be a true Texan if you were born in Connecticut and attended a prestigious Eastern Establishment preparatory school and Ivy League Universities. They'll also tell you how George Bush is a true Texan.

GEORGE II
Born in New Haven, Connecticut.
Spent summers in Kennebunkport, Maine.
After some years of learning in Texas he attended Phillips Andover Academy outside of Boston.
He attended college back at home, at Yale University in New Haven. He averaged a 77%, a C student without an A.
After a brief stint or stunt in the Texas Air National Guard he attended Harvard Business School.
Made over $840,000 with Harken Energy, worked with Spectrum 7 and Arbusto Energy.
Co-owned the Texas Rangers.
Was Governor of Texas and in 2000 obtained the Presidency of the U.S.A.

Because votes were left uncounted George II was selected as President in 2000. George II led the U.S.A. to war with Afghanistan in retaliation to the worst crime/terrorist attack ever conducted in the U.S.A. on 9/11/01. There have been worse atrocities committed by people, but certainly none that were televised live. The live mayhem was most rattling.

SEPTEMBER 11 IN HISTORY
3 B.C. One of many speculated dates of birth of Jesus Christ. (from the book The Star that Astonished the World, by Ernest Martin, 1991)
1297 William Wallace led Scottish to defeat the English at the Battle of Sterling Bridge.
1609 Henry Hudson discovered Manhattan Island and adjacent Hudson River. The Southern tip of Manhattan at the mouth of the river is future site of the World Trade Center and Twin Towers.
1776 Benjamin Franklin, John Adams and Edward Rutledge meet with British General for peace talk. The talks fail and Revolutionary War ensued.
1777 Old Glory Flag first waved in Battle of Brandywine, British victory.
1782 Last battle of Revolutionary War began at Fort Henry.
1792 The Hope Diamond and other crown jewels stolen.
1814 American Navy defeated British in battle of Lake Champlain in the War of 1812.
1826 William Morgan kidnapped.
1857 Known as the Mountain Meadows Massacre, Mormons and Paiute Indians massacred 120 pioneers in Utah.
1906 Gandhi proclaimed September 11 annual celebration of Satyagraha, day of peace and resistance to tyranny through global unity and civil disobedience, meant to last 11 days.
1919 U.S.A. Marines landed in Honduras.
1922 British mandate of Palestine began.
1941 Construction of Pentagon began. U.S.A. navy given permission to fire on threatening German vessels.
1944 First U.S.A. Army Troops crossed border of Nazi Germany. RAF bombed city of Darmstadt.
1948 Muhammad Ali Jinnah, first leader of Pakistan, dies. Day a national holiday in Pakistan.

1955	Dedication of first Mormon temple in Europe, Switzerland.
1961	Formation of the World Wildlife Fund.
1970	Ford Pinto introduced.
1973	Chilean president Salvador Allende killed in violent coup, disappearances, torture and mass jailing ensued.
1978	Leaders from Egypt, Israel and U.S.A. met at Camp David.
1986	Stock market crashed, triggered by computer glitches.
1990	George I mentioned new world order in speech to Congress.
1993	USS Forrestal decommissioned.
1997	Scotland votes to create their own parliament after 290 year union with England.
2001	Pentagon and WTC attacked. Twin Towers collapse at nearly freefall speed, almost 11 seconds. WTC Building Seven nearby, becomes first steel building to collapse without being hit by airplanes at freefall speed. The Twin Towers were one 110 story tall 11.
	New Year's Day in Ethiopian calendar.
	On 9/11 there are 111 days left in the year.

> SYMBOL - **11** The number 11 is considered to be the most powerful number in time and peace. The number 11 symbolizes intuition, knowing needing no verification. 11 and many of its multiples are numbers of mastery and peace. Armistice Day, marking the end of the War to End all Wars, is celebrated on the eleventh hour, of the eleventh day, of the eleventh month.

Different numbers have different significance to different illuminati initiates, but supposedly, they are infatuated with dates, numeric correlations and the power of symbols to influence people. The potential for influence is there whether one notices the influence or not. Supposedly many illuminati believe in magic or the science of mysticism. It is hard to believe that any legitimate representative of any influential institution would believe in magic to the point that they hire magicians, and yet, it's documented.

> FACT: John Quigley was Nancy Reagan's psychic astrologer. Nancy supposedly developed Ronald's calendar according to astrological predictions. Hillary Clinton attended a mystical session and participated in séances.

The fact that the illuminati practice mysticism is strange, how and why is a more strange and perhaps dark mystery wrapped in secrets and confusing information. Knowns contain enough wonderment to question. Actuality is better questioned first, saving magic and mystery for another time. By questioning actuality, mysteries are unintentionally unraveled anyhow. Questioning leads to a better sense of reality, inadvertently nullifying many mysteries.

> "We've never finished the investigation of 9/11 and whether the administration actually misused the intelligence information it had. The evidence seems pretty clear to me. I've seen that for a long time. ~General Wesley Clark

> "I look at the hole in the Pentagon and I look at the size of an airplane that was supposed to hit the pentagon. And I said "the plane does not fit in that hole." So what did hit the Pentagon? What hit it? Where is it? What's going on?" ~Major General Albert Stubblebine, former Head of Imagery Interpretation for Scientific and Technical Intelligence.

If it does not fit, you must acquit or least thoroughly question it. Further escalating the "War on Terror" after the Afghanistan invasion, George II instigated the invasion of Iraq. Amid international protest, and yet, with a coalition of the willing, Iraq was invaded and occupied. Many in the diplomatic community raised concerns; some in the Administration questioned the evidence for the invasion. Later, it was proven to be inaccurate.

Billions of dollars were spent by taxpayers and earned by corporations. The media praised the military, and the military praised itself. When the money flow was on full blast and the regime had fallen, on May 1, 2003, (May Day) a celebratory George II flew onto the USS Abraham Lincoln. He gave a speech with the ship as backdrop, on which hung, a glorious banner that read: Mission Accomplished.

The war was based on official documents that were worth as much as soft tissue for excrement. The officially sourced information was fabrication. No standing army had been able to occupy Iraq in three thousand years, but it didn't matter. The George II administration wanted to invade and they drew up official, institutionalized papers to reason the invasion.

In war, the spiritual and physical are wasted on demise. In Iraq, this demise was based on incorrect or falsified information. The backdrop was the well-lit fear of terror, and adding to the ambience was the necessity of oil. The dish served was stewed taurus cakes a la uranium. Wrong information propagated wrongdoing which served unscrupulous institutionalized. The truth is like an elegant meal, it is ninety percent presentation.

Is it just a coincidence that war is so prominent in history and so profitable to the policy makers? Could the Bush family keep their war and oil interests separate from their politics and military actions which they were in charge of? Is it a coincidence that there is war and it is profitable to prominent individuals and institutions?

Perhaps it is just a coincidence that father and son were both Presidents. Perhaps George II is just another brilliant Yalie. Perhaps the Bush family all have that same heartfelt charisma people are attracted to. Perhaps George II simply used good connections that he had through his family and schooling to become successful. Perhaps corporations unwittingly have stumbled onto fortunes amid death, again. Does it matter when the end result is war?

To keep good connections one must be a good connection. Sometimes all that is needed is the ability to connect people with people, or information or resources. George II and the Bush family have all the connections. Perhaps it was just a friendly combination of connections and brilliance that brought George II to the presidency. Perhaps by being corrupt, other corrupted helped arrange his rise to power. It's been four generations of Bushes involved in policy while correspondingly profiting from war. What are the chances?

> "Once is happenstance, twice is coincidence, three times is enemy action." ~Ian Fleming

It appears Ian didn't think a fourth incident was possible without a reaction to the third, so he didn't bother to write a description of a fourth event. It was safe to assume that after being fired on three times, one would engage the enemy action. The fourth time is institutional operation, and was allowed to happen.

Ian was a writer who invented the James Bond character. He modeled James Bond, in part, after the real 007, John Dee. John signed all of his correspondence to Queen Elizabeth I with the mark 007. The mark looked like two big eyes framed by the seven. John was an alchemist, magician, mathematician, navigator and Queen Elizabeth's astrologer. He also was supposedly her secret agent. The Queen signed her letters with a simple M, for master. John practiced decoding ciphers, and assembled a private library that was one of the most extensive in the 1550s. John coined the term "British Empire."

> FACT: The Democratic and Republican nominees for President in 2004, George II and John Kerry, were both members of the same fraternity or secret club, at Yale University, Skull and Bones.

What is coincidence? What are the chances of the same family setting policy in the U.S.A. for four generations? What are the chances of two people running for President being from the same school and members of the same secret club? Both George II and John Kerry refuse to speak about their secret college frat, of course.

Three presidents out of forty-four graduated from Yale and were members of Skull and Bones. Two other presidents went to Yale Law. Seven Presidents graduated from Harvard University, including Barack Obama. The Ivy League provides some outstanding education, motivation, and connections.

George I had three other sons. Jeb worked for an international bank like his granddaddy and then became Governor of Florida. There he assisted his brother, George II, in catapulting him into the Presidency of the U.S.A. through mismanagement of Florida's voting process in the 2000 Presidential election.

Brother Neil was on the board of directors of Silverado Savings and Loan in the 1980s. Silverado's collapse cost taxpayers one billion dollars. He has been practicing as an advisor to multinational corporations passively raking in millions. Brother Marvin became interested in security and became director of Securacom/Stratesec, a company that had contracts with United Airlines, Dulles International Airport and the World Trade Center. He continues as a business advisor and has expressed interest in politics. The Bush family is as institutionalized as it gets.

The Bush family is blatant in their exploits. Their endeavors in policy are advantageous to their crews, connections and themselves. Why bother with mysteries? Institutions withhold information to distort perspective. If blame arises, it is shirked by presenting partial countering information. They twist what is different into the same and the same into something different. Elite institutions orchestrate, coordinate and manipulate to set secret agendas. Depending on their operations and the knowledge of others, their story shifts, removing truth and presenting distractions.

It is frightening that secret societies believe that they have exclusive and/or esoteric knowledge. It is more frightening though, to think they might actually have valuable knowledge they keep from others and what it could be. It is more frightening still to think that they act based on secret, special information, whether real or not.

FACT: Mitt Romney, is a third generation Mormon, a former Governor of Massachusetts, Presidential candidate and a millionaire who performed public service without compensation. He attended Stanford University and Harvard University. He made his fortune with Bain & CO and Bain Capital, as a consultant. Mitt's father, George Wilken Romney is also a former Governor (Michigan) and also a former presidential candidate who helped make the auto industry what it is today.

FACT: Nancy Pelosi, the first female speaker of the House of Representatives, second in line to the President, has enough money to work for free. Her father was a Representative from Maryland and former Mayor of Baltimore. Later her brother, Thomas L. J. D'Alessandro Jr. III became Mayor of Baltimore too, from 1967-1971.

SHOOTINGS
Baltimore: highest murder rate per 100,000 people in large U.S.A. cities, 2005: 269.
Neighboring Washington D.C.: 169 murders in 2006, down from 482 in 1991.

Democratic and Republican figures perpetuate global institutionalization, global environmental destruction and globalization through war and exploitation within the pyramid system. They run over people, or let people get run over. They globalize instead of localize. They claim connection when there are likable results and separate themselves when developments are otherwise.

Another prominent family of politics currently is the Clinton couple. Bill went to Oxford University, and then to Yale, where he met Hillary. Unlike some of his counterparts, Bill was not a member of Skull and Bones while a Yalie. He had no legacy; as did George II did and John Forbes Kerry. Bill encouraged globalization while in office and continues to do so. Hillary became a New Yorker, and then became the first female Senator from New York. She was also the first former First Lady to run for Presidency and first to become Secretary of State.

FACT: Mission statement of William Clinton Foundation, formed after he left office, "Strengthen the capacity of people throughout the world to meet the challenges of global interdependence."

FACT: Richard John Kerry (John Forbes Kerry's father) attended Phillips Exeter Preparatory and Yale University. He joined the Air Corps, and later worked for the State Department and as a lawyer for the United Nations. John Forbes Kerry is a beneficiary of several Forbes' family trusts. The Forbes family is supposed to have made a fortune in illegally smuggling opium. John Kerry was the wealthiest U.S.A. Senator.

SYMBOL - SKULL AND CROSSBONES #322 The Skull and Crossbones is used today as a symbol for poison. In the past it was used as a warning as well. Pirates are infamous for flying such flags. It meant: face us and face death. Those that fly this flag will never give up; they will fight to the death, by any means necessary. 322 is a symbolic number adopted by the Skull and Bones Society and often depicted with the image. Supposedly it is believed that in

322 BC, the Goddess Eulogia rose to heaven and did not return until 1832, when the society was founded. Members supposedly refer to her as the Goddess of Eloquence.

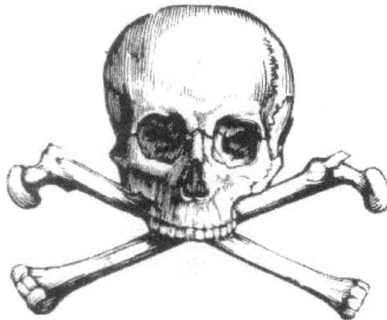

FACT: William Huntington Russell was first cousin to Samuel Wadsworth Russell, who was one of the wealthiest opium dealers of his day. William founded the Skull and Bones Society with Alphonso Taft.

John Kerry and George II are fraternity brothers, distant cousins and the prominent 2004 presidential candidates; these are facts. All the circumstances and speculation about their secret society is secret. Whoever secretly worships or gathers together secretly in institutional pursuits is questionable and potentially corrupt. Bill Clinton is not a member of the infamous Skull and Bones. Bill was on his own mission; as a youngster he became a Boys Nation Senator and met John F. Kennedy in 1963. He was also a member of the Youth Order of DeMolay.

FACT: Jacques DeMolay, the namesake of the Youth Order, was the last Grand Master of the Knights Templar. The King Phillip IV of France imprisoned him for years and ordered his execution. Jacques was accused of being a heretic and denying the divinity of Jesus among many other probable trumped up charges for which he was executed.

The group is said to promote the loyalty that DeMolay exhibited and has nothing to do with the Knights Templar. Bill Clinton later became President and was impeached. Admittedly his lies or rather the lies he was accused of, were small time compared to other suspected and known contemporary lies. The lies of elite liars are normally of great dire. Bill's most well-known lie was a personal one.

Nonetheless, Bill lied about an extramarital affair to a Grand Jury. Newt Gingrich virtually led the hunt to expose Bill of his infidelity and was himself, at the same time, cheating on his own wife. This is a typical hypocritical duality of institutionalized individuals with two hearts. Newt criticized Bill of actions that he was guilty of. And Bill admitted little lies and denied that he would lie otherwise.

A lot of interesting events took place during Bill's Presidency, and Bill led an interesting life before he became President. Bill played music and was famous for admittedly smoking, but not inhaling marijuana, which could have been groovy at parties if he knew how to blow smoke rings. Bill's family is less remarkable than the Bush family. Bill's family is partly unremarkable because there isn't that much known. His father died shortly after Bill's birth.

Bill was presented as the alternative to Bush/Reagan conservatism, but he continued and expanded many of the actions inspired and instituted by Ronald Reagan and George I. He continued and expanded the war on drugs. He expanded the death penalty. And he continued bombing people, cities and stuff.

FACT: Bill Clinton, along with NATO, led by Wesley Clark, bombed Yugoslavia for 78 days from March 24 - June 10, 1999. NATO bombed oil refineries and cities in Europe.

In April 1999, Bill was fined $90,000 dollars for civil contempt of court. This was after the House of Representatives impeached him in December of 1998. Bill also continued sanctions on Iraq and persistently bombed Baghdad. In hindsight, it seems the U.S.A. closed off Iraq and weakened it in preparation for an invasion. Blockades, barricades and bombing campaigns went on for years before the invasion. Yet little connection is made between the degradation and debilitation of Iraq, the promotion of their continued and building threat and the subsequent invasion.

> Some items banned in Iraq by sanctions: baby food, bandages and other medical supplies, clothing, flour, school books, tissues, toilet paper, toothbrushes, toothpaste and wool.

> "Good evening. Earlier today, I ordered America's armed forces to strike military and security targets in Iraq. They are joined by British forces. Their mission is to attack Iraq's nuclear, chemical and biological weapons programs and its military capacity to threaten its neighbors." ~William Jefferson Clinton, December 1998

Did Bill believe Iraq had weapons of mass destruction in 1998? The differences between representatives of republicans and democrats are minimal, no matter the presentation, no matter how they counter each other. Both are equally elite and both focus on globalization and interdependence, though perhaps at times, pursued from different, even opposing angles.

The two parties are interchangeable, intertwined opposition to nothing and everything. Representatives of the two parties flip flop and manipulate information to influence opinion of conditions. The subjects of departure between them are primarily emotional, and rarely correspondingly intellectual. They are countering sides of the same coin. They are opposing angles leading to the same point. They are opposition to one another, not alternatives.

Anyone who zealously, unquestioningly supports Republican or Democrat figureheads will tend to snarl...at the people that inform them of their side's manipulations and not at the manipulators themselves. If people do not question the motivations and actions of politicians, then who will? If leaders make a family business out of leading, shouldn't people question everything about them, including their family activities? If they provide themselves with investment and advisement from institutions beyond government, should they go unquestioned? Should they be allowed secret institutional ties?

George I, Bill Clinton and George II, presidents over a twenty year period and occupants in the White House for almost thirty years, all are supposedly high initiates of illuminati groups. Supposedly, Hillary is a high initiate as well, an illuminati matriarch. What many people consider mistakes and horrible events, may serve illuminati, or elitist interests and gains. Many institutions are crews in secretive gangs.

> FACT: Blackwater USA is a private military contractor and security firm founded in 1996. They operated with immunity in Iraq and train soldiers on a several thousand-acre facility in North Carolina. They experienced a 600% growth between 2001 and 2005. They charged $950 a day per man for security in New Orleans after Hurricane Katrina and paid $350. They were in charge of guarding key facilities in New Orleans, such as Wal-Mart and temporary morgue facilities. In 2009, they changed their name and logo to Xe, pronounced Z.
>
> Rich Devos started Amway, a multilevel marketing company, or pyramid scheme. An abbreviation for the "American Way", Amway has transformed into Quixtar. A 1979 FTC ruling legitimized their pyramidal formation. They paid $25 million in Canada for tax evasion in 1983. They were fined another $45 million in 1989 for another tax settlement in Canada. Rich's son, Dick Devos co-founded Blackwater. The Schmitz family, with extensive ties to politics and the Bush family, were also founders of Blackwater.

Supposedly, certain illuminati groups have shaped global dynamics through institutions for control. One thing is certain, the Bushes, the Clintons, Blackwater, Amway and others akin did not invent the system, they only maintain it and flourish within it. They operate on win-win terms within the pyramid system; even when they apparently lose, they win.

The distribution of information and resources shows they first support institutions and then the status quo and lastly, individuals. Their perspective shows they support institutions over individuals. If decisions are made out of logic or love, it is legitimate to change one's opinion and actions. If decision-making does not make loving or logical sense, it is questionable and probable bull.

Supposedly they, them and the illuminati initiate conflict to ensure financial and political direction suits their agenda. Supposedly they are in control of just about every nation and the majority of information presented. Supposedly, they set up Switzerland as a neutral country with a free-for-all banking system to provide a safe haven for their money during instigated duress in the world. Mysteries mean little when actuality is investigated and hypocrisy dissected.

> FACT: Bin Laden was trained and funded by the CIA and other western intelligence groups to fight the Soviet Army. Al Quaida translates to the base. Not the base of the pyramid or the basis of belief or the student base, but the CIA base where training took place in Khost, Afghanistan.

> ORDO AB CHAO: Order out of chaos. This is a favorite illuminati slogan. Supposedly, it appears on the 33rd degree Masonic symbol, inside a nine pointed star. Bill Clinton is supposedly a 33rd degree Freemason, the highest level attainable.

If there is a problem, there is the people's reaction to it and the new deal or order or solution to solve the problem. There are no new problems, only new solutions. The same institutions that designed the order or solution, have also indirectly or directly designed the chaos. Dr. Jekyll is Mr. Hyde.

Supposedly, they have distorted and outright invented dogma religious ideas in order to manipulate thinking. Though the elite of the elite remain mostly unknown, there are some illuminati institutions that are known. Some illuminati elite, most likely those that mostly pretend to have special information, are active and recruiting. You could be an illuminati initiate in a secretive enclosed pyramid.

The Church of Scientology is blatantly pyramidal, where members have to pay to pray. They claim special information and distribute it within their group depending on one's level. It is an obvious example of a pyramidal illuminati group. The cost of reaching "OT IX readiness", one of the church's highest levels, is estimated to be over $350,000.

The Scientology story was written by L. Ron Hubbard. L. Ron is the Scientology messiah for all intents and purposes, having delivered the scripture. Prior to finding the word, L. Ron was a science fiction writer, who effectively worshipped prescription pills, based on the way he was believed to have popped them. He wrote several fiction books and essays on his theories of the universe.

The Scientology story goes that there is an alien named Xenu who brought mankind to Earth in spaceships that look profoundly like DC-8s, mere human aircraft. Once here, Xenu arranged billions of people around volcanoes (volcanoes are pyramidal) and then dropped atomic bombs onto the people and volcanoes. The resulting explosion and lost souls have been tormenting all subsequent life on Earth ever since "Incident II" with extremely bad vibes. That was 75,000,000 years ago and it was such a terrible event that all beings have been dealing with the trauma ever since. Mind you, Xenu isn't revealed right away from what I understand.

As a scientologist, you would start off with spiritual/religious technology called learning accelerators and Electropsychometers. Along with a qualified operator, the machines would assist you in relieving leftover trauma from the disintegration of the volcanoes and bad vibes from this life. Of course, you would have to buy the product through the church's sanctioned manufacturer and pay the professional operators of the machine, but it could be worth it...

Both devices are similar to lie detectors; the E-meter is used for emotional auditing done by the church approved "auditors." The machines are quite useless without qualified direction. The sessions help remove unacceptable character flaws. That is basically the only auditing going on at the church and their corporate entities. They operate tax free as a religious institution and fixed donations increase as the member's education and indoctrination does.

> FACT: In 1979, L. Ron Hubbard's wife, Mary Sue and other Scientologists, were convicted of conspiracy for their role in infiltrating, wiretapping and stealing documents from government agencies, most notably the IRS. Their infiltration is considered one of the biggest in U.S.A. history. In October 1993, after years of legal and illegal battles, the Church of Scientology received the coveted tax-exempt status it sought.

Church insiders refer to the uninformed or those yet to be indoctrinated as Wogs, which is also derogatory term for certain ethnicities. They label people who question Scientology as suppressive persons, when raising a question is the complete opposite of suppression.

L. Ron claimed exclusive religious knowledge, the very definition of illuminati and before writing Dianetics, L. Ron was an avid science-fiction writer. Today, people the world over continue to join, although the total number of scientologists has apparently declined. The Church of Scientology claims a membership of almost eight million; critics suggest there are less than one hundred thousand members.

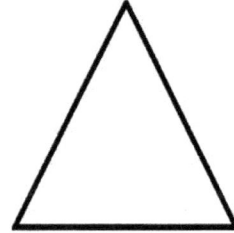

It is perhaps a cockamamie cult, although they are creative, or at least L. Ron was. Though laughable to some, they are the definition of illuminati. It might very well be fun to hang out with Tom Cruise, John Travolta and Priscilla Presley to talk about how caught up in bad memories one might be and learn about Xenu. It might be interesting to hear what Tom has to say about the military base in Fallon, Nevada, where the Top Gun Flight School is now located. He might have an enlightening viewpoint about the bad vibes or toxins exuding from the base.

The Church is known for, or rather touts, successes assisting people in eliminating chemical dependency and drug addiction. An associative group, Narconon, is based on L. Ron's ideas. Narconon has facilities from Arizona to Russia and has been criticized and investigated for various violations in many countries.

The Church of Scientology is scandalous, outrageous, slightly humorous, and are definitively illuminati. The Church of Scientology is darkly glib. There are other recent theological developments as well that are similarly illuminati and occasionally funny.

Mormonism is equally pyramidal and by far, more widely recognized as a legitimate church compared to the Church of Scientology. Next to Xenu, the Mormon story and their talismanic underwear really aren't so strange. The garment of garments reminds the wearer of their promise to God and may offer the truly faithful protection on Earth.

Perhaps, the underwear isn't as holy as the signs on them. When the holy underwear becomes holey or worn out in whatever makes undergarments ready for disposal, the symbols on them are ceremoniously removed and set afire. Only then can the rest of the garment be cast in the trash or whatever one does with used holy undergarments. The symbol is the square and compass on the breast, over the heart.

G is often represented along with the compass and square in Freemasonic symbolism. The G is said to stand for geometry, generations, gold, grand lodge, and God/Goddess. G is the 7th letter of the alphabet, 7 is also symbolic for godly, heavenly transmutation through our 7th and highest main chakra or energy point. In this sense G, along with the compass and square stand for meditative transmutation.

The Skull and Bones is the most famous illuminati frat and one of the most exclusive. Freemasonry is the most prominent illuminati secret society in the U.S.A. Most any properly institutionalized individual be allowed membership into Masonry, while Skull and Bones taps a select few.

Along with the square and compass, other tools of stonemasons are used symbolically by Freemasons. The masons of the past were the builders of complex architecture. It was not because they wanted to work with stone; it was because they wanted power like nobility and royalty. They went where the power resided and provided what they needed and they had the king's ear because they were able to build his castles and fortresses. They knew how to engineer complex feats in stone, and knew how to inspire people to sacrifice their own bone to do so.

The king knew that having a master mason at his side was crucial to build a castle and afterwards. Those who knew the construction's secrets were valuable. The masons participated in the building of society and their engineering secrets were guarded by all involved, to all ends. Today, the secrets of stone engineering are mostly out.

Today, the secretive Freemasons are architects of different structures of society not necessarily made of stone. Today they have the same skills required to build institutions and motivate people to build them, but they do not concentrate their efforts in stone. Once known for sculpting stone and freemasons are now known for shaping perception.

Joseph Smith was the founder of the Church of Latter Day Saints. He and his brother Hyrum were Masons born to a Mason family, in holy Upstate New York. Joseph lost his religion and found a new one, Mormonism. The Church of Latter Day Saints is the largest church inspired by the teachings of Joseph, but there are others. Others worship the teachings of Joseph and operate enclosed communities frequently accused of child abuse and of course operate via restricting access to information.

Joseph was a young treasure hunter and used divining rods to search for things with his father, also a treasure hunting Mason. His mother was supposedly a mystic. Many Mormon rituals correspond with rituals of Freemasonry.

At 14, Joseph was visited by God the Father, and God the Son. They told him that no church on Earth interpreted the word of God correctly and not to join any of them. Supposedly Joseph's grandfather, Solomon Mack had divine visitations from God as well, according to Solomon. It seems God liked the family, or the family liked to believe as much.

Years later, Joseph had another holy visitation. This time from an angel named Moroni. The angel Moroni told him where tablets of gold were buried with the word of God emblazoned on them in an ancient language that he would be given powers to interpret. The tablets were conveniently buried in Upstate New York. Joseph eventually translated them into English with God's help and the assistance of a seer stone or magic rock and looking into his hat, without the tablets present at all, to come up with the Book of Mormon. In 1840, The Book of Mormon was first published and is revered as scripture by many.

Part of their original story is racist, referring to people of color as cursed descendants of Cain and savages. It would seem Joseph or God, was inspired by Masonry, including operating under a pyramid system and sporting the square and compass on holy underwear. The early Mormon tendency toward polygamy is an example of a pyramidal family, the father being the pinnacle, the capstone.

After 'revealing' the Book of Mormon, including the story of Jesus visiting the Americas, Joseph and his followers traveled west from state to state. Not to spread the word of God, but to find a place where they could live unbothered. Everywhere they went they were unaccepted and often violently rejected. Every time they were attacked, Joseph and his followers picked up the pieces and headed west. In 1844, Joseph and his brother Hyrum were murdered by an angry mob in Illinois while locked up in a jail cell.

It is interesting that Joseph found God and founded Mormonism in the same area of Upstate New York, at around the same time, that the Anti-Masonic party began. The Anti-Masonic movement was triggered by the scandalous disappearance of a former Mason and outspoken critic of Masonry. On September 11, 1826, William Morgan was arrested. His bail was paid and he was abducted after being released from jail in Batvia, New York. After his release and abduction William was never seen or heard from again. On September 22, 1827, Joseph was allowed to unearth and see the holy word of God that was buried near his family farm outside of Palmyra, New York.

> FACT: The first "third" party in the U.S.A. was the Anti-Masonic Party. It arose out of vast resentment and suspicion of the group. In 1831, they held the first National Convention in the U.S.A. and issued the first written party platform. The Republicans and Democrats followed their innovations.

Joseph was eventually shot and killed. After the murder of Joseph, Brigham Young became leader of the Mormon Church. Brigham led his followers to Utah and arrived in the Salt Lake Valley in 1847. At the time, Utah was Mexico, but people were far and few between. Northern Mexico was taken as part of manifest destiny in the War for Mexico. Utah became a state and Brigham, the church leader, became Governor of Utah. He served from 1850-1858. It is disputed that Joseph had 33 wives, while Brigham is known to have had some 50.

Some aspects of Freemasonry, Scientology and the Church of LDS are as strange as an LSD trip. Scientology was founded by a science-fiction writer, who wanted to take over the world. The Mormon philosophy is based on the word of a Mason treasure hunter who interpreted the word of God with a magic rock and looking into a hat. Joseph and L. Ron were similar to past prophets in that they were both rejected by most of society and Joseph was even killed, but the similarity may end there.

Mormons use a wide variety of symbols in their church architecture, many are associated with Freemasonry. The square and compass, the beehive, the pentagram, the all seeing eye and celestial spheres, among others, are all used at LDS temples.

> SYMBOL - HIVE
> The honeybee and hive has been used variously as symbols for a high quality group work ethic. The beehive is a Mormon symbol of industry in the shape of a pyramid. It is symbolic of one ruler dominating the entire subordinate hive in pyramidal fashion.

It is estimated that honeybees pollinate $14 billion worth of crops in the U.S.A. every year. In 2006, 2007 and 2008 the bee population in several nations drastically declined like canaries in a cave and most people ignored it. Researching scientists found many causes (pesticides) to the Colony Collapse Disorder. Many people follow institutions to their demise, they lend machines their hearts and exploit brothers and all life and then wonder what happened when the trees and bees are gone. The various causes and consequences of global environmental degradation and destruction are as numerous as the various exploitations of old oligarchies. The exact causes and effects are designed to be difficult to find and explicate. What are killing the bees is arguable, but the truth is the bees suffer in the deteriorated environment.

Many have suggested that Albert Einstein stated, "If the bee disappeared off the surface of the globe, then man would have only four years of life left. No more bees, no more pollination, no more plants, no more animals, no more man." But Albert did not say that. A beekeeper did and though Albert didn't say it, the sentiment is true enough and a valid hypothesis. Albert did say one thing about bees on the record, "It is evident, therefore, that the dependence of the individual upon society is a fact of nature which cannot be abolished - just as in the case of ants and bees."

> So they gave him a piece of broiled fish and some honeycomb. ~Luke 24:42

They gave him broiled fish and honeycomb because they were steadily, readily available. The oceans and bees always provided. When people needed food, they could always count on others with fish and honey. At the current rate, at the end of the unsustainable ride we are on, there might be no more honey and subsequently no more crops, and at the same time, no more fish. The world is poisoned and plundered at high rates and if we don't stop our current endeavors, they will eventually be stopped. There are many living things that will no longer be living things because of our behavior. These may indeed be the last days. The Church of Latter Day Saints may have at least been correct about that. Incidentally, the Church suggests its members keep enough basic supplies for months.

The illuminati practice sometimes hokey and sometimes spooky rituals, sometimes at specific times and places. These rituals often have violent overtones and macabre garb. Supposedly, they wear ceremonial clothing and sometimes no clothing at all. Supposedly, rituals for initiates into The Skull and Bones include masturbating in front of others in a coffin, and kissing a human skull. If the Bush family did this it is laughable and actually inconsequential compared to the tidings since. The silly secrets of their college fraternities are nothing compared to their potential secrets later in life.

Prescott Bush is rumored to have stolen Geronimo's skull from the grave. That is sick and offensive, but minor next to the skulls he may have played a role in delivering to their resting place. George I and II supposedly wanked in a coffin. Big deal. It's the coffins their policies have filled which is real evil and no mystery. What they accomplish out of school is much more notorious and affects many more than the secret wanking ceremonies.

They wear little Robes, masks, hoods, aprons, sashes, and costumes. They dress up like notoriety, ladies, and fabled characters. They hide behind curtains and hold esoteric and ritualistic conversations. Relative to similar such costumes and ceremonies, talismanic underwear is really, not so out of the ordinary.

> **SYMBOL - HOOD**
> The word hood has the same root as hat, to cover, protect. The word hoodwink comes from the 16th century. It means to cover someone's eyes and rob them. The robed and hooded became hoods and robbers. It is symbolic for hiding malevolent secrets, usually crimes.

If they, them and the illuminati have a love for anything, it is for secrets. Trust is developed through keeping secrets or outright lying in order to protect their secrets. It makes one feel involved and embedded in a group when secrets are only known within the group, even if it is only about that one time they beat off in a coffin. If these secrets are important, all the better for the group, but if the secrets are trivial or fictitious it still develops trust and a sense of belonging. It may be as little as knowing that you are wearing the same underwear as another.

The secrets in their societies and in their closed-door meetings could very well be frightening, and they could very well be laughable. The secrets may be important to question, but those questions are relegated as inconsequential without first questioning actuality. George II is a member of Skull and Bones at Yale University as was his father and grandfather. If there is anything evil or notorious about Skull and Bones, it is apparent in what their members do in daylight, not at night.

It is what their members accomplish and represent that makes the groups frightening and perhaps their secrets as well. The overt actualities are primarily scary; hidden secrets may not exist in the first place and may simply be distractions to reality. What we do know about their members is enough. Mystery may remain as much, first actuality needs to be questioned and dissected. What they hide is currently inconsequential to what they have openly propped up and accomplished. What they hide is possibly frightening and worse, but certainly what is known is scary enough.

The known cooperation of opulent elitists is frightening. Their underground secret meetings likely take place to communicate underhanded exploits, but certainly the known outcome is important and often evident of exploitation. Unknowns are potentially frightening, but what is known is the best starting point for investigations. Their public and well-known actions are worthy of serious questioning before inquiry into their secret endeavors. Question what is known first and many unknowns disintegrate.

Albert Pike is a prominent American hero, and renowned Freemason, famous for leading marauding, scalping soldiers rather than having many wives. Al grew up in Boston and was accepted to Harvard, but did not attend for financial reasons. Later the University offered him an honorary degree, he declined. Al fought in the War for Mexico (April, 1846 - February, 1848) and later for the Confederacy in the Civil War, as an advocate of slavery. He remained a Brigadier General for just over a year, before resigning after criticism and arrest. Both during and after the Civil War, he was accused of many crimes, including scalping enemy combatants. Al spent some time in jail, visited Canada and wrote.

After the Civil War, 1861 - 1865, like most Confederate Officers, Al was awarded a presidential pardon from Andrew Johnson, a fellow Freemason. Unlike most Confederate Officers and Generals, Al was commemorated with a statue in Washington DC. Congress approved the statue in 1898, paid for by Freemasons.

April 9, 1865.	General Robert E. Lee surrenders.
April 15, 1865	President Lincoln dies after being shot in the head. Vice president Andrew Johnson takes office that morning.
May 23, 1865	Victory parade is held in Washington D.C.
August 30, 1865	President Johnson formally pardons Albert Pike.
1975	Confederate General Robert Lee received posthumous pardon.

Only certain individuals had to make a special plea to the President, otherwise there was sweeping amnesty and pardons for the Confederacy soldiers. As President, Andrew supposedly met with and pardoned Al, but failed to address the request of General Lee. Al was a prolific writer, working at one time as editor for the Arkansas Advocate. He became a lawyer and at one point had an office in Washington DC, where he also became editor of a newspaper called *The Patriot*. He wrote *Meaning of Masonry, Book of Words* and *The Point within the Circle* among other books. His best known work though, a complex interpretation of world religion, is called *Morals and Dogma of the Ancient and Accepted Scottish Rite of Freemasonry*. Some Freemasons supposedly refer to this book as containing the secrets of the ages. It is over eight-hundred pages long with a two-hundred page index.

Al became the Sovereign Grand Commander of the Scottish Rite of Freemasonry Southern Jurisdiction in 1859 and remained so until he died in 1891. His statue commemorates him, not as a treasonous scalper or Confederate General, but as a Freemason and depicts Al holding his book, "The Morals and Dogma" and a woman sitting below him holding a banner of the Scottish Rite of Freemasonry. The statue is on federal land and paid for by the Scottish Rite of Freemasonry.

Supposedly, Al predicted three world wars and the elimination of religion through deception and nihilists. Supposedly Al stated in a letter to Giuseppe Mazzini (Italian revolutionary), that these wars had to be "fomented" by "agentur." The first two wars so eerily and accurately predicted that it seems to be hindsight, a historical recollection. The description of the third war reads like an embellished current newspaper clipping where the three main monotheistic cultures are pitted against each other to destroy each other, so as to implement a one world religious culture…

There is no specific proof of the letter, perhaps it was made up only recently, but the letter was perhaps first quoted in the 1920s. Regardless whoever wrote the letter had eerie intentions or uncanny powers of prediction, but it may be some sort of crock. Al did claim to be in the company of a spirit guide who dispensed divine wisdom to him, so perhaps he had such powers of prediction or implementation.

Al is not the only American General to claim visions from spirit guides. Supposedly, George Washington claimed to be visited by an angel at Valley Forge in the winter of 1777. Perhaps, it was Lady Liberty herself, or maybe it is an entirely make-believe story started by George or as many note, by a storyteller after George's death.

George helped found the U.S.A. while Al, is alleged to be a founder of the Knights of the Ku Klux Klan. It is well documented that the KKK is an exclusive and violent institution established by former Confederate Generals, rooted in Masonic and demented fantasies. They don hoods, perform ceremonies, promote racial restrictions and some in the group killed people based on race. As a writer, former Confederate General and Grand Commander of a secret society, Al would have made an ideal candidate to create or at least participate in the creation of the KKK and the scribing of their own book, the Kloran, originally "The Precepts" of the KKK.

Al is heralded today by Freemasons, who deny the possibility that he had any role in the KKK. Others say he was one of architects of the murderous, zealous, racist group. The KKK originated in the South. Veterans of the Confederacy organized repression of newly freemen and attempted to maintain white supremacy. They kidnapped, lynched and hung people. They violently intimidated men of color, prevented them from voting and provided all-around repression to those that did vote or did not live up to their racial, national and religious prerequisites.

Despite their members claiming Christianity, the KKK's book is called the Kloran, not the Klible. Their leaders carry titles like the Grand Wizard, Genii, Grand Dragon and Grand Titan. The initiates are called Ghouls, and local dens are governed by a Grand or Exalted Cyclops.

SYMBOL - EYE
The eye is a powerful symbol, like the owl, it symbolizes the powers of true sight or extra vision. To the ancients, the Sun was the all seeing eye of God. Horus, the Son of Isis and Osiris, is hieroglyphically represented as an eye. CBS and AOL, among many other institutions have the eye as their logo. It is symbolic of the all seeing eye, the omnipresence of God or an overseer.

In the late 1960s, during the civil rights movement, the KKK worked overtly and covertly with police departments in various cities and states to disrupt peaceful demonstrations. In their time they have hung, lynched, maimed, burned out, beat up, intimidated and killed countless. There are different levels of initiates and much like Freemasonry the KKK is a compartmentalized pyramidal group, and occasionally violent.

In the 1920s the KKK numbered in the millions. Today, it is estimated that there are 8,000 members of the KKK. In 1998 there were 2.1 million Freemasons, about 15,000 lodges and a Grand Lodge in every state.

"Masonry, like all religions, all the mysteries, Hermeticism and Alchemy, conceals its secrets from all except the adepts and the sages, or the elect, and uses false explanations and misinterpretations of its symbols to mislead those who deserve to be misled, to conceal the truth, which it calls light, from them and to draw them away from it. Truth is not for those who are unworthy or unable to receive it, or would pervert it." ~Albert Pike

In different Masonic orders, there are different numbers of levels or degrees. The first three compromise and compartmentalize the vast majority of members. In each level attained, the initiate performs a certain ritual. This is where the expression "getting the third degree" comes from. In order to receive the third degree, one undergoes intense questioning. The first degree symbolizes birth, the second degree symbolizes life and the third degree symbolizes death. Supposedly, there are two distinct branches of Freemasonry, those on the front and those in the back. There is an order within an order; there are secrets within secrets. Those compromising the first three levels are in front, the rest remain behind the curtain.

"The real rulers in Washington are invisible, and exercise power from behind the scenes."
~Felix Frankfurter, Supreme Court Justice

Freemasonry concepts and crews have influenced many other crews that have taken off in many directions. These organizations are pyramidal, where ignorance prevails and the knowledgeable dominate within the group. Only those at the very top of the pyramid have access to all the information and direction, while those below might not even realize there is other information, other levels above their own. These groups seek to gain and maintain power with information.

There may be more reasons to keep information, and release more mysteries, but quest for power through monopolization and exploitation is an adequate deduction according to known reality. Elitists absorb, ignore, examine, withhold, and manipulate, information to their advantage. They have the worst memory or the most immaculate record keeping depending on whether the information works for or against them.

One moment an institution will cry support of the troops, and the next they will take them for a ride, or run them over. The same institutions that claim support of the armed forces, that armed action equates to patriotism, will allow soldiers to be electrocuted in showers and sickened by filthy water abroad. Soldiers have been getting the sharp end of the stick from their enemies and their employers since first wielding spears.

FACT: In the spring and summer of 1932, veterans of WWI and their supporters marched and camped in Washington D.C. in attempts to convince the Senate to immediately give them their bonus that was promised to be distributed to the veterans in 1945. The protesters remained and eventually President Hoover sent in the infantry to remove the veteran protesters and their families. Some died, many were wounded. Remembered as the Bonus Army, the men who fought in WWI were broken up by new recruits.

"Since I entered politics, I have chiefly had men's views provided to me privately. Some of the biggest men in the United States, in the field of commerce and manufacture, are afraid of something. They know there is a power somewhere so organized, so subtle, so watchful, so interlocked, so complete, so pervasive, that they had better not speak above their breath when they speak in condemnation of it." ~Woodrow Wilson

Who founded the KKK? What is behind the curtain? Where is the garment of garments available? Why are members of secret organizations prominent among global institutions? When will Xenu return? How can one interpret divinity like L. Ron? What really happened with Smedley Butler and the coup? What are the goals of institutionalized families? It doesn't matter. Their mysteries, the mysteries presented and found unsolved, mean less and less in the petrolithic era and nuclear age. Paradigms concerning reality make mysteries less important.

Their vicious college spankings, their elitist foundations and clubs and their exclusive mock sacrifice retreats may hold secrets worth knowing. There may be esteemed information worthy of ponder among them, but their secrets are more meaningless as more facts are known, and are increasingly just distractions away from questioning actuality.

Accidental or otherwise, happenstance or bold conspiracy, matters little to the reality in our face. How we ended up at the wrong location, matters only slightly next to what we have to do to get to the right location. If there is a cross burning in the yard, the history of the KKK is unimportant. Mystery is meaningless next to confronting reality.

Perhaps seeking secrets is a way to actual information. Perhaps there is only one more secret mystery requiring verification as fact in order to induce thought and action. But it is guaranteed that to get to the center of mystery, one has to first question reality. It is always knowledge of reality that changes unknown secrets into known facts.

Pollution increasingly makes the simple actions complex. To question is, in theory a simple act; a simple act of curiosity that becomes complicated depending on who is asked the question and the stakes of the answer. In the petrolithic era, in the nuclear age, the simplest most basic acts have morphed into the most complicated endeavors. Obtaining unpolluted water is increasingly difficult, just as questioning and holding institutions accountable is difficult.

The confines, conditions and consequences of the petrolithic era and nuclear age increasingly make some information more difficult to gather and some resources more difficult to obtain. Secrets may remain so or become knowledge, but until we question the constant, dissonant destruction and eradication of environment, the secrets do not matter, the results do.

They, them -we are all to blame for the results of the petrolithic era and nuclear age. We're caught up in it. Institutions have marched, treaded, stepped on and skipped over individuals and the environment. Apathetic and misdirected individuals allow environmental destruction and exploitation, as results of globalization.

It doesn't matter if the riddle of the ages is solved or an equation for everything posed, we are breathing, drinking and eating from a polluted mess. Our toxins are embedded into all life. The use of oligarchical energy, petrol and nuclear, has layered the whole Earth. In the new world, the greatest scientific achievements mean nothing, if we create demise, reaping environmental catastrophe. Increasingly, getting real answers is as difficult as getting clean water.

> "Today the path of total dictatorship in the United States can be laid by strictly legal means, unseen and unheard by the Congress, the President, or the people. Outwardly we have a constitutional government. We have operating within our government and political system, another body representing another form of government - a bureaucratic elite." ~Senator William Jenner

NOTHING ELSE MATTERS

Mystery matters little next to reality. Unknowns concerning events mean little next to the known outcome of said events. Moreover the past, at least certain aspects of the past, matters little next to the present. Intricacies surrounding and resulting from current conditions might not matter immediately, or at all, next to the intricacies of the present results. History is worth learning, but question the presentation before celebrations. History has led us to the present, and some history is worthy of celebration, but all history is worthy of questioning. If the present is worth celebration, then so too is history. If the present shows San Francisco Bay flooded with 58,000 gallons of heavy duty bunker oil, (November 2007) then celebrating the settlers is morose. A history should be celebrated only if the present is a present, or at least not taxing. If such basics as clean water and open information are unavailable, celebration ought to be canceled for investigation.

> "The drive of the Rockefellers and their allies is to create a one world government combining super capitalism and communism under the same tent, all under their control... Do I mean conspiracy? Yes I do. I am convinced there is such a plot, international in scope, generations old in planning and incredibly evil in intent."
> ~Lawrence Patton McDonald

Larry served four terms in the U.S.A. House of Representatives from 1975 - 1983. Before his death, Larry was outspoken about elements in key institutions that, according to him, promoted the cold war and facilitated actions toward globalization and world government. He called out clandestine cooperation with capitalistic and communistic institutions. He stated that some apparent oppositional actions were actually operating in cooperation.

Larry was opposed to the USSR and communism with what turned out to be good reason. On September 1, 1983, Korean Airlines Flight 007, cruising at 35,000 feet with 269 people aboard, and was shot down by Soviet jets. Larry was onboard and killed along with everyone else. Investigations concluded that the autopilot was set ten degrees off course to the west, causing the plane to accidentally fly into Soviet airspace; giving the Soviets an excuse for their extreme reaction.

Whether the downing of KAL Flight 007 was an accidental unfortunate event or a conspired murder, matters little to the outcome of it. The mysteries of the past, matter little to the facts of the present. Fact is, Larry, and others were shot down and killed. No matter the distinction of the preliminaries, the passenger plane was shot down and people were killed because made up institutional lines were crossed.

The illuminati are steering a plot, international in scope, generations old and incredibly evil, if there were such a thing. If not, they are the elitists in control for now, steering selfish, greedy and temporary, but repetitive elitist plots. If there were a conspiracy to kill Larry, the illuminati would have done so without any more formality than a nod. If the elite of the elitists felt Larry was a threat, they could have eradicated him quickly and easily.

They may be operating in a concerto of covert control or just driving the growth of their long-standing accounts within the long-standing interplay of institutions. Whatever their finite goal, it is apparent they seek to dominate and exploit within the pyramid system, which necessitates that many remain below. Whatever their ends, wealth is power, but money is only a means. Information is real power, greater than mere wealth, information is real strength. Information provides wealth and all sorts of other opportunities.

Elitists and the illuminati hold onto special information and use it over others. They are at the high ranks of world power and hold onto information that should be available to all, in order to take advantage of some. The illuminati are those who sway nations with certain information, concrete or conjured, and yet correspondingly do not share other information in its entirety, or at all.

Institutions become more secretive and more intertwined and elitists continue and profit from exclusive information. Individuals are availed less resources and information than institutions and allowed less privacy and freedom of movement than institutions. Institutions sabotage the level playing field, returning opulence and slant in favor of the few. Information is power, and the elite coordinate and regulate information to monopolize.

Esoteric subjects, transcendence, mysteries, secrets, and that search for refined holy and whole truth, mean less. It is selfish to be concerned with higher intellect and spiritual interpretations if reality is left uncared for. When there is an increasing need for fresh air, clean water and adequate sustenance, the intricacies of space travel and the search for accurate heavenly interpretations mean less. Results, consequences and actualities, not mysteries, are at the forefront of existence. The threats to simple resources and basic liberty outweigh the importance of the search for higher knowledge and increase the need for basic knowledge. Questioning reality is always more revealing and relevant than questioning mystery and now it is more important too. Inventiveness and spirituality are important, but are not useful out there; they are best explored and utilized here, in immediate reality.

FACT: Global climate change has caused many mountain glaciers around the world to shrink. Some glaciers in some areas are growing, but most are shrinking. Himalayan glaciers are the source of the 7 largest rivers in Asia and water for 1 billion people. Because of spring beginning earlier, mountain runoff ends earlier and the rivers dry out earlier in the summer. Water becomes scarcer earlier annually for many people in many parts of the world. Fire season is subsequently longer and more hazardous in such mountain environments as well.

SYMBOL - MOUNTAIN

There are many stories about mountains and peoples' journeys to the peaks of them. These journeys are often symbolic of spiritual development. Upon completion of the journey, they receive special information or visions. The mountain is a symbol of Earth. The peaks are holy places where Gods reside. Mountains are often depicted in the shape of pyramids and share certain symbolic qualities.

The lessons of history are certainly relevant, but the mysteries of the past do not matter and historical fact matters less and less when confronted with the actuality of the petrolithic era. How we have arrived here is worthy of consideration, but finding a more preferable direction is a much better subject of deliberation. If blindfolded and brought to a harsh place, it is more important to learn one's whereabouts instead of deliberating how the abduction occurred.

Throughout recorded time, longstanding institutions have always stood over individuals. The longer an institution had been around, the more refined and trustworthy it used to be, the better its reputation was. Today, the great proclamations of interconnected institutions mean less the longer they've been around. In the petrolithic era, in the nuclear age the older the institution the more responsibility it has for present conditions and circumstances. The older the institution, the more responsible it is for the actuality of the present.

In the petrolithic era and nuclear age time slips away as it always has, but so do fresh air and clean water. Clean water for tea and a quiet place with trees and fresh air to relax and sip tea are dwindling commodities. As the bees convulse and die, as the fish twitch and rise to the surface, institutions that play on, individuals that push the status quo ever forward, are all complicit in the demise of the environment.

One cannot just leave the petrolithic era and nuclear age and clean up in some remote holistic retreat. Petrolithic and nuclear accompaniments are everywhere, in everything consumed and touched. One cannot leave what one is immersed in; it is inescapable. There is no stratum that our industrial excrement does not penetrate. Pollution accompanies every breath you take, every drink you sip, every bite you eat, every drop of blood you have and is layered onto every step you make.

We are all stuck in the petrolithic era, the nuclear age, like it or not, notice it or not. If the ground dried up tomorrow and there was no more petrol, people would still smell it, see it, taste it and suffer its consequences for years, perhaps generations. If we stop burning uranium and stop stockpiling nuclear weapons we will still have to deal with it for thousands and thousands of millennia. And until the time arrives when we stop burning these fuels on a global scale, the side-effects will only increase.

Secretive information used by elitists, who put fortune and finance above future and sense, should be collected and redistributed, and then used to better situations. And yet there is no secret needed, currently actuality is enough to question and act on. There is enough information available through simple observations to conclude certain institutions and institutionalized influences should be renovated or overtly eliminated. The longer institutions have existed, the more likely they promoted, profited from, and provided for the environmental destruction of the planet and exploitation of people.

The search for mysteries and research into the essence was once a noble pursuit. Transcendence is meaningless, if at the same time as one seeks and gains knowledge, one lets the physicality of one's surroundings succumb to the poisonous byproducts of one's existence, and the existence of surrounding institutions and individuals. Mental and spiritual transcendence means nothing if future children are born into a decrepit physicality where they don't see trees and do see air. Transcendence is impossible while effectively living in one's own effluence. No intellectual or spiritual progression is important when there is murk, funk and junk in what should be fresh air and clean water.

All of the physical architectural stature and grandeur of society, all of the information acquired in all of time is meaningless when the status quo continues in physically unsustainable manners. Every great creation theory and cosmology, every great observation of the universe, spiritual or scientific, every great discovery and device is useless in a polluted and bereft environment. All higher pursuits are useless in nature tainted if not directed to remedy the taint.

Just as everyone knows what is right; people also know when something is wrong, unless institutionalized or burdened by accumulated tolerations. The wrong supplied of the petrolithic era and nuclear age is so complex and changes so rapidly that it may be difficult to explain. Because the soot is everywhere, it may be hard to sense. Things may be difficult to explain, difficult to understand, perhaps because of acquired tolerations, but simple unobscured observations increase awareness and betters explanations.

The truth may sway, but what is right stays. That is, many things can be true and then not be true. One thing forever true is things don't remain the same forever. Yet violence is always wrong, killing is always wrong, exploitation of people, and destruction of one's environment, is always wrong.

Opinions are not always based on truth; they may be based on things that were once true or things that are entirely false, or derived from illogical fears and other feelings. Institutions monopolize information to convince one that doing wrong is right, that a lesser evil can be for the greater good. Some people repeat dogmatic belief and act wrongly in accordance with it, perpetuating conditions of the status quo. People's feelings about situations might be as valid as the opinions of others with logical explanations. Underneath layers of beliefs, tolerations and fears, people might simply feel conditions lack complete and/or sensible explanation. People might feel a situation contains elements wrongdoing without particular information, for people are capable of valid intuitive feeling, though in fear or other negativity there is loss of accuracy. Institutions are not capable of intuition, nor are institutionalized individuals.

Specific and factual information concerning wrongdoing may be unavailable or difficult to obtain when conditions have been wronged for so long, as in the petrolithic era and nuclear age of big business and big war. Inundated as we are it is difficult to accurately understand conditions, let alone imagine alternatives. After heavy opinionated institutionalization, understanding reality might be hindered with covered senses, but individuals still have feelings. People might simply feel there is reason to pursue questions and answers. Of course institutions and the institutionalized would deny individual feeling at all, let alone feeling leading to curiosity and questioning their direction.

> "Condemnation without investigation is the height of ignorance." ~Albert Einstein

Institutions and the institutionalized will deny that it is possible to accurately feel something for they have no heart and it is impossible, for them. Individuals may not know the specifics and shifts of the multitudes of truths, the facts and statistics that exist and relate to actuality, but individuals can still know what is right and what is wrong, no matter how buried under toxic waste, no matter how burdened by tolerations. People may not know what is clouding the river, but they know it's not right. It may be impossible for people to spell it out conveniently and clearly, but generally people know when something is amiss, they feel it. And generally institutions like to quell the idea of that individual power.

Some information may be dispelled in overwhelming presentation of other information, but everyone unburdened and not institutionalized knows when conditions are exploitative or degenerative, because they can feel it. Idiots, zealots and elitists keep grinding away, sacrificing themselves and others for bites of extravagance and yet, they hear whispers, they see hints and they have feelings too. Unless institutionalized and burdened by tolerations, unless wearing blinders and earplugs and stuffing their mouths, people know wrongdoing.

Humanity has island-hopping tendencies, people went from here to there using an area's resources and then moved on. Only now, the island is Earth and there is nowhere else to go. We are becoming as isolated as Rapa Nui in the South Pacific.

The poisons and toxins of our status quo are sickening and killing life as we know it. Which creation theory you adhere to is meaningless next to the chorus of destruction. Different pursuits become meaningless and are nullified next to the near unison of destruction sown. All the scientific and philosophical research into ancestry and space travel is meaningless when we see our end through the regimentation of the status quo. Mysteries concerning cosmology and everything else are belittled next to our eschatology. Our beginnings mean nothing next to our potential end.

The mysteries concerning world events are unimportant. It does not matter whether the reason for the invasion of Iraq was fabricated lies or great mistakes, the outcome is the same. Wrong is wrong, and many wrong conditions are perpetuated when unquestioned and unaddressed. It does not matter where global warming is from, when global pollution continues and is a known detractor to the quality of life with known sources. It doesn't matter if one's liberty is taken for the implementation of safety; it is taken. A response is required no matter the mystery.

Mysteries are meaningless next to actualities. Presently, there is no mystery of the past that is worth considering compared to the results and actualities of the present. The Earth is riding on a human-made downward spiral trending toward complete environmental destruction. Nothing else matters. There are life threatening consequences and conditions made by extracting and burning coal, oil and uranium.

Throughout recorded time, it has always been the same type of scoundrel that has hindered people, foreign or domestic. Before the Boston Tea Party and since, it has always been the same type of institutions that patriots have questioned and battled in mind and with heart. It has always been patriots versus institutions and the institutionalized, patriots attempting to awaken idiots and zealots and free them from elitists. There have always been three types of institutions that continuously and sometimes maliciously interlink to engulf all and always individuals battling such leviathan constructions.

The trinity of monopoly is made up of institutions derived from, and/or latched onto state, religious or corporate formations. In 1773, at the big steep, the original patriots not only tossed The Company's tea into the sea, but they tossed the British Parliamentary authority and King's laws overboard as well, and all support from the church that supplied the royalty with the divine right of kings. At the Boston Tea Party, the patriots rebelled against all three interwoven institutions.

Corporations seek growth. The bigger the corporation, the more global growth they intend, the more likely they are to exploit variously. Corporations seek to dominate, monopolize and create dependencies the world over. The franchise fast-food industry is an example of one such corporate globalization and monopolization. Oil corporations are another example of expansive global monopolistic institutions. Company commitment and brand loyalty are enough to inspire some to exploit others of differing religious, national or corporate institutions.

States seek growth. They seek to expand their sphere of influence or conquer and takeover. The cold war was about advancing one way of operating throughout the entire world. All wars and deals by states are meant to advance their possession of influence, resource or territory. Jingoistic national beliefs are enough to inspire people to war on others of different national, religious or corporate institutions.

Churches seek growth. Proselytism is an underlying urge and principle in the world's major religions, in which a church seeks to dominate the globe through conversion. Some among Islam believe one should convert or die. Christianity sent missions of conversion the world over for centuries. Monotheistic religions formations are especially institutional and frequently lead people astray instead of showing them the way. Ardent religious beliefs are enough to inspire people to exploit and war on others of different national, religious, or corporate institutions.

It has always been a battle between institutions and individuals. A battle waged by elitists, they, them and the illuminati against some patriots, some farmers and others who still had heart enough to feel the wrong. Throughout recorded time, the trinity of monopoly has manipulated individuals and destroyed environment for reward. It has always been patriots who questioned exploits on behalf of themselves and their peers, and patriots who questioned individual tolerations that lure some to think of others as part of a collective to exploit.

Throughout recorded time, there has always been four types of people in the world; idiots, zealots, elitists and patriots, and three types of institutions; church, state and corporation. The exact interests of all four types of individuals differ infinitively, the way in which people react to relevant information and conditions coincides and is the fairest way to understand people. The aims of the three different institutions have sprouted out of infinite human interests, but lean toward controlling people in specific ways. Understanding relationships between the four types of individuals and the three different types of institutions is easy and only requires open observations and relevant questions.

IDIOTS, ZEALOTS, AND ELITISTS VS. PATRIOTS

"I believe our heavenly father invented man because he was disappointed in the monkey." ~Mark Twain

It is possible to learn a lot from observations of reality and simple questions. Simply by observing nature, questions have been asked and answered. Through the observation of animals, people have not only learned about animal behavior, but also about the mechanics of the world, the universe and themselves. Observations of animals have influenced everything from the design of martial arts to the engineering of space technology. Open observations and questioning lead to insight into a wide array of conditions and subjects, including the mentality of others and oneself.

Monkey see, monkey do. Simpletons mimic, but do not learn. They observe and then perform the action, without understanding what it is they are doing. Monkeys are capable of imitation. They are intelligent, they can perform, they have hands, but they can't adequately question. Monkeys can imitate in limited capacity, but without being able to formulate relevant questions about the action they mimic, they may perform it incorrectly, or without the intended results.

Some subjects are beyond the comprehension of monkeys. Scientists concluded that monkeys are capable of empathy, and lean toward what is termed the prosocial option. Observations of Capuchin Monkeys found they predominantly share food with their peers in equal portions. Scientists concluded the monkeys received satisfaction from sharing. Monkeys have a tendency to copy and also to share. Similar studies show the same tendency to share among domestic dogs. Some subjects are basic notions to monkeys. Humans too, when unburdened of tolerations, also tend to share when there is the opportunity and plenty, but sometimes people cease sharing and begin asking questions towards the very opposite of sharing.

There is an ancient adage and image that depicts the thinking and being of people by way of four archetypal monkeys. Variously known as The Wise Monkeys or The Three Wise Monkeys they are typically depicted sitting next to each other in a row. One covers its eyes, blinding itself. The second covers its ears, deafening itself. The third covers its mouth, restricting speech. They are the three wise monkeys, but none seem much the wise character, each known for hampering itself in one way or another. The accompanying phrase: See no evil, hear no evil, speak no evil.

Typically there are only the three monkeys depicted, yet there is a fourth wise monkey. The least commonly depicted fourth monkey is the only monkey who seems wise at all. The fourth monkey is depicted with its arms folded over its abdomen. In Asia people conceptualized that all movement, physically and metaphysically, begins and is anchored in the abdominal region or dantien, an energy point just above the belly button. The fourth monkey looks, listens and communicates, but has ceased action, probably based on what is seen, heard and said. The fourth monkey is unafraid and unflinching. And the fourth monkey is often invisible or disappeared because he is the distinct of the four, the patriot.

There are four wise monkeys, even though the fourth is often omitted and forgotten; see no evil, hear no evil, speak no evil and fear no evil, also known as do no evil. There are not three wise monkeys; there are three frightened monkeys who monkey-around and one wise monkey.

Fear no evil, the fourth monkey, is all but deleted from the archetypal presentation of the wise monkeys. Similarly in *1984* the Brotherhood are similarly deleted. *The Theory and Practice to Oligarchical* Collectivism in *1984* states that there are three types of people in the world, the high the middle and the low. In *1984*, the Brotherhood is mentioned only as a rumored group, while in the book within the book they are not included as an actual characterization in the world. The fourth monkey, the patriots resembling the Brotherhood, are practically always belittled and disappeared.

In *1984* the monopolization was complete, and perhaps there were only three types of people. It is also possible that the Inner Party attempted to delete the notion of the existence of the Brotherhood by presenting three instead of four. George Orwell originally wanted the title of *1984* to be *The Last Man in Europe* instead of *1984*. Winston Smith is made to believe he is the last man in Europe, the last person who questions, who looks, listens and speaks. In *1984* the rebellious Brotherhood is mentioned as a rumor, a fourth vague possibility. In the "Theory and Practice to Oligarchical Collectivism", the book within the book, the fourth grouping goes unmentioned. There is only the high, the middle and the low presented.

In *1984* and in the ancient adage of the wise monkeys, the fourth characterization is mostly absent from the presentation. The Brotherhood is unmentioned in the book within the book, because it had already been distorted. The fourth monkey, the Brotherhood and patriots are ignored, omitted and distorted by institutions and the institutionalized. In *1984*, the notion of the Brotherhood was deleted. In reality, with the archetype of the wise monkeys, the fourth monkey, fear no evil, is deleted in just the same way.

By observing and questioning actuality, the four types of people are realized and further examination is granted. Institutions can use the three monkeys, but they cannot use the fourth monkey. The mentality of the fourth monkey, fear no evil, frightens institutions. Institutions delete and distort the notion of fear no evil, the Brotherhood and patriots because they are unafraid and thus useless to institutions that operate by manipulating fear and burdening tolerations.

In reality, institutions attempt to remove the notion of patriots and transform patriotism into idiocy, zealotry, or elitism. Institutions in reality attempt to distort and confuse the meaning of patriot and eliminate the notion of them altogether. Institutions would prefer that people see only zealots, idiots and elitists claiming to be patriots. Institutions prefer to keep patriots mixed up with the others, for when the definition is clear, they and them cannot hide behind preconceptions.

In *1984* the Inner Party adopted Big Brother as the image or the archetype to represent them. Big Brother is not in the Brotherhood. The words are transmutable in the mind. Big Brother is an Inner Party institutional creation, associated with the disappeared Brotherhood. Institutions mix themselves up with patriotic ideas and words and at the same time, eliminate the understanding of patriot or the Brotherhood or fear no evil. Institutions transfer and confuse words and ideas in the same manner as the Inner Party with the conjuring of Big Brother and the elimination of the Brotherhood in *1984*. Institutions delete patriots, and at the same time they attempt to adopt the archetype, take the words and flip them.

The archetype of the four wise monkeys is considered to be one of the oldest axioms with a corresponding image. The original concept has its roots in Chinese philosophy and can be traced back to at least the 8th century. In Japan, it is interpreted as akin to the Golden Rule and is also a play on words. The Japanese word for monkey is saru and the expression in Japanese uses verb forms that sound like the word monkey; mizaru, kikazaru, iwazaru and shizaru. The predominant presentation of the wise monkeys around the world lacks the fourth monkey, fear no evil, shizaru.

Institutions always attempt to cancel the notion of fear no evil, the patriot. Institutions operate in threes, in pyramidal formation. There are four types of people, four modes of political thinking, but only one is a threat to institutional monopolization, hence institutional preference to reduce four to three. If institutions cannot eliminate the fourth monkey, if elitist institutions cannot eliminate patriots, they distort and confuse what it means to be a patriot. They remove traits and present their own qualifications, consisting of being more idiot, zealot or elitist than patriot.

In physics, special relativity and general relativity, as theorized by Albert Einstein, states that reality is four dimensional; time, length, width and depth. Four is symbolic for completion. There are four types of people in the world; those who are afraid to look, those who are afraid to hear, those who are afraid to speak and those who are unafraid to look, listen, speak and face evil without flinching, idiots, zealots, elitists, and patriots.

"Few are those who see with their own eyes and feel with their own hearts." ~Albert Einstein

---

Richard Wilhelm translated many Chinese philosophical works into German, among them the Secret of the Golden Flower and the I Ching. Richard's translations are considered to be among the finest. Both books were printed with commentaries written by Richard's friend, Carl Jung. The Secret of the Golden Flower reveals Daoist and Buddhist techniques for development through meditation. The book presents ideas to look for what is missing by looking at what is there. It relates the idea of feeling rather than intellectualizing situations.

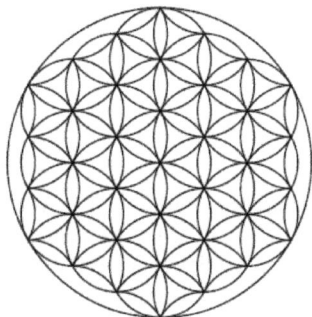

SYMBOL - FLOWER OF LIFE
The Flower of Life is a geometrical design associated with the Tree of Life. Many mathematical and theoretical designs are within the Flower of Life. It symbolizes the sacred oneness and equality of all living beings. The oldest known examples of The Flower of life design are in Egypt, at the Temple of Osiris. These depictions may be more than 10,000 years old. Different religions and cultures all over the world depict the Flower of Life.

The archetype of the four wise monkeys is one of the oldest adages in existence. It is also likely one of the most commonly misunderstood and partially distorted images. It is an old example of a missing whole truth and a partial presentation. The absence is normally unconsidered or trivial, but helps to point out the very lesson of the wise monkeys maxim. Observe reality and openly communicate with others about the nature of conditions to find what is hidden by way of what is there.

Institutions maintain lies by partial presentation and proceed as if the absent never existed. Institutions insist that they have the correct math and there is no reason to question it, only a need to believe it. Institutions insist that there are three when there are four.

The pronunciation of the word "four" in Japanese and Mandarin is similar to the word for death. In Japan and most of China, death and four are near homonyms and the relation instigates fear and aversion of the number. Four is a number that evokes fear in parts of Asia and is superstitiously avoided as one would avoid word of death.

Buddhists and many others interpret the wise monkeys as a karmic reminder of sorts not to participate in any form of evil, but it is more than that. This traditional interpretation states that one should not see, hear or speak of inconsequence. It is true that avoiding irrelevance is wise, but this is only part of the truth.

"A man should look for what is, and not for what he thinks should be." ~Albert Einstein

If one was ignorant of lions and tigers and bears, they might still hurt and kill you. The same is true today. Just because one is ignorant of reality does not mean that one is safe from it. There are some things that need no inquiry, but ignorance is not bliss. Ignorance is bliss - until the moment arrives when knowledge is needed immediately. Ignorance is strength to institutions. Institutions instill ignorance because ignorance results in fear and fear results in dependence.

The four wise monkeys are reflective of the four archetypal reactions to information. The four wise monkeys are the idiot, zealot, elitist and patriot. Idiots shut their pupils to all information and do not learn. Zealots close their ears and do not hear what's really going on. Elitists keep their mouths shut and do not disclose what is seen and heard. Patriots, the least common of the monkeys, use all their senses and stops activity. Some statues depict the monkeys in varying order, but the fourth monkey, fear no evil is always on the right.

The three wise monkeys are an incomplete depiction of mentality, but still provide valid representation of certain lessons, in particular the point that one should discontinue communicating rumors and lies. In a similar manner, Socrates used what he called the Test of Three to verify if information was worthy of communication. As the story goes a man approached Socrates and told him that he had something to tell him about an acquaintance. Socrates asked the man if what he had to say was verifiably true. Then he asked if it was in goodness. Finally he asked if the information was useful. The man's statement was not verifiably true, good or useful and Socrates declined to listen to the rumor. The three monkeys are allegorically aligned with this sentiment. If information is untrue, negative and meant to be destructive, it is not worth communicating. If information meets one or more of the three filters, it is potentially worthy of communication.

Gandhi lived a lifestyle free of possessions. Gandhi lived as the fourth monkey; fear no evil. Excluding the clothes on his back, his spectacles, sandals and comb, Gandhi's one possession was a porcelain statue of the three wise monkeys. He received it as a gift from Chinese admirers. Gandhi functioned as a fourth monkey on every level and in every facet of his life. Today there are statues of the three wise monkeys at Gandhi's one time residence, where he began his march to protest the taxation and monopolization of sea salt in 1930.

The interpretation of the wise monkeys varies and is of course layered, but if monkeys were wise they would certainly maintain all of their senses. If monkeys were wise, they would not participate in evil true; but they would also stay informed and alert like the fourth monkey. If monkeys were wise, they would not ignore evil in one way or another, but would ignore irrelevance in total. Wisdom is noted by quality vision, understanding ear, thoughtful speech and courage. If monkeys were wise, they would be as the fourth monkey and cease action, not hinder their senses.

> "Non-cooperation with evil is a sacred duty." ~Gandhi

People are not like monkeys. There are shared characteristics, but people are capable of much more than monkeys. When information and resources are available people can do anything, be it positive or negative. People are all alike; everyone wants clean water and liberty for instance and everyone should be entitled to at least such basics. The difference between people is in how they react to information. Their reactions are based on prior information, experience and acquired tolerations or fears.

There are four types of people in the world. All types can potentially intertwine in an individual and reveal themselves depending on the circumstances and subject matter. The characterizations are concrete, yet people can transpose from one to the other depending on the conditions and circumstances. People are people; it is our reaction to relevant information that defines us.

Idiot	One who refuses to question information, the blind monkey.
Zealot	One who refutes countering information, the deaf monkey.
Elitist	One who withholds information, the mute monkey.
Patriot	One who questions information, the still monkey.

Patriots do not necessarily want to change unless change is necessary to implement what right or cancel wrong. Patriots do not seek change; however, they are able to embrace change, including stopping, by openly questioning new information. Patriots are willing to implement change through their action and inaction. Patriots use their senses and cease participation in the perpetuation of manipulated information. Patriots are a rarity in society, like four leaf clovers in the forest, but they indeed exist.

Patriots are not afraid to stop, look, listen and speak up. Patriots do not fear repercussions of their speech, they are unafraid to speak the truth. Most everyone is afraid of something; afraid of what evil they might see, hear or speak of. Monkeys and most people are fearful.

Children have basic, animalistic and irrational fears. Children display uncontrollable fear of what is seen, heard and said demonstrated by instinctual reactions. Children shut their eyes and cover them with their hands when afraid of the dark or something else the eyes reveal. Children clasp their ears when they want to avoid hearing or learning something. And children literally clasp their mouth shut when they realize, for whatever reason, they should hold their tongue.

Monkeys attack out of fear, as well as take things and take flight. Patriots may be afraid at times as well, everyone is afraid sometimes; only patriots are not afraid of obtaining or supplying any information. Patriots are unafraid of obtaining information or speaking out on their perspective of the truth. Patriots are unafraid of taking action or halting action on behalf of what is right. If patriots are wary of anything, it is the outcome of the fear and ignorance, continuation without information.

Idiots do not want to change their thoughts. When idiots are informed of the dangers of fire, they will shut their eyes in fear and later get burned. When zealots are told about the dangers of fire, they won't hear the words because they are transfixed with the appearance of the flames and later get burned. If elitists learn about fire, they will look and listen and later remain silent while others get burned. In all likelihood, the elitists will have bandages ready to sell to the idiots and zealots who burn themselves, and may have set the fire to begin with.

Patriots learn about fire, patriots question the heat and light of fire and do everything in their power to inform others about the dangers of fire and also its potential usefulness. If the others ignore the patriots, patriots stop, patriots remain grounded, until the others open their eyes and ears. Patriots will not gather fuel for the fire, their arms are crossed and they cease until the others learn. Patriots look, listen, speak up and cease to supply the fire.

Idiots and zealots shut their eyes and clasp their ears to new information that could possibly change their mindset about subjects as dangerous as fire. They would rather be ignorant. They know that asking questions risks revealing new information, which can make it extremely difficult to continue their course in the status quo, more difficult even than nursing burns.

Idiots storm out of rooms and flee from new information in every way imaginable. They support the status quo by refusing to see and hear new information. One could point out they are shackled and being played, but they don't want to know. The best way to convince idiots to question is to provide them with information. Idiots are passive and slow to react. It takes time to inspire questioning among them. The best way to reach idiots is by informing them of parallels and relevant correlations to subjects they hold interest in, whether it is sports or whatever.

The best way to confront an idiot is by giving them new information, as much as they can handle, a little at a time. If one has enough information, it is possible to instill enough emotion to clear a room full of idiots in a few moments. Idiots are easily lied to, that is, they are so passive that they will accept lies that sound pleasing and ignore truths that are not. Idiots need information, but only a little. Their eyes adjust slowly.

Idiots and zealots may be frightened to go outside the cave to look and listen; one has to show them it is possible. Gripped by fear, they need to see and hear what's outside the cave before they will go outside, and go outside before fully contemplating outside.

Zealots attack information opposing their perspective with all sorts of sensible or pointless criticism. If passionate enough about the subject, they will senselessly attack the deliverer of alternative information. One could point out that they are transfixed with false evidence, but they won't listen.

Zealots are more easily roused to violent action than idiots. They are impassioned, deaf to their surroundings and their influences, intently holding onto their perspective. Zealots have received and reviewed information counter to their opinion and dismissed it all as mumbo jumbo, lies, bullshit and the propaganda of one ethnicity or nationality, or other group who are out to get them. Not all zealots are racists, but all racists are zealots. Zealots do not fear all new information. They pick and choose the information they acquire to present the appearance of being unafraid. If it is potentially frightening, displeasing or disagreeable they simply don't accept it in the first place. Differing information and alternative perspectives mean nothing to zealots; they continue to march on and over.

Zealous belief system do not morph or transpose, unless shown just the right bit of information. Zealots support their own demise with the utmost passion when they are presented with appropriate and acceptable institutionalized information. They always take rigorous action within the status quo even if it means their own destruction. Zealots may react in confrontational manner if presented with differing information. They might attack the unconnected deliverer of information when the information differs from and threatens their worldview. Zealots charge over whomever at the indirect suggestion of institutions or under direct orders of institutions supportive to their worldview. Zealous aggression rolls right over people.

It is difficult to make an impression on zealots, but if one can connect just the right dots, find just the right key and unlock certain validated information, it is possible to convince zealots to open their perspective, or witness a breakdown. One could easily raise a room full of zealots into a frenzy with the wrong information or emotional hit. Just as easily, with the right piece of information, zealots might question their preconceptions.

The best way to confront zealots is to give them the benefit of the doubt - as much as intellectually possible - and admit they could be correct. If one can admire their point, even rationalize their perspective further and then break it down in their terms and add it up, one can convince zealots to openly question it. They may have never had anyone reasonable agree with them and analyze it to come to the next logical question and conclusion, which may trigger them to think.

It is possible to translate zealous ideas into logical reasoning that hits zealots emotionally and exposes doublethink. But beware, zealots are reactive, and they tend to void reason besides their own reasoning. It is possible to lead them into questioning the truth about their own perspective, but dangerous. Zealous opinion is derived from some information, be it falsehood, partial truth or otherwise. With that in mind, it is possible to steer zealots into open-minded evaluation of information. Show zealots the source of the light and imagery and they may then question openly and uncover their ears.

Elitists act solely based on what will work to their advantage. They repel ideas that work against their agenda and promote information that benefits them and their crew. They will do anything in their power to initiate their own comfort and control. The trampling of anyone who is not in their group is acceptable and endorsed. They support the status quo actively and sometimes do so just by keeping their mouth shut.

In their quest for information, elitists might pose questions as open-mindedly as patriots, but do not do so openly. Elitists are always thinking of ways to make information work for them, and against others. Elitists question information, but toward further selfish manipulation. Elitists withhold and distort information and cast imagery to confine and confuse others. Patriots question information in attempts to bring people out of the cave, elitists question in attempts to capture and hold people in the cave.

The best way to confront elitists is to catch them in the middle of doublespeak and loudly, boldly proclaim the facts they omit and the perceptions they twist. Speak out, let the elitists know you know, and let their supporters, the idiots and zealots, know too.

Elitists are supreme liars and manipulators of information. The information used to confront elitists must be concrete, but when confronted with undeniable information, their supporters may see them for the liars or manipulators of information they are. Elitists need to be smacked with information as boldly and publicly as possible. Elitists nearly always have a counterpoint, slander, or whatever is needed to defeat their opponent's idea or character. The information that reveals their doublespeak must be weighty, loud and always accompanied by further information in anticipation of their counter or slander. Ask elitists about subjects you know a great deal about and in a way that subtly says to them that you don't know much about the subject, allow them to dig into their lying and then call them out.

> "If you do not change direction, you may end up where you are headed."
> ~Lao Tzu, Reputed Author of Tao Te Ching

Exploitative institutional mechanics can be dismantled and bettered. Individuals can ascend institutional walls. The fire casting the imagery can be put out, and will go out if left unattended, if we cease fueling it. The idiots and zealots can be alerted to the fact that they are blinding their eyes and plugging their ears to relevant information and reality. The elitists might be informed that they are exploiting others, their surroundings and themselves. Just as people are capable of creating institutions, people are capable of halting or developing exploitative institutions as well. Institutions after all, are only structure and machinery.

If evil is about, the only way to cancel it is to look, listen, speak up about it and cease support of it without fear. To eliminate evil: stand up forthrightly, unafraid and use one's sight, hearing and speech like the fourth monkey. The fourth monkey does not cooperate with evil, but faces it. The fourth monkey ignores irrelevant images, speculations, speeches and remains silent when irrelevance is spoken of, but does not ignore evil. One way to cancel irrelevance is to ignore it, but ignoring evil simply conceals it and allows it. Ignoring irrelevance is efficient in its cancellation, but evil must be addressed and faced with foreknowledge of surrounding conditions to be eliminated. Ignoring actuality is only wise when it is irrelevant and any evil about, is never irrelevant. Only by using the senses and refusing to serve evil, can one make monkey-work out of canceling evil that lurks.

TO BE OR NOT TO BE - FREE

> To be or not to be, - that is the question -
> Whether 'tis nobler in mind to suffer
> The slings and arrows of outrageous fortune
> Or to take arms against a sea of troubles,
> And by opposing them end them? - To die - to sleep -
> No more; and by a sleep to say we end
> The heartache, and the thousand natural shocks
> That flesh is heir to, 'tis a consummation
> Devoutly to be wished: to die, to sleep.
> To sleep, perchance to dream. Ay, there's the rub;
> For in that sleep of death what dreams may come,…
> Shakespeare - Hamlet Act 3, Scene 1

There are differences between freedom and liberty. Freedom is undefined. Freedom might be any formulation from refined to crude, while liberty is the legislation of the Golden Rule. There are also differences between violence and destruction, and similarly, there are differences between destruction and cessation.

Freedom is not liberty. Liberty would never allow institutions to have the rights of individuals. To be with liberty or to be without liberty - that is a big question. To be or not to be at all - that is the biggest question. To continue or to cease - that is the question. To be inquisitive or to ignore, to stand up or sit down, to continue or to forfeit, to choose anew or operate in catch 22 fashion - that is the question.

Suicide by continuation, like a sick chain smoker, that is the petrolithic era and nuclear age. All is flipped and distorted in an increasingly depleted environment, when providers are also exploiters. Continuation doubles dilemmas in the petrolithic era and nuclear age, pausing prevents the continuation of certain problems.

Revolutionaries, activists and patriots are those who would cease participation in chopping down the last tree, while institutions insist it be cut down and used for the fire. To stop wrong that we are responsible for is to live, to be. To continue unconcerned despite resulting destruction, to perpetuate the con of the status quo in the petrolithic era and nuclear age, is to commit slow Hara-kiri. The fourth monkey stops, folds its arms and has no fear because stopping is supremely powerful.

Revolution and evolution do not have to be violent; in fact anything revolutionary today would be nonviolent. Violence is normal, part of the status quo. A change, one type of revolution would be simple nonviolent approaches. Violence is stagnancy and perpetuates sameness, while revolution is change, something different from the status quo. Violence is a common denominator in the status quo. Violence is not revolutionary and revolution does not require violence.

Only those who continue the madness of the status quo in the petrolithic era would stick with violence, for violence necessitates institution over individual. Change may very well happen overnight and nonetheless be nonviolent. Revolution simply means to turn, to change. Change is revolutionary, whereas war is war.

Patriots do not have to be extremists to enact revolution. In fact, anything antiestablishment and revolutionary might also be opposite of extreme, as the establishment in the status quo is the epitome of extreme. Simply adjusting one's spending habits to promote fair treatment of workers around the globe can have an intense, rippling power. Corporations all over the world heed to the power of the consumer and ultimately the will of people. One can eliminate or decrease purchasing products made through slave and exploited labor. That is a potential change. One can stop buying products, as much as possible from nations who sell the most weaponry around the world and the nations that manufacture the most nuclear energy/waste and they are basically the same countries. Gandhi only owned a small porcelain statue of monkeys. What are your needs?

> "Great doubt: great awakening. Little doubt: little awakening. No doubt: no awakening."
> ~Zen Saying

Technological revolutions and societal revolutions induce great change and yet, might slide through history with violent quakes and bloodshed. The Berlin wall came down in a celebration without blood and fire. If you have aggression, take it out on walls, not people. Hitting a wall is destructive, not violent. Pushing a person down is violent. Society can evolve and change with as little drastic drama as the rejoining of Germany or the advancement from beepers to cell phones.

> FACT: Cell phones contain lead, mercury, arsenic, cadmium, beryllium, and antimony. These are persistent bioaccumulative toxins that often are burned into the air and buried into the ground on disposal. Studies indicate that the use of cell phones may cause cancer.

Poisonous elements find their way into plants, animals, food, children and you. Simple devices and products might be part of complex problems. Through socially responsible investing one can make a powerful statement and change. Stop supporting cellular phone companies, get a landline. Purchase natural alternatives as opposed to petroleum products, not because of global warming, but for the health of others and yourself. Corporations want your money bad enough to change for it, but you have to stand for it.

Stop investing in a communication network that provides cancer and pollution. Stop investing in formations that supply such negativity and deny alternative. It is not just cell phones; one could pick and choose from any number of dire networks of demise to actively disengage from, there are plenty. It is impossible to cease support for all displeasing aspects of the status quo totally and permanently, but it is possible to cease support totally and temporarily or partially and permanently. Such discontinuance performed in chorus is enough to steer institutional direction to supply individuals and eliminate the negative results.

> "A long habit of not thinking a thing wrong gives it the superficial appearance of being right, and raises at first a formidable outcry in defense of custom. But the tumult soon subsides. Time makes more converts than reason."
> ~Thomas Paine

The power of the consumer is vast; the powers of consumers together directly influence corporate policy, state law and church dogma. If everyone or even half of the people/consumers stop purchasing with a statement, corporations would change; they want your money that much. The power of the dollar can convince individuals to do wrong and institutions to do right. Removing support for institutions, whether dollar or attendance, instigates action.

People have power to change without violence and in spite of violence. People also have the power to influence and change situations regardless of their finances. Depending on the situation and the environment one resides in, there are different actions that might be initiated or ceased to influence conditions in the status quo. Depending on one's location, there are options regardless of income level. One's environment dictates one's capabilities first and foremost and then one's imagination.

In the city, one is in a unique position to announce a boycott of gas stations. One may already use public transportation out of convenience and not own a car, and if so, announce a boycott. In the city it is impossible to boycott petrol completely as the facilitation of food is dependent on petrol, but it is a place to start and make a statement. The manufacturing and shipment of every product is dependent on petrol and many products are made from it. It is currently impossible to boycott petrol completely in the interdependent inner city, yet it is always possible to do something.

In the city, the most powerful form of patriotism is to inform, communicate. No matter the power one has to influence and rebel, the best outlet is to inform one's peers and neighbors. Question, communicate and speak out to and with others, but don't take anyone's word for it.

> "Patriotism means to stand by the country. It does not mean to stand by the President or any other public official."
> ~Theodore Roosevelt

In a rural environment, one is in a unique position to announce a boycott of certain suppliers that might not meet one's standards. In the country, one might not have the use for certain services in the first place, and if so, announce a boycott of mismanaged corporations, whether one has use for them or not. Seek to gain the support of one's peers by communicating about global franchises or any other number of locally available examples of oligarchical collectivism.

In the country, a powerful form of patriotism is to inform, but perhaps the most powerful form of patriotism in the country is to care for the land and produce sustainable resources. In the country, there might not be as many people to inform, but there might be more land to care for and opportunity to produce resources for oneself and others.

The power of money is vast. The power of one person alone, without cash is much deeper, no matter where one resides. The power of informed voice and actions can be greater than the power of communication through spending. The power derived from the First Amendment is more powerful than any stack of Benjamins. Money is potent, but the greatest power and the greatest equalizer of power, is information. Question the monkeys around you. Look, listen, speak, question, and if need be cross your arms in defiance like the fourth monkey. No amount of cash can equal the power of the fourth monkey.

People are alike. It is the reaction to information that makes us different. It is the conceptualizations in our brains and mentality that makes us different, not the appearance of bodies or any other distorted division. Further, it is how people think that differentiates, not necessarily what people think. This alone is a new concept, one that has gained prominence with the trinity of liberty and a land of immigrants. It is a basic and rising idea of the U.S.A. that all people are created with equal rights and potential. Throughout recorded time, ideas of liberty and equality have been scorned by institutions and still are in many regions in the world.

People have ability; people are valuable. Yet throughout recorded time individuals have been held back and restricted of self-evident potential through institutions. Institutions throughout the world restrict the better sensibilities of people and betterment of people through unequal distribution of information and restrictions on liberty. The functions of institutions belittle individual alternatives and development and praise the maintenance of mechanics. Institutions portray themselves as holding the truth; however the truth is self-evident, not mechanized. Power and potential are also self-evident. People make institutions worthy in the first place, not the other way around.

> "One person can make a difference and every person should try." ~John Fitzgerald Kennedy

Before institutions, before the trinity of liberty, before plastics and cell phones, people roamed and settled the planet for tens of thousands of years. People survived ice age and drought without institutions, people settled in and adapted to all of creation without institutions. For millennia, there were no institutions to assist, just people. The will and partnership of people enabled the accomplishment of amazing feats without amazing mechanization or prominent institutions. People together were able to survive, create and flourish.

People develop and invent, at times, through institutions, for they are simply tools of, for and by people and as tools are used to help and at times, hinder. Language is a similar tool of, for and by people. Both conceptualized language and concrete institutions might be used to explain and accomplish, or misused to restrain and maintain.

Possibly the oldest continuously inhabited community in the U.S.A. is Old Oraibi, in the Hopi Nation, Arizona. It is estimated that the settlement was established in approximately 1100 AD. The Four Corners region of Arizona is an extreme climate, a dry desert in the summer and a frozen desolation in the winter. There is little water available and the arid winds blow the top soil around, making it difficult to grow anything, yet the Hopi established a flourishing farming community there. With all the land in all of the Americas available, why did they choose one of the least hospitable climates?

The Hopi believe that the Four Corners region is the center of the Earth and the center of the universe. The Hopi also reasoned that by going to an inhospitable place, they would depend on each other and develop a mutual reliance on each other. If they went where things were easy they would cease to rely on one another. They settled in the desert because it was difficult, the climate would draw them together. The only institution they needed was local and all-inclusive, it was each other.

By pursuing loud and quiet questions, and acting on answers, the world has been changed. By the loudest and most notable exclamations of truths has the world turned. Great change is possible by questioning and revealing answers. People are able to better themselves and their surroundings through simple questions, communication and cooperation.

Complete information is a rare occurrence; complete answers are fleeting, if ever. There is always more to know and more to question about reality, as it is in flux, perhaps more so in the petrolithic era and nuclear age. For the last ten thousand years, there has been a lot of ice at the poles, today not so much, tomorrow maybe none or maybe a whole lot more. The Earth changes on its own and is changed by people. Knowledge, sometimes found outside the light, is the key to grasping forever morphing reality. When you lose your key or your way, sometimes looking outside the light is the key, it is the way.

The global formations and institutions now in place may seem great and powerful, impossible to replace. This is an institutionalized thought, an acquired toleration. Many institutions are not necessary; many are not beneficial, many offer continuous complications, hindrance with assistance. No institution is necessary and everything under the Sun changes, the Sun itself goes through changes. Institutions come and go; clean elements are the only things that are absolutely necessary and global pollution is making such rarer.

Allowing the crap of machinery into the water is wrong. When obvious wrong is stopped, if only briefly, right might be uncovered. Simply stopping wrong may reveal a more righteous option that was always there, just impossible to notice with all the wrong whirling around.

Individuals manifest institutions, and there is nothing mind can wrong that heart cannot right. Any misaligned institution, no matter how systematically and technologically superior, no matter how integrated, is replaceable. There is no institution that cannot be abandoned and undone, dismantled, or ignored and retooled. No institution is so sacred that it supersedes individuals or what is right. All institutional walls fall and are surmountable in some way.

Patriotism scales institutional walls. There are five stages to patriotism. They tend to follow in the order presented, but sometimes the order in which they are enacted differs. There are many ways to accomplish change, progression, revolution or evolution through patriotic measures; all of which fall under one of five stages. The specific order and potency of the stages should be left up to individual conditions and individual decisions, based simply on observations of actuality and pursuance of liberty.

The Boston Tea Party is the archetypal patriotic response to oligarchical collectivism. Those who participated in the Boston Tea Party planned and conducted their operation in a peaceful manner to make a statement. The defining act was particularly defiant and definitely destructive, but it was nonviolent. No one was hurt save a few who were punched and booted, and at worse bruised, for attempting to pocket tea and degrade protest into theft. Violence and theft turn noble protest into riot lacking statement.

First they questioned the institutional exploitation. Next they communicated the confirmed exploitation. Then they spoke out publicly in voice and in print about the exploitation. Following speaking out, they stopped participating in their exploitation and boycotted the tea. Finally the original patriots, with reasoning based in liberty and bettered through discussion, acted out of a redress of grievances and tossed The Company tea into Boston Harbor.

To be a patriot is to act in accordance with the basis of the trinity of liberty. The First Amendment of the Bill of Rights, ratified December 15, 1791, guarantees people rights and also provides the description of and prescription for patriotism, keeping these rights. The First Amendment is the formula for patriotism. It not only protects the rights specifically, but unifies them together in one Amendment equating to and directing patriotism itself. The First Amendment is an amalgamation of rights because they all pertain to the mutual concept of patriotism. The First Amendment is not only an indication of secured rights, but also the formula to patriotism's fundamentals, which conveniently secure procedure to keep the rights. The First Amendment provides individuals with the right, and the direction to, patriotism.

It is the formula followed by the original patriots, dressed as American Indians at the Boston Tea Party. It is so important a formula that it is the first right, in one of first documents of its kind. The First Amendment provides the right to act patriotically and presents the step-by-step course of action for individuals to keep their liberty. The following nine Amendments are further assurances that institutions respect individuals if the First Amendment doesn't secure liberty. If the peaceful patriotic actions of the First Amendment do not end exploitation, but result in attack, then there is the Second Amendment and so on. The Bill of Rights not only provides a set of rights, but the formula to protect individuals and individual rights at the same time.

Since 9/11 the Writ of Habeas Corpus has fallen by the wayside like so much boxed tea in Boston Harbor. The Writ of Habeas Corpus was a specific response to institutional "abusive detention of persons without authority." The English Parliament adopted the Habeas Corpus Act in 1679, rooted in older laws, the critical individual right was adopted by the trinity of liberty as well. It provides individuals the right and opportunity to stand up to their captors in court.

The Writ of Habeas Corpus specifies the time frame, that upon arrest, one must be arraigned, charged, held over for trial or dismissed, and tried by a jury of one's peers. Without Habeas Corpus individuals might be jailed indefinitely without reason and without ability to be heard or seen. The U.S.A. Constitution states: Habeas Corpus shall not be suspended unless in cases of rebellion and invasion, the public safety may require it. The first time Habeas Corpus was suspended in the U.S.A. was by Abraham Lincoln during the Civil War and the Reconstruction period.

George II suspended the right after 9/11. Anyone labeled an unlawful enemy combatant might be held indefinitely at Guantanamo Bay. In 2006 the Military Commissions Act was passed determining that Habeas Corpus was not applicable for unlawful enemy combatants. Later several courts decided this decision went against the Constitution. The First Amendment is incapable of doing much good wherever Habeas Corpus is absent.

The rights designated for all might be gathered for a few, if people were prevented from questioning and speaking up. The rights intended for all individuals might be increasingly extended to institutions if people didn't stand up and speak out. Some laws and acts benefit individuals, but many place restrictions on us.

The Patriot Act is definitely more like an act or an image in a show of patriotism rather than a real patriotic act. It enhances surveillance procedures and diminishes privacy. One's spending habits, travels, reading material, bank accounts and communications are all now freely monitored. In fact The Patriot Act is the very counter to the First Amendment, the real patriot act. Why is liberty removed for security? Terrorist acts are deplorable and threatening, but perhaps a more real threat is the reaction to remove liberty because of a threat. How do individual and institutions react to information?

The Patriot Act acts, it is not real patriotism. The real patriotic act, the original formula to patriotism cannot be replaced. The First Amendment, the first right of in The Bill of Rights of the U.S.A., Amendment A#1 is the original patriot act. The prescription to properly confront the trinity of monopoly and oligarchical collectivism is presented in the very First Amendment in the U.S.A. Bill of Rights. The First Amendment is the formula to nonviolently confront the trinity of monopoly. It is the way in which change, revolution, is conducted without hostile confrontation. The First Amendment defines patriotism.

All other Amendments are straightforward and pertain to particulars whereas the First Amendment is a mix because it is the explanation of patriotism, put in the form of, and protected as one right. There are five distinct parts to the First Amendment, five parts to the whole. These five distinctions spell out five separate rights and stages essential to form patriotism. These five rights and procedures were formulated by the original patriots through their diplomatic, rhetorical and martial experience against the forces of the most powerful empire the world had known.

Throughout recorded time, the individual rights described in the First Amendment have been coercively and institutionally stomped out. Normally the stomping is done on a perceived "them" among an imagined "us" denoted by some institutionally conjured character judgment or fear based assumptions. Exploitation has been institutionally and individually driven, but when individuals are run over on a large scale it always begins with the removal of their First Amendment rights.

The First Amendment, the patriotic formula, was deciphered, enacted and scribed by the original patriots. There are five distinct parts to the First Amendment. To be a patriot one must question, communicate, speak out, stop and act. These rights are more commonly known as the Five First Amendment Freedoms.

Normally the First Amendment Freedoms are interpreted and presented as the freedom of religion, speech, press, assembly and petition. Everything is open for interpretation. This traditional presentation is not personal or individual enough, not formulated as simple individual orientation. The First Amendment protects these basic rights and provides direction to implement patriotism by making them as five fingers to one hand, and no matter how institutions would like First Amendment rights of man, it is meant for individuals.

To be a patriot one must always question information in an unbiased manner without conniving intentions to make gains over others from answers. When a subject arises requiring scrutiny, one must communicate with others. The next step is to speak out in print or loud voice to the public at large about the subject in question. If the subject continues to be questionable, one stops participation in protest with others. If questions are left unanswered, if the subject remains questionable, if exploitation continues, then defiant action is taken.

To meet the requirements of a patriotic action there must not be harm done to others and nothing can be stolen. Essentially there must be no sin involved in the action. Actions might remain patriotic as long as no harm comes to the wellbeing and liberty of others. Such peaceful patriotic actions tend to be impenetrable to institutional operations and distortions. One must always defend oneself if physically threatened; this is the Second Amendment. Self-defense is primordial and legal action and unless one wants to make a statement like Gandhi in the face of institutional sticks, legitimate. Patriotic statement and action requires at least one attempt at nonviolence. Realistically, when more than one attempt is made toward nonviolence before the use of force in self-defense, there will likely be little chance for institutional distortion of events.

When the right to free speech and free press is used to say some bullshit or splatter insults, it's no longer patriotism, it's just a right. If one uses the right to question the interpretation of God simply to insult, divide or manipulate others, it is no longer patriotic. If people use these rights, this formula peacefully and in liberty, to instigate thinking, then and only then, are these actions patriotic.

> "Threats to freedom of speech, writing and action, though often trivial in isolation, are cumulative in their effect and, unless checked, lead to a general disrespect for the rights of the citizen." ~George Orwell

STAGE ONE: QUESTION
Congress shall make no law respecting an establishment of religion, or prohibiting the free exercise thereof;

The beginning to every invention, every story, development, action, indeed every institution, religious and otherwise began with questions. Questions concerning the specifics and generalities of God are the most rippling questions of all. Congress shall make no law prohibiting the free exercise of questions pertaining to the interpretation of God and all other subjects.

Individuals have the right to question the world and the universe, any theory, any portion of reality and the interpretation of God, in whatever manner they see fit. People have the right to question any subject up to and including the interpretation of God herself through any religion or other discipline. People have the right to question any subject, even established religious interpretations however. No individual shall face repercussion for their interpretation of God and any other question, other than being told another perspective. Everyone has the right to question everything and exercise individual interpretations of everything, even God herself. When one is allowed to question religious and individual interpretations of God, then questioning all else is granted. No subject is above questioning and no institution is above questions, even those of God. Everything changes and sometimes people lie, requiring open questions.

The original patriots knew the power of questioning and they did so, perhaps over a cup of tea, while discussing tea. "Who? What? Where? Why? When? And, how?" They asked.

> "All religions, arts, and sciences are branches of the same tree." ~Albert Einstein

STAGE TWO: COMMUNICATE
or abridging the freedom of speech,

"Congress shall make no law" is implied to stage two and each of the following stages of patriotism. Individuals can communicate with anyone, any of the answers they find, even those relating to the interpretation of God. Individuals have the right to speak amongst themselves about any information, in any manner they see fit, without repercussion and without notification of sorts.

People can say whatever they want about whatever they want, including, but not limited to religious, spiritual and atheistic interpretations of God and the universe. Everyone has the right to question and reveal answers and interpretations that may or may not be desired. Everyone has the right to exchange information and answers, to communicate about everything with anyone, even differing religious interpretations, without repercussions.

Everyone has the right to speculate on and question any statement and interpretation about God or otherwise delivered via an institution or individual. People have the right to communicate on matters concerning God or government and also have the right to speculate on the communication of others.

The original patriots communicated in order to find answers when The Company monopolized tea. "This is who, what, where, why, when and how."

STAGE THREE: SPEAK OUT
or of the press,

Individuals have the right to express information to any and all in any form of media and can demand information of any and all publicly. Individuals are allowed to access and distribute any form of media to enable their public statement. Individuals have the right to publicly ask any question to any institution and disclose and distribute any answer, information or the lack of it.

Individuals have the right to question and report on any other institution or individual, even those who claim to be God's representation on Earth, even the government. Institutions have latched onto the right to speak out and do so with wide platform, often with specific biases, but it is individuals that enable this right. Individuals have the right to distribute information on any situation, in spite of institutions that also distribute information, commercially or otherwise. To speak out, one must be able to openly research and present information on any event, individual or institution, no matter how sacred. Institutions prefer partial truths, patriots seek the whole truth and distribute it openly.

The original patriots communicated the exploits, probably without tea, their energy amplified by simple information and opportunity to communicate their exploitation. The original patriots printed articles, editorials, political cartoons and stories revealing information. "The questions and answers must be known, here are some questions and some answers." They expressed.

> STAGE FOUR: STOP
> or the right of people peaceably to assemble

The prerequisite to assembling peaceably is stopping the status quo. In order to peaceably assemble one has to discontinue normal routine and participate with others. People have the right to stop and gather with any number of other people in a peaceful manner, for any reason. People can stop their normal activity. People may change their plans and decide to go somewhere different or not to go at all. People can publicly peaceably gather to worship any interpretation of God or for no reason at all, whenever they want. Individuals and entire communities can stop, for any reason or no reason at all.

This was first done by the original patriots at protests of taxation without representation and all out Company monopolization. There probably was no tea and little heat. "We have answers and we cease support of the exploitation." They announced.

> STAGE FIVE: ACT
> and to petition the government for a redress of grievances.

We all have the right to hold every individual and institution accountable and have the right to petition action accordingly. Every institution under the governance of the U.S.A. and the government itself is accountable to the people and bound to the concepts of the republic. A redress requires a declared problem, a wrong that needs to be set right. The grievance is the announcement of a problem; the redress is the removal of the problem. Accountability is upheld; gatherings and actions take place until the problem is fixed. Until the grievance is addressed and the problem solved, institutions face petition for redress by people.

The government may be the cause of grievances; they are accountable to the people through the trinity of liberty. The government can be addressed to hold any institutions in its governance accountable to people's grievances, including its own branches. If there is wrongdoing, people have the right to ask questions concerning all grievances of any institution and demand answers and solutions.

Every institution in the U.S.A. is subject to answer the questions of people and to address their grievances. People have the right to demand change in the cause of their distress. If they do not get it, they have the right to act peaceably.

This was first done, without tea, in the cold, amid peril at the Boston Tea Party. "We're mad as hell and we are not going to take it anymore!" They showed.

Throughout recorded time, oligarchical institutions have controlled, limited and restricted the five stages of patriotism in one way or another. The original patriots formulated the First Amendment by combining the timeless elements of individual empowerment. The power of individuals using the First Amendment is what makes the U.S.A. a great nation.

Freedom of religion guarantees the right to question everything including one's existence, God's existence and one's relationship with God and the universe. Freedom of speech provides the right to express any question and any answer. Freedom of the press guarantees people the right to question events and distribute answers. Freedom to assemble gives people the right to question anything and anyone, and do so anywhere with anyone. Freedom to petition and redress grievances enables people to ask questions, exchange answers and provoke answers.

The First Amendment, like any group of words, images, or events, is open for interpretation. These individual interpretations are based on information, the events and circumstances of the time. However there are also institutionalized tolerations which might influence individual interpretations. Misleading institutional beliefs might interfere with accurate interpretations of the First Amendment or any number of conditions. The First Amendment inarguably allows questioning of interpretations in the first place and enables them to be bettered.

Many interpret the First Amendment as protecting their rights to worship and gather as they please and as an assurance of the freedom of speech, but it is more than that. The First Amendment protects liberty and instructs patriotism. The First Amendment protects these rights, but also prescribes direction to patriotism in five stages. One might interpret there to be more or less rights described in the First Amendment. Interpretations may vary, but the intent is inarguable. The First Amendment describes, prescribes and defines patriotism.

The First Amendment presents five different rights that independently provide for liberty. Together they are interrelated and interconnected, prescribing patriotism's fine points. Patriotism secures liberty and the First Amendment exemplifies, clarifies and secures patriotism. The five stages are rarely enacted altogether separately. They are distinguished concepts that form together in varying concentrations. Each of these rights could stand alone, but like people together, they are more powerful combined. Patriotism has five stages, as presented in the First Amendment, practiced and put into law by the original patriots. The same formula is applicable now, as was applied at the big steep.

STAGE ONE: QUESTION

To question and persevere in seeking answers is what separates mankind from monkey-kind. Many other animals have opposable thumbs on their hands and feet. The difference between humans and animals is in the mind; curiosity and inventiveness set man apart. The ability to question and develop with answers defines humanity. Asking questions and persistence in seeking answers is a primordial trait and gift of people that makes five fingers useful.

No matter the individual or institution, if questions go unanswered, if questions are not promoted, there is suspect manipulation of information. It is the instinct of people unburdened by tolerations to question all things great and small. When obvious and subtle questions go unasked, the cause is likely acquired tolerations or manipulations.

Elitists and monopolistic institutions would prefer fewer relevant questions be asked. They perform to eliminate questioning. These performances are done flagrantly and delicately, noticed and unnoticed. Institutions obviously and subtly portray themselves as having all the answer act as if they don't require questioning.

It is not that children are curious and adults grow to lack curiosity; rather adults normally acquire tolerations to apathy. Adults also acquire tolerations to speaking lies. Adults speak more lies more easily than children because they have developed the ability to do so. People speak more lies, more frequently, more smoothly as they age and at the same time question actuality and the presentation of actuality less frequently.

"We must distinguish between speaking to deceive and being silent to be reserved." ~Voltaire

There is no prerequisite for asking questions. Intelligent questions require no degree or official title and neither do intelligent answers. Perhaps breath alone is the only requirement to question and hypothesize. Individuals do not need to be scholars or professionals to legitimately question conditions or situations in actuality. Some of the most profound and difficult questions arrive from children who have yet to master language and from apparent ignoramuses who know only the slightest of the subject in question. Some of the most brilliant and inventive people were not scholastic or official at all. Anyone can ask questions and hypothesize and everyone is entitled to answers.

One need not be in a position of authority in order to ask questions and provide answers. To ask questions and to seek answers is the right, and perhaps instinct, of everyone. Yet throughout recorded time, many oligarchical institutions have attempted to remove the right to ask questions. Questioning is the natural reaction of everyone over the age of two and the defined right that is fully utilized by few. Children instinctively ask "why?" again and again endlessly.

> "Question with boldness even the existence of a God; if there be one, he must more approve of the homage of reason, then that of blindfolded fear." ~Thomas Jefferson

The same question can be seen as mundane curiosity or outright rebellion. What is in the water? Where does meat, produce and tea come from? Are oil corporations in control? Does institution Y intersect with institution X in order to control A through Z? How are institutions financed? How are donations to various religious denominations spent? Are political families simply involved in politics? What is the difference between an RPG and an IED? Why? Why?

The point is to question. Question the questions, and question the answers. As long as you question every truth, lies can't reside. Question this story, but question their story as well. Question my individual interpretation, but also, more importantly, question institutions that spend fortunes on media, public relations, advertising and propaganda in creating or recreating their images.

> In 2000, Coca-Cola spent $1.7 billion on advertising. In 2004, Procter & Gamble spent $5.5 billion on advertising.

> FACT: Over 1 billion people have no access to safe drinking water. The UN estimates that 2 out of 3 people will not have access to water by 2025.

Please question this information as it may be wrong, after all, the information here has been filtered through institutions and then through me, an imperfect author. There may be information that could be expanded on, there may be typos or misprints in the book; there may be lies that were accepted as truths at the time of printing, and there may be truths that have changed, so question this. But more importantly, question those who claim they cannot be wrong and those who claim to have the complete truth. Above all, question those who seek blind, deaf and dumb allegiance, those who would have you believe that they have the truth and it does not change.

Question official institutional authorities that pretend they cannot be wrong or do wrong. Question those who claim that the truth is steady and right and wrong change. Question those who would openly enact wrong for something they claim is greater than right. Don't believe every fact or statistic, quote, or symbolic interpretation, but look into it for yourself. Question the interpretations and observations of others. Perhaps it is fair to suggest that the more institutions spend encouraging people to do, buy, or believe something the more they ought to be questioned.

I implore everyone to question the accuracy of the information I assembled, for I am individual and I have made mistakes before. There might be misnomers or misquotes for I don't know everything. The statistics change and possibly were inaccurate to begin with, interpreted by some machine, but I tried to keep numbers accurate, letters aligned and quotes straight. But I may have made mistakes in categorizing the information or ignorantly perpetuated some jive; however any mistake is likely inconsequential to the overall theory and practice as presented. Any mistake is irrelevant to the point; the First Amendment theorizes patriotic practice, practicing The First Amendment empowers individuals.

The truth may be disagreeable to established opinion, but the truth is always worthy of further exploration. Seeking and considering new information is the first requirement of a patriot. It was that search for truth that was done prior to the Boston Tea Party, and it is that search for truth that continues today. The Complete Patriot's Guide is admittedly incomplete; the subjects at hand, the truth, can only be expanded and improved on. Patriots question everything, even that which is deemed by institutional authority to be unquestionable and infallible. What is in the water your tea and coffee are steeped in?

> FACT: Water is the most abundant substance on the planet, yet only 2.5 percent of all the water on Earth is fresh water and most of that is frozen. Water is considered to be the main prerequisite to life. It is the only element on Earth that is found naturally in gas, liquid and solid.

Lacking questions allows transgressions. The lack of questioning permitted and enabled the invasion of Iraq. The U.S.A. House of Representatives were presented with manipulated and false information and investigations were left undone, questions unasked. There are countless hearts and minds who wish they questioned more, or at all. Many representatives themselves profess that they wish they questioned more as well. The official report was deemed unquestionable, and whoever did question it or the program for war, were themselves questioned or deemed unpatriotic. Practically no one questioned or read the Patriotic Act either. We might as well have had monkeys in office.

Installed as a solution, going to war was unquestioned. The war was based on information that was later found to be bullshit and advantageous to the agenda of a few institutionalized strangers. Who knows what their agendas were? But it is obvious and evident that invading Iraq was made to happen. The "Mission Accomplished" banner may well have been true. Perhaps the mission had been accomplished. Perhaps billions upon billions of missions were accomplished.

The information used to install the war was untrue, and yet was written and employed by official authorities, trusted institutional branches within the U.S.A. government. If reputable institutions within the U.S.A. government with resourced information can be wrong, any institution can be wrong. Also any unofficial individual may be correct, not automatically, but it is possible anyway. You can't trust institutions, at least not always, and you can trust individuals, at least sometimes.

Observe reality and question people's actual actions. Investigate and understand how people react to new information. By doing so, one can deduce people's intellect, interests and intentions. Do they question new information or do they refuse it? Do they avoid information altogether? Do they wonder what to do about it, or do they wonder what to do to avoid it? Do they pick and choose the information they consider? Do they prevent others from obtaining information? Do they wonder how to change wrong or do they wonder how to profit from it? Do they question from an open perspective in broad terms or as a narrow-minded, institutionalized individual?

Some people may become emotionally unpredictable when it is revealed that an institution that gained their empathy is guilty of reprehensible behavior. They be so institutionally focused they may have lost sight of others and don't want to hear them. Many people respect institutional characterizations more than real strangers they share the street with. Emotional confusion and acquired tolerations make it easier to accept believing an institution with a track record of lies over an individual. These people are true victims/enablers of societal Stockholm Syndrome, living in fear of darkness, dependent on dim light and imagery.

Perhaps the polar bears are not hunting each other to extinction. Perhaps people around the world are not sickened from a polluted and degraded environment. Perhaps continuous manufacturing of weapons is meant to deter their use. Perhaps building prisons is meant to scare away would-be criminals. Perhaps marijuana is illegal to protect people. Perhaps global slavery doesn't exist. Perhaps institutions are not interlinked in a trinity of monopoly.

There is information within this book that may be inaccurate, but don't assume as much, question it. Verify or deny through experience and confirmation, through other information. Many things outside the book may be incorrect as well, but find out for yourself. Don't take my word, but definitely don't take their word for it, don't believe institutions just because they are institutions. Question, or carry on. Question, or keep listening to institutions. They're glad to tell you what is happening, where you should go and how you should think.

The more you question, the more you know. The more you know, the less likely you will be taken for ride somewhere or held in your place; the less likely you will be manipulated or lied to. The more you know, the more you can see things as they are, for yourself. The more you know, the more questions you can answer yourself instead of singing someone else's song.

Practically no information presented within the Complete Patriot's Guide to Oligarchical Collectivism: Its Theory and Practice is cited. All facts, statistics, quotes and symbols discussed are from my own research and formulation. Barring certain references to prove a point, the information presented lacks sources. This is intended to inspire individuals to question for themselves. Is it new information one has never heard before? Question this, but question institutions that would have your opinion steered with part truths and officially sourced lies more.

Question all information, but especially question information from those who have power and influence. Instead of official institutional information and institutional truth, this is unofficial information, and unofficial truth. Which is more respectable or reliable? Which has more potential to be used adversely?

If there is debate on a subject, look it up yourself, at least for verification and possibly enhancement of contemplation. People have to ask the difficult questions in order to uncover the difficult answers and complex information. Who will ask, if not individuals? Do corporate media institutions answer your questions, or do they answer their questions?

Will national institutions ask your questions? Will banking institutions seek answers with you? Do think-tank investigative institutions answer your questions? Will religious institutions, perhaps, find the answers pertinent to you and the future of your children? Will your favorite corporation and their "Marlboro Man" help you find the answers? You have to ask.

Question the theory of the First Amendment. Perhaps there is a better way to decipher and use it. Perhaps the First Amendment defines actions other than patriotic procedure. Only you would know, only an individual can come up with that notion. Look into the statements of individuals and institutions. Look into the presentation and coordination of established authorities. Look into information provided by well-established institutions. If an individual, who happens to be the representative of an apparently courageous institution, or even the President, tells you something, question it. Often what is stated is different from what is meant, and what is meant is different than what is interpreted.

No matter what type of information is presented, complete or partial, rhetorical or factual, theoretical or practical, all information needs questioning in order to realize if it is reality or fiction. After being inaugurated to his second term as President, George II announced his Ownership Society Plan. The plan was to inspire economical responsibility and stimulate individual ownership. Years later, beginning in 2008, taxpayer money from the Federal Reserve rescued many failing financial institutions, while many homeowners lost their properties and many individuals lost their shirts.

> "I think every citizen - every citizen - has got the capacity to manage his or her own money."
> ~George II, 2005

> "We do not torture."
> ~George II

> "Read my lips - no - new - taxes."
> ~George I

> "I am not a crook."
> ~Richard M. Nixon

> "I did not have sexual relations with that woman, Miss Lewinsky. I never told anyone to lie, not a single time."
> ~Bill Clinton

In the world of elite power play, the black and white of illegal and illegal and right and wrong are contrasted and conned to benefit the few. Truth, lies, real, unreal, moral, immoral, legal and illegal are transposed and confused into the grey area. Presidents are not only capable of lying, but more than likely are coached professionals, capable if needed. Anyone is capable of lying, but when someone does it on behalf of an institution, the lie expands. The big lies are not merely dependent on the subject matter, but also on the size of the audience. An institution can lie about a little thing, but when it reaches a lot of people, it becomes a big lie.

You can't believe everything you see and hear, and you have to open up your eyes and ears. Question, research, learn and read. Tell other people information, and encourage them to challenge it and question it themselves. Read what authorities accomplish, as well as what they state. There are verifiable facts out there. One can explore for oneself. Ask questions. Read. Get multiple sources of information, read. Read because the truth is like an elegant meal, it is ninety percent ambience and presentation. Read and question in order to know what you are being served.

> "There are three kinds of lies: lies, damned lies and statistics."
> ~Attributed to many, including Mark Twain and Benjamin Disraeli

Mathematical statistics and calculations might be obviously and subtly distorted. Statistical interpretation of situations was first taken into account by empires in the 1600s. Goddfried Achenwall first termed the phrase statistic, meaning science of the state. Goddfried received financial support from King George III. Statistics was also called "political arithmetic" in its beginnings, but statistics sounds less diabolical I guess. It is not considered to be mathematics, but uses math.

Freedom is the freedom to say two plus two equals four, but it is also the freedom to question answers when the arithmetic is more complicated. Liberty allows for complicated mathematics that explores different questions. Freedom is the freedom to ask questions of institutional addition, if that is granted, all else follows. The more you know, the more prepared you are to put two and X together and come up with the answer. The more that is known, the less likely institutions will be successful in obscure and exploitative agendas when they present incomplete truth or damned lies. Question them when complex mathematics arrives at simple answers or simple mathematics answers complex questions.

The system of checks and balances, the very basis of the framework of U.S.A. government, exists to enable questions. It is the underlying concept, the very essence behind the design of the good old U.S.A. To question, to ask, to research, is the most fundamental and at the same time, special right that people have. To check and question new information, balances.

Justice is blind because she asks questions without bias. Justice refuses to see and hear irrelevant concepts so as to get the whole story, without the irrelevance of preconceptions or heresy. Justice investigates reality's entirety while refusing irrelevance. Justice temporarily holds secrets so as not to affect the outcome of a situation. The court system is designed to openly ask fair and relevant questions. One is innocent until proven guilty through thorough questioning. The three wise monkeys, on another layer, are wise only when their attributes are used temporarily as allegorically performed by Justice in refusing to observe or speak of irrelevance.

Question yourself and others. When one questions the interpretations and actions of oneself and others, it is easier to understand and control situations in one's surroundings, even violent situations. And if violence can be understood, it can be stopped, and when violence is ceased all else is granted. By simply questioning, one embarks on a journey.

> "Never open the door to a lesser evil, for other and greater ones invariably slink in after it."
> ~Balthasar Gracian

> "All that is necessary for evil to succeed is that good men do nothing."
> ~Edmund Burke

Many simple questions have been labeled dissent merely because the question threatened to get at the other side or underside of a situation within the status quo which would reveal institutional exploitation. Questions become dissent when they uncover, inquire or dissect institutional domination or distortion of information. Institutions seek to maintain aspects within the status quo, and sometimes institutions hold off change even if the change would better individuals and their surroundings.

All that is necessary for evil to succeed is that relevant questions are unasked. Questions actualize the noblest progress. Questions exist for answers, and answers lead to a better understanding of reality. If a question leads to information other than truth or incomplete truth, it is just more questionable information. If people do not seek the truth then what do they seek? And who will then seek the truth?

In the story of the Garden of Eden, Adam desired to know what everything in the garden tasted like. Adam questioned everything. Buddha sought to be enlightened and left the greatest palace in the world to find answers. To seek the truth is the most righteous and most primordial goal.

There are more than two sides to every story, to every question and every issue. When a situation is presented as having just two options, there is usually an amalgamation of both that makes more sense than either and often there is an alternative solution somewhere in the dark, unimagined or unperformed presently. There are many truths and many solutions outside the box, outside the light.

Options are rarely, if ever, limited to this or that. The timeless argument of nature or nurture is a prime example of a debate between two extremes with a mix making more sense. The argument of art imitating life or life imitating art is also another timeless example of two opposing ideas combined making a more sensible answer. Presenting only two options is limiting and likely as ridiculous as the question "What came first the chicken or the egg?"

The distinction between good and evil stays, while the truth sways. The truth is often an amalgamation of two presented extremes. The truth expands, morphs and evolves, but what is right is ever constant. Good and evil are forever distinct. The interpretation of right and wrong changes, yet the difference between the two is steady. The truth is sought while right and wrong remain the same. The complications of acquired tolerations, the consequences, conditions and confines of the petrolithic era and nuclear age, make the distinction of right and wrong shrouded. The truth is likely hidden by elitists and the partial truth is probably pumped by zealots and idiots who find it acceptable. And without the truth, properly understanding the distinction between right and wrong is jeopardized.

Right and wrong do not shift. Perceptions of right and wrong shift, likely through misinformation and burdened tolerations. Within the status quo, within pyramid system and oligarchical collectivism, wrong may seem right, but likely only because of lacking truths and falsifications. When stopped, it is easier to shed confusions, shrouds, tolerations and fears to gain truth through questions and contemplation. The distinction between right and wrong is clearer when such shackles are shaken off and reality is impartially explored.

It is not always the truth on one side only. It is not always the correct on one side and the incorrect on the other. Information and the truth arrives in layers. The truth is more layered and fluid than its polarized institutional presentation, and right and wrong are more static. Whenever there is a choice in society, there are always more than two options. Institutions attempt to control situations and present polarized and limited options. There is always another choice. Step one toward invention, prevention of exploitation, progression, is to question. The truth is forever sought, the distinction between right and wrong is forever.

STAGE TWO: COMMUNICATE

In order to communicate truly openly, it is important to accept all information and openly share all information to everyone. Be accepting to everyone, but do not just accept anything anyone tells you without questioning it and communicating its basis. Be skeptical of answers, but also be skeptical of skepticism. All is questionable. Do not refuse information as institutions often do, global institutions do not acknowledge certain information from certain sources. Individuals have the right and the instinct to accept and question information from all sources and communicate concerns with any to develop information or decry falsehood.

Biased information is abundant, yet this is not reason to castoff information before contemplation and communication; this is reason to acquire more information from more sources. It is as equally important to question confirmed information, as it is to question confirmed liars. Ignorance is excusable; acceptance of elitist lies is not. Question information and source it for yourself. Communicate your answers and their answers with others.

The ability to encourage, consider and disperse all information is a rarity among individuals and practically nonexistent among institutions. Individuals are capable of open communication, yet this ability is not always engaged. Institutions and the institutionalized normally restrict and limit the information they consider and deliver. Institutions do not accept all answers, even if the truth is therein.

All institutions, especially states, do not accept information from certain sources. They do not meet the particular institutional qualifications to be heard, seen and spoken of. Those that do not meet whatever requirements are ignored as if they were nonexistent. Institutions do not recognize new information unless it is from a source deemed acceptable, then they eat whatever is fed to them without asking what's in it. They negate some information, and lack consideration of information that they have accepted. Institutions are guilty of another contravention of communication, withholding information that they have accepted and may or may not have considered. Institutions are not capable of open communication. They always distort or withhold information predominantly to close parameters and not open them.

To question all information, to consider and discuss with others is not only a right, it is human nature. Communication is a primal instinct that has enabled man to fly and have light at night, we have to be institutionalized and trained to not communicate. To seek, consider and reveal information openly removes a cornerstone from the pyramid system. The fundamental structure of a pyramid is compartmentalized architecture, which is liberated by open exchange of information. Institutions and authorities withhold information to essentially divide and conquer, or at least divide and prefer that others do the same. Individuals can open their eyes, ears and mouth to observe and communicate about situations; institutions normally do not openly communicate. Equal dispersal of information and basic resources is a prerequisite to equality and liberty.

Let everyone know who is capable of understanding, because ideas are bettered through communication. Most media sources, it seems, function to distribute limited interpretations of reality rather than simple investigative reports of reality. Institutions prefer swift stories because the machine is constantly moving.

Most people enjoy exchanging information with others. No matter how alienated people are, they cannot be fooled when in possession of information and become less alienated with information. In the same way Capuchin monkeys tend to share food, people tend to share information. People desire open communication and when unburdened of institutional tolerations tend to share resources as well.

Imagine a General Electric owned media outlet, be it NBC, Disney or Time doing a story on GE's pollution of the Hudson River, or Housatonic River, or Saratoga County, Spokane County, Henderson County or Puerto Rico. Their story would probably be limited in scope, if presented at all.

Perhaps there is innocent ignorance to such stories of institutional interconnectedness. Perhaps the bias and lack of complete information is purposeful. Perhaps GE and others would like to present GE as an ignorant polluter of the early petrolithic era and nuclear age. GE would like people to believe they are innocent of wrongdoing, and not question how they have fought to avoid cleanup of, and compensation, for the messes leftover from their profits worldwide.

If there were only one source of information, as GE presumably would like it, then there would be less variation of ideas, less instigation of questions and little progression. The fewer sources of information, the less likely consequences and conditions will be properly considered. The larger the institution presenting information, the more likely their information is going to be distorted or misguided in some way by some confluence at their roots.

Open exchange of information is the best way to impart liberty for all. Allowing people to speak openly without repercussion is part of liberty. If they are wrong, tell them, if they are exploiting, defame them, by all means redress them. However, let them speak and expose themselves for how wrong they are, and then maybe more people will question them next time. The ability to communicate openly, without threat is the founding principle of the U.S.A. Threatening communication is unpatriotic and akin to Neanderthal reaction. Enabling the right to open communication is patriotic and moreover, human. If they are wrong, tell them, tell your peers, tell everyone, but let them communicate without threat.

Be wary when informing others of valid, but disputed or disagreeable information. Beware, because societal Stockholm Syndrome may cause some to react in a threatening manner to protect their captors/providers. Someone who becomes physically threatening will have no logical argument and will do whatever they believe it takes to defend their captors. They will attack the messenger instead of acknowledging and disputing the information. If information is sensitive in one way or another, they will attack syntax, accent or neck, but always disregard the message.

> "He who strikes the first blow confesses that he's lost the argument." ~Chinese proverb

Idiots are so passive that they actively seek to remain ignorant to maintain their passivity. They expend energy avoiding relevant information to maintain their perspective. They do this because they know that new information might lead to new conclusion, which would consume a tremendous amount of energy in changing perspective. They clench onto their perspective, but generally won't attack. Idiots run away from reality, or just sit there and shut their eyes.

Zealots are active. Instead of running away to eliminate new information, zealots may run towards to eliminate the messenger of new information. Zealots clench onto their status quo and might approach anyone counter to their belief system with bashing of character and body. Zealots charge ahead while deafening themselves to alternate information.

Elitists may react violently to new information, but generally not in public, not directly. Elitists withhold information. If one presents information that they would rather keep silent, elitists will try to silence. They counter opinion that goes against their interests. They use clandestine attacks to discredit those against their agenda and hold their tongue.

Idiots, zealots and elitists act to maintain the status quo, or their end of it. People are afraid of change, yet it is the only constant. The status quo cannot continue, in terms of resources, the status quo cannot continue without eventually coming to a dead end. Scared of change? Then cover your eyes, ears and mouth. Scared of being ignorant of change? Then question and communicate.

Idiots do everything in their power to steer clear of information and truth. Idiots decided that the truth is more horrible than ignoring it. They avoid new information because ignorance is steady and easy. Chocolate is tastier when one is certain that it was harvested by family farmers and not slaves. Thriving off of exploitation is easy if one is unaware of it. Drinking tainted water or milk is fine, if one is unaware of it.

> To each his sufferings: all are men,
> Condemned alike to groan,
> The tender for another's pain;
> The unfeeling for his own.
> Yet ah! Why should they know their fate?
> Since sorrow never comes too late,
> And happiness too swiftly flies.
> Thought would destroy their paradise.
> No more; where ignorance is bliss,
> 'Tis folly to be wise
> ~Thomas Gray, Poet, 1716-1771

In the petrolithic era and nuclear age ignorance may get you killed. To simply enjoy the beauty of one's surroundings was once completely satisfying and carefree. Today, one has to take care to be sure that the surrounding environment is not dangerously polluted and that the water is safe to drink or swim in.

Idiots refuse relevant information. Since they can't question openly, they cannot openly communicate either. Idiots would swim in a polluted river or live next to some sort of petrolithic or nuclear facility without seriously questioning why they are sick. Idiots would rather remain ignorant of surrounding toxins and exploits and do not have pertinent questions or answers concerning relevant actuality.

Zealots do everything in their power to defeat alternative ideas that expose their perspective as supportive of horrible conditions. Zealots are completely passionate about their river or opinion and refute consideration of actuality that may endanger the river or themselves, in order to maintain conditions. They are reactionary to ideas inconsistent with their belief system and potentially snap, on hearing or learning of actuality that differs from their beliefs. No matter the evidence or rationality in presentation, zealots may irrationally attack.

Zealots refute relevant information. Zealots will say and do anything in whatever voice they are accustomed to repeating; in whatever archetype they've adopted, in order to maintain perspective. Zealots look at new information, but only information corresponding to their preconceptions. Since they can't openly question information, they too cannot openly communicate.

Elitists provide nonsensical arguments that, if peeled apart, can be exposed for their irrationality and often elusive support of some institutional agenda. Elitists are highly skillful at coercing information to suit their opinion. They are capable of showing the right and slipping the wrong. At times they use the same information to present opposite arguments. Elitists are masters of information, dispersing or clenching it, depending on their agenda. Elitists do not ask their questions out loud, do not openly act or communicate.

Be wary, but let people know. As more people learn, the less spectacular or dangerous information becomes. Withholding information is dear to institutions and authorities, while equal dispersal of information is dear to individuals.

The sentiment of powerlessness often prevails when the status quo is exposed for its exploitations. "What can I do then?" is a reasonable question. A better question is "What do we do now?" How can we stand up to and get out of the intertwined institutionalized pyramid system? There is no need for an intricate plan. No drastic action is required. Sharing open and unbiased information may be enough to sway situations and unburden tolerations.

The best thing to do with relevant information is to share it openly. Once that information is available, new information is uncovered and developed. Truth can always be improved upon with more truth. The more questions are answered, the more knowledge is improved upon. The shaking caused by paradigms is slighted and made smooth when open dispersal of information is acceptable and practiced.

Tell everyone, even if they feel they are being told off. The truth may be insulting, but one need not be insulting simply because there is truth in the insult. Don't withhold relevant information, but don't accept every idea. Be accepting to everyone, but question everyone's delivery of information, not as insult, but as courtesy. Individual information is normally irrelevant information, and individuals can have secrets, as long as they are not manipulating and exploiting in the process, personal information and personal insult are irrelevant.

Questioning dismantles bad ideas, betters good ideas and finds the difference between the two. If, by being divided we are conquered, then by being united we are unconquerable. To be united, information and resources must be shared, and be openly available to all. Unity requires an understanding of others, to understand others question and communicate.

Only by functioning in alternative terms can one create an alternative to the pyramidal system, the status quo. To truly defy and alter the pyramid system, be alternative to it. Be peaceful and treat others as equal. Ask questions, question questions and relay answers for further questioning. Speak out to those lacking information no matter the resulting disturbance. By accepting everyone and telling everyone everything, the elitist viewpoint that only certain privileged persons should be in the know, is defeated. By sharing information one distributes power and equality.

By telling everyone everything, pyramidal slant is flattened. The pyramid system wreaks havoc upon fairness; it thrives off of separation, repression, and exploitation. Accepting people and openly providing information unites and eliminates problems derived from categorizing whole populations based on their location, heritage, origin, appearance, or some other conjuration. Understand how people think, according to how they react to information, instead of judging people on how they appear, where they live or who they are with.

> "We must not confuse dissent with disloyalty. When the loyal opposition dies, I think the soul of America dies with it." ~Edward R. Murrow, Reporter

Information is power. When whole and true information is openly exchanged, a whole and true point of view is better enabled and established. When the presentation of information is intentionally limited, it is in order to control certain situations by controlling perceptions. Patriotic communication openly and equally presents everyone with information and might be enough to coordinate what is right. Communication alone can indirectly and directly eliminate and defeat oligarchical collectivism.

Diplomacy is communication between national institutions. Institutions of state and war either accept information from other institutions or deny information presented from unallied institutions. This is just an example of how institutions have steeply slanted biases concerning what information they accept and distribute. Institutions deny the existence of actual nations that are real and perhaps equally established. Those who do not walk and talk mutual institutional lines are ignored.

Sometimes people repeat institutionalized political diatribe they heard from others. Perhaps one is able to see and hear that their opinion is based on an institutional perspectives and preconceptions. Instead of merely pointing that out, it is important to question their expressions. If one can notice manipulation in others it is possible to notice it in oneself and then, open and improve communication.

Those who believe differently are not necessarily unworthy of computing alternative information. Their different opinion is from different information. If you want people to listen to you, listen to them and question your own beliefs as well as theirs. Remind those of differing opinions that open dialogue is mutually empowering and will only lead to a better understanding for all.

Open exchange of information leads to more coherent observations and bettered inventions. Most opinions are just derivatives of what people have seen and heard before, not what they learned or deduced. With information, people may develop their own opinion, and invent better tools, but only through communicating questions and answers.

Opinion does not require critical thinking. Opinion often requires as little critical thinking as a tape recorder. Opinion is often generated by people who refuse what they see and refute what they hear so they don't have to speak about certain conditions. Opinion may be derived from hocus pocus and old, partial, misleading information and ideas.

Opinion does not necessarily derive from critical thinking; opinion may result from lack of critical thought. Many people's perspectives exist only because they've heard others voice such opinions and then they've adopted them. Often, opinion is based more on emotional information than factual and lacks critical thought entirely. If critical thought has not led to opinion, it still can. When people accept a more true and open discourse and debate, progression and evolution of information and opinion follows.

If people are less emotional and more critical, they are better able to develop and progress opinion and action. If idiots' fear was quelled, they might be more capable of critical thought. If zealots' zest was paused, they might form an opinion based out of critical thought. If elitists' greed was replaced, they might open their critical thinking. Question and communicate answers openly, simply and sharply if need be.

STAGE THREE: SPEAK OUT

They came first for the Communists, and I didn't speak up because I wasn't a Communist.
Then they came for the Jews, and I didn't speak up because I wasn't a Jew.
Then they came for the trade unionists, and I didn't speak up because I wasn't a trade unionist.
Then they came for the Catholics, and I didn't speak up because I was a Protestant.
Then they came for me, and by that time no one was left to speak up.
Martin Niemoller, Theologian

The open exchange of information and unbiased communication without repercussion is a higher function and coordination of people. Possession of information and a willingness to pass it to others exemplifies higher intellect, a developed and evolved mentality. Those who readily speak out to strangers are among the bravest. No other animal can present explanations, exclamations and proclamations. Only people have the ability speak out on behalf of themselves and others, and only the brave do so.

When you speak out, you introduce yourself as a voice, for you open up and speak in public and express your opinion. When you are otherwise a stranger, people only recognize you for what you express and nothing more. Often they might think you represent an agenda of sorts or an institution. Perhaps one's opinions are based out of an institutionalization of sorts. Realization of the institutionalization of oneself and others is more likely when you speak out.

Speaking out develops opinions, for speaking out publicly cries for response and discourse. Before speaking out prepare for debate. You will find there are many interpretations to what you say and many counterpoints that may not have been considered. The process of respectful open debate with anyone should be encouraged and the presentation of information, no matter how consequential or trifle, should never be met with consequences, unless it is elitist lies.

There are many means to speak out. Printing some form of literature or image using a press is the best example of speaking out, but not the only way. In the late 1700s, when the First Amendment was drafted, the printing press was the pinnacle of technological tools used by people to speak out. In the information age one's voice is amplified and enabled by the exponentially expanding ability to communicate and express ideas.

When speaking out, strangers are exposed to your point of view, often without saying anything. You may carry a sign to speak out. You may not have to say a word or carry a sign, but may speak out simply by stopping and being part of a gathering. Speaking out informs, as does communication, which disrupts the pyramid system. It may be information that people already know about, but they don't know you know too. They don't know how you think until you speak out. Speaking out is standing up and defying the majority and the empowered, if necessary, to place or better the truth.

Speaking out communicates, sometimes without words, to the public at large and institutions among them. Communication relays information, while speaking out shares answers to peers and strangers alike, for their own interpretation. A good communicator listens and develops ideas out of questions and answers. One who is good at speaking out has already developed ideas. Speaking out requires an understanding of actuality and a brave heart to face informed or ignorant opposition. Speaking out may take place among an audience that is too large to communicate with or an audience that won't communicate. To speak out, one has to stand up and inform others, often without the possibility of exchanging direct communication, but rather to stimulate overall communication.

People gathered to speak out or gathered to do nothing are as legitimate a group as any institution. It is perhaps more meaningful of an event that people come together to merely communicate and speak out on an idea instead of some institutional directive. Institutions have podiums protected by physical authority. Individuals need to grab moments to speak out when they can. Individuals normally have less access to the audience that institutions have and less protection from aggressive reactions. Individuals without podiums need to join together when speaking out, or yell.

Institutions respect and answer to individuals, but only when the numbers of the group are adequate. If there is a protest of five individuals who speak out, they probably will be ignored or vacated by authorities. If there is a protest of five hundred, they will probably get beat up or broken up and locked down by authorities, perhaps protests numbering five thousand would be similarly violated. But if there is a protest of fifty thousand or five hundred thousand, the authorities will allow the protest to take place. Attempts to neutralize the effectiveness of the protest may take place in one way or another, but they have to listen to large and persistent numbers. When enough individuals unify, they quantify institutional recognition.

Institutional branches are designed to hold back and break heads; the institutionalized who wield the nightsticks are trained to break it up. If institutionalized arms of authority are given legal reason or opportunity to enforce violently, they will. Opportunity sometimes arises from simply lacking numbers or someone crossing whatever arbitrary line is drawn. Institutional authorities want to stop protests, while protesters want to stop.

Numbers matter to institutions. Numbers measure people and money and numbers sway the interests of institutions. Institutions have no heart, but machines can count. A group who speak out on an issue as a unit can have real sway concerning the actions of institutions. By speaking as one, people together can instigate right among wrong.

Alone, one can speak loudly and some may hear. Together, people can speak softly and many will hear. Alone in the square random strangers will hear, together wherever the rigidly blind, deaf and silent become aware. There are times when a lone individual could yell a phrase that might be heard by many. But united people are always powerful.

Any voice stating a legitimate standpoint is powerful. One need not be a trained public speaker or institutional authority to speak out. Many politicians have been notoriously bad at public speaking. One lone voice is powerful. It does not matter if one is unaccompanied by institutional backing. It is not your accent or literacy that is important, or which institution supports the statement, it is what you say and how you think. George II was arguably one the worst presidents at public speaking, and it never stopped him from becoming a two-term President.

FACT: In the 2000 presidential election, many votes went uncounted including votes from

---

servicemen and women overseas. A disproportionate amount of black people's votes were also eliminated. Florida decided it would be too much trouble to do a proper recount.

"…you know what I'm talking about, some of ya…if you're running a nursery, you know what I'm talking about…if you got a chicken factory…a chicken pluckin' factory or whatever you call 'em, you know what I'm talkin' about." George II

Do not let your lisp, stuttering speech, misspelling, lack of colorful metaphor or anything else stop you from exclaiming the truth. Join together with others and don't say a word, only stand up and speak out. Scream it in the hallways or legislate it in office, just speak out. Write an article, start a magazine, stand up and speak out. You may stutter and utter only a half of one insight, you may speak or write nonsensical, incomplete sentences, and if only chicken-pluckers understand, at least someone made sense of what you're talking about. Next time you will be better at it as well.

The original patriots were well aware of the pyramid system the trinity of monopoly used. They gave power to the individual states, local governments and individuals for this reason. They separated the institutions of church, state and corporate to prevent their unification and oligarchical collectivism. They enabled freedom of information, for equal information levels the status quo. The trinity of liberty attempted to flatten the pyramid system and disconnect the trinity of monopoly, in part through allowing individuals to speak out. Whether downtown on a crate or in an institutional debate, speak out.

The trinity of liberty protects individual rights. Institutions have latched onto the rights of individuals and used them to promote their own interests, while many individuals do not use the rights prescribed to them. You have more rights than AT&T, Proctor & Gamble, GE and any other institution. They have more power, but they do not have heart. Individuals are alive, institutions are not. Institutions are tools.

Institutions can be everywhere, all the time, if the people are foolish or fooled. There are not enough of them to ignore all questions and voices. But there are enough of them to eliminate observations and prevent the circulation of questions. The status quo is too grand to be controlled with only force. But nothing is too massive to be controlled with information.

"It is true you may fool all of the people some of the time: you can even fool some of the people all of the time: but you can't fool all of the people all of the time." ~Abraham Lincoln

But they can try and try they do. If they can fool enough people sometimes, the fools can fool more by being fools. When people who aren't fooled speak out, they not only succeed in exerting possible influence over the fooled, they also show people who aren't fooled that there are others who were not fooled as well. The freedom of the press is the freedom to express and progress truth, and eliminate potential foolishness.

"There's an old saying in Tennessee, I know it's in Texas, probably in Tennessee. That's says fool me once… shame on… shame on you…eh fool me, can't get fooled again." ~George II

The saying is actually much older than the Republic of Texas. The Chinese proverb that the Exeter, Yale and Harvard educated George II so eloquently said or tried to say: Fool me once shame on you, fool me twice shame on me. Ironically, George II was speaking about Iraq and Saddam Hussein supposedly misleading the world concerning his possession of weapons of mass destruction. Who fooled whom? The People of the U.S.A. were told they were being fooled by Saddam, when actually people were fooled by the George II Administration into thinking they were fools. Only by not questioning do people become fools, idiots and zealots lied to by elitists. The world was told that intelligence had investigated and found factual information, and no one that had influence pertaining to the march to war questioned it.

If only someone in power or a quantifying group questioned, "Can we stop for a moment?" "Can we think about and debate this?" These are great starting questions. Only criminals and tyrants demand no debate and no questions. Only institutions propel continuation no matter the conditions that call for change.

Get involved in your local government. Petition and pester your representatives. Speak at government meetings. Run for office. Gather together and say something. Question the interconnectedness of institutions and extremely polarized presentations. Go to a meeting of intertwined institutions and toss over a table, scream, "Why?" Jesus would, Jesus did. Just make sure no one stubs a toe. Change things with your voice from the outside or inside.

There are not enough of them to be in every facet of every institution. In local government, you are given a forum and others have to listen. Sign up for local government and join other institutions to speak up from within. Change things by changing oneself. Join something or create something to join. Speak out from the inside as an individual. Sometimes it is effective to throw over the table, other times it is more efficient to sit at the table.

If circumstances are fair, pleasant and do not need change, then leave well enough alone. If subjects are questioned and not wrongful, then play on. However in the petrolithic era and nuclear age, the rarity of gold is eclipsed by the rarity of conditions that would not benefit from change.

If there is institutional intertwinement resulting in wrong, stand on a street corner and let people know, if you dare. One person can make a difference. One person's advice or assistance can make a difference. When you really need help, who do you need? One person, that's who. The power of one exists. Speak out from the outside, inside and wherever. Write editorials, the press is free to question and be questioned. Call them out on their interconnectedness and exclaim the institutional transgressions over individuals when observed.

In the great and free U.S.A., the downtown plaza is just as much a valid place to speak out as any political forum or office. Stop and speak, see what happens. You might teach someone something and you'll likely learn something as well. The U.S.A. is based on free speech and open questions. This provides that anyone be given forum, whether in official hallowed halls or green hills under trees and anywhere in between. People have the right to communicate and also to stand up and speak out, no matter the setting.

Demand that the hard copies of your votes be created and counted. Just the mere possibility that electronic voting machines could miscount or be tampered with should convince people of every county to question their exactness. Speak up, speak out or stay in line and shut up.

Do you like the tradeoff of the petrolithic era and nuclear age? The tradeoff is easy access to abundant energy, which results in war, pollution and reinforced oligarchical collectivism. Do you want nuclear waste in exchange for nuclear power? Do you want your government proclaiming that preemptive nuclear strikes are acceptable? If you let institutions speak for you, they will. If you do not express the need or desire by asking for it, most likely you won't get it. You better say something. You don't have wings, but you do have vocal chords. Maybe people weren't meant to fly, but we were certainly meant to speak up and speak out.

FACT: GE and Du Pont contributed to the U.S.A. Army Hanford Nuclear Reservation. The reservation supplied the material for the first A-bomb exploded in Alamogordo, New Mexico and the bomb dropped on the city of Nagasaki, Japan. The reservation polluted air, water, soil, plant and animal life in the surrounding area. During the 1940s and 50s, the plant released radioactive particles into the air carelessly and in experiments to see what would happen. In 1963, GE performed other experiments. These experiments were done on willing participants. The willing participants were inmates from nearby Walla Walla, Washington. They irradiated the testicles of prisoners to see what would happen to their reproductive system.

"All our lauded technological progress - our very civilization - is like an axe in the hands of a pathological criminal."
~Albert Einstein

Nuclear waste is already so abundant they can't safely get rid of it. Besides the usual release of radioactive materials from weapons tests, processing and reprocessing, power plants, satellites and submarines, more and more industries increasingly use radioactive materials for more and more diverse applications. Food and other products are irradiated by radioactive rays. Meat, meals, juices, fresh fruits and vegetables are sterilized using the irradiation process, euphemistically labeled cold pasteurization.

FACT: There are over 400 operating nuclear power plants in the world.
1,054: Number of nuclear test explosions conducted by U.S.A.

715: Number of nuclear test explosions conducted by Soviet Union.
210: Number of nuclear test explosions conducted by France.

"I am not only a pacifist but a militant pacifist. I am willing to fight for peace.
Nothing will end war unless people themselves refuse to go to war. " ~Albert Einstein

Nuclear bombs are exploded on the surface of the Earth and underneath waters and underground just to investigate their destructive power. Used radioactive waste is buried to be rid of its dangers. It has been launched into outer space and into gaseous Jupiter. All life on the planet was risked in the process of an acceleration technique called the slingshot. Definitely one and perhaps more than one satellite loaded with nuclear waste was launched around the moon to return to Earth where it was effectively slung into space through interaction with Earth's gravity on return. If the Soviet calculations were off, people might have experienced plutonium rain. They bury it, dilute it and shoot it into space, but there is already mounting, rotting nuclear waste. It is a permeating toxicity, an extreme hazard. Nuclear power is not clean energy, it is institutionalized and monopolized energy.

FACT: The Federal Energy Department planned to transport 77,000 tons of radioactive commercially spent fuel and high level defense waste from around the country, to Yucca Mountain 90 miles from Las Vegas.

Yuck, stay away from Yucca if that were to happen. What happens in Vegas isn't the only thing that stays around there. Until then the waste sits in spent fuel pools nearby the reactors. Don't let anyone call you a fool when you are providing information you know is true. Sometimes in an argument, varying and opposing sides might be partly correct. When the benefactor is the captor, it is easy to get the facts mixed up, confusion is not only possible, but likely. Many times people argue because they believe others are wrong, not because they know they are right.

If people have no counter to your argument and only insults, tell them as much and tell them to look up facts before arguing based on assumptions. If you have questioned your own bias and asked unbiased questions, then you can dissect and break down their argument as being form the point of view of an idiot, zealot or elitist. Then call them out on it, speak up and shut them down.

Imagine the insults that were thrown at the people who first said that some in the Catholic Church had been abusing children for decades, and that others were covering it up in a worldwide ring. Imagine suggesting the natural world is a globe, when it suits the authorities that it is flat. The human world is a pyramid.

People become furious when institutions they believe in, that they've put on a pedestal and blessed with their energy are found to be oppressors, our captors. It is a painful event to be relieved of Stockholm Syndrome, to come out of their light into the light, to realize that they always had a grip on you, but the door was always open.

If someone is lying, sing "God Bless America" or anything else to drown them out. That would be something if people wouldn't let liars speak, by singing! Imagine if one person started singing and then another and another while elitists attempt to spin lies. Liberty provides you the right to tell them to beat it, sail off into the sunset and shove their lies where the Sun don't shine. If they lie, if their opinions are grounded in incomplete information, then sing when they speak, yell when they lie and tell everybody why.

The truth may be excited or calm, but lies are always cool, calm and collected. Liars generally speak slowly and clearly to maintain their lies and steady their eyes. Truth can arrive in lecture, whisper, wink, drawl, slang, song, jokes, conversation, yells or screams, but information of any sort is far more readily acceptable when presented in a calm manner. If liars' lies are filling the area with false information, speak out. If their lies frustrate and anger you, yell angrily, sing angrily. Sing a song that others will join in, and the liars will have to do the same and pretend like they know the words.

"Nothing gives a person so much advantage over another as to remain always cool and unruffled under all circumstances." ~Thomas Jefferson

Liars package manipulated information in pleasing tones. People who hold and seek the truth do not care what they sound like. Liars comb their hair smooth and sleekly edit their speeches. People with the truth are excited, especially among liars, but the truth does not need to be cool or unruffled. Truth is energetic, especially when among lies. Holding the truth can make one extremely excited especially when newly seen by eyes largely accustomed to old lies.

Yell at them, sing at them, if you cannot remain calm, let it out. If the truth is inexplicable at the time, sing the national anthem. Sing alone or sing with others, say anything to dispel their lies. Speak, yell, sing anything to halt their lies, if only momentarily. Go by yourself if you have to, but better to speak or sing with others for singing in unison takes some measure of cooperation and spontaneous or preconceived cooperation frightens institutions which may make some representatives fumble their lies. Lone individuals and groups speaking influence institutions.

STAGE FOUR: STOP

"Any fool can make things bigger, more complex, and more violent. It takes a touch of genius - and a lot of courage - to move in the opposite direction." ~Albert Einstein

There are certain things people need, things people will continue to need always and every day. The most immediate concern is clean air; we need that every few seconds. Next we need clean water, every day. We steadily need food, shelter and clothing as well. For sanitation and sanity, we need an assortment of toiletries and amenities. People need those basics, and people need the companionship of others. Everything else is a luxury, a bonus, but clean air, water and access to the essentials is a constant need; the right of everyone breathing.

FACT: Proctor & Gamble raked in $68 billion in 2006. They make toothbrushes, toothpaste and toiletry supplies, and they use chemicals known to cause cancer in their cosmetics and other products. PETA reported appalling animal cruelty and circumstances practiced by Proctor & Gamble owned IAMS. Some of their factories in China are employed by temporary workers, who work 12+ hour days.

There is no reason that people ought to stop living comfortably. There is no reason people should stop having fun. There is no reason people should stop anything that is not wrong. There are plenty of good reasons to stop many things that don't appear wrong, but serve wrong within the pyramid. The wealthy who splurge, ought to think about what they need to live and what is obtained for status and other superfluous reasons. The poor, who go without food, ought to ponder why they go without the basics.

Needs and wants are different. All people need clean air, water, food and companionship; all people have a right to basics and liberty. Many people have tolerations to greed that makes them think they need a whole slew of other things. Many people want things because they have been mediated to want them.

What is most important in life? If there is clean air and water, if there is adequate food and resources, all else is granted. Any myriad of interests are possible and acceptable when provisions, companionship and liberty are available. If simple requirements are not met, questions are necessary or tolerations ensue.

If simple requirements are eliminated or restricted by conditions, the conditions must be ceased. Drastic efforts must be made in securing fundamental resources. If certain practices must be ceased in order to obtain clean air and water, in order to cease exploitation, then que sera, sera. Stop, or continue and get drunk, and try to stop thinking about it or thinking at all.

FACT: Adolph Coors, born in 1847, founded Coors Brewing Company in 1873. It remains family owned and operates the world's largest, single brewery in Golden, Colorado. During prohibition Coors began manufacturing porcelain ceramics and brewing malted milk. After prohibition, milk was out, beer was back. The ceramics company continued and became CoorsTek. CoorsTek manufactures industrial ceramics. Coors ceramics were used in the first atomic bombs developed at Oak Ridge. Joseph Coors, Adolph's grandson, attended Cornell University and was a member of a secret society there, The Quill and Dagger. Coors generously donated money to many institutions including the Hoover Institution and American Defense Institute. Coors put up $250,000 of beer money to found the Heritage Foundation. In 1990, Coors was fined $650,000 for pollution violations and in 1993 they were fined another $1,000,000.

FACT: The Heritage Foundation is a public policy research institute based in Washington DC with offices abroad. Among their mission goals are to promote the American way and defense. Since the original stake from Coors, the Heritage Foundation has received many big checks from Amway, Exxon/Mobil, Proctor & Gamble, Pfizer, South Korea, Lockheed Martin, GlaxoSmithKline, Microsoft and many private individuals.

It is quite easy to make one's own beer and wine. It requires no stirring, only time Within the petrolithic era and nuclear age even a simple beer is simple no more. Don't stop drinking. If you must drink, stop buying, make it yourself or with peers, or know from what you are buying it from.

Don't stop eating food of course, rather start growing it, trading growers for it, and source your food closer to home. Don't stop eating, but you have the ability to eat differently. Diverse nutrients are available locally, or could be.

It is possible to stop eating temporarily; no panic should ensue if one misses a meal. Gandhi fasted frequently for health and as a form of protest. The longest fast in protest is attributed to Terence Macswiney, 74 days to death. Terrence was an Irish writer and politician arrested by the British Government on charges of sedition in 1920. He immediately began a hunger strike protesting his internment and trial before a military court. Terrence died in Brixton Prison.

People routinely fast for various reasons. Other people routinely go without food all over the world, this is not fasting. A fast is a temporary pause, hunger is constant desperation through malnutrition.

As a youth, Prince Siddhartha enjoyed the indulgent life of pleasure in the king's palace. Later, he

renounced worldly life and became an ascetic; he experienced the hardship of torturing his mind and body. Finally, not long before attaining enlightenment, he realized the fruitlessness of these two extreme ways of life. He realized the way to happiness and enlightenment was to lead a life that avoids these extremes. He described this life as the middle path. These three ways of life may be compared to strings of different tensions on a lute. The loose string, which is like a life of indulgence, produces a poor sound when struck. The overly tight string, which is like a life of extreme asceticism similarly produces a poor sound when struck and is moreover likely to break at any moment. Only the middle string which is neither too loose nor too tight, and is like the middle path, produces a pleasant and harmonious sound when struck.
~Story of Buddha

Stop, observe the elements. Find out who is pulling the strings and contemplate their rigidity. Don't stop everything, just tighten the strings or loosen them, whichever is needed. Wrongdoing occurs during extremes. This was an important concept in the Story of Buddha and continues to be important today as well. Stop and relax, think. You, acting in unison with other people, can change the world by reducing your consumption, or stopping completely, if only briefly. You, acting in unison with others, can change the way institutions function. Cease institutional support for a day, stop something for a week, stop one thing or another for a year. Stop, for stopping is the best way to start something new.

If corporations think of you as a consumer, power rests in your spending habits. To the machine, simply stopping is a powerful act. Stop spending and stop fueling. The machine is fireproof and bulletproof, but needs constant and maintenance to continue.

The best things in life are free, and that which is priceless you can't buy. Family, friends, peers and potential new friends are priceless. Moments and time are priceless. Fresh air and fresh water are priceless. Institutions and machines on the other hand are lifeless. So stop in order to enjoy life and break the machine.

Stopping completely is absurd and impossible. To cease all actions that support exploitative institutions is reasonable and possible. Cease wrongdoing simply because it is the right thing to do. Stop simply to end one wrong or another. Stopping allows change, continuation is just that.

To stop specific actions completely is not absurd when to continue manifests such hazards. It is a difficult notion to accept and a difficult action to perform, because it is not among the building blocks of the status quo, not within the pyramid system. Next to other solutions, revolutions and actions, stopping wrong is massively easier and exponentially more effective. It is cheap as well, with potential for extraordinary, even lucrative results for stopping allows starting. To stop is not within the confines of the status quo, stopping is an alternative to the status quo, stopping is outside the box. Stopping influences institutions because they are machines that require people's continuous support. To cease allows the facilitation of alternatives, it does not mean the end. Stopping activities and endeavors, is decried by some as rebellious and un-American, in fact it is righteous and un-institutional.

If a loose group of individuals called a boycott of new automobiles, idiots, zealots and especially elitists, would snarl at the threat to the economy. Yet who can argue with stopping what is wrong? Is stopping not the best way to start? Is the continuation of one form of economic growth more important than clean air and water? Those who demand no one stop wrong show themselves as wrong and dependent on it.

Institutions put massive amounts of energy into all sorts of functions, many of which have enormously negative consequences. Institutions insist on continuation regardless of negative outcome. Who will argue stopping what is wrong despite the consequences? Who will argue discontinuing riding in the shiny status quo with rotting underbelly? Those who feed off it, that's who.

The petrolithic era and nuclear age contains conflicts, consequences, conditions that confine existence. The petrolithic era and nuclear age is a con; we've been conned and fleeced of air and water and for convenient temporal comforts. Cooperation with our natural surroundings and sustainability has yielded to mechanization and institutionalization. Coexistence between people, places and things is possible, but less likely the more rigid surrounding institutions.

"Now we put our minds together to see what kind of world we can create for the seventh generation yet unborn."
~Iroquois Great Law of Peace

FACT: The Mohawk Nation was part of the original Iroquois Confederation. They have a prophecy, which is shared by many native nations. It is the prophecy of the seven generations. It states that seven generations after the arrival of Europeans to the Americas, people would see the elm trees die. Animals would be born deformed, without proper limbs. The rivers would burn, and the air would burn the eyes of men. Fish would die in the water and birds would fall from the sky.

FACT: Through 2006 - 2008 inexplicable die-offs of birds all over the world occurred. Birds literally fell from the sky. In 2009, Pelicans along the entire West Coast began dying, breeding adults fell from flight.

The Iroquois Great Law has been orally passed down from one generation to the next for centuries and is also recorded on belts kept in the Onondaga Nation. There are three main principles in the Iroquois Great Law, the first component in the Iroquois tradition is righteousness. Everyone should be treated as equals and share with others, and there are certain acts that will always be wrong and most everyone instinctively knows what wrongdoing is. The second component is healthy reason and the third is power. All three components require thorough investigation and explanation of surrounding information for accurate interpretation.

The Iroquois principles are concentrated on seeking harmony instead of hostility, and providing availability instead of acting restrictively. The Great Law concentrates on general principles rather than rigid specifics. The principles are based on expanding peace, eliminating war, distinguishing conditions that lead to peace or war and realizing what might be eliminated to decrease negativity. The Iroquois principles are symbolically represented in The Great Tree of Peace, the white pine tree is depicted as having four roots and an eagle perched atop. The four roots symbolize peace growing in all four directions, for if peace does not expand, it erodes.

It is always possible to stop the machine. What will take place when the machine stops is unknown, but we do know the actuality of its continuation, the conditions and consequences of the petrolithic era and nuclear age are apparent. We know what takes place when the machine is on. To understand the future is extraordinary, to understand the present merely requires open observations of actual and conceptual horizons.

Individuals are always capable of standing up to institutions, no matter how few march with them or against them. Many are convinced via fear that they cannot, but all people are able to stand up to institutions and cease serving machines. No matter the powers authorities may display, people are always able to stand up to authority. There is no institution that people cannot stop by standing together righteously and reasonably. There is no institution that can force people to continue, as well, there is nothing some institutions won't do to stop individuals from standing up to them and stopping wrong.

In June 1989, there were protests throughout all of China. The protests were countrywide, but were centered in Tiananmen Square, Beijing, one of the largest public spaces in the world. People gathered to peacefully protest and soldiers aggressively converged on students and citizens. Fighting amongst the armed soldiers and angry civilians ensued. The timeless archetypal story of unarmed local oppressed peoples gathering together to be confronted by armed soldiers began again. The scene might have been St. Petersburg, 1905.

Possibly thousands were killed in Beijing, definitely hundreds. Many more were injured, the exact numbers are unknown. What is known is that the protest and unrest was a bloodbath. People were confronted with the people's armed forces. People expressed themselves by communicating, speaking up, and gathering together to stop the status quo. They were confronted by the guns and boots of their own regimented armed forces. Soldiers shot at civilians.

Tanks eventually arrived on the scene to secure the area. On the morning of June 5, a column of tanks began a procession around Tiananmen Square. One lone individual stepped in front of the lead tank and stopped. He just stood there, preventing the parade of tanks and the show of force. He stopped while carrying an apparent bag of groceries and a book bag. The column of tanks all stopped and some turned off their engines. He climbed onto the tank and yelled at the driver. Eventually, he was taken away by people who are theorized to be police. The unknown rebel was never to be seen or heard from again. The predominant theory is that he was executed.

Take a stand, stop. Stop, if only for a few minutes like tank-man or days and weeks like the original patriots, Gandhi and so many countless others. Keep in mind that tanks are likely to run you over if you step in front of them, but there are infinite ways to diminish the power of machinery, even tanks.

You don't have to stand up to take a stand. Rosa Parks was by no means physically helpless; but she was a small woman armed only with conviction and intention. Stopping and peaceful refusal to participate contains the greatest power for change. It diffuses the biggest institutional machines and the most complicated exploitations.

Rosa sat down, she stopped, and she discontinued a mandated, official exploitation and wrongdoing. She was the catalyst for the people who knew the institutional situation was wrong. She is a hero because she enacted the power of one, one person stopping. She deciphered the wrong present and stood up to the supportive authorities. Most everyone, besides racist zealots, agreed; there should be no race based classism. The people ceased participation in exploitation and change ensued.

252

Stop participating in the institutional exploits. The provider is the captor, and there is a way out of the cave. It is difficult to imagine ceasing dependence on oil because it delivers everything in our daily life. It can be difficult to imagine, but there are other ways. There is plenty more petrolithic and nuclear fuels available, they are just more complex to extract, process and deal with. Mined and refined elements are plenty, but their use comes with a hefty environmental burden. There are numerous ways to obtain energy; it's just that they perpetually serve individuals, and not institutions. There is clean, constant, renewable energy available, but such unlimited energy does not serve elite institutions.

A patriot's primary concern is to cease wrongdoing, not to know what to do after wrong is ceased. The primary concern of patriots is to understand actuality and cease wrongdoing. No one can predict the future in absolutes; we can only know the present, and then hardly absolutely. Patriots seek to understand the actuality of the present, not predict the possibility of the future.

Patriots might plan for the future, but might also act in spontaneity. Whatever the turbulence in the aftermath of change is not a concern for patriots, stopping wrong is. It is the righteous right to cease and stop wrongdoing. If enough wrongdoing is stopped, right alternatives are better conceptualized and actualized.

It is a lofty goal to reduce oil consumption and nuclear waste production and institutions have no idea how to develop such reduction. When institutions don't know how to proceed, they don't know how to proceed in a direction that won't jeopardize their control within the status quo. There are many different ways to go about things outside the box, outside the cave. Institutions and the institutionalized don't know how to proceed outside the pyramid system that serves them.

SOLAR ELECTRIC
Jimmy Carter installed solar panels on the White House, Ronald Reagan removed them.
The Earth receives more energy from the Sun in one hour than the whole world uses in one year.
Documented speed record for electric vehicle: 245 mph.
Documented distance record for electric vehicle: 478 miles in a delivery van.
Uses no water comparable to coal, nuclear, and natural gas energy cycles that use and destroy massive amounts of water.

Solar power could free the world from permanent reliance on institutional delivery of energy. Solar power is not expensive, it is free. Combined with renewable wind power, geothermal power and hydroelectricity from current and waves too, there would be no concern for energy resources. There are numerous sources of natural and perpetual energy, it is here, occurring now all around. It is only a matter of tapping into it. Hemp could also be grown as a complete alternative for energy and industry oil. Wind, wave and solar energy are constant and clean sources of energy.

There are many sources of energy that are more sensible for the individual than petrol. There are many sources of energy available that would provide equal power to people with fewer complications than petrol. However, there are not many forms of energy that would provide equal power to institutions with as many compliments.

Sometimes the wrong prevents us from seeing the right way, as if smoke settled on the scene. Humanity could have free energy for most means and ends that would be relatively pollutant free. It would cost billions, but what is the cost of petrolithic era and nuclear age?

FACT: Peabody Coal Corporation is the world's largest private coal supplier. The corporation extracts billions of dollars of coal from the Arizona desert and other locations around the U.S.A. This same land could produce massive amounts of solar energy and not be left bereft of clean water, and near useless in the process. The only slurry line in the U.S.A. is a billion dollar Bechtel project. The slurry line floats and transports coal 273 miles with precious desert groundwater.

Individuals operate within the pyramid system among the mechanization that benefits some and degrades many. Free and renewable energy is a great idea for people, but not for the institutions and not for the status quo. Free energy is not conducive to elite control, free energy sheds dependence on institutions.

FACT: Declining air quality and reduced visibility in the remote Grand Canyon is deduced to be anthropogenic. The haze is manmade pollutants and particles in the air. Santiago, Chile is in a valley surrounded by mountains.

Because of this, it sits shrouded in its own thick smog and pollution. The geography and problems are similar in Los Angeles, California, Cairo, Egypt and Beijing, China. Egyptian pyramids, Aztec pyramids, and ancient sites elsewhere, that survived thousands of years, are now being eaten away by acid rain and pollutants in the air.

Petrol and nuclear are foul, while solar is clean. Which do you want? Solar power is possible even on foggy coastlines and in overcast climates. In space, the mechanical satellites in orbit are powered by rechargeable batteries and solar panels, though many nuclear reactors were sent into orbit as well. People have the power to harvest energy without negative consequences. The result of humanity's unbalanced energy consumption is global environmental destruction.

The wars in Iraq and Afghanistan since shock and awe until beginning of 2007: One half of one trillion dollars, $500,000,000,000. What does oil cost? The price may remain cheap, the resulting octane may be cost effective to business, but the total environmental costs are unconceivable. Petrol and its accompaniments may be immediately cheap, but burning and morphing it globally has global consequences. What does oil earn?

What does war cost? Millions of lives and trillions of dollars is a starting estimate. War costs a lot of money, but someone is getting paid. Cost corresponds with profit. What does war earn? Institutions are founded and funded with war. Wars cost the people who fight them and the people living among the fight. War costs limbs and dreams and war earns for elitists, corporate cabals and other institutions. War costs liberty, locals and land. War pays institutions.

"What is more immoral than war?" ~Marquis de Sade

The complications of the petrolithic era and nuclear age physically tax individuals through environmental pollution and exploitative situations. The U.S.A. could put an army in the southwest to build viable solar energy stations with less complications and financial cost than war. However, doing so would be costly to the architecture of the status quo, complicating institutional control. Institutions need people to act on their behalf for simple maintenance, stopping threatens machines because then one can start anew.

In 1943, after the attack on Pearl Harbor and during WWII, the U.S.A. Army Corps of Engineers built a road over fifteen hundred miles long through virgin forest and over unknown mountains and terrain. Eleven thousand troops built the road to Alaska through unmapped territory. An army or the Army could easily build a solar facility the size of Death Valley instead of bringing death to valleys. There is nothing too complicated to accomplish, for war is commonplace and there is nothing more complicated than war.

Why have people in the U.S.A. stopped seeking independence? People sacrifice all that is right to proceed with initiating institutional interdependence and yet, actual independence is avoided. Are people more likely to march for dependence and war or toward independence and peace?

When one pays, another earns. The Federal Reserve has been pulling money out of thin air for decades to fund all sorts of mischievous miscellanies. Why not pull some cash out of whatever hole they get it from to construct a solar panel project in a desert, a desert where no one resides?

The controllers capture and captivate, yet provide and protect as well. They are both benevolent and malevolent. It is difficult to imagine alternatives because every day they say they have the way. They feed you, but it makes you sick. They clothe you and hold you.

Institutions do not want free energy; this would remove a cornerstone in the pyramid system. By being independent, they would lose power, because free energy provides independence. Humanity could have had limitless, free energy a long time ago, but institutions prefer to maintain the status quo. Why provide something for free when they can get paid for it?

Automobiles use a large amount of petrol and correspondingly source a large amount of pollution, cars mostly driven in individual pursuits. Pollution is embedded into glacial ice as far and removed from man as can be. Individuals and institutions are negatively altering the planet with cancerous pollutants. Such degradation of the environment furthers dependence on institutions.

Perhaps global warming is just a passing phase, but the toxicity is verifiable and can be diluted no more. The high and mighty seas can no longer disperse man's wake of pollution, the wide skies and winds can no longer blow it away, just around. The fault lies with us all, but certainly institutions, the trinity of monopoly, hold more responsibility than individuals. People are subject to the institutions if they do not stand up, and institutions are subject to people when people do stand up.

Stop pollution because it is toxic. Stop buying their pollutants because they are included in your food and coursing through the veins. Not only does responsibility lie with us all, but toxins lie within us all as well. Waiting for proof that toxins are causing dramatic climate change is stupid when we know the toxins cause illness.

The next time someone says that the current cold called winter disproves global climate change and global warming explain the poo allegory. If there is large pool with two chunks of ice in the pool (like Earth's ice capped poles) the ice will melt at a certain rate depending on the overall temperature of the pool. If it becomes warmer the ice will melt quicker, releasing more cold water into the pool thereby cooling the overall temperature of the pool.

> FACT: Thousands of new chemicals are being manufactured and released into the environment. Many species subjected to industrial chemicals experience a feminization due to increases in certain hormones. The chemicals have feminized fish, birds, reptiles and insects. Scientists report that the unchecked release of chemicals poses a serious threat to future wildlife in certain areas.

> FACT: Milk from all mammals contains essential nutrients and enzymes for growth and the lifelong health of offspring. On top of the essentials mother's milk contains persistent poisons including DDT, PCBs and a wide assortment of other varying chemicals and harmful minerals now in the environment. During the natal period, bioaccumulative toxins, poisons and pollution gathered over lifetime are released through mother's milk.

Welcome to the petrolithic era and nuclear age where we are all taxed by environmental degradation and destruction. Individuals experience while institutions do not drink or breathe and therefore do not measure the purity of air and water or feel. Remnants in the water or poison in breast milk are incalculable to institutional agendas.

Is physically taxing pollution not reason enough to stop? Many of the chemicals in breast milk and blood did not exist prior to the petrolithic era and nuclear age; their long term effects are unknown. Is it not a crime to perpetuate pollution for profit? It is seemingly impossible to stop supporting the energy and oil corporations, but it is possible to slow down. And it is possible to use well-founded, currently subjugated, alternatives. It is impossible to exit the environment, but it is possible and occasionally practical to leave institutions.

Gasoline is required for nearly everything, however there are alternatives. Earthen oils power manufacturing, the delivery of goods and peoples' commutes. It may seem there is no other way. Just stop and take a moment to think, for yourself. There are always other ways. Quit and get another job that is not so far away or move to your employment. Do the math. Is it worth it? You could walk or bike there. They built a road to Alaska. They went to war in (insert location here). Lewis & Clark walked over eight thousand miles.

If you invest in oil, stop. If you work for a nuclear plant, quit. If they do not have the people's support, they will attempt to develop it. There are other ways to harness energy, other ways worthy of support. If idiots, zealots and elitists are blind, deaf, dumb and close-lipped concerning conditions of the environment, we are all abandoned.

Under institutions, people become shells of their former selves. People act as the institution when they don a uniform. Those inside institutions normally will not notice the rattling and destruction that the institution makes, just as being on the streets makes it difficult to see the cityscape.

When institutions begin to hinder more than help, they are removed or remade, but the actuality of institutional performance matters less, relative to what people believe about the performance. When institutions no longer serve a purpose or worse, people leave. When people leave, institutions transform into new tools. Walk out of institutions that exploit and pollute reality.

Institutions are not individuals, but they are made of and dependent on people, even, perhaps you. Doing the right thing is difficult, but it starts with stopping that which is wrong. When wrong continues, it buries and blights the right, but as soon as wrongdoing ceases, what is right may blossom like spring flowers after a deluge.

Don't sign up for war, defend by all means, but walk out of institutions that profit from, and conduct war. Stop the violence. There are other ways to support and defend your country, your people and your ideals. There are other ways to take out your aggression. There are other ways to build character. There are other ways to see the world. There are other ways to make money. Ask a veteran or enlisted soldier. Ask a recruiter too, just know their perspective.

At worst, you will be dismembered or killed, used for a stranger's agenda. There are other ways. War is war. Sign up for the military if it suits you, but build a road, don't bomb people on roads. Refuse to kill at the will of institutions no matter if they are stately or claim to represent God.

Stop supporting those that market war. If you invest in war, move your money into socially responsible funds instead or better yet, remove it and invest it locally. Stop not to end, but to begin. Stop to start, instead of clinging onto someone else's pyramidal construct.

Don't work for a weapons manufacturer. War is perpetuated by those who think it's going to happen and invest in it.

Support something other than the war machine. Support an individual's cause if right, and stop supporting the exploitative agendas of institutions if they are wrong.

To stop wrong altogether, all at once, is next to impossible. Yet, it is not impossible. It is next to impossible to invade and occupy foreign nations, but it is done. Is it madder to invade and war or to stop and cease supporting institutions that conduct war? Which is insane: continuation or conclusion?

Minimize. Stop your support for wrongdoers one at a time if need be. If you can't stop altogether, cut down. Do you really need that new cell phone?

Try water over soda. Gather your own herbal tea. Question institutional operation, and then deny their exploitative goods and services. Find ways to become more independent.

Try to buy locally for a month. See if it is possible in your area to live on locally grown and produced food. You will be supporting your close neighbors, and you might learn something. Try to consume food from a one hundred mile radius or more if need be.

Act locally and think globally, but think localization. Buy goods from China and elsewhere, but buy local crafts and not globalized crap. Try to buy local, organic and/or certified fair-trade products. People the world over depend on trade. Not all manufacturing and agriculture is ruinous to the rivers and repressive to people. If institutions are exploitative and if questions go unanswered, cease support. You have the choice to stick with their products and systems or leave them behind.

If a stranger in China is being screwed for your new cell phone, shirt or shoes, are the products still satisfying? Sometimes people have the information and resources that allow for protests and progression, other times outsiders may have the capacity to stand up for others. When the trinity of monopoly link, they restrict information and/or resources to prevent people from gathering.

FACT: On May 1, 1886, workers protested for rights and fair treatment in the U.S.A. As many as 80,000 people participated in Chicago. Similar subsequent strikes were carried out all over the U.S.A. for the eight hour work day. Around 350,000 people across the U.S.A. participated in the general strike that went on for days. On May 3, Chicago police opened fire on protesters, killing four. On May 4, the protests continued. In Haymarket Square, Chicago, tensions peaked when police ordered the protesters to disperse. A bomb was thrown at the officers, they retaliated, firing indiscriminately, killing four protesters and six fellow officers and wounding an unknown number of individuals. Without evidence, in an unfair trial, seven men were convicted of being involved in the bombing.

The bomb tossed on May 4, 1886, was thrown by an unknown individual, but on November 11, 1887, four men were hung. The night before the execution a fifth killed himself with dynamite, implicated in building the bomb and helping the bomber. Years later, in 1893, the Governor of Illinois pardoned others who remained in prison and stated that the jury was essentially rigged and the hanged men were victims of hysteria. Many unions and companies began adopting the eight hour work day and many laws were subsequently passed improving labor conditions. Yet only in 1938, was the eight hour work day entirely implemented with the Fair Labor Standards Act.

"Gentlemen of the jury, convict these men, make an example of them, hang them and you save our institutions, our society." ~Julius Grinnell, Chicago Prosecutor

---

There are many lessons to be learned from the 1886 protests. If you're an officer of the law, don't use force to break up the gatherings because more protesters will come. If you shoot gathered people, you might kill them and fellow officers. Killing loses the moral authority and will eliminate support one may have had and gather more for opposition. Society changes, and then institutions.

If you are a protester don't bring a bomb or any other means of violence to the protest, eliminate the possibility of violence. When machines for violence go unused and self-defense is prepared and done solely with the self, moral authority is kept and the cause expands. Be ready for violence though, because authorities are often assembled solely to use their boots and sticks. The legitimate authorities will wield their power along with illegitimate powers as well. If peace is met repeatedly with violence, there are always options other than fighting and fleeing. And there are always many ways to fight and many ways to flee.

If you have a message, do not shoot people or explode people. No message gets through murder. Violence perpetuates stagnancy and more violence. Why are wars fought? Peace and nonviolence, is in itself, a statement and promotes messages. Peaceful protests and stopping may be the most powerful form of individual resistance to oligarchical collectivism, while violence and war are the oldest institutional tools to maintain it. Complicated machines do not require active dismantling to stop; they might just be left alone.

When institutions want to prevent a movement from succeeding, the individuals are labeled violent. Sometimes this takes place in complicated plots that implicate the peaceful. Sometimes it is done by committing violence on them and then presenting their self-defense as attack. If they can turn peace into violence, they will. Institutions use violence in one way or another in order to elevate their position. Some historians speculate that the person who threw the bomb was an agent provocateur possibly working for steel corporations that had a lot to lose if workers gained rights. Like the majority of history, there are known unknowns in the story.

> FACT: The Industrious Workers of the World (IWW) was founded in Chicago, 1905. Their motto: An injury to one is an injury to us all. The organization was met by violence and repression around the U.S.A.

That sums up the perspective of the IWW. The IWW is a union of unlimited solidarity. If the workers who manufacture plastic widgets for cell phones are being taken advantage of, they protest and strike. The folks who make the buttons strike too, as do the people selling groceries and those making coffee. Those connected and those totally unconnected all strike. All down the line everyone involved and uninvolved strikes, assuring that your cell phone is made by people who are being treated fairly. At one time, the IWW numbered approximately one-hundred-thousand members. Today there are only a few thousand.

People assembled together are always powerful. Political protests and gatherings are made up of people from the pressurized levels reacting to and rebelling against continuation of manipulation via those in the upper levels. When many people on one row protest and stop, change may occur, starting is enabled by stopping. If a small portion protests or stops, it goes unnoticed to the rest of the pyramid's architecture. Only when a significant portion of a row, or small parts of many rows remove themselves is change instigated and the pyramid shook.

All problems, as small as land disputes and overdevelopment, or as great as global environmental destruction, can be solved by first stopping. Stopping is the most powerful and sure act amid the constant calamitous status quo. There is no reason to stop completely and permanently, just momentarily. Ending allows beginning, socially and environmentally. The simple act of discontinuance is nearly impenetrable to agent provocateurs as well.

> FACT: Highly polluted and disputed parcels of land, partitioned and abandoned, have become havens for wildlife. Simply by stopping, the area around the Chernobyl nuclear accident is booming with life, despite suffering from the effects of radiation, life is thriving. Simply by leaving them alone, the borderlands between the Koreas and between India and Pakistan have become practical wildlife refuges.

Pause, reflect and cease support and maintenance of environmental destruction, stop layering petrolithic residue and nuclear dust on the only suitable rock around. Stop support of steeply slanted elite institutional advancement. It is your right and stopping does no wrong. Don't leave the controls suddenly; shut down the parts of the machine that might overload first, unless of course you work at a nuclear power plant then you, or someone like you, will have to be there for the next...?

The words separation, abolish, and dissolve appear in the Declaration of Independence. It proclaimed departure from exploitation. Stopping is perhaps the most powerful form of nonviolent action for change. The controlling institution's harsh reaction is what normally leads to violence or is violent.

Regardless of the outcome and difficult shift, it is possible to cease participation in our own exploitation and degradation. Regardless of global reach and power, it is possible to dismantle institutional architecture that enables exploitation. Even if they are part of a company that works for royalty, sanctioned by a religion claiming correspondence with God, if wrong is the result, stopping actively rejects them. To stop is the right thing to do and is increasingly, the necessary thing to do.

It is impossible to say what will be found when people stop. Perhaps one will have the chance to finally notice what went unnoticed while in a constant state of continuance. The lacking smell of the flowers, the tint in the skyline, the taste in the water, is reason enough to stop. Stopping allows one to notice what is normally unnoticed. How could people know what would happen or what they will notice?

FACT: Global dimming is the decrease of irradiance from the Sun due to an increase in particulate matter in the Earth's atmosphere. The particulate matter arrives from industrious pollution, the incomplete combustion of petrol and the contrails or emissions of aircraft. After 9/11 there was a near total shutdown of civilian air traffic for three days. During this time, scientists observed a change in the environment, a warming, due to a decrease in the emissions of airborne particulates.

At least someone was asking questions after 9/11. Certain civilians were able to fly during those days, namely the Bin Laden family. After they all were gathered together for their safety, they bailed the country one week after 9/11. Of course the FBI questioned the family, on the plane prior to their departure. Osama's half-brother, Shafig was in the U.S.A., apparently at a Carlyle Group meeting with George I when 9/11 went down. They were allowed to leave the country with little interview. FBI documents contain mistakes about the number of suspects. Regimented routines of criminal investigation were tossed aside -freeze the movement of a suspect, or those with potential knowledge of a suspect.

Global dimming is a consequence of industrial soot, the particulates of waste, being ejected into the atmosphere. For instance, a car has exhaust and in that exhaust is particulate which become airborne. Minute particles block sunlight and have an overall dimming and cooling effect. This is not a balancing act. Global dimming does not equalize global warming. The combination makes the dire and detriment of both warming and dimming less noticeable, until theoretically, an environmental tipping point is reached, which is a euphemism for the beginning of the end. Stop, you never know what you might find out.

To stop, to cease, to declare independence, is the only act that fights overtly without fighting at all. It is passive, powerful, peaceful resistance, yet active and aggressive towards institutions at the same time. It is not passive-aggressive behavior, which is at least in part rooted in fear; it is standing up to wrongdoing without fear and causing ripples by doing so. Peaceful resistance is active. It accomplishes by requires people to join together unafraid. Stopping is an act that is difficult to subvert covertly and manipulate because it is outside the status quo. Stop, look and listen, you never know what might happen.

Stop to communicate. Stop to research or experiment. Murphy's Law is the notion stating anything that can go wrong will go wrong or if there is more than one way to do something, and one way will result in disaster, then someone will do it that way. Edward Murphy was an aerospace engineer who is credited with originating the phrase, but it is an old sentiment and perhaps originally described potential predicaments of ships at sea instead of components for flight. Murphy's Law: what can go wrong will go wrong, and probably will go wrong at the least opportune moment, when one is farthest from shore. Murphy's Law is only a negative portion of a much older law, a much older secret.

The secret behind Murphy's Law is not what may break, will break. This is a wise and preventative notion before heading out to sea, but the secret is more than that. Knowing what could break and then preventing it is the obvious intention of the statement. Knowledge of what can happen is the precursor to the real knowledge, the real secret. When you know something negative is possible, you can prevent it. But there is more, when you know something is possible you can allow it and actualize it. The secret is not limited to 'what can happen, will happen.' The secret is 'what you will, can happen.' Every invention is first imagination. That which you will is possible and more likely the more you will it. Will it, and it will be.

Murphy's Law most always refers to negative occurrences. This is only part of the truth, for what can happen is possibly positive as well and just as easily willed. When things go wrong people notice more, thus Murphy's Law, but the secret is constantly in effect. What can go right will go right, if you will it right. Mentally will it, and it will be. The real secret behind Murphy's Law precedes the origins of the name Murphy, the real secret is older than any name.

The secret might be called psychomentalemotional actualization. Manifesting actuality begins with imagination, whether it's successfully sailing through troubled waters or actualizing invention. Mind over matter is all a matter of mind. Information is powerful in part because of perspective that influences negative or positive psychomentalemotional actualization. Murphy's Law limits the secret. Information and open observation enables one to better understand and influence actuality. Perspective alone creates the ability to will possibilities. Knowledge not only recognizes actuality and possibility, but serves to expand possibility as well.

STAGE FIVE: ACT

If institutions and authority will not bend to the questions, communication, voice, and boycott of the people, then action ensues. Patriotic actions are nonviolent, noteworthy, and frequently noisy with many people saying "no." Patriotic actions require words, only standing up and stepping out of line in order to make a statement for good. The results are often so powerful that violent reactions occur from peaceful actions. When institutions and the institutionalized react to peaceable protests with violence, they gain transparency and lose their legitimacy.

Action causes reaction, if the reaction or effect one seeks is a violent one, violence is enacted, for violence is a likely result of and reaction to violence. If one wants effects other than violence, one must perform actions other than violent ones. When there is a violent reaction to peaceful protests and gatherings, it is to destroy the movement through harm. The intention behind institutional violence is to intimidate and eliminate or to instigate and discredit. If people do not back down and do not retaliate, violence might be diffused and overcome.

In feudal times, a patriot was an individual of the patriarchy. The patriarch was the top elitist and the patriots consisted of everyone else. In a republic, in the U.S.A., a patriot, or matriot, is an individual of the country. Today, patriots act on behalf of liberty, not the head honcho, and openly question instead of simply following the directives from the king, the capstone.

Do something righteous. Do something daring, creative and nonviolent. Stop something exploitative and violent. In order to instigate change do something alternative. To instigate revolution, do something revolutionary, evolutionary. To counter the pyramid system requires an alternative to pyramidal formation. To initiate real change, alternative systems or shapes are instigated instead of simply countering shapes. Do something that is neither idiotic, zealous nor elitist.

Simply stopping is a powerful action toward further change. If enough people stop together, it results in rapid change, but sometimes stopping may not be enough; more accurately sometimes there may not be enough people who stop together.

If there are unanswered questions, if there is exploitation, enact civil disobedience. Disrupt the status quo to instigate the investigation of exploits and the evolution of liberty. All forms of nonviolent protest are rooted in active discontinuance and stopping from The Boston Tea Party, to Sit Ins and Occupy Wall Street.

One can stop and act at the same time. One can cast off acquired tolerations and do the right thing in spite of institutional steering. What would you do if you were unafraid? What would you will?

The most powerful form of protest and revolt, the most productive, inarguable and non-injurious feat is inaction. Discontinuance of support and performance for institutions disables them. To boycott and cease support of institutions is the most powerful, nonviolent and inarguable act to initiate change and ease the steep slant of the pyramidal system of the status quo.

If individuals, who otherwise support an institution, boycott instead the institution would crumble or rapidly change. If many more individuals boycotted or discontinued support of multiple institutions, the foremost superfluous institutions would fall by the wayside soonest. The most unsustainable elements of the pyramid would reveal their structural instability the soonest. The institutions most needed by people would remain, and the most useless of them would quickly transform into vacant space.

Everyone could stop buying new petrol-powered automobiles. Everyone could explain that until automobile manufacturers increase mileage significantly or manufacture 100% electric vehicles, they would not buy into their program further. There is no doubt that if enough people discontinued purchasing new cars, automobile manufacturers would find some patent, in some secret file that would benefit the individual over the institution and enable durable electric vehicles.

> "Truth often suffers more by the heat of its defenders than from the arguments of its opposers." ~William Penn

Economic authorities claim that if the overwhelming majority of citizens and consumers in the U.S.A. stopped spending their extra money and started saving it, the economy would go into recession, if it wasn't in one already. If most everyone stopped spending their money with one corporation, that institution would change or collapse. If the spending power of people is enough to collapse the economy it is enough to promote and demote institutions. They would be forced to change their ways or blow away. The power is in your hands.

Money has a grip on many, but can provide many with a powerful grasp as well. One person with a million dollars could possibly change the world, but even better is one million people with one dollar. One person can eventually be the architect of structure, but many people can erect the same structure at exponential speed. The same of course is true concerning the dismantling or remaking of institutions.

If enough people decided to live using significantly less power until the grid sharply increased its solar and renewable energy sources, energy providers might scramble to find a way to get your money quickly. They would suddenly figure out a cheap and easy way to install solar panels on some sunny and unused property. Many institutions endorse the statement that free energy is expensive to initiate. This maybe so, but how is free energy expensive?

Institutional privileges could be canceled by simply abandoning their systems. Institutions crumble when they lose the support of people's money and mentality. It is good to boycott now and then anyway. Among other reasons, it reminds them that at any time people can shake their institutions. Institutions despise change partly because initially change is difficult or even expensive. In addition, if they didn't make it happen or let it happen, chances are they don't gain from it.

If people are suddenly without their wants, there might be volatility, but people would adjust. If suddenly needs were unavailable, there might be chaos, but people would adapt. Problem solving turns problems into new directions.

If institutions are faced with options where they would either lose a lot or be eliminated, they might change, but first they would try to hold on in institutionalized format. Institutions are not as adaptable as they are maintainable, like all machines. Institutions do occasionally develop, but largely institutions act to maintain situations rather than progress them.

When storms hit machines are sunk, unable to go with the flow. Individuals go with the flow, flow with the flow, swim upstream, across currents and undertows, individuals adapt. At times individuals act rashly during change or strong currents, usually based on some sort of institutionalized toleration.

Katrina made landfall in the U.S.A. just about four years after 9/11/01. The Hurricane and storms like it, was enabled by overdevelopment and climate change. The marsh buffer zone that dotted the coastline and used to weaken storms before they made landfall is mostly gone, mostly from initiation of petrol production machinery.

For years after 9/11, the U.S.A. had increased its emergency spending and preparation for sudden problematic events and shakeups. Billions were spent for emergency preparedness, emergencies like unpredictable terrorist acts and predictable environmental catastrophes that would leave people suddenly in need of assistance and rescue. Despite the resources spent, evacuation and supplying victims with water was horrendously slow. Where did all the money go? Why didn't they pay the police in Gretna to open their bridge?

Hurricane Katrina swept in after the U.S.A. spent a fortune preparing for emergencies from sudden, drastic terrorist attacks or other devastations. Institutions were blank from the landscape of New Orleans immediately afterwards, except some of the local police force.

KATRINA ASSISTANCE
Pfizer contributed over $2 million and provided medicine.
Prudential Financial pledged to contribute $5 million.
General Mills provided truckloads of food.
Levi Strauss distributed 125,000 items of new clothing.

FACT: In 1999, Pfizer paid $20 million in fines after pleading guilty in an international conspiracy to fix prices.

Many institutions were able to lend a hand when times were tough. Wal-Mart was able to help out, in some instances, more rapidly than FEMA. Hugo Chavez supplied discounted fuel and even Citigroup lent a hand and bent the rules, eliminating loan costs and announcing no foreclosures for a time. But the oil corporations that swell the Gulf with platforms and line Louisiana's coastline were busy taking care of their own, looking for lost platforms and repairing their own infrastructure.

Certainly some institutions are capable of goodness. Perhaps oil corporations, among other institutions were never capable, and will never be capable, of such. The oil corporations power the war machines and the war machines power the oil corporations; one supports the other. Institutions cannot stop, they are not made to stop; people have to stop.

Institutions, in the complexities of the status quo, distort situations that strip people of their instinct to question. What is the best action in any given situation? When a situation is questionable, one should follow through by questioning it. The greatest actions against the worst wrongs were first manifested with a question. It is not what you think that is most important, it is how you think.

A common sentiment among people is that they are powerless. This notion has perhaps never been more prevalent considering the power that people do wield, the information at their disposal is correspondingly greater than ever. Information is power and it is plentiful. Despite all that people have at their disposal, despite all of our responsibility and our complicity, people still ask, "But what can I do?"

That is the question. Only don't ask it believing that things will go wrong, ask it believing that things will go right. Don't ask it doubting yourself; ask it doubting them. "What can we do?" Patriots are activists. Patriots first acquire information, and then act on it. Perhaps many activists have also been rebels or instigators or anarchists of sort, but no matter if one is throwing tables or sitting at them, asking certain simple questions is rebellious and threatening to institutions and the institutionalized.

Activism must continue, but ceasing must begin. Movement and participation is essential to life. In the petrolithic era and nuclear age, inactivism is a powerful means to an end. Declaring independence and active discontinuance is, at times, essential to life, liberty and the pursuit of happiness. The fourth monkey is unafraid to look, listen, question and cease activity; the fourth monkey does not lash out or leap away.

In the petrolithic era, because of past treading, because of destruction unleashed on the natural world, inactivity, stopping, is the only activity that is powerful and manageable. In the petrolithic era and nuclear age, patriots discontinue wrongdoing and become inactivists simply because clean water, which is required for tea, is threatened.

The machinery of the status quo in the petrolithic era must be abandoned, or it will eventually abandon those who ride with it. In order to protect, life, liberty and the pursuit of happiness, people must stop and fold their arms. To ensure life and to slow the desertification and environmental destruction of Earth, to make certain that we become ancestors to future patriots, today we must become inactivists. Wrongdoing must be abandoned for our wellbeing, let alone our pursuits and dreams.

FACT: A Cornell professor of ecology and agricultural sciences concluded that 40% of deaths worldwide are caused by pollution of water, air and soil.

Inactivism implies laziness to those who would disagree with stopping wrongdoing. It actually takes tremendous effort to stop performing for the status quo, to leave the cave, and stop wrongs they claim are right. In the petrolithic era and nuclear age, wrong is abundant, intermixed in physicality and mentality as pollution and misinformation. If one lacks persistent questioning one might consume poisons without knowing it.

The petrolithic era and nuclear age is inescapable. There is no silent oasis, no place left undisturbed. Everywhere is touched by pollution no matter how distant from industry and city. Petrolithic and nuclear toxins are in the waters of deep wells and in the high reaches of the atmosphere as well. There is no vacating the petrolithic era, but one can still cease and evict exploitation. There is no going backwards, but you can stop.

FACT: In 21st century, scientists discovered contamination of remote waters, ice, earth and air via pesticides and chemicals sourced thousands of miles away.

If institutions or individuals argue against stopping wrong, you know that they are wrong, dependent on wrong and that there is likely something deeply wrong with them. Stopping wrong is inarguable and becomes more essential as the petrolithic era and nuclear age continue. When institutions and individuals argue over stopping wrongdoing that directly and negatively influence the livelihood and likelihood of life on the planet, you know something is deeply wrong with them.

"Each species on our planet plays a role in the healthy functioning of natural ecosystems on which humans depend." ~William H. Schlesinger, Biogeochemist

EXTINCTIONS

In 2003, there were an estimated 23,000 African lions, compared to 1953 when there were an estimated 200,000. In 2005, 1,212 of the Earth's 9,775 species of birds were in imminent danger of extinction, while over 700 were considered near threatened. It is estimated that there are 30 wild Chinese tigers left. It is also estimated that 656,000 people die in China every year due to indoor and outdoor air pollution; another 95,000 succumb to polluted water. Human-made air pollution is responsible for an estimated 2 million human deaths worldwide, annually.

Many scientists refer to the end of the twenty-first century as the beginning of the sixth mass extinction of the planet. A majority also believe it may be the fastest rate of extinction, eclipsing even the sudden doom of the dinosaurs, the last mass extinction. The planet's sensitive ecosystem that we are dependent on for our breath, water, life and depth of thought is being dismantled, disfigured and destroyed.

The ability to question and answer is the distinguishing characteristic of man. Other beings have heart and mind and may notice things, but they cannot question and cannot manipulate an answer into being. Questioning is both the result of evolution and the instigation of it. Curiosity is God's gift to people that makes hands useful. The lion has cunning, teeth and claws; man has reasoning, voice and hands.

At times lions will not hunt; as well there are times when people do not question. Sometimes it is not necessary to question and sometimes the lion may not be hungry. Other times there are strange circumstances or sickness leading to questions going unasked or a lions ambling past grazing gazelles.

The confusion of changing truths and actualities with the corresponding, yet unchanging concept of good and evil is perhaps the original dilemma and most consequential mix up, causing misdirected action. Adam and Eve had the Tree of Life and all the other trees of the Garden of Eden to eat from, yet they were coerced into eating from the one tree they were not supposed to eat from, the Tree of Knowledge of Good and Evil.

In the Genesis Story, God commanded people not to question, or eat from the Tree of Knowledge of Good and Evil, for I propose, it is the only subject that does not change form, the only subject that just is. Good and evil remain so, always, the only unchanging concept in the universe. Interpretation of the distinction changes, tolerations of evil sway, but its actuality is stable. Deception, exploitation and violence towards one's brothers are always wrong.

The original sin is not the knowledge of good and evil, but questioning and manipulating the distinction of good and evil. It is the only concept one knows innately, no matter how buried under burdened tolerations. Even then, underneath the tolerations, the subconscious knows, but it may not be awake. The one subject that requires no question or investigation is the difference between good and evil. Only complete information pertaining to events is required.

> Love yourself and be awake-
> Today, tomorrow, always.
> First establish yourself in the way,
> Then teach others
> And so defeat sorrow.
> To straighten the crooked
> You must first do a harder thing-
> Straighten yourself.
> You are your only master.
> Who else?
> Subdue yourself,
> And discover your master
> ~Buddha

The one subject that is permanent requires no questioning for it just is, always has been and always will be the same. Acceptance of evil changes, the distinction between good and evil does not. It is human nature to question. To question the difference between good and evil is not necessary, it is known innately. If the distinction is not apparent, one's own tolerations require questioning, one's own acquired tolerations.

It is the design of institutions to be like the serpent and distort information and pile on tolerations of right and wrong. Institutions build their own trees, but like the serpent, slyly insist that actuality is steady and that the difference between right and wrong changes. In this millennia old creation story, possibly the most frequently retold story for centuries, there are four characters. They each display personality archetypes of the idiot, zealot, elitist and patriot. Adam is the idiot, Eve the zealot, serpent the elitist and God the patriot.

> ### SYMBOL - SERPENT
> The serpent is apparent and important in most every religion and mythology worldwide throughout recorded time. The serpent is often depicted as Godly and always in possession of special information, it always powerful, but it is not certainly evil. The serpent is universally symbolic for possession of wisdom and special information and is sometimes interpreted as being malevolent and other times as being benevolent.

To question and act to seek answers is humanity's primary glory and should be celebrated. To question and dissect the intricacy of the simple apple and the complex universe is our right and our divinity. However, there is no need to question the distinction of right and wrong, it just is. There are no ifs, ands or buts about it. There are certain acts that are always wrong. Violence is wrong. Exploitation is wrong. Environmental destruction is wrong. Slavery is wrong. Withholding, distorting or otherwise tampering with information is wrong. Bringing harm and impeding the liberty of others is wrong.

The components of the status quo tend to be wrongful. Individuals lean toward what is right unless burdened by tolerations and conditions presented in the status quo. Everything is questionable, except the knowledge of the difference between good and evil, which just is.

In the petrolithic era and nuclear age, stopping increasingly becomes necessary in order to continue. Stop or be stopped. To discontinue, to stop and to become an inactivist as much as possible, with as many others as possible, is the way to change. Stopping proves to individuals and institutions that people hold power. To stop is the most powerful action for a revolution, or a turn, a change.

> CHOCOLATE $ In 2000, people in the U.S.A. spent $1.9 billion on Easter chocolate and candy and about the same on Halloween candy. On Christmas, about $1.4 billion was spent

and on Valentine's Day another $1 billion was spent on chocolate and candy.

To walk away from the mass of wrong, the status quo, is the best form to dismantle it. It is fighting without fighting. The best way to start is to first stop. Stop buying slave sourced chocolate and start something else for instance. Stop buying cars. Stop using power for a day. Stop war permanently. Leave the left wing and the right wing of the status quo and walk off, let the bird fly away. The new world of the petrolithic era requires a new kind of activism - inactivism. In the petrolithic era separation from the wrong as much as possible, is required.

Forget their poisonous plastics, their genetically engineered food, their pharmaceuticals, their pesticides and all the other poisonous plundered crap that you don't need. Forget their chocolate. Stop purchasing their plastic disposables and ineffective effects. Stop following serpents on institution branches.

Forget working for, and in the format of their sham, forever promising future benefit and providing permanently headache. Forget lining up to round up all that is around in order to capitalize and construct a pyramid of capitalization within and according to the status quo. Stop temporarily, partially or permanently.

The environmental consequences of the petrolithic era and nuclear age call for individuals to stop, to change. And in the U.S.A. as long as one doesn't impede or traverse over others in the process, charge or pause in liberty. Institutions however are not designed to stop or pause and contemplate in limited mechanized capacity. They are not alive and have no heart, yet they present Ronald McDonald personas that seem immortal, even though they are not alive and not real. Institutions continue on as long as the status quo does. There is no way that humanity can continue at this rate of consumption and pollution, but institutions would herald otherwise according to their limited contemplations.

FACT: Chevron has invested billions of dollars into alternative energy and is the biggest producer of renewable energy among the oil corporations. Other oil companies have invested fortunes into sustainable energy as well. Chevron holds and refuses to release many patents to many inventions that would be beneficial to individuals and potentially decrease use of petrol.

Mother Earth, God's creation, this random rock in a limitless realm, may not thrive as it once did thanks to the instigation and continuation of the petrolithic era and nuclear age, thanks to our activities and tolerations. Nature is balance, individuals and institutions have interrupted its balance, but nature will balance itself out way or another.

The status quo must be stopped by choice or it will be ceased without choice. The most powerful and entirely disruptive act in the petrolithic era is inactivity. Peaceful resistance, nonparticipation and non-cooperation with institutional wrongdoing are the best ways to dismantle oligarchical collectivism. To implement right in the petrolithic era first requires stopping wrongdoing.

Laws have been made and broken in the evolution of ideas, sometimes laws have to be broken. Laws do not always correlate with what is right. Sometimes tradition must be broken, but institutions always bend, break or change in the evolution of ideas, in revolution of ideas. There are many defiant acts that have also been criminal acts, but now are looked at as heroic. One can commit a crime that is nonviolent, be punished and still be in the right. Laws govern the lesser man and we all face a greater judge.

Perhaps the petrolithic era and nuclear age will lead to a full well of benevolence and benefit instead of malevolence and toxins. Maybe great wrong will eventually a far cry from the present day, bring some good, but only through stopping, reacting and changing it.

"The true history of my administration will be written fifty years from now, and you and I will not be around to see it."
~George II

Universally, in nature and society, transformation not only takes place slowly in the calm stream, but also and perhaps more often, suddenly in the volatile flood. As nature goes, so goes society, the interplay between individuals and institutions. Individuals have more interests than institutions. The trinity of liberty, beginning with the First Amendment, provides and prescribes the method to protect individual liberty among institutional monopoly. Patriotic actions may be deliberate and prolonged or sudden and temperamental, but thorough questioning and peaceful, cooperative hands are qualifications for patriotic action.

Institutions strive for growth and expansion. People want life, liberty and happiness. People want clean air and water among other simple essentials and more complex resources and rights, but institutions want to monopolize mind, or matter or both.

Stopping is not against the law, it is a nonviolent, powerful alternative to the megalomaniacal, monopolistic, institutionalized and popularized mechanizations of society. To stop is a powerful statement and it is earsplitting to institutions when discontinuance is chorused. Environmentally and socially, it is logical and spiritual to stop. Stop trespasses on liberty, locals and land and stop others from trespasses and treading.

Inactivists commit no crime, or at least no wrong, and yet could change the world with a week of meditation, soccer, rallies, or any distraction other than the continuation within the status quo. In a week of discontinuance, or a year of partial discontinuance, the world would change. Instead of worldwide events and historical events constantly consisting of war, people could declare and carry out a worldwide event of peace and cease. A worldwide event as notable as any invasion, any battle or any bloodletting, it could be a mark on the timeline that was not the mark of war.

There are many reasons for a declaration of independence in the petrolithic era and nuclear age. It would be an open letter to the world, of course. He, in reference to King George III, would be substituted with They, in reference to the institutionalized elite. The indictments concerning their offenses and trespasses, would be different, yet the essence would be much the same.

If the infallibility of the global royal system of yesterday can be cast away, then too can the global oligarchical system of today. The majority in Colonial America could not believe that the kings and all the kings' men would one day be meaningless. Today, there is a similar disbelief concerning the present integration of oligarchical institutional control.

In the petrolithic era and nuclear age, stopping, inactivity increasingly is the most sensible option. The original patriots declared their non-participation and today, the next generation patriots would hail a similar message. Today, patriots must rattle the zealots and inform the idiots, and cast off the elitists just as transpired in the late 1700s.

Institutions are not designed to cease, they last lifetimes without aging. War is a temporary adjustment for many institutions, a planned disruption that they may benefit from however for people it can be a permanent disembarkation from Earth. The underlying philosophy of the trinity of monopoly is to forego what is right to perpetuate their system, their profit and their agendas. They operate legally and illegally, though they definitely prefer the gray area in between. The gray area is a confusing legal and moral limbo, where actions may not be right, but are not illegal either.

If a wrongful act is committed, people consider it wrong whether or not it is also unlawful. Institutions and the institutionalized do not know right from wrong, they just know to keep chugging along in legal and illegal terms. Institutions instill any action in order to profit or fulfill agendas, including running over people in the gray area. How could institutions that sell something dirty and deadly manifest anything other than dirt and death?

Sometimes, it takes a criminal act to demonstrate that the entire philosophy behind the act being illegal is criminally wrong, but if the crime is violent, even accidentally, the point is dulled. One cannot be violent and expect a message to come across, even if that violence is accidental. And even if that violence is towards you, even if that violence is conducted by someone else, if it can be spun, it will be.

Animals are capable of vicious violence, as are people. In small groups without technological advantage, man is capable of more tireless violence and destruction than all the rest of the animal kingdom. No monkey can match man's destructive potential. At the same time, a distinction of man among animals is the ability to act and react in nonviolent capacity. People have the distinct ability to help and heal.

Man is probably the most destructive entity the planet has ever known, and yet we are the only species to possess higher intellect, curiosity and compassion. Man is the only species that can question, answer, build and show compassion to kin and strangers alike. Peaceful action is always the higher path to more powerful place.

Violence typically profits strangers, mostly those strangers who manufacture weaponry and power tanks. Violent acts, despite any reason presented, are in the interest of violence, it is defeating and distracting to any cause except more violence. The first electrical impulse and reaction may be to fight or take flight, but there are always more than two choices, and both these options are fear based.

Fight or flight is perhaps the archetypal primordial choice. Constantly thinking in this manner perhaps promotes the "us and "them" mentality. It is our initial emotional reaction to situations from the reptilian brain, but there are always other choices for a free individual pursuing liberty.

In the petrolithic era and nuclear age there is no one institution to fight and no place one can run away to. Today there is nowhere to run, nowhere to hide and wars are not winnable, there is no one to fight. And there are always more than instinctual, fear based choice

FACT: Part of the human brain is called the reptilian complex. This primal part of the brain controls, rage, xenophobia, and fight or flight decisions.

Though people are capable of demolishing all, people are also capable of caring for all. Peaceful action, stopping for instance requires no confrontation, and dismantles wrongdoing by not maintaining it. Violence sanctioned and perceived as justified is always wrong, while at times, crime of a nonviolent sort, while criminal, can become legend of morality that surpasses tolerations of the time. Violence, no matter the proposed good, is simple violence. There is nothing wrong with self-defense, but kindness does not equate to weakness, and strength is not violence capability. Nonviolence is powerful.

Rosa parks went to jail. Nelson Mandela was imprisoned for a lifetime. Countless unnamed people have been imprisoned for breaking the law and doing the right thing. Standing up to face wrong, practice civil disobedience, conscientious objection through peaceful resistance is always right.

People who are tossed inside a box without cause and then break their cage asunder are always right, no matter what is broken getting out of the cage. Patriots stand up, speak up and if need be, act up. No matter the legality, patriots first deal in morality, no matter how outnumbered they are.

The Nation of Gods and Earths is a community organization in NYC. The group, distinct from Nation of Islam, was founded by Clarence 13X, a member of Malcolm X's NOI congregation, before Clarence and then Malcolm left the NOI. The Nation of Gods and Earths, or Five Percenters, numerically theorized the pyramid system and the outnumbered and often missing, patriots. They broke down the percentages that equate the status quo and cement the pyramidal oligarchy.

The theory is that 85% of people are lost, easily misled and are being manipulated to ignorantly kill themselves without knowing who their true nature. The 10% are the slave makers of the poor and lost 85%. The 10% are responsible for and benefit from the manipulation. And then there are the 5%, who attempt to do the right thing and free the minds of the 85%, who are under the thumb of the 10%. The 85% are known as the dumb, deaf and blind, or the idiots and zealots. The 10% are referred to as the slave makers, or the elitists. And the rare 5% are known as the poor righteous teachers, or the patriots.

The Nation of Islam, despite being counter to much of the status quo, is of it as well, as they seek to expand their religious institution. The Nation of Gods and Earth is alternatively community based and are unaffiliated with The Nation of Islam. They seek to distribute information and benefit local communities, while religious institutions seek to monopolize situations.

The Nation of Gods and Earths, among others, did the correct arithmetic, their math adds up. The percentages may sway with time and paradigm, but the status quo depends on the pyramidal steadiness of the formula of 85%, 10% and 5%. Throughout recorded time slight shifts in numbers don't altered the essential structure of the status quo.

85% are on the bottom. The 5% are squashed amongst them and the 10% reside in the capstone. The status quo, the pyramid system, depends on this mathematical stability. If a portion of the idiots and zealots began to behave as patriots, the pyramidal architecture rapidly becomes archeology. If the 5% were increased to 11% or more, they would outnumber the elitists and their numbers would exponentially increase in 100th monkey fashion. 11% is the tipping point.

The identity of the 5%, 10% and 85% may be difficult to distinguish. The distinguishing characteristics of the poor righteous teachers, the slave makers and the mentally oblivious may not be obvious, but realization of how they react to new information reveals their identity. The formula of the pyramid system is steady. The identity of the 85%, 10% and 5% is often obscured and debated, but questioning how people react to and act on new information reveals who they are, how they think.

In order to bring about change, in order to progress, the 5% has to increase. The 10%, the numbers of exploiters and elitists, vary very little. They are content exploiting the 85%. Rarely do the elitists give up their position at the apex. If there were more of them, there would be too many, and if there were less there wouldn't be enough, therefore their numbers are more or less constant.

The 5% must grow and to do so must gain numbers from the 85% to eclipse the numbers of the 10% in a revolution of consciousness. The 10% does not give up. The 85% must accept reality and learn actuality. It is extremely difficult to get them to look away from the light and imagery, but it is possible with information. The only way to disengage the formula of the status quo is to enhance the numbers of the 5% by decreasing the numbers of the 85%. New information leads to new ideas, the 85% need information in order to be released from the rigid entrapment of the status quo. Until the 85% is informed, the 5% remains compressed and restricted among them.

"As we are liberated from our own fear, our presence automatically liberates others."~Nelson Mandela

THE PYRAMID SYSTEM

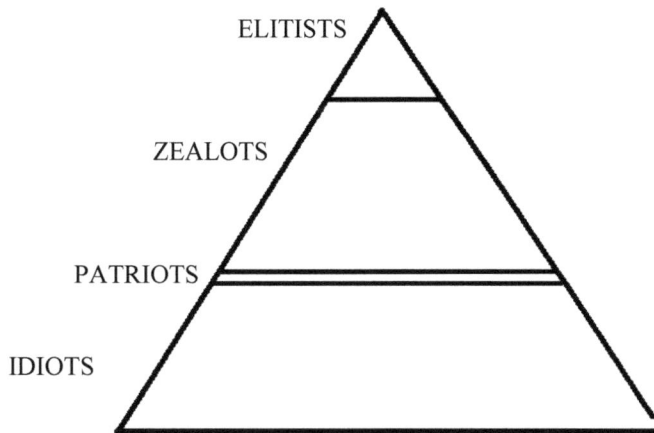

```
        ELITISTS       /\
                      /  \
                     /----\
       ZEALOTS      /      \
                   /        \
                  /          \
      PATRIOTS   /------------\
                /==============\
               /                \
      IDIOTS  /                  \
             /_____\
```

> "There is natural ignorance and there is artificial ignorance. I should say at the present moment the artificial ignorance is at about eighty-five percent." ~Ezra Pound

> "Five percent of the people think; ten percent of the people think they think; and the other eighty five percent would rather die than think." ~Thomas Edison

Thomas Edison came up with a lot of ideas. On top of numerically conceptualizing the pyramid system, Thomas invented an assortment of tools people still use today. He had well over one thousand patents on his inventions, among them were improvements to alkaline batteries for electric automobiles. Before petrol became standard, electric vehicles were commonplace and Thomas believed they were the best option. He invested a decade of work into improving electric batteries for vehicles, but by the time he finished, the electric starter made petrol powered vehicles more acceptable.

Thomas is best known for recognizing the formula to make the light bulb work; however someone else had already written the formula. Thomas invented many things besides the carbon filament for light bulbs, but Joseph Swan originally came up with the idea years prior.

Thomas is known to have sat at his desk in contemplation of mechanical concepts and problems for hours at a time. Albert Einstein is known to have similarly sat contemplatively for hours at a time. While contemplating, Thomas would eat or smoke opium. He would sit at his desk, high on opium, studying a certain problem. During his inquisitive stupor he would hold ball bearings in one hand. As time passed, his sedation grew and eventually he would pass out. The instant Thomas fell asleep the ball bearings from his hand onto the floor, waking him up.

In this dream state, the mind has much higher cognitive abilities than usual. It was not the opium, though Thomas may have believed as much, it is the mind. When you first fall asleep, you enter the dream state and engage a different, open state of mind. In the dream state, all around is entirely understood, for it is all via your own mind. In that moment when you first enter the dream state, you understand everything being manifest, intoxicated or not. If gently awakened when the mind is accustomed complete comprehension entirety is conceivable, including the intricate functions of machinery, if only briefly.

Thomas would sleep on it, if only for an instant and gain access to ideas. This brilliance is available to anyone who dreams, if only for an instant. Instead of a lucid dream, when you know it's a dream and are in control, this is more lucid reality, when you know you are awake, but comprehend reality in totality as if it were your dream.

> "Sleep is the best meditation."
> ~Fourteenth Dalai Lama

The dream state is apparently more attainable in that first moment, when you first fall asleep and are gently awakened. Though, it is possible to experience the meditative effects in varying degrees, at various points during sleep and not just that first instant. A meditative mindset is likely the only prerequisite. One has to relax, concentrate and go to sleep, all at the same time. You cannot reap the benefit of the dream state unless you wake up. You have to wake up and act, otherwise you are just dreaming.

SYMBOL - LIGHT FLASH
The lightning bolt is symbolic for a flash of enlightenment, a sudden idea. The light bulb is also symbolic for the flash of an idea, just as the idea supposedly came to Thomas, in a flash.

FACT: In Livermore, California a light bulb has burned for over 100 years. The filament reads "on."

The requirements to benefit from the dream state are meditative contemplation, relaxation, and shifting consciousness. Opiates or drugs of any sort are not a requirement. Only by being meditative and by waking up is one able to pull ideas from the mind in a dream state and not from a mind state in a dream as the 85% seem to live.

The 5% principal is a powerful conservationist, fund raising and empowerment idea. If people stop just 5% of their wrongdoing, i.e. pollution and exploitative consumption, the world would be polluted by a significantly less tonnage of poisons. If people donate 5% of their income into an idea, the 5% combination soon magnifies into figures institutions recognize.

5% is also considered to be a tipping point. Something new, be it fashion or any other revolutionary idea, usually takes a while to catch on. With quality marketing, and advertising investment, it may take a long time for one percent to turn into two percent and two percent to turn into four but, when five percent is reached growth accelerates, explodes. From five percent on, growth is exponential and easy. Five percent is the key to change. The 5% have changed the world.

FACT: Many scientists refer to human environmental alteration as approaching a tipping point. The tipping point will create an environmental emergency and calamity from which there is no turning back.

The original patriots and those who sought independence in 1773 were the 5%. The vast majority in the Colonies thought those who would challenge the Crown were bloody batty. The original patriots, those who threw the Boston Tea Party and those who authored and enacted the trinity of liberty, were at first a tiny minority among the majority who believed their actions crazy or futile, less than 5%.

Nelson Mandela changed the world, at first with a minority of less than 5%. The ideas of the 5% are often, so counter to the status quo that initially their numbers remain below 5%. Civil rights in the U.S.A. were enabled by the 5%. Perestroika and Glasnost, the Velvet Revolution, the liberty experienced in Eastern Europe, the fall of the Berlin wall and the separation of the USSR were all initiated by the 5%.

Peaceful revolution is possible and accomplished when the 10% allow the 85% to follow the 5% out of the cave into reality without repercussions. Peaceful change is possible when people are unafraid to stop and go and institutions have no choice but to let go of their hold. Peaceful revolution is possible when the 10% cannot convince the 85% to react violently in attempts to maintain control of the status quo and eliminate the 5%.

The 85% are the idiots and zealots. For whatever individual and collective reasons, the 85% are unable to reasonably question. The 85% move together. They purchase the same goods and have the same priorities and take holidays at the same time. The 85% tend to accommodate to the formations and shapes of institutions, instead of making institutions better suit them.

When there is a disagreement, it is in the concept of either-or, one or the other. Alternatives are outside their scope, they go by the institutional program, the institutionalized balance of one or the other, like Democrats or Republicans. They think one way or the other way, either zealous or idiotic. They are deaf and blind to creative problem solving and thinking for themselves because they've been led away from their true nature.

The 10% are the elitists. Though they are excellent at concealment and many are unknown, the results of their exploits are everywhere, impossible to hide. Their processes may be clandestine, but the results are blunt. It can be difficult to know the

10%, the exploiters, the elitists because they operate by deception and manipulation of information. It is possible to know elitists by examining actuality, by putting two and two together.

It is impossible to extract oneself physically from the environment of the petrolithic era, and seemingly impossible to extract oneself from supporting the 10%, but it is possible. Most of the 85% and 10% do not know they are killing themselves. At times it is directly obvious, but mostly it is indirect subtleties that add up. Sometimes the equations to actuality are easily put together, but mostly the deductions are ignored. When the 85% know they are killing themselves, they will start to question.

Everyone is wrapped up in the status quo so completely that they can only see solutions within the framework of the status quo. These are not solutions as much as they are actions in continuation in the same formation which caused the problem in the first place. Stopping the wrong is the only way to end wrong; everything else, even countering operations, serves only the maintenance and continuance of the status quo.

If the 5%, the patriots, grow to be 11%, then the poor righteous teachers would outnumber the 10%, the slave makers of the poor, the elitists. The 85% would be no more and exponentially more people would learn and be swayed toward what is right. The pyramid system of oligarchical collectivism would be no more if the 85% decreased and the 5% increased. Percentages aside, one person has changed the world many times over too.

The murder of Archduke Ferdinand was a catalyst for WWI. The war was bound to happen, many nations were readying for war, but the assassination was the catalyst that fed its beginning. A secret society called the Black Hand, threw a car bomb at the Archduke's vehicle. The explosion failed to find its intended victim, but did cause casualties. Later, the Archduke and his wife visited the victims of the blast at the hospital and were shot in their car. If a few people can change the world with bomb and gun, then 5% can change the world with nothing besides voice and hand. If an army can change the world, then so too can an unarmed and unregimented group.

SYMBOL – HAND
The human hand is symbolic for man, manifestation and manipulation. The hand is symbolic for power, healing, and creation. The hand can be composed into different signals to communicate anything and everything from stop and go to evil and peace. Hands are best for sharing, being open.

"It is easier to be critical than correct."
~Benjamin Disraeli

When words are unable to inspire righteous questions and natural curiosity, actions take place to arouse questioning. To get a message across through action, one must be completely correct and safe. One must coordinate every aspect and prevent every onset of violence or mishap. If any individual is hurt, the activist's message is potentially lost. People will wonder what is wrong with the purveyors of violence and not what they were trying to say.

To get a message across through inaction, one does not have to worry about mishaps. To discontinue, to stop is the simplest, nonviolent course to change. It is the most powerful and loudest message to those who participate in wrong and are dependent on wrong, for wrongdoing is ceased. Stopping rocks the boat and exposes the wrong to the unquestioning majority, the 85%. Stopping wrong reveals the wrong, it does no wrong. Stopping is not in the status quo and it is not harmful. Stopping provides the 85% with glimpses of actuality, instigating questioning and better direction on a higher path. By stopping, there is ending and by ending, there can be beginning.

If many stopped wrongdoing there might be repercussions, rattling and shaking. There might be turmoil resulting from people stopping and innocent individuals might suffer. Of course, institutions would blame this on the inactivists and not the institutionalization, integration of wrongdoing and their lack of accommodation. Change is frightening, but continuation of the status quo leads to individual suffering and reasons change. Continuation of the status quo is dangerous to the environment and the happiness of individuals, conclusion is dangerous and rattling to institutions. Stop what is wrong, regardless of the consequences. They continue regardless of the consequences. Which is more acceptable? Which is more dangerous?

There are many actions and many institutions that could cease and life would go on just as pleasantly as before if not more so. One doesn't have to think about stopping work unless your employer is working people. Keep having fun; keep working, just discontinue the support of institutions that run over liberty, locals and land -fairness, peers, and nature.

All information varies and is questionable. Question the Complete Patriot's Guide to Oligarchical Collectivism: Its Theory and Practice, because no source of information is complete. There is always more to the story. Question this story, but more importantly question their stories. Check and double check all verified and unverified information. Question and check their math. Freedom is the freedom to question their math. Question your own doubt of holding the answers, and more importantly, question the surety of others who provide answers.

Don't be afraid of what might be seen or heard and don't be afraid to speak up. Question, keep questioning and act on the answers. A patriotic act must be carefully thought out. Every act must be considered and coordinated if one intends to voice a message. It is tremendously difficult to do things that are correct and just in protest. When a group of people is large enough, there will be antagonists who are offended or offensive, even potential agent provocateurs whom can detract from the intention. Inactivity, even unorganized inactivity disallows any potential for their disruptions. Even unorganized inactivity without protest or gathering, without signs, is perhaps more powerful, productive and inarguable than one with toss away signage. Ten million whispers are louder than ten thousand screams, many small actions can bring about vast change.

To cease wrong hurts no individual, but it does make institutions shudder, crack and change. To cease presents power to people. No farmer should stop growing, but they should stop growing GMO. No doctor should stop healing, but they should stop supporting exploitative pharmaceutical corporations. They could question homeopathic and allopathic treatment and not simply refer to instituted and regimented cut and dose procedures.

> FACT: 80 million people around the world took Vioxx, a drug manufactured by Merck. Merck withdrew the product and its successor after it was found to increase risk of heart attacks among other complications including death. Merck faces thousands of lawsuits, has paid out millions and has set aside billions.

Stopping participation in wrong, no matter the outcome, is never wrong. When there is negative result from simply stopping wrong, it is because of the integration of wrong, not the action taken to call attention to and correct the wrong. Collectivized oligarchies might act in rigid formation to make situations less tolerable for more people when their exploitative mechanics are called into question. When there are negative results from ceasing it is because of the dependency on wrong, not because of rocking the boat.

To stop wrong, stop wrong. There is no complete disconnect from the petrolithic era; it is here and will be here for the foreseeable future. There is no air, water or soil that has escaped the consequences of the nuclear age. It is impossible to leave the environment, there is no going back, but it is powerful and possible to cease support of institutional wrongdoing. It is possible to walk out of institutions. Negative consequences are often the only thing people notice, but stopping wrong is inarguably not wrong.

While authorities and powers try to stop protests, they cannot do anything about a stop protest. To cease participation in wrongdoing is the most inarguable and powerful reaction to wrongdoing; fighting wrong often fuels it. The most powerful act is to stop, cease support of wrong. Be a poor righteous teacher, each one, teach one. Continue to question, communicate and speak out, but fold your arms across your chest like the fourth monkey and fuel the fire no more. Assist others out of the cave into the sun. Refuse to move. Toss their tea. Stop.

The best way to restore balance in a world overwhelmed by institutionalized wrong, is to simply stop it. Wrong can only be accomplished with constant stoking of institutions, and institutionalized individuals. Walk out of the pyramid, walk out of the cave. It is tremendously difficult force out wrong and yet it soon slithers and slips away if left unattended. Of all acts possible, the most powerful and the most inarguable is to stop. It is your right, and it commits no wrong.

> "Far better it is to dare mighty things, to win glorious triumphs, even though checkered by failure… than to take rank with those poor spirits who neither enjoy much nor suffer much, because they live in a gray twilight that knows not neither victory nor defeat." ~Theodore Roosevelt

Idiots are afraid to dare mighty things and zealots are afraid to leave rank. They are those poor spirits who live in gray twilight and know neither victory nor defeat. Elitists exploit their fears by manifesting and maintaining the gray twilight. Patriots dare the mightiest of actions, to stop. They suffer or enjoy the outcome, but stop wrong and let the chips fall where they may. Patriots rock the boat by practicing the First Amendment thoroughly and roughly if necessary, but never violently, just as the original patriots did at the big steep and with the Declaration of Independence. Conditions must be addressed and faced, no matter how checkered by failure. Avoiding actuality, remaining in gray twilight, not questioning and facing wrong is humanity's greatest detriment.

Before the First Amendment was written, the original patriots practiced its elements. Today the equivalent tea party in the would treat petrolithic and nuclear industries as the enabler of the exploiters, though we cannot throw oil into the sea or coal into the bay, as water is too tainted already. Today, we must abandon petrolithic and nuclear accompaniments in war and environmental destruction for what is right. Liberty must expand or else it contracts.

> FACT: A gyre of trash the size of Texas swirls and collects in the Pacific Ocean north of Hawaii. The multi-continental trash swirl of the Pacific is a mass of humanity's remains due to ocean currents. There are many such gyres in the oceans.

Prior to the big steep, the refusal and boycott of The Company tea led to the three chartered ships floating in Boston Harbor, waiting, with no place to sell their goods. The Dartmouth waited for weeks while the Eleanor docked for days and the Beaver had arrived the night before the big steep. If no one wants their goods they will have to halt the facilitation. A defining aspect of the original patriot's defiance was the discontinuance of tea consumption, not only tossing the tea into the sea.

A petrolithic era and nuclear age tea party might be appropriately an actual tea party, where people peaceably gather together to drink tea and exchange ideas on alternative direction. To gather and have tea, one must first stop. More and more, there are less and less suitable places to stop and have a tea party and more reasons to have one like the big steep. Stop the routine and have a tea party.

Institutions are masterful at presenting two choices which are countering opposites and yet not alternatives. Normally one is a great wrong and the other, a lesser evil. One side or the other side of the coin is presented; conditions are polarized leading to limited doublethink. The multitudes of alternatives available in liberty are lacking. The choice is simple, but either choice is continuation of wrong and often constructed options. No wrong and no lesser evil ever built or manifested any good. When an institution presents two choices, one a dead end and the other a dead end for someone else, choose neither.

> FACT: The Cuyahoga River flows into Lake Eerie. The River was briefly part of the U.S.A. border until the land was taken from tribes on the other side. The Cuyahoga began sporadically catching afire in 1936. In 1969, there was a fire that caught the attention of people and since then, the Cuyahoga River has improved. The fires brought attention to pollution and influenced environmental legislation.

To be an activist in the petrolithic era and nuclear age, become an inactivist. Stop feeding the fire supplying the dim light which casts their imagery. Unsustainable continuation is the firestorm of the petrolithic era and nuclear age. This fire can't be fought, for fighting the fire also feeds it. We didn't start the fire, it was always burning, but we fuel it, we maintain it. The fire must be left alone to burn itself out. Stopping is increasingly the only logical solution, as well as the most loving option. It is also an action that they, and them are less able to manipulate and take advantage of.

Stop, for if we do not stop, we will be stopped. Who knows what, where, when, why or how, but the dramatic global burning of petrolithic and nuclear fuels is sure to come to an end one way or another. Natural events become enhanced catastrophes in the confines of the petrolithic era and nuclear age.

A Tsunami that struck Indonesia from a 9.0 earthquake in December, 2004, killed some 230,000 people. This is an example of the unsustainable and easily disturbed architecture of the petrolithic era. A cyclone hit Myanmar in May 2008. This is another example of unsustainable actualities and consequences of the petrolithic era amid naturally occurring events. Some 140,000 people died there.

Also in May, 2008, more than 80,000 people died as a result of a 7.9 earthquake in China. Their deaths were mainly caused by unsustainable overdevelopment. The architecture literally fell, and many couldn't get out in time. Scientists later hypothesized the construction of a reservoir near the epicenter may have triggered the earthquake. The weight of the newly accumulated water may have added pressure on the fault and lubricated it causing aggravated movement and the earthquake. Overdevelopment was initiated in spite of the rattling and overdevelopment induced the rattling itself.

In June, 2008, a typhoon sunk a ferry in the Philippines. The ferry took hundreds of people down to Davy Jones locker and ten tons of pesticide too. Recovery operations were postponed until the toxins were no longer threatening, some sought to ban the pesticide in the area afterwards. This is an example of unsustainable, easily disturbing chemical creations. On 3/11/11 the earthquake and tsunami in Japan off the Fukushima coast killed approximately 30,000 people and caused a nuclear catastrophe at the six reactor facility on the coast, one of the largest nuclear experiments on the planet.

The conditions of the petrolithic era and nuclear age increase the hazards of naturally occurring events such as storms and other acts of God. The rain, floods and earthquakes are a more extreme threat because of overdevelopment and overuse of petrolithic chemicals without consideration for liberty, locals and land. The global steady environmental poisoning and pollution is enough reason to stop, let alone the jeopardy from extreme spills due to natural events. The accidental chemical spills might happen at any time, because storms can happen anytime. The obvious and constant environmental destruction conducted by man, combined with the elusive eventualities of nature are potent reasons to stop and act.

The exploitation of peoples and environment is potent reason for change, and stopping is potent recipe to change. The power to change is in your hands. Reasoning to take power over another is all imagery in your head. Victory and peace.

V FOR VICTORY
Extending the index finger and middle finger up creates a V. The expression symbolizes victory, peace and screw-off. The V is the shape of an upside down and open triangle, symbolizing a pyramid turned upside down and opened. Patriots exclaim victory, peace and similar expletives to exploitative institutions, all at the same time.

PEACE
Peace is symbolized by a triangle or pyramid within a circle being pierced through the middle and opened by a straight line.

"A heavy black volume, amateurishly bound, with no name or title on the cover. The print also looked slightly irregular. The pages were worn at the edges, and fell apart easily, as though the book had been passed through many hands."
~George Orwell, Description of Theory and Practice of Oligarchical Collectivism in 1984

If The Complete Patriot's Guide inspired you to stop, look, listen and speak up more often, please pass it along.

Please consider leaving a review for The Complete Patriot's Guide to Oligarchical Collectivism on amazon.com, it makes all the digital difference to Ethan Indigo and indie authors.
Please consider other written works by Ethan Indigo Smith like The Matrix of Four The Philosophy of The Duality of Polarity, The Terraist Letters, 108 Steps to Be in The Zone, Down and Out in Mendocino and The New Printed Threat, The Little Green Book of Revolution and the international bestseller The Geometry of Energy How to Meditate.

Lightning Source UK Ltd.
Milton Keynes UK
UKHW05f2109191018
330852UK00026B/426/P

9 781499 539455